Synthesis Lectures on Computer Architecture

Series Editor

Natalie Enright Jerger, University of Toronto, Toronto, Canada

This series covers topics pertaining to the science and art of designing, analyzing, selecting and interconnecting hardware components to create computers that meet functional, performance and cost goals. The scope will largely follow the purview of premier computer architecture conferences, such as ISCA, HPCA, MICRO, and ASPLOS.

Yuhao Zhu

Visual Computing For Architects

Imaging, Rendering, and Human Vision

 Springer

Yuhao Zhu 🆔
University of Rochester
Rochester, NY, USA

ISSN 1935-3235   ISSN 1935-3243 (electronic)
Synthesis Lectures on Computer Architecture
ISBN 978-3-032-05017-5   ISBN 978-3-032-05018-2 (eBook)
https://doi.org/10.1007/978-3-032-05018-2

This Springer imprint is published by the registered company Springer Nature Switzerland AG
The registered company address is: Gewerbestrasse 11, 6330 Cham, Switzerland

If disposing of this product, please recycle the paper.

Preface

This book attempts to present a unified view of visual computing, looking at it as a series of signal transductions across different domains—optical, analog, digital, and semantic—along with the processing that happens within each. Any sufficiently complex visual computing system worth studying will likely involve both transductions and processing in all of these domains.

Take Augmented Reality glasses as an example. The input signals—light—are in the optical domain. These first need to be converted into electrical signals by an image sensor so that a computer system can process them to extract semantic information—say, the orientation of a table in a room. The system then simulates light transport to generate photorealistic, context-appropriate virtual objects—perhaps a mug correctly oriented on that very table. Finally, these virtual objects must be transformed back from electrical signals, in the form of pixels, into optical signals by the display.

But wait, we are still not done! The light emitted by the display enters our eyes, where photoreceptors in the retina convert the optical signals back into electrical ones. The retina and, further downstream, the brain, process these signals, eventually giving rise to our perception and cognition: we see a virtual mug sitting naturally on a real table.

With this perspective in mind, the main motivation for writing the book grew out of a simple observation: in our community, visual computing is often approached primarily as an acceleration problem. This is, of course, crucial work, because performance and energy efficiency are always important goals. But most of these optimizations target the digital domain. Electrical signal processing is, in a sense, "just" one stage in a much larger, end-to-end visual computing system.

The other forms of transduction and processing are often less familiar to computer architects. This book aims to introduce them, and we will do so from first principles. At times, therefore, the material may seem far removed from computer architecture. Why, for example, should we care how photoreceptors work? But if anyone can appreciate this kind of question, it is us architects. After all, how a transistor works seems light-years away from how modern AI systems operate, and yet none of us would argue that understanding the former is not foundational if we hope to optimize the latter.

The style of the writing is influenced by two books: Brian Wandell's *Foundation of Vision* and Sönke Johnsen's *The Optics of Life: a Biologist's Guide to Light in Nature*. I strive to get close to the amazing level of technical clarity of the former, and the latter keeps reminding me just how much could be derived from how little. I am also grateful to Natalie Enright Jerger, who encouraged me to embark on this project, and to Timothy Sherwood and Abhishek Bhattacharjee for their thoughtful feedback. All remaining errors are mine alone.

Writing a book forces one to step back from one's own research and try to paint a broad-stroke picture of the field. In doing so, one gains new perspectives, which I have greatly enjoyed. I hope you enjoy reading the book as much as I did writing it.

Rochester, NY, USA   Yuhao Zhu
July 2025

Competing Interests The author has no competing interests to declare that are relevant to the content of this manuscript.

Contents

An Invitation to Visual Computing

1

1.1 What Is Visual Computing?

We can think of many things when it comes to visual computing. Cameras? Yes; they turn the world into visually pleasing images. Computer Graphics? Yes; they simulate how visually pleasing images are captured as if there was a camera placed in the scene. Computer vision? Yes; it interprets visual information (i.e., images) to infer semantic information of the world (e.g., object categories). Displays? Yes; they generate visual information (i.e., lights) to represent an intended scene. What about Augmented Reality (AR) and Virtual Reality (VR)? Of course; in fact, AR/VR requires all the above to work seamlessly together.

But what are the fundamental connections of the multitude of things that we can all loosely associate with visual computing? Fig. 1.1 shows the key concepts that unify the different fields of visual computing: (1) representing the physical world in three fundamental signal domains, i.e., the optical, electrical, and semantic domains; (2) processing signals within these domains; and 3) transforming signals across these domains.

We will use the Human Visual System (HVS) as an example to walk through some of the key concepts (Sect. 1.2). We will then expand to three more visual computing domains (computer imaging, computer graphics and rendering, and machine vision), comparing and contrasting how the signal representations, processing, and transformations are exercised in different systems (Sect. 1.3). We will introduce a power abstraction that governs any visual computing system. This abstraction allows us to reason about the limits of a system and design ways to improve a system (Sect. 1.4).

1.2 Human Visual System as a Visual Computing Platform

Imagine taking a walk through the woods and seeing a butterfly. How does your visual system allow you to notice the butterfly and that it is flying? The inputs to an HVS are lights from the butterfly and the trees in the physical world; they are information represented in the optical

© The Author(s), under exclusive license to Springer Nature Switzerland AG 2026   1
Y. Zhu, *Visual Computing For Architects*, Synthesis Lectures on Computer Architecture,
https://doi.org/10.1007/978-3-032-05018-2_1

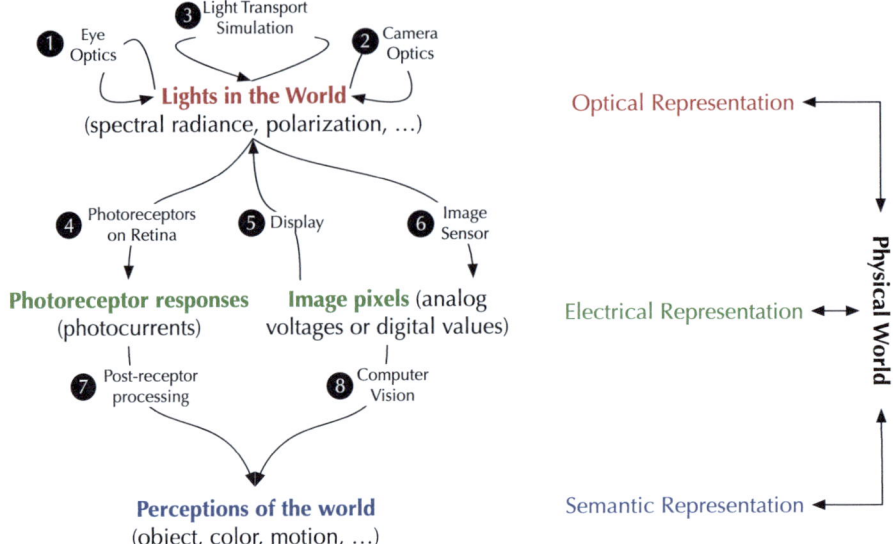

Fig. 1.1 A framework unifying visual computing. The fundamental building blocks are the signals represented in three fundamental information domains: optical, electrical, and semantic. Visual computing systems transform signals across, and process them within, these domains

domain. The output of the HVS is semantic information, e.g., the color and motion of the butterfly. The HVS extracts semantic information from optical signals through a sequence of signal transformations illustrated as ❶→ ❹ → ❼ in Fig. 1.1.

1.2.1   Signal Representations, Processing, and Transformations in HVS

1.2.1.1 Optical Signal Processing

First, lights enter your eyes by traveling through the ocular media in your eyes, such as the cornea, pupil, and lenses, and eventually reach the retina. Just before the lights get processed by the retina, the optical signal is already being processed as lights propagate through the eye. This is illustrated by ❶ in Fig. 1.1. For instance, the ocular media absorb photons of certain wavelengths and transmit photons that are unabsorbed. The pupil controls how many photons are allowed in at any given time, and the lens bends and *focuses* lights on the retina—the chief goal of the eye.

The optical information after eye optics and right before being processed by the retina is usually called the *optical image*. An optical image is a lossy and aberrated version of the optical information in the scene, because the optical signal processing in the eye is lossy. For instance, by focusing on the butterfly, which is at a particular depth, objects at other depths, such as the trees in the background, are blurred. The ocular media also absorb photons selectively across wavelengths, so the true light spectra in the scene are lost.

1.2.1.2 Optical to Electrical Signal Transduction

The optical image gets transformed into an electrical representation by the photoreceptors on the retina. This is step ❹ in Fig. 1.1. Photoreceptors absorb incident photons; once a photon is absorbed, it could, through *phototransduction* cascade (Wald 1968), generate electrical responses in the form of photocurrents or, equivalently, photovoltages across the cell membrane of the photoreceptor. The responses of all the photoreceptors form the electrical representation of the optical image. The rest of the visual system is "just" a hugely complicated circuit that processes the electrical signals from the photoreceptors. In this sense, the optical to electrical transformation is the first step in seeing.

This optical to electrical signal transduction is once again lossy. Photoreceptors sample and integrate signals spatially, temporally, and spectrally. As a result, much of the optical information of the incident light, such as the incident angle of the rays, the wavelengths of the photons, and the polarization of the light, is all lost. The main information that *is* retained, light intensity, is fundamentally limited by sampling and integration, which establish the limits of vision.

1.2.1.3 Electrical to Semantic Signal Transduction

The electrical signals produced by the photoreceptors are first processed by the rest of the neurons on the retina and then transmitted in the nervous system to the rest of the visual system, first to the Lateral Geniculate Nucleus (LGN) and then to the visual cortex, where the electrical signals undergo further processing and eventually the semantic meanings of the scene arise. You might now realize that the object is, in fact, a red lacewing butterfly (object recognition), that the color of the butterfly is an astonishing bright red and pale brown interlaced by black and white (color perception), and that the butterfly is flapping and flying (motion perception). We lump all the processing stages after the photoreceptor and call them "post-receptoral" processing, which is denoted by ❼ in Fig. 1.1.

The post-receptoral processing progressively extracts richer and higher-level information as the signal progresses through the retina-LGN-cortex pathway. The retina encodes information such as the spatial/temporal frequency, contrast, and, to a large extent, color. This set of information is generally regarded as "low-level" information, which does not, in any way, suggest that the information is somehow inferior; rather, they are the building blocks for higher-order visual processing.

It is no small feat that our retina can extract such information: the retina must reliably do so across a very wide range of illumination conditions. For instance, the retina adapts to different illumination levels spanning several orders of magnitude. Perhaps somewhat surprisingly, much of the adaptation takes place within the photoreceptors, whose sensitivity changes based on the incident light intensity. This suggests that photoreceptors are not merely signal transduction devices.

The LGN and early areas in the visual cortex extract information such as edge and orientation, and other higher-order areas further refine the signals to extract information such as motion, depth, and object category. Eventually, all these individual bits and pieces are knit together in our brain to give us perception and cognition, i.e., the semantic signals. Information processing in the visual system is not purely feed-forward. There are many feedback paths between cortical areas and between the cortex and the LGN (Gilbert and Li 2013; Briggs 2020). We hasten to add that while we know a lot about the *correlation* between the electrical responses and the semantic signals, we cannot yet say much about the *causation*.

1.2.2   The Transformations Are Born of Necessity

This complex sequence of transformations that turns the physical realities into one's subjective percept is born of necessity. A comparison is another sequence of transformations that computer architects are perhaps more familiar with. To have a computer solve a problem for us, we first describe the algorithm in a program written in a high-level language and then transform the program to a low-level, machine-understandable language (i.e., the Instruction Set Architecture), which is then executed on the microarchitecture implemented using circuits and, eventually, moving electrons. If we could directly talk to the electrons and instruct them to move to solve our problem, this sequence of transformations would not be strictly necessary. Similarly, if we could crack open one's head and manipulate the neuron spikes at will, we could perhaps directly impose certain percepts on humans. But since we cannot (easily), the sequence of signal transduction is necessary. Of course, the sequence of transformation in the computer systems is purposefully engineered to be that way, whereas the one in the HVS is naturally evolved.

The fact that there is a sequence of transformations involved suggests that we can study the HVS at different levels of abstraction. This idea is illustrated in Fig. 1.2, where, again, we compare the HVS with a computer system. The goal of a computer system is to solve a problem for us, and we can study how a computer system solves the problem at different levels of abstraction. Similarly, the HVS reacts to physical stimuli that are presented to it, and we can study, at different levels, how an HVS reacts to the physical stimuli.

First, we can study it at the psychological level to understand how human psychology, i.e., different forms of perception, cognition, and action, varies under physical stimuli (e.g., lights). This is the field of *psychophysics*. The psychological experiences one has are results of the collective behaviors of the neurons in the HVS. Naturally, the second way to study the HVS is to relate the behaviors of the neurons and the neural networks to the physical stimuli. This is the field of *systems neuroscience*. Finally, the behavior of a neuron is fundamentally a result of how cells and molecules function inside and between neurons, so one can study

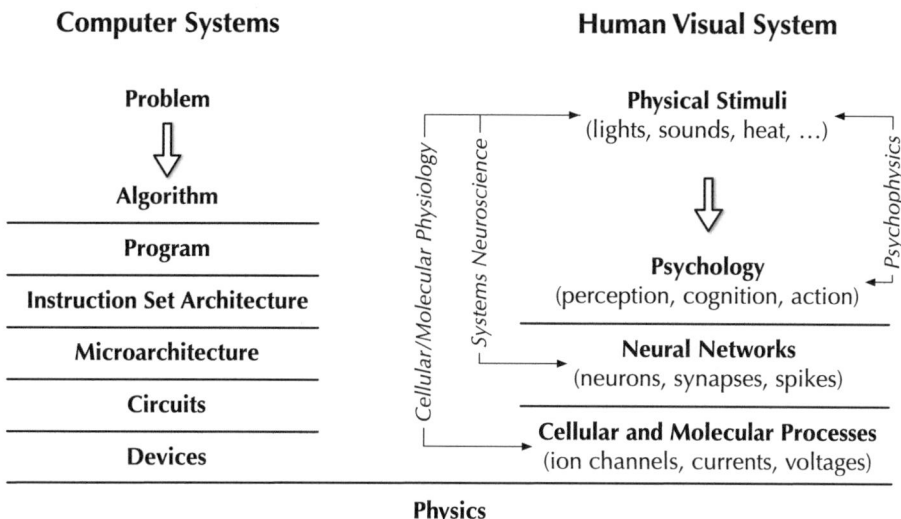

Fig. 1.2 Just like in a computer system, HVS also involves a sequence of transformations and can be studied at different levels of abstraction

the underlying cellular and molecular processes given physical stimuli. This is the field of *cellular and molecular physiology*.

1.3 Engineered Visual Computing Systems

While the example above is drawn from a biological system, engineered visual computing systems such as smartphones are fundamentally no different in that they all involve visual information represented in and transformed between different domains. We will consider three examples of engineered systems and compare and contrast them with those in the human visual system.

1.3.1 Computer Imaging and Digital Photography

Imaging refers to the task of capturing images of the physical world. Photography is sometimes used interchangeably with imaging. Just to be pedantic, however, photography is a special case of imaging where the goal is to capture *visually pleasing* images for the human visual system. Scientific imaging is another branch of imaging, where the goal is to capture *physically accurate* information for scientific inquiry. Examples of scientific imaging include astrophotography, microscopy, and Computed Tomography (CT). We will focus on photography here. Conventional photography is purely analog; think of dark rooms and film development. Modern imaging is computer-assisted, hence the name "computer imaging", not to be confused with "computational imaging" or "computational photography", which we will see later.

An end-to-end photography system is a complicated sequence of signal transductions involving ❷ → ❻ → ❺ → ❶ → ❹ → ❼ in Fig. 1.1. Lights enter the camera and are first processed by the optics in the camera with the main goal of focusing lights (❷), similar to the eye optics. Camera optics are designed completely by humans and we can, therefore, specifically engineer them to achieve a particular performance, whereas eye optics do not enjoy such flexibilities. An example is compound lenses, where a combination of lenses of different kinds are cascaded together to correct various aberrations that a single (spherical) lens introduces.

After the lenses, lights hit the image sensor, whose main job is to transform optical signals to electrical signals (❻). This is achieved by an array of light-sensitive photodiodes, or pixels, that convert photons to electric charges—using the *photoelectric effect* (Einstein 1905a, b) (the discovery of which won Albert Einstein his Nobel Prize)—which are then converted to digital values, i.e., image pixels. From the signal transduction perspective, the pixels in an image sensor are "just" like photoreceptors on the retina. Vision scientists might take offense at this comparison, because the photoreceptors, as alluded to earlier, are much "smarter" and do a lot more than the pixels, e.g., visual adaptation. In fact, an active area of research is to design pixels so that they adapt like photoreceptors (Liao et al. 2022).

Eventually, an image needs to be displayed for the human visual system to see. The display performs an electrical to optical signal transduction, turning digital pixels to lights (❺). The photons from the display then enter human eyes, and what we have discussed before about the HVS applies.

1.3.2 Computer Graphics and Rendering

Computer graphics and rendering systems generate images, where photorealism is the main goal (although not the exclusive goal). What does it take to render photorealistic images? A rendered image is photorealistic if it almost looks like a photo taken by a camera, so to render something photorealistic, we want to simulate how a photo is taken! To that end, we must simulate two things: (1) how light transports in space before entering the camera and (2) how lights are turned into pixels by a camera, which follows the signal chain in an imaging system.

Comparatively speaking, the second simulation is easier; it amounts to simulating the image formation process in a camera (i.e., ❷ → ❻). Since cameras are built by humans, we know exactly how they work, at least in principle. The first simulation is much harder, because it requires simulating the nature: modeling the complicated light-matter interactions (❸).

This is why most compelling rendering systems are physically based. The kind of physical models used for rendering are *phenomenological* in nature; they describe the empirical rules governing the light-matter interactions but are not always derived from first principles. An example is that we sometimes model light scattering within a volume using the Bidirectional Scattering Surface Reflectance Distribution Function (BSSRDF), which maps energy from incident rays to exiting rays while abstracting away the details of how photons interact with particles in the material, for which one has to turn to the theory of radiative/energy transfer (Chandrasekhar 1960).

Using phenomenological models is sometimes the only option when the actual underlying physics elude us. More importantly, however, simulating physics at the lowest level is simply unnecessary for rendering (which cares about photorealism rather than physical realism) and is computationally too costly for real-time rendering. A recent trend in graphics is neural rendering (Mildenhall et al. 2021), which parameterizes the phenomenological models using deep neural networks and learns such models from actual images, which, by definition, are precisely simulated—by nature.

Similar to photography, the rendered images will also go through an electrical-to-optical signal transformation by the display, whose output is then consumed by the HVS.

1.3.3   Machine Vision Systems

For better or worse, machine vision systems are prevalent in modern society. Autonomous vehicles use machine vision to navigate the environment, drones are used in agriculture to monitor crop health, and facial recognition technologies are increasingly used for security authentications. A machine vision system has two main components: (1) an imaging sub-system that, as discussed above, transforms the optical information in the scene to the electrical information encoded by the image pixels (❷ → ❻) and (2) a computing sub-system, which uses computer vision algorithms to interpret the images and extract meanings from the scene (❽).

At the risk of once again downplaying the capabilities and complexities of the HVS, one can argue that a machine vision system largely emulates the HVS—from a signal transduction perspective. Both aim to extract semantic information from the physical world, and both do so by first turning the optical information in the world to its electrical representation. One can even go as far as saying that today's dominant paradigm toward computer vision, i.e., deep learning, is heavily inspired by the HVS. The field of neuromorphic computing explicitly aims to mimic the structure and operation of the human brain.

A key difference between imaging in machine vision and imaging for photography is their respective consumer: the output of a photograph is meant to be consumed by an HVS, so visual quality is the main consideration, whereas images captured by, for instance, a robot are meant to be consumed by the downstream computer vision algorithms, which do not care about the visual appearance as long as the semantic information can be decoded from the images. This difference influences the design of the imaging system used in photography and for machine vision.

1.4   A Powerful Abstraction

A visual computing system enlists the work of multiple stages of signal transformation. At every stage in an application's pipeline, we have decisions to make. These decisions should not be made locally to optimize for a specific stage. Much of the exciting research in visual computing focuses on jointly designing and optimizing all stages of an end-to-end system. This section provides two concrete examples. But before we can entertain them, we first introduce a power abstraction that will allow us to reason about these research ideas.

1.4.1   The Encoding–Decoding Abstraction

We can take an information-theoretical perspective and abstract virtually any end-to-end visual computing pipeline as an encoding–decoding process. Decoding is the ultimate goal, but encoding is necessary, because it transforms signals to a domain that can be processed by the decoder. Take, for instance, human vision and machine vision systems; while the ultimate goal is to generate percepts of the physical world, information in the world must be first encoded as electrical signals (through imaging), which are what the brain and computer vision algorithms can process. Imaging itself can also be regarded as an encoding–decoding pair, where the optical information of the scene is first encoded in the electrical domain and the computational algorithms, acting as a decoder, reconstruct an electrical representation that faithfully captures the information in the original scene.

A more complicated example is visual display devices such as a VR headset. When developing a VR application, we usually have a scene in mind, e.g., a red lacewing butterfly flying in the woods. We hope that users will perceive the object (butterfly), color (the astonishing bright red and pale brown interlaced by black and white), and motion (flapping and flying), but we cannot simply impose these percepts on humans. Instead, we generate visual stimuli on the display to encode the desired percepts. This encoding is done through a combination of rendering (generating electrical signals) and display (converting electrical signals to optical signals). The entire HVS then acts as the decoder, which ideally would provide the intended percepts to users.

1.4.1.1 Encoding Capabilities Set the Limits on Decoding

Once we take this encoding–decoding abstraction, we can start reasoning about limits of a visual computing system. The decoder consumes information generated by the encoder, so its utility is fundamentally limited by the encoding capabilities. Ideally, the encoder should faithfully capture all the information in the world. But in practice, encoding is almost always lossy—for a number of reasons.

First, the actual encoding device used in a system, be it biological or engineered, usually uses fundamentally lossy mechanisms such as sampling and low-pass filtering (e.g., integration). Take HVS as an example, where the optical information of the scene is encoded as photoreceptor responses. The photoreceptors sample the continuous optical image impinging on the retina. The sampling rate dictates, according to the Nyquist-Shannon sampling theorem (Shannon 1949), how well the original optical image can be reconstructed, which in turn limits our ability to see fine details. Even before the photoreceptor sampling, the eye lens blurs signals in the scene not currently in focus, and the pupil, when very small, further blurs even in-focus objects through diffraction, setting the first limit of vision. Blurring is a form of low-pass filtering and is one of the many optical aberrations introduced during the optical signal processing in the HVS.

Second, an encoding device might completely disregard certain information in the incident signal. For instance, the polarization information in the incident light is simply ignored by the photoreceptors, whose responses are, thus, invariant to the polarization states. As a result, humans cannot "see" polarization. Some animals, such as butterflies, have polarization-sensitive photoreceptors. So it is not surprising that monarch butterflies make use of the light polarization for navigation (Reppert et al. 2004).

1.4.1.2 Jointly Design Encoding and Decoding

The encoder–decoder abstraction also allows us to design strategies to enhance a visual computing system, both augmenting its capabilities and improving its execution efficiency. For instance, when certain information is not needed for an accurate decoding, it need not be encoded in the first place and, of course, will not participate in decoding, reducing both encoding and decoding costs. Alternatively, if we know what information is crucial for decoding, we can design the encoding system to specifically capture such information. We can also "over-design" the encoder to encode signals in a higher dimensional space than the space to which the information is to be decoded; this essentially introduces redundant samples to improve the robustness to noise.

Ultimately, exploiting these ideas amounts to modeling and, often times, jointly designing the encoder and decoder, considering the end-to-end requirements of task performance, efficiency, and quality—of both the humans and the machine. We will discuss two concrete examples.

1.4.2   Encoding–Decoding Co-design: Two Examples

1.4.2.1 Computational Photography

The optical to electrical signal transduction in the image sensor is lossy due to various forms of signal sampling and integration. The signal transduction process itself is also not perfect due to fundamental physical limitations (e.g., quantal fluctuation in photon arrivals) and practical engineering considerations (e.g., sensor size). As a result, the sensor output, which is usually called *raw pixels*, is noisy (especially in low-light conditions) and does not accurately represent the luminance (especially under bright illuminations) and color information in the scene; certain information such as light-field and polarization is completely lost.

To overcome these limitations, modern smartphones and advanced imaging systems use computational algorithms to correct those imperfections, reconstruct the lost information, and sometimes can even add an artistic touch to the photo. Critically, such computational algorithms are usually jointly designed with the imaging system, i.e., the optics and image sensor. This is computational photography, co-designing camera optics, image sensors, and the computational algorithms to overcome fundamental limitations that conventional imaging systems face.

A classic example of computational photography has to do with a practical problem in photography. As a contemporary reader, you most likely have had the experience where you want to use your smartphone camera to capture a scene that has both a very bright region (e.g., the sunny sky) and a relatively dark region (e.g., a street corner). In technical terms, such a scene has a very high *dynamic range* (HDR), in that the ratio between the highest and lowest luminance in the scene is huge. The challenge is that image sensors on smartphones cannot capture a wide dynamic range: information at low-luminance regions is noisy, and high-luminance regions saturate pixels. So how do we capture the full luminance range in the scene? This is the task of HDR imaging.

People over the years have come up with a variety of clever ideas for HDR imaging. The most well-known idea is perhaps exposure bracketing, where we take multiple captures of the scene, each with a different exposure time, and then computationally combine the captures to synthesize the full dynamic range in the scene. Another approach is Google's HDR+ algorithm (Hasinoff et al. 2016), which takes multiple exposures using the same (low) exposure time to ensure high luminance regions are accurately captured, which is then followed by denoising algorithms (e.g., frame averaging) to recover low luminance information. Yet another approach is the time-to-saturation (TTS) image sensors (Stoppa et al. 2002), which measure the time it takes for each pixel to saturate and use that time to extrapolate the luminance information.

These HDR imaging techniques are all examples where the imaging system, i.e., the encoder, is intentionally designed to capture critical information (luminance) that is otherwise lost (either due to noise or due to saturation).

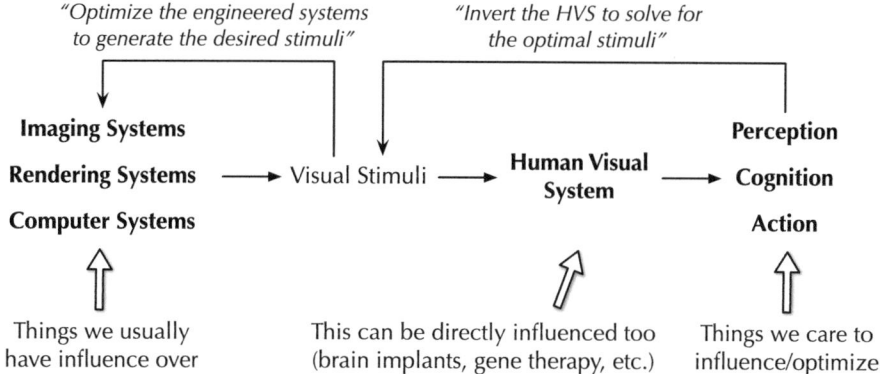

Fig. 1.3 In visual displaying devices such as AR/VR and smartphones, the engineered systems (imaging/rendering/computer systems) act as an encoder and the HVS acts as a decoder. By understanding the the decoding process, we can then better engineer the imaging, rendering, and computer systems to maximize end-to-end performance both for humans and for machines. Brain implants and gene therapy can directly influence the decoding process and must be designed with the encoder in mind, too

1.4.2.2 Perceptual Rendering

Perceptual rendering is a classic example that leverages the characteristics of HVS (decoder) to inform the design of visual display systems (encoder) such as AR/VR or even just smartphones. We illustrate the basic idea in Fig. 1.3, where imaging, rendering, and computing systems encode information that is then decoded by the HVS. The output of the decoder, i.e., the perception, cognition, and action of a human user, is what we care to influence, but what we actually have influence over, for the most part, is the encoding system (for imaging, rendering, and computing). If we have a good understanding of the HVS, we can then invert it to solve for the optimal stimuli, and from there we can then figure out how to optimally engineer the encoding system to deliver the desired stimuli while maximizing the system efficiency.

Gaze-contingent rendering is a well-known technique in AR/VR that exploits this opportunity. Our peripheral visual acuity is extremely bad: we could not tell the details of an object in our peripheral vision. This is mainly a result of: (1) a higher degree of low-pass filtering due to neural convergence in the periphery, and (2) a lower rate of sampling in the periphery due to drastically fewer photoreceptors. When immersed in a virtual environment with a VR headset, the majority of the pixels rendered and displayed fall in the periphery of the retina. Therefore, one could improve the rendering speed by generating low-quality visual stimuli for the periphery with impunity (Patney et al. 2016; Guenter et al. 2012). We could also alter pixel colors in the periphery to reduce display power without introducing artifacts (Duinkharjav et al. 2022).

Modern science and engineering have also empowered us to directly influence the decoder itself through techniques like brain implants and gene therapy—just imagine how powerful it would be to directly control a function whose outputs we care about. An example is the artificial retina (Gogliettino et al. 2023; Muratore and Chichilnisky 2020), an electronic retinal implants that converts optical signals to electrical signals that mimic actual retinal responses or codes; this holds the potential to restore vision to blind individuals. Similarly, these mechanisms must be designed with the encoder in mind in order to deliver the desired output.

1.5   The Rest of the Book

Why Should Architects Care?

It is not controversial to observe that architects are perhaps one of the most interdisciplinary groups in CS. We architects go out of our way to bridge software and hardware. By the nature of classic computer architecture, we dabble at the boundary between software and hardware, and the prevalence of domain-specific accelerators, where we drive computer systems designs by deep understanding of algorithmic characteristics, only accentuates this nature of our research community.

Now is the time to push that to the next level. We should be the ones that connect computing with other (traditionally) *non-computing* domains such as imaging and human visual perception. In some sense, it is nothing more than asking us to expand the scope of computing to all forms of signal transduction, be it optical, analog, digital, or biological, in which perhaps conventional computing is concerned with only analog and digital signal transductions.

Here is another way to think of this. When we talk about "software" in the context of software-hardware co-design, what we often really mean are "algorithms"—predefined pieces of code crafted to solve (part of) a problem. But as architects, our scope should go beyond algorithms to encompass the **problems** themselves; see the distinction between "problem" and "algorithm" in Fig. 1.2. There is no reason we must constrain ourselves to algorithmic solutions handed down by others. On the contrary, we should be the ones driving the development of solutions, because we understand what it takes to implement them efficiently and effectively.

To design good solutions, we must understand the entire stack: optics, image sensors, light-matter interactions, human visual perception, and more. The goal of this book is to build a foundation in these areas so that you can confidently understand and, better yet, design solutions that span across them.

That said, we invite you to indulge in the pursuit of fundamental sciences—even when they might not have immediate applications. As Edwin H. Land wittily and emphatically put it, the true application of science is that "we finally know what we are doing."

Goals, Non-goals, and Other References

We will cover mostly the signal transductions between the optical representation and electrical representation (①–⑥ in Fig. 1.1) while being very light on the electrical to semantic transduction (⑦ and ⑧ in Fig. 1.1). In particular, we will not touch computer vision at all, simply because there are too many excellent texts and it is arguably the most well-understood by architects.

We will not attempt to be comprehensive—no one understands everything, and no one needs to understand everything in order to get started. Our goal is to take a first-principled approach, so that you can build a solid foundation and feel confident learning new concepts in the future. There are many excellent references on the various topics we cover in the book if you want to dig deeper. Here are a few of my suggestions.

For human vision, the monumental book by Wandell (1995) is a must read. Rodieck (1998) is a breathtaking walk-through of the early stages in vision (eye optics and retinal processing), which we focus on in this book as well. Rodieck was an engineer (which is evident from the fact that he insisted on using frequency rather than wavelength in spectral plots) and approached vision with an engineering approach where every step is described *operationally* rather than just conceptually. In the end, you get the sense that the "The Astonishing Hypothesis" by Francis Crick might actually be true. Goldstein and Brockmole (2017) and Yantis and Abrams (2017) are popular introductory texts to human perception (vision and beyond).

For rendering, Pharr et al. (2023) and Glassner (1995) are golden references, and Dorsey et al. (2010) covers many aspects of physically-based rendering particularly relevant to this book. There are comparatively fewer texts on imaging. The one I particularly like is Rowlands (2020). I would also highly recommend Johnsen (2012); it has few equations but beautifully demonstrates how much insight can be gained from just a few basic principles.

References

Briggs F (2020) Role of feedback connections in central visual processing. Ann Rev Vis Sci 6(1):313–334

Chandrasekhar S (1960) Radiative transfer. Courier Corporation

Dorsey J, Rushmeier H, Sillion F (2010) Digital modeling of material appearance. Elsevier

Duinkharjav B, Chen K, Tyagi A, He J, Zhu Y, Sun Q (2022) Color-perception-guided display power reduction for virtual reality. ACM Trans Graph (TOG) 41(6):1–16

Einstein A (1905) On a heuristic point of view about the creation and conversion of light. Ann Phys 17(6):132–148

Einstein A (1905b) Über einen die erzeugung und verwandlung des lichtes betreffenden heuristischen gesichtspunkt

Gilbert CD, Li W (2013) Top-down influences on visual processing. Nat Rev Neurosci 14(5):350–363

Glassner AS (1995) Principles of digital image synthesis. Elsevier

Gogliettino AR, Madugula SS, Grosberg LE, Vilkhu RS, Brown J, Nguyen H, Kling A, Hottowy P, Dąbrowski W, Sher A, Litke AM, Chichilnisky E (2023) High-fidelity reproduction of visual signals by electrical stimulation in the central primate retina. J Neurosci 43(25):4625–4641

Goldstein EB, Brockmole RJ (2017) Sensation and Perception, 10th edn. Cengage Learning

Guenter B, Finch M, Drucker S, Tan D, Snyder J (2012) Foveated 3D graphics. ACM Trans Graph (TOG) 31(6):1–10

Hasinoff SW, Sharlet D, Geiss R, Adams A, Barron JT, Kainz F, Chen J, Levoy M (2016) Burst photography for high dynamic range and low-light imaging on mobile cameras. ACM Trans Graph (ToG) 35(6):1–12

Johnsen S (2012) The optics of life: a biologist's guide to light in nature. Princeton University Press

Liao F, Zhou Z, Kim BJ, Chen J, Wang J, Wan T, Zhou Y, Hoang AT, Wang C, Kang J et al (2022) Bioinspired in-sensor visual adaptation for accurate perception. Nat Electron 5(2):84–91

Mildenhall B, Srinivasan PP, Tancik M, Barron JT, Ramamoorthi R, Ng R (2021) Nerf: representing scenes as neural radiance fields for view synthesis. Commun ACM 65(1):99–106

Muratore DG, Chichilnisky E (2020) Artificial retina: a future cellular-resolution brain-machine interface. In: NANO-CHIPS 2030: on-chip AI for an efficient data-driven world. Springer, pp 443–465

Patney A, Salvi M, Kim J, Kaplanyan A, Wyman C, Benty N, Luebke D, Lefohn A (2016) Towards foveated rendering for gaze-tracked virtual reality. ACM Trans Graph (TOG) 35(6):1–12

Pharr M, Jakob W, Humphreys G (2023) Physically based rendering: From theory to implementation, 4th edn. MIT Press

Reppert SM, Zhu H, White RH (2004) Polarized light helps monarch butterflies navigate. Curr Biol 14(2):155–158

Rodieck RW (1998) The first steps in seeing. Oxford University Press

Rowlands DA (2020) Physics of digital photography, 2nd edn. IOP Publishing

Shannon CE (1949) Communication in the presence of noise. Proc IRE 37(1):10–21

Stoppa D, Simoni A, Gonzo L, Gottardi M, Dalla Betta GF (2002) Novel CMOS image sensor with a 132-dB dynamic range. IEEE J Solid-State Circ 37(12):1846–1852

Wald G (1968) Molecular basis of visual excitation. Science 162(3850):230–239

Wandell BA (1995) Foundations of vision. Sinauer Associates

Yantis S, Abrams RA (2017) Sensation and perception, 2nd edn. Worth Publishers

At the center of visual computing is human vision, which is important for two key reasons. First, many visual computing systems (such as cameras and AR/VR headsets) generate image signals that are ultimately consumed by humans. It is therefore essential to understand how the human visual system processes and interprets these signals. Second, although not the focus of this book, machine vision systems are still, in many ways, striving to match the capabilities of human vision. A deeper understanding of human vision may help inform and inspire better machine vision designs.

Our discussion will primarily focus on the eye's optics and retinal processing while touching only lightly on cortical processing—for three reasons. First, eye optics and retinal processing are *relatively* better understood in the scientific community compared to cortical processing. Second, many visual behavioral characteristics—such as spatial and temporal resolution, contrast sensitivity, and visual adaptation—can be largely explained by the eye's optics and retinal function. These characteristics are frequently exploited in engineering optimizations aimed at improving efficiency. Finally, the systems and architecture community is already relatively attuned to cortical processing, thanks to the substantial body of work on spiking neural networks. For further exploration of cortical mechanisms, we refser readers to those specialized texts.

From Light to Visual Perception: An Overview

2

2.1 The Big Picture

Before studying the HVS, it is useful to start by discussing why we care about the HVS at all—after all, if you are a computer science and/or engineering student, why would you care? We will then discuss the methodology we will use when studying the HVS.

2.1.1 Why Do We Study HVS?

Why do we care about studying the HVS? First and foremost, for the science itself— it is extremely satisfying to just understand "how stuff works", is it not? Understanding the basics of the HVS will also allow us to investigate the unknowns of the HVS, and computer scientists have a lot to off. For instance, modern computational methods, especially deep (artificial) neural networks, have provided us a new toolbox to better understand the biological neural networks: if a signal representation or a learning paradigm is effective in deep neural networks, would it be possible that our HVS uses a similar representation or can learn based on similar representations?

For computer scientists and engineers working on visual computing systems, there is another reason, which is already illustrated in Fig. 1.3. The psychological experiences of the users of a computing platform, be it an AR/VR headset or a smartphone, are what we want to influence, but we, for the most part, exert that influence *indirectly*, by designing and optimizing the imaging, rendering, and computer systems. The outputs of these systems, i.e., the visual stimuli coming out of the display, become the input to the HVS of a human whose psychological states we care to optimize. So if we understand the HVS, we could invert the HVS process, given the desired psychological states, to solve for the optimal visual stimuli, and from there we can then think about how to best design the various engineered systems.

© The Author(s), under exclusive license to Springer Nature Switzerland AG 2026   17
Y. Zhu, *Visual Computing For Architects*, Synthesis Lectures on Computer Architecture,
https://doi.org/10.1007/978-3-032-05018-2_2

Understanding the cellular, molecular, and neural processes in the HVS has also inspired people to better engineer systems such as imaging systems (Liao et al. 2022; Wodnicki et al. 1995) and deep neural networks, even though the output of these systems is not meant to be consumed by the HVS (Idrees et al. 2024).

2.1.2 How Do We Study HVS?

How do photons in the real world give rise to perception and cognition in our brain when they enter our eyes? We want to show you that there is really no magic here. The perception and cognition we experience are fundamentally a result of the complicated, first optical and eventually electrical, signal processing in the physiological system—our eyes and brains.

This relationship between low-level electrical signals and high-level behavioral responses in humans is conceptually no different from one that we find in computers. This comparison is shown earlier in Fig. 1.2. For someone unfamiliar with computer systems and chip design, it would seem rather magical that a computer does what it does. But we know that the high-level, observable behaviors of a computer program are a result of low-level processing in the electrical circuits. Similarly, the experiences humans have in response to visual stimuli are a result of the collective behaviors of the underlying neurons in the nervous system, whose behaviors result from the cellular and molecular processes within and between individual neurons.

The circuits in a computer are made of engineered material such as transistors, whereas circuits in the HVS are made of biological materials such as neurons. Fundamentally, however, it is all physics—electrons and/or ions move around and cause changes in voltage potentials and currents, and these changes are how information is propagated.

With the advancements in modern science and engineering, we can now measure, at a neuronal or even sub-neuronal level, the electrical responses of the HVS when presented with visual inputs. These measurements allow us to *correlate* electrical responses to perception and cognition, which, in turn, allow us to say something like "this part of the HVS supports or is responsible for that particular function (e.g., object detection)." It is important to note, however, that we still do not know why the electrical responses *cause* our perception and cognition. The causation problem, for the moment, is at best a philosophical problem or, if you will, a religious one.

The goal of this chapter is to give you an overview of the Human Visual System (HVS). We will focus on the main components and key facts of the HVS so that you can start appreciating the connections between signal processing at the physiological level and perception, cognition, and action at the behavioral level while leaving many details to later chapters.

The signal processing in the HVS consists of three main components; this is illustrated in Fig. 2.1. First, lights are processed in the optical domain as they enter our eyes and go through the eye optics. The optical signals then reach the retina and are first converted to electrical signals by the photoreceptors (cones and rods), which are further processed before

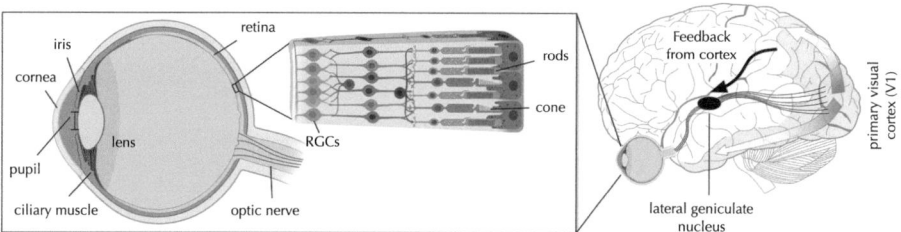

Fig. 2.1 Pupil, under the control of the iris, lets in lights. Cornea and lens focus light with the former contributing the most optical bending power. Lens contracts and relaxes to accommodate object depth under the control of the ciliary muscle. Retina transforms optical signals to electrical signals, which are further processed and exit the retina through the optic nerve. Retinal signals go through the Lateral Geniculate Nucleus and then are projected to the visual cortex. This retino-geniculo-cortical pathway carries the main information flow in the HVS, with the cortex also providing feedback to the LGN. Adapted from Selket (2007); the blown-up view is drawn in BioRender with a publication license

exiting the retina. The retina output neurons, i.e., the retinal ganglion cells, encode low-level information such as wavelengths, contrast, timing of object motion, etc. The retinal outputs are then transmitted to the Lateral Geniculate Nucleus (LGN) and, for the most part, relayed to the visual cortex. Cortical processing essentially knits together the low-level, upstream information to give us vision. The retino-geniculo-cortical pathway is the main pathway for the electrical signals.

2.2   Eye Optics

The optical signal impinging on the retina is called the **optical image**, which is a 2D continuous signal in that at any position on the retinal surface we can ask: how much optical power is there here?[1] Ideally, the optical image is a perfect perspective projection from the 3D physical world, with no loss of information other than the projection. The reality is much more complicated.

2.2.1   The Main Goal Is to Focus Lights

The main goal of the eye is to focus light on the retina. To focus light the optics need to bend light, which is achieved collectively by all the ocular media in the eye, including the cornea, aqueous humour, lens, and vitreous humour. This is illustrated in Fig. 2.2. Lights bend because of the difference in refractive index between adjacent ocular media. Most of the bending is done by the cornea because there is a large difference in the refractive index

---

[1] The power at an infinitesimal point is called irradiance; see Sect. 5.3.

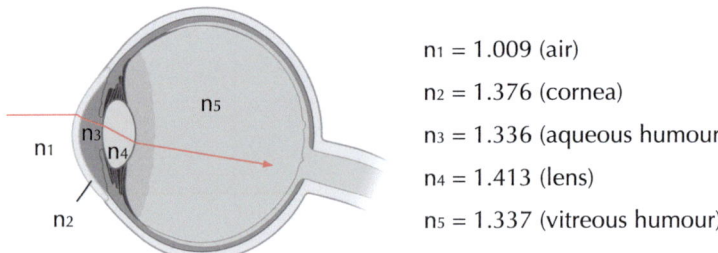

$n_1 = 1.009$ (air)

$n_2 = 1.376$ (cornea)

$n_3 = 1.336$ (aqueous humour)

$n_4 = 1.413$ (lens)

$n_5 = 1.337$ (vitreous humour)

Fig. 2.2 Much of the optical bending power in the eye is contributed by the cornea, which has a large refractive index difference with respect to its adjacent ocular media (Snell's law). The lens also contributes to light bending, albeit with a lower contribution. Cornea is rigid but the lens is malleable, so accommodation is attributed exclusively to the lens. Data from LaValle (2023, Fig. 4.25)

between the cornea and the air. The lens also contributes to light bending, albeit with a lower contribution, because the differences in refractive index between the lens and its adjacent media (aqueous fluid and vitreous fluid) are relatively small.

The cornea is fixed in shape. Lens, in contrast, is malleable in its shape. The ciliary muscle controls the contraction and relaxation of the lens, which changes the focal length, and thus bending power, of the lens, and by extension the entire eye optical system. Adjusting the focal length to bring an object into focus is called **accommodation**.

But if the ciliary muscle cannot properly adjust the lens, we get defocused blur, which is a form of optical **aberration**. There are a number of other optical aberrations; astigmatism and chromatic aberration are two common ones found in eyes. While not an optical aberration, diffraction also contributes substantially to visible blurs when the pupil size is very small (e.g., under strong illumination).

For our purpose, "imperfections" introduced by eye optics (aberration and diffraction) can be modeled by the Point Spread Function (PSF) of the optical system, which we will see later in Sect. 8.4.

2.2.2 Ocular Media Absorb Light Selectively

While all the ocular media are generally transparent, they still absorb some amount of light. Critically, the absorption and, by extension, transmittance, are strongly wavelength dependent. Color vision is fundamentally tied to the power distribution of light over wavelengths, so the selective absorption of light by the ocular media significantly influences our color vision.

Boettner and Wolter (1962) [Fig. 7] measured the spectral transmittance of the eye, which defines the amount of light allowed to transmit through the media at each wavelength. The transmittance spectrum of the ocular media is generally lower at short wavelengths, which means the ocular media generally absorbs blue-ish lights; so if the incident light is white-ish, the light would appear yellow after traveling through the ocular media.

2.3   Retina: Basic Facts

Now the photons have arrived at the retina. The retina is where optical signals are transformed into electrical signals. The electrical signals undergo further processing on the retina and are then carried by the optic nerve to the brain. The signal transduction and processing are carried out through layers of neurons on the retina, of which there are five categories (each of which has sub-categories). They are the photoreceptors, bipolar cells, horizontal cells, amacrine cells, and retinal ganglion cells (RGCs). This is illustrated in Fig. 2.3.

The main information flow starts from the photoreceptors, flows through the bipolar cells, which synapse with photoreceptors and send their outputs to the RGCs. The horizontal cells synapse with the photoreceptors (and other horizontal cells), and the amacrine cells connect with both the bipolar cells and the RGCs (and other amacrine cells). Identifying the different classes of neurons and their connections is largely due to Santiago Ramón y Cajal, who won the Nobel Prize in 1906.

Interestingly, while we might be used to neurons communicating through spikes, i.e., action potentials (which were first recorded by Edgar Adrian, a Nobel Prize laureate in 1932 who developed the all-or-none theory of action potentials; Hodgkin and Huxley (1952), who shared the Nobel Prize in 1963, explained the ionic mechanisms underlying the action potentials), the RGCs are the only type of neurons on the retina that spike. The rest of the neurons are non-spiking neurons; they communicate through graded potentials.

2.3.1   Optical-to-Electrical Signal Transduction Takes Place in Photoreceptors

Photoreceptors are where optical signals are transformed into electrical signals. Photoreceptors absorb incident photons; once a photon is absorbed, it could generate electrical responses through the process of **phototransduction** cascade (Wald 1968). George Wald won his Nobel Prize in Physiology or Medicine by essentially elucidating this process. The electrical response can be represented as photocurrents or, equivalently, photovoltages across the cell membrane of the photoreceptor. We will have a lot to say about this process later in Sect. 3.1.

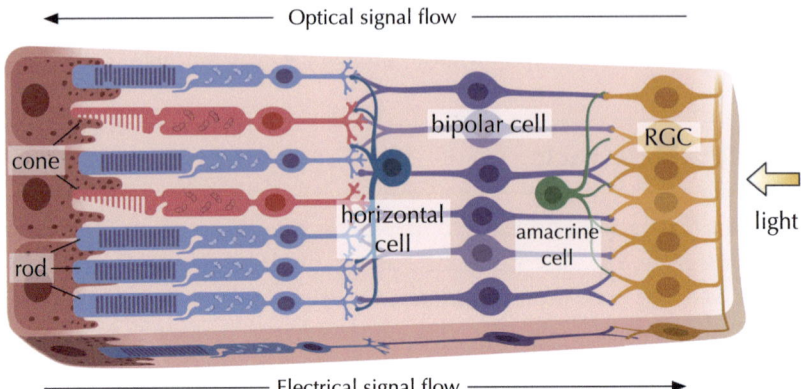

Fig. 2.3 The basic neural network on the retina. The photoreceptors convert optical signals to electrical signals. The electrical signals go through the bipolar cells and then to the retinal ganglion cells, which carry all the output of the retina. Horizontal and amacrine cells mediate lateral interactions, giving rise to important features such as the receptive field. Since the RGCs are at the outer most layer of the retina, the optical information and the electrical information flow in opposite directions

2.3.2 Functional and Anatomical Organizations of the Retina Are Opposite

The functional organization of the cells is opposite to the anatomical organization of the cells. This is illustrated in Fig. 2.3. Functionally, the first layer of the retina is the photoreceptor cells, which convert photons to electrical responses, and the last layer is the RGCs, which carry all the retinal output information and are directly connected to the optic nerve, which are effectively the axons of the RGCs. Anatomically, however, the RGCs lie at the outermost layer of the retina, and the photoreceptors are the innermost layer. Therefore, photons upon reaching the retina first hit the RGCs and then go through other neurons before eventually hitting the photoreceptors, where the signal transduction takes place. As far as a photon is concerned, neurons before the photoreceptors are transparent and simply let the photon through without doing much about it—with an exception that we will see soon.

2.3.3 Blind Spot Exists Because of the Routing Issue

An implication of the anatomical organization is that the optic nerve must be routed from the front of the retina and *through* the retina at a single location, which is called the **optic disk**. The optic disk must be free from any neurons, including photoreceptors, simply for the optic nerve to exit. Since photoreceptors sense light, the optic disk is also called the blind spot. This is illustrated in Fig. 2.4. Some vertebrates, like the octopus, do not have this "wiring" issue, since their retinal signals exist from the back of the retina.

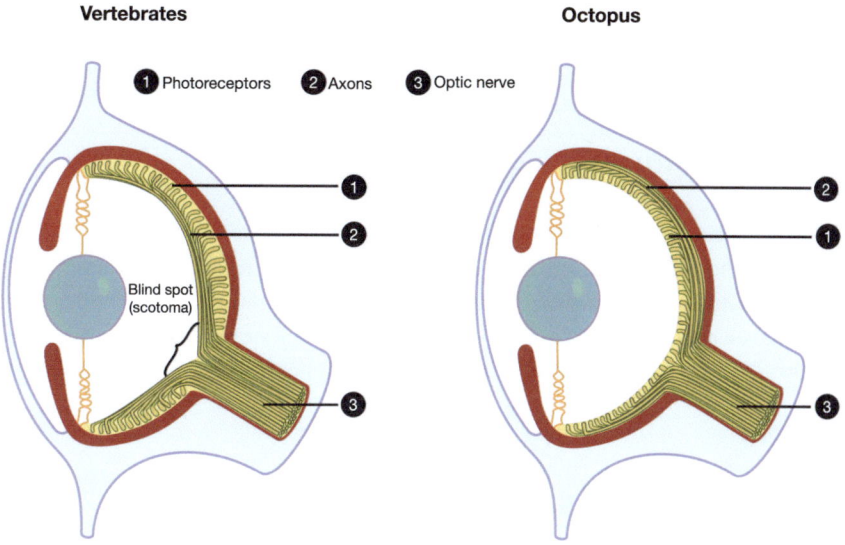

Fig. 2.4 Vertebrate eyes have a blind spot (scotoma) because the RGC axons exit the retina from the *front* of the retina. It is purely a "wiring" issue. Octopus eyes do not have this issue. Adapted from Caerbannog (2016)

It is unclear whether there are evolutionary advantages of having a blind spot on our retina, but it does not seem to be a disadvantage: we clearly do not notice the blind spot in our daily life—the downstream visual system fills in the missing information there. Our head and eye movements further mitigate the impact of the blind spot.

2.3.4   ipRGCs are Light-Sensitive But Do Not Contribute to Image-Forming Vision

Photoreceptors are the only type of neurons on the retina that are sensitive to light *and* contribute to image-forming vision. There is another type of neuron, a sub-type of the RGCs actually, called the **intrinsically photosensitive RGCs** (ipRGCs) that are also sensitive to light (i.e., they absorb photons and convert optical signals to electrical signals), but interestingly they do not (primarily) contribute to image-forming vision.

The ipRGCs were discovered fairly recently, and it is fair to say that the discovery was a big deal for the field (Berson et al. 2002; Hattar et al. 2002). For the past 150 years or so, human vision could be adequately explained by photoreceptors being the only light-sensitive neurons. Now, if the ipRGCs are also light sensitive, do we have to rewrite the science behind human vision? It turns out that while the ipRGCs do respond to lights, they primarily contribute to non-image-forming vision (but see Dacey et al. 2005). For instance, they are shown to impact circadian rhythms, mood, and pupillary light reflex (Lazzerini Ospri et al. 2017; Do and Yau 2010).

2.4 Retinal Structure and Functions

Retina is organized to perform a set of low-level tasks that are crucial to vision. "Low-level" here refers to the fact that information encoded by the retina forms the building blocks for more complicated visual functions later in the HVS. At the risk of over-simplication, each task is achieved by a **visual stream** of neurons. These visual streams are also called **parallel pathways**. This section briefly discusses a set of basic functions of the retina and their visual streams.

2.4.1 Rod Versus Cone Specialization

2.4.1.1 Sensitivity and Kinetics

There are two types of photoreceptors: rods and cones. Perhaps the most important difference between the two is that rods are much more sensitive to light than cones. This is evident in Fig. 2.5, which compares the single-photon response of rods and cones in primates. The response here is represented by the photocurrent, the change of current that flows into the photoreceptor as a result of photon absorption.

Due to the high sensitivity, rod responses saturate quickly as the ambient light level increases, so they are primarily responsible for vision at low illumination levels (e.g., at night); rod-mediated vision is called the **scotopic vision**. Cones are much less sensitive, so they are responsible for vision at normal illumination levels, such as during the day. Cone-mediated vision is called the **photopic vision**. The sensitivity range overlap, so there is a luminance range where both rods and cones contribute to vision, which is called the **mesopic vision**. This is illustrated in Fig. 2.6.

Cones also have faster response kinetics than rods: cone responses rise and fall much faster than rods; this is illustrated in Fig. 2.5. The faster kinetics allows cones to track moving

Fig. 2.5 Illustration of single photon responses (photocurrents) of rod and cone. Rods are more sensitive with a slower kinetics. Angueyra-Aristizábal (2014, Fig. 1.4C) reports an actual measurement on a primate

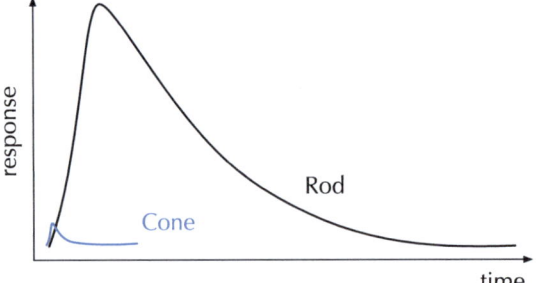

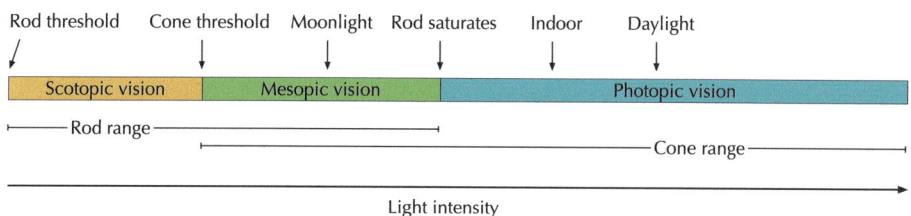

Fig. 2.6 Sensitivity range of rod-mediated vision and cone-mediated vision

objects better than rods do. To reason about the influence of the response kinetics, think of a camera where the exposure time is very long: the resulting image is (motion) blurred. Shorter exposure/shutter time captures motion better. Cones have a shorter effective "exposure time" than rods.

2.4.1.2 Spectral Sensitivity and Color Vision

Yet another important difference between rods and cones is that the cone-mediated vision provides color information whereas rod-mediated vision encodes only light intensity but not color. This is because there is only one class of rods but three different classes of cones, each with a different (linearly independent) wavelength sensitivity function. Fundamentally, color arises from the wavelength information in incident lights. Having three types allows cones to have a stronger capability of encoding wavelength information than rods. The entire Chap. 3 is devoted to color vision; for now, let us just appreciate how different cones have different wavelength selectivities.

One way to measure the spectral differences between photoreceptors is using a technique called microspectrophotometry (MSP), which measures the fraction of photons that gets absorbed by a photoreceptor at each wavelength. Using MSP, Dartnall et al. (1983) collected data for cones and rods from human donors, shown in Fig. 2.7. The y-axis plots *absorbance*, which is $\log(I_{\text{incident}}/I_{\text{transmitted}})$, i.e., the log ratio between the incident light intensity and transmitted (i.e., unabsorbed) light intensity.[2]

While many cones were measured, there were only three distinct spectra, whose absorbance peaks at relatively long, medium, and short wavelength, respectively. We call them the L, M, and S cones. The rod's peak is in-between that between the S and the M cones. Note that the spectra in Fig. 2.7 are normalized to peak at unity. The absolute absorbance of rods is slightly lower than that of the cones.

Notably, the L and M cones exhibit greater similarity to each other than to the S cones, suggesting that the S cones are quite different from the L and M cones. This is a clue about

---

[2] absorbance $= \log(I_{\text{incident}}/I_{\text{transmitted}})$, and the fraction absorbed, i.e., absorptance $= 1 - I_{\text{transmitted}}/I_{\text{incident}}$. Therefore, absorptance $= 1 - e^{-\text{absorbance}}$. Numerically, absorbance is approximately absorption when absorbance is low, which is the case here when using MSP to illuminate the photoreceptors.

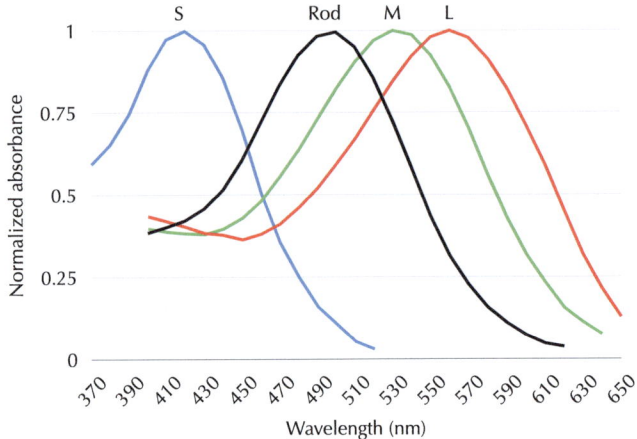

Fig. 2.7 The absorbance spectra of the three cones (L, M, S) and the rod (R) in humans; data reported in Dartnall et al. (1983). The spectra are normalized to peak at 1

the evolution of the three cone types. Most mammals have only two cone types, one that is sensitive to short-wavelength light and the other that is sensitive to long-wavelength lights; the former is evolved into the S cones, and the latter separated into the L cones and M cones through a local gene duplication (Jacobs 2008). Since the duplication is relatively recent (about 30–35 million years ago), the L and M cones are rather similar. Bowmaker et al. (1978) shows similar data for a macaque. There, the L and M cone spectra are also closer to each other than to the S cone spectrum, indicating that the divergence between the L and M cones occurred *before* the split between modern Old World monkeys and great apes (including humans).

2.4.1.3 Spatial Distribution

There are about 120 million rods and about 6 million cones. Curcio et al. (1990) is the first to measure the spatial distribution of rods and cones on human retina. Figure 2.8 shows the distribution of both cones and rods on the retina. Almost all the cones are concentrated at the **fovea**, a small, central pit on the retina that is approximately 2 mm in diameter and subtends a visual angle of about 1°. The position in the fovea that has the peak cone density is defined to have an **eccentricity** of 0°. As eccentricity increases, the density of cone photoreceptors reduces sharply. There are no rods in the fovea; all the rods are placed at the retina periphery, peaking at about 20° away from the fovea. There is a small retinal area where there are no cones or rods: the blind spot (Fig. 2.4).

There are many important implications of the photoreceptor mosaic and distribution. First, the visual acuity decreases in the visual periphery. Think of photoreceptors as sampling the continuous optical image impinging upon the retina. A higher density leads to a higher

Fig. 2.8 Cone and rod distribution on the retina; the *x*-axis is the eccentricity (angular distance from the fovea, which has an eccentricity of 0°). From Cmglee (2021)

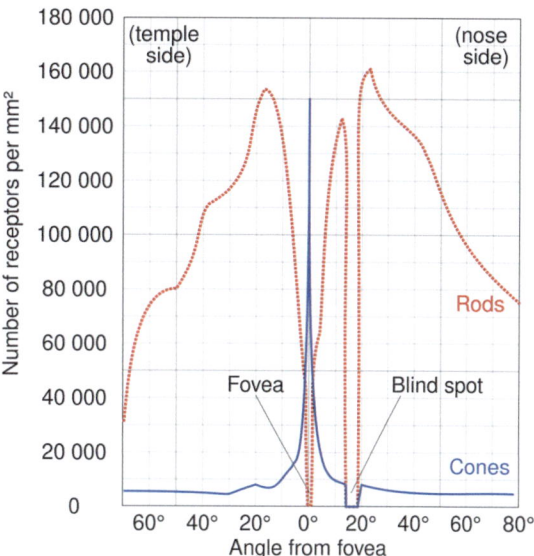

sampling rate. In addition, larger cone sizes in the periphery are equivalent to higher degrees of blurring, since photons hitting a cone are integrated together just like by a camera pixel (although, critically, the electrical response of a photoreceptor is *not* proportional to the photon count, unlike a camera pixel), and integration is a form of low-pass filtering.

We hasten to add that the lower acuity in the periphery is *not* exclusively attributed to the photoreceptor mosaic. As we will see shortly, how photoreceptors communicate with other neurons on the retina plays an important role, too.

Second, since the fovea has the highest visual acuity, our ocular motor system has evolved in such a way that when we want to see fine details of an object, we move our eyes so that light from the object is captured by the fovea. This means that we cannot see fine details of an object in dim environments if we fixate at it. Instead, we would have a better chance of seeing details if we intentionally placed the object in our peripheral vision.

2.4.1.4 Rod Versus Cone Pathways and Visual Streams

Rods and cones have their own pathways initially and merge later. This is shown in Fig. 2.3. Both rods and cones synapse with bipolar cells, but they synapse with distinct bipolar cells. That is, an individual bipolar cell receives information from either rods only or cones only. The rod pathway and cone pathway are parallel streams at this point. The bipolar cells then feed their outputs to the RGCs. A RGC can mix information from both rod and cone bipolar cells. This mixing is enabled by amacrine cells, which synapse with both the rod and cone bipolar cells and with the RGCs. Thus, the distinct information in the rod pathway and the cone pathway gets merged in the RGC layers.

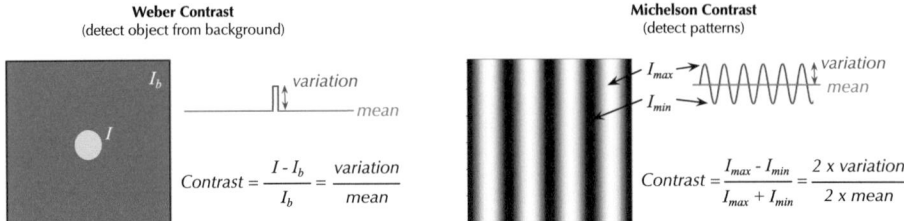

Fig. 2.9 Weber contrast is often used for detecting objects against a uniform background, and Michelson contrast is used for detecting patterns. The two definitions are compatible: they both describe the ratio between the maximal variation of the signal over the mean

Why are rod and cone pathways initially parallel but merge later? The initial parallel pathways allow rods and cones to extract low-level information, such as contrast, independently under different lighting conditions, but once the information is collected, it is processed similarly, so there is really no need to duplicate the processing circuitry.

2.4.2 Contrast Detection and Adaptation

Another important function of the retina is to extract contrast information. Arguably most interesting information in the physical world exists all in image contrast, i.e., local differences in light intensities. Take a look at your surroundings; uniform light levels where there is absolutely no change in light are rare and do not present much useful information. Fine details of an object are really encoded in contrasts.

This imposes two requirements on our visual system. First, we need to extract contrasts and encode them in neural signals so that they can be processed by the rest of the brain. Second, we must reliably encode contrast across a wide range of ambient light levels. Before discussing how the RGCs meet these requirements, we must first define contrast more rigorously.

2.4.2.1 Contrast is Variation Over Mean

Intuitively, contrast describes how much *variation* there is in a signal relative to the average strength of the signal. There are two commonly used definitions, both of which are compatible with this intuition. They are usually used in different scenarios. Figure 2.9 illustrates the two definitions.

Weber contrast is often used in scenarios where there is a small object against a relatively uniform background. The contrast C_w is defined as:

Fig. 2.10 Illustration of how the dendritic field size increases with eccentricity, indicating a higher degree of neural convergence at the periphery. Wandell (1995, Fig. 5.7) (which is after Dacay and Petersen (1992, Fig. 2A) plots the actual data for two RGC subtypes

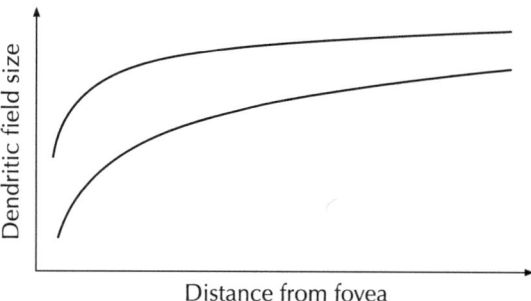

$$C_w = \frac{I - I_b}{I_b}, \tag{2.1}$$

where I_b is the background luminance and I is the object luminance. If the object is small, the mean luminance of the entire field is approximately the background luminance, and naturally $I - I_b$ is the maximal variance over the mean.

The Michelson contrast is used in scenarios where we want to detect patterned signals. Taking a sinusoidal pattern as an example (and recall any arbitrary pattern can be decomposed into sinusoidal basis patterns), the contrast C_m of a sinusoidal signal is usually defined as:

$$C_m = \frac{I_{max} - I_{min}}{I_{max} + I_{min}}, \tag{2.2}$$

where I_{max} and I_{min} are the highest and lowest luminance, respectively, of the signal. We can see that C_m can also be interpreted as the ratio between the variation and the mean of the signal. A higher C_m would mean that the pattern is more easily detected, and vice versa.

2.4.2.2 RGC Pools Signals from Many Photoreceptors

There are about 120 million rods, 6 million cones, and 1 million RGCs on the retina. Therefore, a single RGC *necessarily* receives signals from multiple rods and/or cones. Pooling signals from multiple neurons into a single neuron is generally called **neural convergence**, a many-to-one mapping. Evidently, there is a much higher degree of neural convergence in rods than in cones. The fovea, which, recall, contains only cones, is an extreme case where there is no neural convergence. In fact, each foveal cone sends its signal to multiple RGCs, so there is a one-to-many mapping there.

The higher degree of neural convergence in the rod pathway is another reason why rod-mediated vision is more sensitive than cone-mediated vision: the responses of different rods that are pooled together to the same downstream RGC, so that the RGC could generate responses faster to the brain than if the RGC receives input from only a single cone at the fovea. The flip side of the higher degree of convergence is that rod vision offers low spatial acuity. If an RGC generates a response, we could not resolve the source of that response since it could come from anywhere within a large group of photoreceptors being stimulated. From a signal processing perspective, summation is a form of low-pass filtering (equivalent to convolving the signal with a box filter), which naturally reduces the frequency of the signal.

The degree of neural convergence increases as the eccentricity increases. Figure 2.10 shows the dendritic field sizes of two RGC subtypes; the size increases with the eccentricity. The higher degree of neural convergence is another reason why peripheral acuity is much worse than that at the fovea.

2.4.2.3 RGCs Have a Center-Surround Receptive Field

Neural convergence gives rise to an important concept called **receptive field**, which is central to contrast encoding. The receptive field of a neuron is the *retinal* area that influences the neuronal activity. For an RGC, its receptive field is the collection of photoreceptors whose output signals converge at that RGC. Due to the one-to-one mapping relationship at the fovea, the RGCs that are connected to the fovea cones have a receptive field of only one cone.

The way an RGC aggregates information from the receptive field is *not* to simply sum up the signals from the individual photoreceptors. If we illuminate the entire receptive field of an RGC uniformly, the RGCs respond similarly regardless of the illumination intensity. This is a form of *light adaptation*, which we will discuss shortly. Let's call the RGC's response rate under a uniform illumination its spontaneous rate.

If uniformly changing the light levels does not change the RGC's response rate, what does? It turns out that you need to have *variations* in the illumination within the receptive field. The RGCs respond best to variation patterns that have a center-surround structure. For about half of the RGCs, their response rate is maximized if we present bright lights to the center photoreceptors and dark lights to the surround photoreceptors. These are called **ON-center, OFF-surround** RGCs, since they have an excitatory center (excited by light) and inhibitory surround (inhibited by light). The other half prefers the opposite pattern: dark at the center and bright at the surround. They are the **OFF-center, ON-surround RGCs**, since they have an inhibitory center and an excitatory surround. The RGCs are said to have a **center-surround** receptive field. Figure 2.11 illustrates the receptive fields of the two RGCs.

Haldan Keffer Hartline, who won the Nobel Prize in 1967, measured the RGC responses from horseshoe crabs (Hartline and Graham 1932), using which he famously demonstrated inhibitory signals (Hartline 1949; Hartline et al. 1956); he was also the first to use the term receptive field (Hartline 1938, 1939, 1940a, b). Barlow (1953) demonstrated the inhibitory signals in a frog's RGC, and Kuffler (1952, 1953) was the first to demonstrate the center-surround receptive-field structure in a mammalian (cat) RGC, with Barlow also making significant contributions (Barlow et al. 1957).

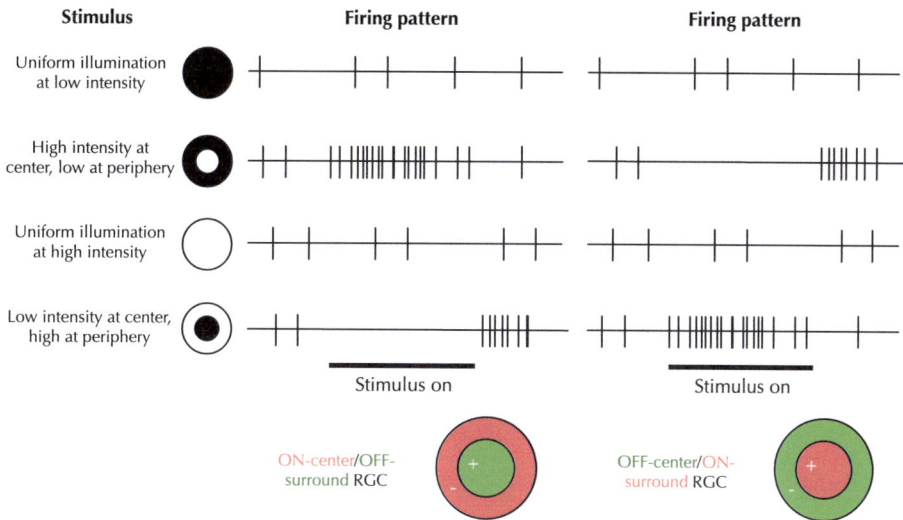

Fig. 2.11 RGCs have a center-surround receptive field with two types. The ON-center RGCs are excited by stimuli presented at the center but inhibited by stimuli presented at the surround (stimulus 2 on the left); OFF-center RGCs have the opposite response (stimulus 4 on the right)

2.4.2.4 Center-Surround Receptive Fields Are Designed to Encode Contrasts

Looking at the preferred stimulus of the two RGC types in Fig. 2.11 (stimulus 2 for ON-center and stimulus 4 for OFF-center), evidently the RGCs are designed to extract illuminant variations, i.e., contrast. If a visual field has a high (positive) Weber contrast, i.e., there is a small object that is significantly lighter than the background, the ON-center RGC would respond well to it. Similarly, an OFF-center RGC would respond well to a dark object placed against a light background.

We can also quantify the how the center-surround receptive fields respond to patterns of different Michelson contrast. A complication is that a pattern is described not only by its contrast but also by the frequency. At each frequency, we determine the minimal amount of contrast needed to produce a criterion level of RGC response (say 30 spikes/second).[3] The contrast sensitivity at that frequency is defined as the reciprocal of the threshold contrast. We then sweep the frequency and repeat this exercise for each frequency. The result of such a measurement is called the **Contrast Sensitivity Function** (CSF); Fig. 2.12 shows one such example.

We can see that the RGC's CSF is *bandpass*, where there is a preferred frequency to which an RGC responds the best. When the frequency is too low, the signal is equivalent to a uniform background; when the frequency is too high, the positive and negative cycles of the signal cancel each other. In both cases, an RGC would respond weakly.

---

[3] The implicit assumption here is that once the RGC responses reach a criterion level, the pattern becomes subjectively detectable at the behavioral level.

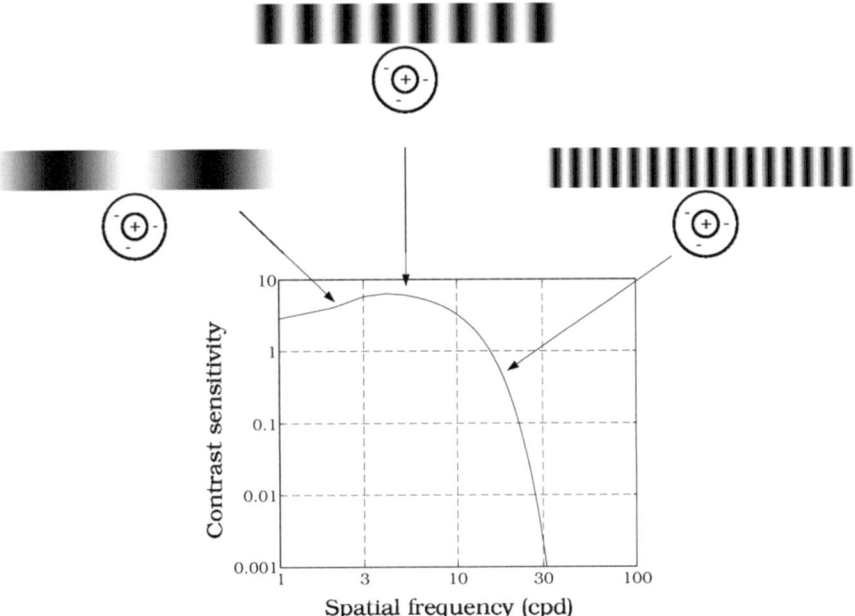

Fig. 2.12 Contrast sensitivity function (CSF) under a center-surround RGC. CSF is bandpass. It is worth emphasizing that the spatial frequency on the x-axis refers to the frequency of the retinal signal, not the signal in the world space. Depending on the viewing distance, the same world-space signal results in different retinal signals. From Star Whitt-Frousiakis (2013), which is from Wandell (1995, Fig. 5.18)

The CSF above allows us to study the joint effect of spatial frequency and contrast in detecting a patterned signal. In general, the ability of pattern detection depends on a number of other factors, such as the spatial frequency, eccentricity, color, and temporal frequency (if the stimulus is time-varying) (Mantiuk et al. 2022; Ashraf et al. 2024). Customarily, this high-dimensional data is plotted as a set of different CSFs, each quantifying the contrast sensitivity as a function of other factors.

Functionally, detecting contrast allows us to detect edges and contours: information across the two sides of an edge has the highest contrast. We will see shortly how later processing stages in the HVS leverage the contrasts to extract more specific information from the visual field to aid tasks such as object recognition.

2.4.2.5 RGCs "Discount" Background Illuminations: Light Adaptation

Looking at Fig. 2.11 again, the RGC responses do not change much with uniform illuminations (stimulus 1 and stimulus 3) regardless of the illumination level. This is true for a wide range of illumination levels. In some sense, the RGCs are able to "discount" the ambient

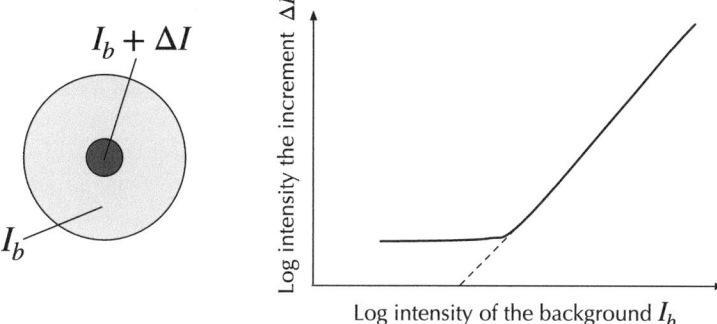

Fig. 2.13 Illustration of the RGC adaptation. Through the increment-threshold experiment, we show that, over a wide range of the background intensity I_b, the threshold ΔI needed for the spot light to be detectable is linearly proportional to I_b. That is, the minimal detectable contrast $\frac{\Delta I}{I_b}$ is roughly constant, a.k.a., the Weber's law, the result of light adaptation. The extended dashed line shows that the Weber's law does not hold for all the luminance levels. Enroth-Cugell et al. (1977, Fig. 6) and Sakmann and Creutzfeldt (1969) report actual data for cat's RGC

light level so that the contrast is reliably encoded at arbitrary light levels. This is called **light adaptation**.

Figure 2.13 illustrates an experiment showing the effect of light adaptation. It uses the "increment-threshold" paradigm, where there is a uniform background light with an intensity of I_b and a spot light is superimposed over the background; the spot light has an intensity increment ΔI over I_b. The entire stimulus (background + spot light) is impinging on the receptive field of an RGC. The goal is to adjust the increment of the spot light so that the RGC's response reaches a criterion level (e.g., 30 spikes per second). The plot in Fig. 2.13 shows the minimal amount of increment (y-axis) under different background intensities (x-axis).

We can see that over a wide range of background intensity I_b, the threshold ΔI needed for the spot light to be detectable is linearly proportional to I_b. That is, the minimal detectable (Weber) contrast $\frac{\Delta I}{I_b}$ is roughly constant. We could also perform this increment-threshold experiment *behaviorally* on human participants, through which we can derive the minimal ΔI needed for the spot light to be detectable to humans (Blakemore and Rushton 1965; Fuortes et al. 1961; Aguilar and Stiles 1954; Barlow 1957). Perhaps unsurprisingly, the same trend holds: over a rather wide range of background levels, the increment threshold varies linearly with the background intensity. This means, behaviorally, the minimal detectable contrast is also constant, and this constancy could potentially be accounted for by the physiological constancy.[4]

---

[4] We emphasize "potentially" because while correlation is easy to establish, claiming causation requires ruling out other factors.

Minimally detectable contrast being constant over different background intensities is called the **Weber's law** or the "Weber-Fechner law". A direct interpretation of the Weber's law is that stronger signals are needed at high ambient light levels for a signal to be barely detectable. It is almost like our visual system is "desensitized" at higher ambient light levels. This desensitization is very well documented for photoreceptors (Matthews 1988; Nakatani and Yau1988; Fain et al. 2001), and it is unsurprising that photoreceptor desensitization can lead to (although does not fully account for) the desensitization observed in the RGCs and in the behavioral experiments (Dunn et al. 2007).

This desensitization allows us to extract contrasts rather than absolute light levels, which is of significant advantage to us. The ambient level varies over several orders of magnitude, but the contrast of a scene is relatively stable regardless of the ambient light level. Consider our ape ancestors who need to find apples from a tree to survive. As the ambient light level increases, both the apple and the tree become brighter, but the contrast is relatively constant. To be able to reliably detect the apple, an ape needs to reliably extract contrast at all light levels but not the absolute light level itself.

Sharp readers like you have most definitely noticed that Weber's law does not hold at all background illumination levels (Kolb et al. 2005, Part VIII-Light and Dark Adaptation). The extended dashed line in Fig. 2.13 indicates that Weber's law fails at very low background levels. When the ambient light level is very low, Weber's law fails because the retinal responses are dominated by noise, both retinal internal noise (called dark light or dark noise) (Barlow 1957; Blakemore and Rushton 1965; Donner 1992) and external photon shot noise (Rosae 1948; De Vries 1943). At extremely high background levels, Weber's law also fails because of photoreceptor saturation. All in all, however, Weber's law holds reasonably well under a very wide range of normal lighting conditions that we encounter in every life.

Stated more formally, the Weber's law says:

$$\Delta I = k I_b, \tag{2.3}$$

where k is a constant representing how fast the threshold increases with the background and is called the Weber's constant.

When Eq. (2.3) is written in the log-log domain, as is plotted in Fig. 2.13, we have:

$$\log(\Delta I) = \log(k) + \log(I_b). \tag{2.4}$$

We can see that in the log-log plot, the Weber's constant affects the intercept of the threshold-vs-background line (the intersection of the dashed line and the y-axis). For the Weber's law to hold exactly, the slope of the threshold-vs-background line in the log-log plot must be 1, which is roughly the case in Fig. 2.13 (for the range where the relationship is linear). In many measurements, the slope fit from the data is not exactly 1. To account for this, the Weber's law is extended to take the following form:

$$\Delta I = k I_b^d,$$
$$\log(\Delta I) = \log(k) + d \log(I_b), \tag{2.5}$$

where d is a free parameter that allows for this additional degree of freedom.

Finally, although we will not discuss it in detail, a concept related to light adaptation is **dark adaptation**. Dark adaptation deals with the situation where the eye is first exposed to light at a certain level and then the light is removed. We can all tell from experience that our visual sensitivity is terrible when the light is just removed but will improve over time as we spend more time in the dark. Dark adaptation is concerned with quantifying the dynamics of the visual sensitivity recovery at different times in the dark. Once again, dark adaptation can be studied both psychophysically (Hecht et al. 1937; Crawford 1937, 1947) and physiologically (Lamb and Pugh 2004, 2006).

2.5   Post Retinal Processing

The signals leaving the retina are first routed to the **Lateral Geniculate Nucleus** (LGN) and then to the cortex, where vision is formed.

2.5.1   Lateral Geniculate Nucleus

Different classes of RGCs project to distinct LGN layers with virtually the same RFs: midget RGCs project to the Parvocellular layers (P cells) in the LGN (forming the P pathway/stream), parasol RGCs project to the Magnocellular layers (M cells) in the LGN (forming the M pathway/stream), and bistratified RGCs project to the Koniocellular layers (K cells) in the LGN (forming the K pathway/stream).

Similar to the RGCs, the LGN neurons also have center-surround receptive fields, and their receptive-field organizations are almost exact copies of that of the corresponding RGCs. This is why, by and large, LGN has been thought to be mainly a relay station, transmitting information from the retina to the brain. Interestingly, the way the LGN relays information to the brain is to gather information from one hemifield and send it to the other side of the cortex.

If LGN simply relays information, why does it exist at all? It turns out that LGN receives about 90% of its inputs from the cortex (Sherman and Koch 1986). This is different from the retina, which is a "closed" system that does not receive information from the rest of the brain. The feedback from the brain serves to regulate the visual signals before they are sent to the brain. Higher-order brain regions encode cognitive information such as attention, and one can imagine how attention can be used to influence what subsequent information is sent to the brain (O'Connor et al. 2002). If the brain were to send the feedback signals to the retina, the blind spot would have been 10 times larger, so the LGN seems like a convenient and cost-effective place where the feedback-driven regulation can take place.

2.5.1.1 Another Example of Parallel Pathways

Rods versus cones is an example of parallel pathways in the HVS. The parvocellular vs. magnocellular pathway is another example; they encode different spatial/temporal frequency information. The magnocellular pathway responds to high temporal frequency well, is sensitive to low spatial frequency, and responds strongly to contrast changes. The parvocellular pathway, in large part, behaves oppositely. It is worth noting that these two visual streams start from the retina, where they start from distinct RGC cell types, and remain physically separated all the way into the primary visual cortex V1. This is different from the rod vs. cone pathways, which start at the photoreceptors and merge at the RGC layer.

2.5.2   Visual Cortex

Once in the cortex, the visual signals are first processed in the **primary visual cortex**, also known as visual area 1 (**V1**) or the **striate cortex**. V1 neurons primarily encode edge orientations but are also tuned to edge lengths, object motion direction, and specific colors. David Hubel and Torsten Wiesel, who won the Nobel Prize in 1981, were the first to elucidate the responses of V1 neurons and the architecture of V1 in general (Hubel and Wiesel 1959, 1962, 1968).

2.5.2.1 V1 Simple Cells Are Orientation Selective

Perhaps the most striking feature of V1 neurons is that they are orientation selective. The left panel of Fig. 2.14 shows the responses of a cat V1 neuron, recorded by Hubel and Wiesel (1959), when presented with a slit of illumination at different orientations. This neuron responds best to a particular orientation (vertical in this case) and responds very weakly, if at all, to other orientations. The right panel in Fig. 2.14 plots the neuron responses (spikes/second) as a function of the illumination orientation; a plot like this is called the neuron's orientation **tuning curve**.

Why would this neuron be tuned to a specific orientation? It must be because its receptive field is oriented: when the orientation of the stimulus coincides with the excitatory (or inhibitory) region of the receptive field, the neuron is optimally stimulated Hubel and Wiesel (1959, Fig. 1). Other orientations would involve both the excitatory and inhibitory regions, reducing or abolishing the response. V1 cells with such a receptive field are called **simple cells**. Different simple cells might have different preferred orientations; for instance, the first cell in the right panel of Fig. 2.14 prefers a 90° orientation.

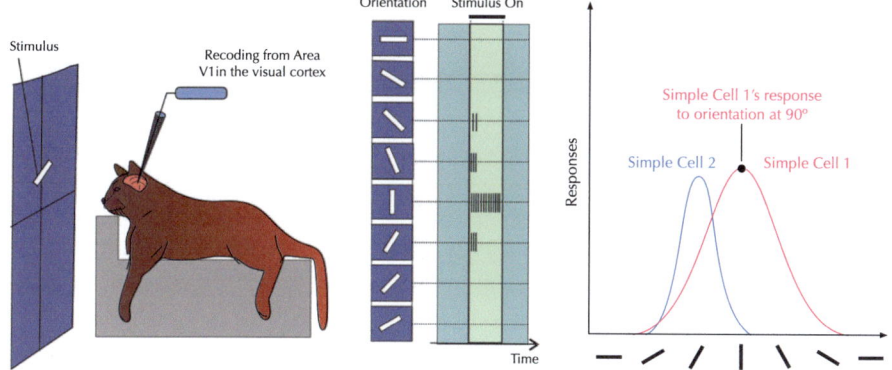

Fig. 2.14 Left: Orientation selectivity of a cat V1 simple cell; adapted from Pancrat (2012). Right: Orientation tuning curves of two illustrative V1 simple cells (do not necessarily correspond to the experimental data on the left); different cells can have different preferred orientations

Fig. 2.15 An orientation-selective V1 simple cell (left) can acquire its receptive field structure by synapsing with multiple center-surround LGN cells (right)

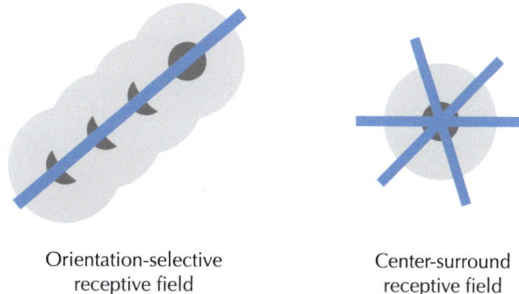

Orientation-selective
receptive field

Center-surround
receptive field

How would a V1 simple neuron acquire such an oriented receptive field? It turns out that an orientation-selective receptive field can be constructed from a collection of center-surround receptive fields—as long as they are wired in a particular way. Figure 2.15 illustrates the model suggested by Hubel and Wiesel (1962), which is supported by later electrophysiological results (Clay Reid and Alonso 1995). Each V1 simple cell synapses with and sums the inputs from multiple LGN neurons (which, recall, also have the center-surround receptive fields as the RGCs), whose receptive fields abut on the retina and are arranged in an oblique angle. When those receptive fields all have the same ON-center (or OFF-center) structure, the simple cell would tune for an oblique, elongated edge. Therefore, even if center-surround cells do not have orientation selectivity, V1 simple cells can.

2.5.2.2 Direction, Length, and Binocular Vision Emerge from (Hyper)Complex Cells

The majority of neurons in V1 are actually not simple cells. Three-quarters of the V1 neurons are **complex cells**. Complex cells have more complex selectivities. Fundamentally, their receptive fields cannot be subdivided into excitatory and inhibitory areas. That is, they do not respond to a spot light no matter where the light is placed in the receptive field. Therefore, their responses to complicated geometries cannot be explained/predicted by their responses to spot lights, unlike those of simple cells.

The complex cells are also orientation selective, but unlike simple cells, many complex cells respond only to a properly oriented edge *sweeping* across the receptive field *as if* (but not actually) the entire receptive field is excitatory. However, they do not respond at all, or only weakly at the onset or turning off, when we present a properly oriented, stationary edge. This further shows that the responses of complex cells are not a linear superposition of responses to spot lights.

Interestingly, about one-fifth of the complex cells prefer movement in a particular direction, showing the **direction selectivity** of many complex cells. Hubel and Wiesel (1968) measured the direction selectivity of V1 complex cells in monkeys; many complex cells are optimally stimulated by a properly oriented edge moving across a particular direction, but not the opposing, orthogonal direction.

Hubel and Wiesel (1968) also discovered a set of what they call the **end-stopping** neurons or hypercomplex cells in V1. Those neurons are tuned to properly oriented edges with a specific length, beyond which the neurons are inhibited. These neurons play a role in encoding corners, curvatures, and sudden breaks in lines (Hubel 1995, p. 85).

Finally, Hubel and Wiesel also found that some V1 neurons respond to stimuli only from the left eye or only from the right eye, a property termed **ocular dominance**. There are also binocular cells that can be stimulated independently by stimulus from either eye. There cells represent the first stage where information from the left and right hemi-fields converge, which is critical for depth perception.

2.5.2.3 "Be More Specific"

An obvious conclusion we can draw from comparing the V1 neurons and the retina/LGN neurons is this: as we progress along the visual pathway, the stimulus we present to the visual system must be more specific. Put another way, our visual system increasingly extracts more specific information as signals progress in the pathway.

Being more specific is critical, as that allows us to recognize objects by their subtle details. For instance, the RGCs/LGN neurons provide the contrast/edge detection capability, but virtually any object has contrasts and edges, so they are not terribly useful in recognizing specific objects. The V1 simple neurons, however, allow us to detect orientations, and that is critical to our vision—from orientations we can then infer shapes, as we recognize objects mostly by their shapes.

Critically, however, the V1 simple neurons offer orientation selectivity *precisely because* the RGCs/LGN neurons have contrast/edge detection capabilities, as demonstrated in Fig. 2.15. This is why we say the early visual system extracts low-level information, but

Fig. 2.16 Once in the cortex, signals are projected from area V1 to other areas, each generally specialized in a particular information process. The two main pathways from V1 are the ventral pathway ("what") and the dorsal pathway ("where"). There is top-down feedback in the cortex from higher-order areas to lower-order areas. Adapted from Selket (2007)

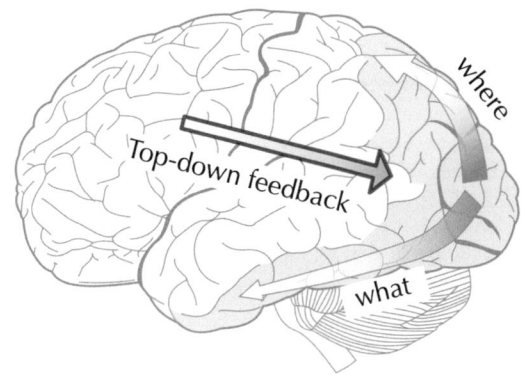

the later visual system extracts high-level information: the former is used as the building blocks by the latter.

2.5.2.4 The Rest of the Cortex

From V1, signals are projected to other areas such as V2, V4, IT, MT, etc. There are two main projection pathways (Nassi and Callaway 2009; Ungerleider and Mishkin 1982; Mishkin et al. 1983), as shown in Fig. 2.16. The first is the **dorsal** pathway, which is concerned with observing objects in space, such as their spatial location and motion, information that is also useful to guide actions (Goodale et al. 1991). Therefore, this pathway is also called the "where/how" pathway. The other is the **ventral** pathway, or the "what" pathway, that carries information of the details and identity of objects and supports visual functions such as object recognition, facial recognition, and color perception. The two pathways interact. For instance, to guide visual action we not only need to know the position and motion of the objects but also the shape, color, etc.

The discussion so far focuses on the bottom-up information flow, the flow of information from lower-order representations in the hierarchy, such as V1, to higher-order representations, such as V4 and beyond. There is also a top-down information flow from the higher regions to the lower regions. This information flow provides feedback information such as attention, knowledge, and expectation to influence the early information processing in the cortex (Gilbert and Li 2013; Briggs 2020). Combining the bottom-up and the top-down flows, the HVS acts essentially as a self-adaptive system that automatically optimizes its performance for a given task.

References

Aguilar M, Stiles W (1954) Saturation of the rod mechanism of the retina at high levels of stimulation. Optica Acta: Int J Opt 1(1):59–65

Angueyra-Aristizábal JM (2014) The limits imposed in primate vision by transduction in cone photoreceptors. PhD thesis, University of Washington Libraries

Ashraf M, Mantiuk RK, Chapiro A, Wuerger S (2024) castlecsf-a contrast sensitivity function of color, area, spatiotemporal frequency, luminance and eccentricity. J Vis 24(4):5–5

Barlow HB (1953) Summation and inhibition in the frog's retina. J Physiol 119(1):69

Barlow HB (1957) Increment thresholds at low intensities considered as signal/noise discriminations. J Physiol 136(3):469

Barlow HB, Fitzhugh R, Kuffler S (1957) Change of organization in the receptive fields of the cat's retina during dark adaptation. J Physiol 137(3):338

Berson DM, Dunn FA, Takao M (2002) Phototransduction by retinal ganglion cells that set the circadian clock. Science 295(5557):1070–1073

Blakemore C, Rushton W (1965) Dark adaptation and increment threshold in a rod monochromat. J Physiol 181(3):612

Boettner EA, Wolter JR (1962) Transmission of the ocular media. Invest Ophthal Vis Sci 1(6):776–783

Bowmaker J, Dartnall H, Lythgoe J, Mollon J (1978) The visual pigments of rods and cones in the rhesus monkey. Macaca Mulatta. J Physiol 274(1):329–348

Briggs F (2020) Role of feedback connections in central visual processing. Ann Rev Vis Sci 6(1):313–334

Caerbannog (2016) Comparison of structures in vertebrate's eye (left) with octopus' eye (right); CC BY-SA 3.0 license. https://en.wikipedia.org/wiki/Blind_spot_(vision)#/media/File:Evolution_eye_2.svg

Clay Reid R, Alonso JM (1995) Specificity of monosynaptic connections from thalamus to visual cortex. Nature 378(6554):281–284

Cmglee (2021) Human photoreceptor distribution; CC BY-SA 3.0. https://commons.wikimedia.org/wiki/File:Human_photoreceptor_distribution.svg

Crawford B (1937) The change of visual sensitivity with time. Proc Royal Soc Lond Series B-Biol Sci 123(830):69–89

Crawford B (1947) Visual adaptation in relation to brief conditioning stimuli. Proc Royal Soc Lond Series B-Biol Sci 134(875):283–302

Curcio CA, Sloan KR, Kalina RE, Hendrickson AE (1990) Human photoreceptor topography. J Comp Neurol 292(4):497–523

Dacey DM, Petersen MR (1992) Dendritic field size and morphology of midget and parasol ganglion cells of the human retina. Proc Natl Acad Sci 89(20):9666–9670

Dacey DM, Liao HW, Peterson BB, Robinson FR, Smith VC, Pokorny J, Yau KW, Gamlin PD (2005) Melanopsin-expressing ganglion cells in primate retina signal colour and irradiance and project to the LGN. Nature 433(7027):749–754

Dartnall HJ, Bowmaker JK, Mollon JD (1983) Human visual pigments: microspectrophotometric results from the eyes of seven persons. Proc Royal Soc Lond Ser B. Biol Sci 220(1218):115–130

De Vries H (1943) The quantum character of light and its bearing upon threshold of vision, the differential sensitivity and visual acuity of the eye. Physica 10(7):553–564

Do MTH, Yau K (2010) Intrinsically photosensitive retinal ganglion cells. Physiol Rev 90(4)

Donner K (1992) Noise and the absolute thresholds of cone and rod vision. Vis Res 32(5):853–866

Dunn FA, Lankheet MJ, Rieke F (2007) Light adaptation in cone vision involves switching between receptor and post-receptor sites. Nature 449(7162):603–606

Enroth-Cugell C, Hertz BG, Lennie P (1977) Cone signals in the cat's retina. J Physiol 269(2):273–296

Fain GL, Matthews HR, Cornwall MC, Koutalos Y (2001) Adaptation in vertebrate photoreceptors. Physiol Rev 81(1):117–151

Fuortes M, Gunkel R, Rushton W (1961) Increment thresholds in a subject deficient in cone vision. J Physiol 156(1):179

Gilbert CD, Li W (2013) Top-down influences on visual processing. Nat Rev Neurosci 14(5):350–363

Goodale MA, Milner AD, Jakobson LS, Carey DP (1991) A neurological dissociation between perceiving objects and grasping them. Nature 349(6305):154–156

Hartline HK (1938) The response of single optic nerve fibers of the vertebrate eye to illumination of the retina. Am J Physiol-Legacy Content 121(2):400–415

Hartline HK (1939) Excitation and inhibition of the "off" response in vertebrate optic nerve fibers. Am J Physiol 126:527

Hartline HK (1940) The effects of spatial summation in the retina on the excitation of the fibers of the optic nerve. Am J Physiol-Legacy Content 130(4):700–711

Hartline HK (1940) The receptive fields of optic nerve fibers. Am J Physiol-Legacy Content 130(4):690–699

Hartline HK (1949) Inhibition of activity of visual receptors by illuminating nearby retinal areas in the limulus eye. Fed Proc 8(1):69

Hartline HK, Graham CH (1932) Nerve impulses from single receptors in the eye. J Cell Comp Physiol 1:277–295

Hartline HK, Wagner HG, Ratliff F (1956) Inhibition in the eye of limulus. J Gen Physiol 39(5):651–673

Hattar S, Liao HW, Takao M, Berson DM, Yau K (2002) Melanopsin-containing retinal ganglion cells: architecture, projections, and intrinsic photosensitivity. Science 295(5557):1065–1070

Hecht S, Haig C, Chase AM (1937) The influence of light adaptation on subsequent dark adaptation of the eye. J Gen Physiol 20(6):831–850

Hodgkin AL, Huxley AF (1952) A quantitative description of membrane current and its application to conduction and excitation in nerve. J Physiol 117(4):500

Hubel DH (1995) Eye, brain, and vision. Scientific American Library/Scientific American Books

Hubel DH, Wiesel TN (1959) Receptive fields of single neurones in the cat's striate cortex. J Physiol 148(3):574–591

Hubel DH, Wiesel TN (1962) Receptive fields, binocular interaction and functional architecture in the cat's visual cortex. J Physiol 160(1):106

Hubel DH, Wiesel TN (1968) Receptive fields and functional architecture of monkey striate cortex. J Physiol 195(1):215–243

Idrees S, Manookin MB, Rieke F, Field GD, Zylberberg J (2024) Biophysical neural adaptation mechanisms enable artificial neural networks to capture dynamic retinal computation. Nat Commun 15(1):5957

Jacobs GH (2008) Primate color vision: a comparative perspective. Vis Neurosci 25(5–6):619–633

Kolb H, Fernandez E, Nelson R (2005) The organization of the retina and visual system. In: Webvision-the organization of the retina and visual system

Kuffler SW (1952) Neurons in the retina: organization, inhibition and excitation problems. In: Cold spring harbor symposia on quantitative biology, vol 17. Cold Spring Harbor Laboratory Press, pp 281–292

Kuffler SW (1953) Discharge patterns and functional organization of mammalian retina. J Neurophysiol 16(1):37–68

Lamb T, Pugh EN Jr (2004) Dark adaptation and the retinoid cycle of vision. Progr Retinal Eye Res 23(3):307–380

Lamb TD, Pugh EN (2006) Phototransduction, dark adaptation, and rhodopsin regeneration: the proctor lecture. Invest Ophthalmol Vis Sci 47(12):5138–5152

LaValle SM (2023) Virtual reality. Cambridge University Press

Lazzerini Ospri L, Prusky G, Hattar S (2017) Mood, the circadian system, and melanopsin retinal ganglion cells. Ann Rev Neurosci 40(1):539–556

Liao F, Zhou Z, Kim BJ, Chen J, Wang J, Wan T, Zhou Y, Hoang AT, Wang C, Kang J et al (2022) Bioinspired in-sensor visual adaptation for accurate perception. Nat Electron 5(2):84–91

Mantiuk RK, Ashraf M, Chapiro A (2022) stelacsf: a unified model of contrast sensitivity as the function of spatio-temporal frequency, eccentricity, luminance and area. ACM Trans Graph (TOG) 41(4):1–16

Matthews H, Murphy R, Fain G, Lamb T (1988) Photoreceptor light adaptation is mediated by cytoplasmic calcium concentration. Nature 334(6177):67–69

Mishkin M, Ungerleider LG, Macko KA (1983) Object vision and spatial vision: two cortical pathways. Trends Neurosci 6:414–417

Nakatani K, Yau K (1988) Calcium and light adaptation in retinal rods and cones. Nature 334(6177):69–71

Nassi JJ, Callaway EM (2009) Parallel processing strategies of the primate visual system. Nat Rev Neurosci 10(5):360–372

O'Connor DH, Fukui MM, Pinsk MA, Kastner S (2002) Attention modulates responses in the human lateral geniculate nucleus. Nat Neurosci 5(11):1203–1209

Pancrat (2012) Direction-selective response of striate cortex neurons V1; CC BY-SA 3.0. https://commons.wikimedia.org/wiki/File:Orientation_V1.svg

Rose A (1948) The sensitivity performance of the human eye on an absolute scale. J Opt Soc Am 38(2):196–208

Sakmann B, Creutzfeldt OD (1969) Scotopic and mesopic light adaptation in the cat's retina. Pflügers Archiv 313:168–185

Selket (2007) The ventral vs. dorsal stream; CC BY-SA 3.0. https://commons.wikimedia.org/wiki/File:Ventral-dorsal_streams.svg

Sherman S, Koch C (1986) The control of retinogeniculate transmission in the mammalian lateral geniculate nucleus. Exp Brain Res 63:1–20

Star Whitt-Frousiakis (2013) Contrast sensitivity vs. spatial frequency; CC BY-SA 3.0. https://commons.wikimedia.org/wiki/File:Contrast_Sensitivity_vs._Spacial_Frequency.png

Ungerleider LG, Mishkin M (1982) Two cortical visual systems. In: Ingle DJ, Goodale MA, Mansfield RJ et al (eds) Analysis of visual behavior. MIT Press Cambridge, MA, pp 549–586

Wald G (1968) Molecular basis of visual excitation. Science 162(3850):230–239

Wandell BA (1995) Foundations of vision. Sinauer Associates

Wodnicki R, Roberts GW, Levine MD (1995) A foveated image sensor in standard CMOS technology. In: Proceedings of the IEEE 1995 custom integrated circuits conference. IEEE, pp 357–360

Color Vision

3

3.1 How do Photoreceptors Work?

Color vision starts from the photoreceptors. We will take a brief look at how photoreceptors turn optical signals into electrical signals, and derive the spectral sensitivity functions of the photoreceptors, which serve as the basis of color encoding further down the line.

3.1.1 Counting Photons: Principle of Univariance

Anatomically, a photoreceptor has two parts: an inner segment and an outer segment. Photons enter from the inner segment, which for the most part can be thought of as a waveguide that funnels the photons to the outer segment. The outer segment contains the photon-absorbing pigments. This is illustrated in Fig. 3.1.

Conceptually, we can think of each photoreceptor as a bucket that collects photons. There are millions of buckets sitting on the retina, taking a shower of photons. Many photons entering the eye will not hit any bucket: they are absorbed before they reach the bucket (e.g., by the lens). Any photon that does hit the bucket has a certain *probability* of being absorbed. The absorption probability varies with the photoreceptor type and the photon's wavelength.

Fundamentally, a photoreceptor can absorb photons because it contains light-sensitive, photon-absorbing pigments, each of which is able to absorb one photon. Each rod photoreceptor has tens of millions of such pigments (Milo and Phillips 2015; Nathans 1992, pp. 142–147). Why is a photon's absorption probability not 100% once it enters a photoreceptor? For one, a photon might not meet a photopigment as it travels through the photoreceptor before the exit. Even if a photon hits a pigment, its absorption is still probabilistic, as absorption is dictated fundamentally by quantum mechanics.

Once a photon is absorbed, it has a certain probability of "exciting" or "isomerizing" the pigment. A pigment **excitation** or **isomerization** generates a certain level of electri-

© The Author(s), under exclusive license to Springer Nature Switzerland AG 2026
Y. Zhu, *Visual Computing For Architects*, Synthesis Lectures on Computer Architecture,
https://doi.org/10.1007/978-3-032-05018-2_3

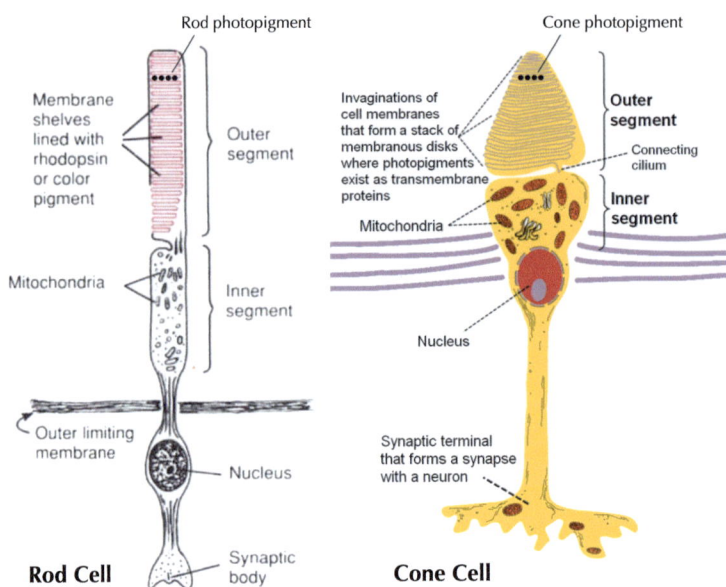

Fig. 3.1 Anatomical structures of rods and cones. The outer segment contains photon-absorbing photopigments, each of which has the capability of absorbing a photon and being excited/isomerized after absorption. Adapted from Ivo Kruusam gi (2010) and Kosigrim (2007)

cal signal—in the form of a current or voltage change across the cell membrane of the photoreceptor. The excitation probability once a photon is absorbed is called the **quantum efficiency** of the pigment. Quantum efficiency is about two-thirds in the visible spectrum, and is not wavelength sensitive (Dartnall 1972; Fu 2010; Kropf 1982). A pigment excitation is also called pigment **bleach**, since the pigment after excitation is no longer responsive to light as if it is bleached.

The process of initiating an electrical response upon a photon absorption is called photo-transduction. It is important to know that for a given class of photoreceptors, the electrical response caused by a photon absorption is constant regardless of the photon's wavelength. This is called the **Principle of Univariance** (Naka and Rushton 1966; Rushton 1972a, b): each photon that generates an electrical response has the same effect as any other photon that does so. In other words, the only effect that wavelength has is to impact the probability a photon gets absorbed; the wavelength information is lost after absorption.

A crucial implication of this principle is that any two lights that are equally absorbed/excited will be seen as the same light by the human vision. For the purpose of comparing two lights, think of each bucket as having a counter; every time a photon is absorbed and excites a pigment, the counter gets incremented by 1. If two lights lead to the same counter value, they are perceptually the same. Crucially, if a bucket's counter is, say, twice as high as another's, it does *not* mean the electrical response produced by the first photoreceptor is twice as high as that of the second.

3.1.2   Spectral Absorbance and Absorptance

To understand vision in everyday scenarios, what we care about is not the probability of how a single photon is absorbed and excites a pigment, but the collective behavior of a flux of photons that enter our eyes. Conveniently, when we have a large population of photons, the probability that an individual photon causes an excitation translates to the *percentage* of incident photons that are absorbed and/or cause excitations. In fact, the percentage of absorption is the quantity that we can directly measure.

As discussed on Sect. 2.4.1.2, a common way to estimate the absorption rate of a flux of photons is using a technique called microspectrophotometry (MSP). The idea of MSP is to shine a beam of light through a photoreceptor and then measure, at the other side, the percentage of photons that are transmitted, i.e., unabsorbed (Bowmaker 1984). Ignoring back-scattering,[1] photon absorption by photopigments in a photoreceptor can be modeled using the Beer-Lambert law (Sect. 7.2.1). The **transmittance** at wavelength λ is defined as the ratio between the amount of transmitted photons $I_d(\lambda)$ and the amount of total incident photons $I_0(\lambda)$:

$$T(\lambda) = \frac{I_d(\lambda)}{I_0(\lambda)} = e^{-\epsilon(\lambda)cl}, \tag{3.1}$$

where $\epsilon(\lambda)$ is called the absorption coefficient and is wavelength dependent, c is the concentration (the number of pigments per unit volume), and l is the optical length, the length through which a photon has to travel.[2] Both c and l are inherent properties of a photoreceptor and are not dependent on photon wavelength.

Absorptance $a(\lambda)$, the percentage of absorption at λ, is naturally $1 - T(\lambda)$. **Absorbance** $A(\lambda)$ (also called the **optical density**), whose spelling is subtly and annoyingly different from that of absorptance, is defined as:

$$A(\lambda) = -\ln(T(\lambda)) = \epsilon(\lambda)cl. \tag{3.2}$$

---

[1] Without back-scattering, we can assume any unabsorbed photons will be transmitted through, and measured at the other side of, the photoreceptor. In reality, a very small amount of some photons might be scattered backward toward where they come from and will not be measured either, but the effect is small.

[2] $\epsilon(\lambda)$ so-defined has a unit of m^2, and c so-defined has a unit of m^{-3}. In the literature, sometimes people define $\epsilon(\lambda)$ to be the **molar absorption coefficient**, which has a unit of $m^2 \, mol^{-1}$, and define c to be the **molar concentration** (the number of moles of pigments per unit volume), which has a unit of m^{-3}.

Therefore, absorptance $a(\lambda)$ and absorbance $A(\lambda)$ are related by:

$$a(\lambda) = 1 - e^{-A(\lambda)}. \tag{3.3}$$

We would repeat this experiment over a frequency range and obtain the axial absorbance at each sampled frequency. The resulting plot is usually called the **absorbance spectrum**. One such example is shown in Fig. 2.7, measured by Dartnall et al. (1983) on humans. Much such data has been obtained in the literature, the earliest of which is perhaps by George Wald and his colleagues (Brown and Wald 1964; Marks et al. 1964) who identified three distinct absorbance spectra in cone-mediated vision and, thus, provided direct physiological evidence for the existence of three classes of cones. The three cone types are generally referred to as the **L**, **M**, and **S** cones, since their absorbances peak at, relatively, long, medium, and short wavelengths.

Decades before the work by Wald et al., Ragnar Granit, who shared the Nobel Prize in 1967 with George Wald (and Haldan Keffer Hartline), measured the spectral sensitivities of the retinal ganglion cells (Granit 1941, 1943, 1945a, b). Granit showed the existence of two classes of RGCs: (1) one that has a broader spectral sensitivity whose peak shifts to shorter wavelengths from photopic vision to scotopic vision, and (2) one whose spectral sensitivities are narrower and fall generally into three main groups. The former is the physiological version of the Purkinje shift that we will discuss in Sect. 3.4.2, and provides direct evidence for the convergence of the rod and the cone vision pathways (Sect. 2.4.1.4 and Fig. 2.3). The latter is the first direct evidence of the existence of three dinstinct wavelength encoding mechanism (albeit not at the photoreceptor level), essential for the trichromatic color vision.

3.1.2.1 Normalization

Quite often, the absorbance spectrum is normalized to peak at unity, as is the case in Fig. 2.7. According to Eq. (3.2), normalizing absorbance across different wavelengths is equivalent to normalizing ϵ across wavelengths, since c and l are not wavelength specific, whereas ϵ is. c and l might vary across species and across individuals and might differ between different illumination methods (see below), but ϵ, which is fundamental to the photopigment, does not. Therefore, the normalized absorbance spectrum tells us something fundamental about the wavelength sensitivity of the photopigments.

Perhaps a subtlety but quite confusing when perusing the literature, the maximum absolute absorbance across all wavelengths (i.e., the peak of an absorbance spectrum) is usually simply called the "optical density"; "peak optical density" would have been more accurate, as optical density is wavelength specific. Using the peak optical density and the normalized absorbance spectrum, we can reconstruct the absolute absorbance spectrum; from there we can get the absolute absorptance spectrum.

While not shown here, the peak absorbance between rods and cones is not that different. The peak absorbance of rods is about 0.475, and the value is about 0.375 for foveal S cones and 0.525 for foveal L/M cones (Bowmaker and Dartnall 1980; Bowmaker et al. 1978). The large sensitivity difference between rod vision and cone vision is not primarily attributed to the difference in their ability to absorb photons.

3.1.2.2 Correcting for Transverse Illuminations

There is one more complication. With MSP, we illuminate a photoreceptor *transversely*, i.e., the light passes from one side of the photoreceptor to the other side. In reality, when a photon enters a photoreceptor, it travels *axially* from the inner segment through the outer segment. The main difference between these two scenarios is the optical length that a photon has to travel. A photoreceptor is tall and skinny, so its width is much smaller than its length, about 2.5μm wide and 35μm long for a fovea L/M cone (Polyak 1941).

Therefore, we need to first calculate the absorbance per unit length, called the **specific absorbance**, and then scale the specific absorbance by the axial length of the photoreceptor to obtain the axial absorbance, from which we can estimate the axial absorptance using Eq. (3.3). This is shown below (omitting λ for simplicity):

$$A_{\text{transverse}} = -\ln(p_{\text{transverse}}) = \epsilon c l_{\text{transverse}} \tag{3.4a}$$

$$A_{\text{specific}} = \frac{A_{\text{transverse}}}{l_{\text{transverse}}} = \epsilon c \tag{3.4b}$$

$$A_{\text{axial}} = A_{\text{specific}} l_{\text{axial}} \tag{3.4c}$$

$$T_{\text{axial}} = e^{-A_{\text{axial}}} \tag{3.4d}$$

3.1.3   Response Versus Light Intensity

The Principle of Univariance tells us that the electrical response from a photon absorption is constant without regard to the photon wavelength, but it does not tell us how the *magnitude* of the electrical response varies with the *number* of photons absorbed. With the basic understanding of phototransduction, we can now turn to this question. You might be tempted to think that the relationship is linear, and you would be wrong!

3.1.3.1 Peak Response is Not Linearly Proportional to Light Intensity

Figure 3.2 shows the normalized photoreceptor (peak) response of macaque rods under flash lights of different intensities. If the relationship between the response magnitude and the light intensity were linear, the curve would be a straight line. But in reality, we can see that the response grows quickly initially, but the growth slows down soon. What does the actual relationship tell us about photoreceptors? Let's define the photoreceptor's sensitivity, or its response rate, to flash lights as the additional response per unit increment in light intensity.

The sensitivity/response rate is given by the derivative of the curve, i.e., the slope at every point on the curve. Evidently, the response rate slows down as light becomes more intense; in other words, the photoreceptor becomes less sensitive as light becomes more intense. While the discussions here focus on photoreceptor responses to flash lights, the conclusion holds for responses to steady background lights as well.

This non-linear relationship can be used to explain our brightness perception. Our perceived brightness is not linear with respect to the light intensity. Imagine you walk into a dark room and turn one light on; the perceived brightness changes a lot (literally from 0 to 1); then you turn another light on and another light on; every time you turn on an additional light, your perceived brightness increases, but not as much as before. As you continue, the additional brightness you feel from turning one additional light on becomes smaller: you probably would not notice it if someone turned on one more light when there are 1,000 lights on already.

This non-linear relationship between perceived brightness and absolute light power is important when deciding how to effectively allocate digital bits when encoding pixel values. A classic example is the gamma encoding/compression in the popular sRGB color space, a topic we will turn to in Sect. 4.3.2.

The reduction of sensitivity under stronger lights is called **desensitization**, and is stereotypical of photoreceptor **light adaptation**. A curious question is, does desensitization provide us any benefits? Do we not want our photoreceptors to be more sensitive to light? Without desensitization, i.e., if the initial response rate was maintained, the rod would saturate at about 47 pigment excitations, as shown in Fig. 3.2. The desensitization allows the photoreceptors to extend their operating range, which, in turn, allows our vision to operate at higher light levels.

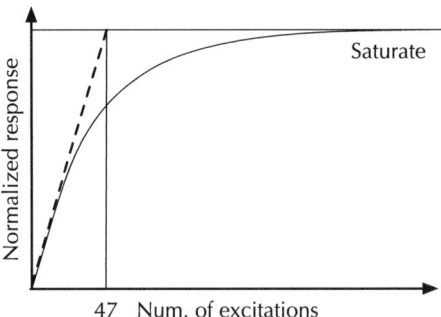

Fig. 3.2 Illustration of the photoreceptor normalized (peak) response as a function of flash intensity (which is proportional to the actual number of pigment excitations); Rodieck (1998, p. 178) and Baylor et al. (1984, Fig. 1) show actual data. The tangential line shows that only 47 pigment excitations would saturate the photoreceptor *if* the photoreceptor does not desensitize

3.1.3.2 Linear Range

If you observe Fig. 3.2 closely, you will see that the response versus flash intensity is lin-ear when the lights are dim. This linear relationship is used to estimate the single photon response: we cannot easily measure the response of a single photon as it is difficult to pre-cisely deliver just one single photon, but this linear relationship in the dim range allows us to estimate such a response by scaling the response of a dim light by its intensity.

Mathematically, the response versus intensity relationship is modeled in literature either by a negative exponential function (when negative feedbacks are weak) (Baylor et al. 1984; Kraft et al. 1993; Lamb et al. 1981) or by the Michaelis equation (when negative feedbacks are not negligible) (Baylor and Fuortes 1970; Baylor et al. 1974, 1979; Fain 1976; Ingram et al. 2016; Normann and Perlman 1979; Schneeweis and Schnapf 1995). The negative expo-nential model would look something like $r/r_{max} = 1 - e^{-ki}$, where r, r_{max}, and i denote the response, maximum response, and flash light intensity, respectively; k is a constant fit to data. The Michaelis equation, which is also called the Naka-Rushton equation (presumably because Naka and Rushton 1966 was the first to use it), looks like $r/r_{max} = \frac{i}{i+\sigma}$, where σ is a constant fit to data. Sometimes it would fit the data better to use the generalized Michaelis equation, which takes the form $r/r_{max} = \frac{i^n}{i^n+\sigma^n}$, where n is the additional control parameter. Both models can be approximated by a linear function when i is small. This linear region perhaps also explains why the sRGB encoding is a piece-wise function where the encoding is linear when light levels are low.

3.1.4   Cone Fundamentals: Cornea-Referred Spectral Sensitivities

Our discussions so far have focused on absorption by the photoreceptors, but for a flux of photons arriving at the cornea about to enter our eye, they are also absorbed even before reaching the photoreceptors. Accounting for these **pre-receptoral** filters is important to model human vision. Spectral sensitivities that account for these pre-receptoral filters are what we call the *cornea-referred* spectral sensitivities.

3.1.4.1 Cone Fundamentals From Physiology

There are two such pre-receptoral filters: the ocular media (Sect. 2.2.2) and the macular pigments, which are located at a small area in the fovea. Macular pigments absorb light presumably to counter some of the aberrations from the ocular media and to protect the retina from light damage (Snodderly et al. 1984). Both ocular media and macular pigments absorb light selectively over the spectrum, just like photoreceptors do.

We can model $E(\lambda)$, the fraction of photons arriving at the cornea that are absorbed by the photoreceptors:

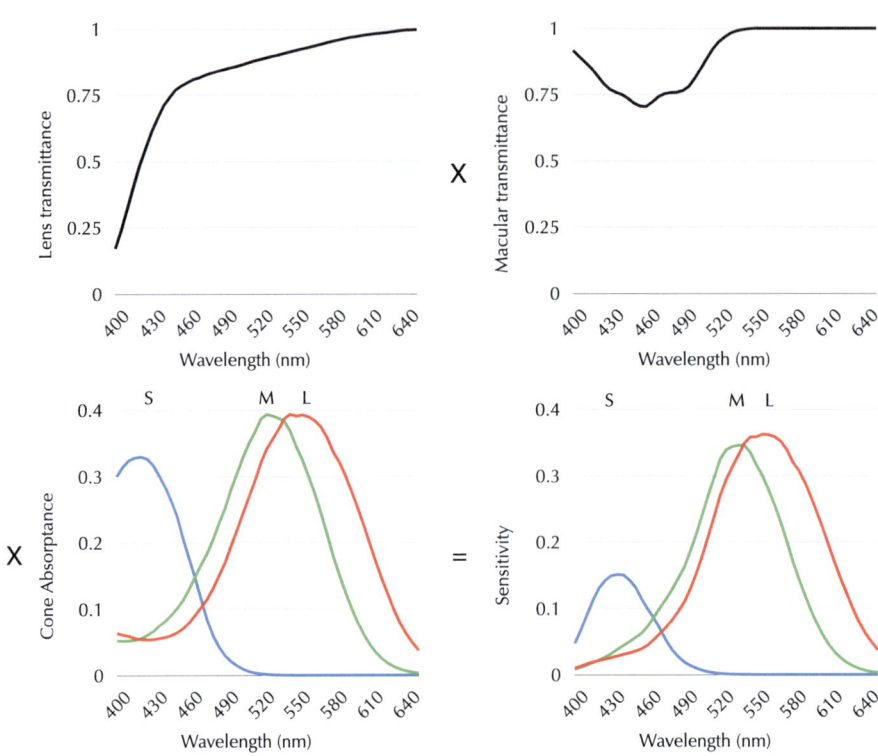

Fig. 3.3 Cornea-referred spectral sensitivity function measures the percentage of photons arriving at the cornea (about to enter the eye) that are absorbed by each photoreceptor type at each wavelength. The cone versions of this are called the cone fundamentals and are visualized in the bottom right. The sensitivity metric relates to the rate of pigment excitation only by a constant scaling factor (i.e., the photoreceptor quantum efficiency, which is about two-thirds). It is a product of ocular transmittance (top left), macular transmittance (top right), and photoreceptor absorptance (bottom left). The macular transmittance and lens transmittance are from Stockman et al. (1999); the cone absorptance spectra are estimated from Stockman and Sharpe (2000) (different from the Dartnall et al. 1983 data used in Fig. 2.7; see the methodology in CVRL 2025)

$$E(\lambda) = l(\lambda)m(\lambda)a(\lambda) \tag{3.5}$$

where $a(\lambda)$ represents the photoreceptor absorptance spectrum, $l(\lambda)$ and $m(\lambda)$ represent ocular and macular transmittance spectrum, respectively, i.e., the fraction of photons at λ *unabsorbed* by the ocular media (e.g., lens) (Boettner and Wolter 1962; Norren and Vos 1974) and the macular pigments. Figure 3.3 illustrates this process.

We call $E(\lambda)$ the cornea-referred spectral sensitivity function, since it is calculated with respect to the incident lights at the cornea surface. When $a(\lambda)$ is replaced by the absorptance spectra of the three classes of cones, the resulting sensitivity functions are more commonly referred to as the **cone fundamentals**.

We can make a few general observations about the cone fundamentals. First, the cone sensitivity drops to 0 beyond the 380 and 780 nm range, a range we usually call the visible spectrum, since there will be no pigment excitation beyond that range: lights beyond that range are invisible. Second, S cones are generally the least sensitive of the three cone types, but it is not because of the photoreceptors but because of the pre-receptoral filters, which absorb mostly low-wavelength lights.

3.1.4.2 Cone Fundamentals From Psychophysics

The spectral sensitivities discussed above are measured physiologically. We can also measure such functions through psychophysics using the increment-threshold method. A typical set up is one where there is a uniform background illumination and a spot light superimposed at the center of the background. We ask a participant to adjust a knob to control the intensity of the spot light so that it is just noticeable from the background. The sensitivity is then defined as the reciprocal of the threshold intensity. We repeat this experiment for each sampled wavelength across the spectrum to obtain a sensitivity curve. This method is first used in the pioneering work done by Stiles (1939, 1959, 1964), and is adopted in virtually all later work (Smith and Pokorny 1975; Stockman and Sharpe 2000; Stockman et al. 1999; Wald 1964).

A curious question is how we can separate the sensitivity of different photoreceptor types, given that the spectral sensitivities of the four photoreceptor types overlap. There are two methods to isolate rods from cones. We can either use very dim lights, to which cone responses are too small to contribute to vision (Crawford 1949), or we could measure from people with rod monochromacy—individuals who have only rods. When measuring cone sensitivities, we will use intense lights that almost completely saturate rods.

Isolating the three cone types from each other is generally challenging with individuals with normal vision. W.S. Stiles' initial work (Stiles 1939, 1959) designed special conditions of background illumination to suppress the sensitivity of two unwanted cone types while sparing the one under study. Modern studies usually turn to color-deficient individuals who lack one or two cone types. Isolating S cones is done by measuring from S-cone monochromats (Stockman et al. 1999). Isolating L and M cones is challenging because individuals with only L or M cones are very rare and the spectral sensitivities of the L and M cones overlap substantially. Instead, a common approach is to resort to Protanopes and Deuteranopes; the former has only M and S cones, and the latter has only L and S cones. To isolate M (L) cones from the S cones, we measure from Protanopes (Deuteranopes) using lights that have high spatial and/or temporal frequencies, to which S cones are known to be insensitive (Smith and Pokorny 1975; Stockman and Sharpe 2000).

3.1.4.3 Physiological and Psychophysical Sensitivities Match Well

We can then compare the spectral sensitivity data from physiology and from psychophysics. Baylor et al. (1987) makes such comparisons for both rods and the three classes of cones. Overall it is fair to say that the two sets of data match well.

Think about what this comparison means. What we measure in psychophysics is the threshold intensity (at each wavelength) needed to evoke a criterion level of human *behavioral response* (i.e., just noticeability). The threshold intensity in the physiological measurement represents how much light is needed (at each wavelength) to cause the same amount of pigment absorption and, by the Principle of Univariance, the amount of *electrical responses*. The fact that the two sets of data match suggests that the amount of electrical response we need to evoke a just-noticeable level of perception is a constant regardless of wavelength, a perhaps unsurprising inference.

Interestingly, the physiological data used in Baylor et al. (1987) is obtained from macaques, and the psychophysical data is from humans. The fact that they match well suggests the similarities of the visual system among primates—we have come a long way since the monkey days, but our photoreceptors have not changed much. Other studies obtaining the physiological sensitivity data from humans show similarly good matches with human psychophysical data (Bowmaker and Dartnall 1980; Crescitelli and Dartnall 1953; Kraft et al. 1993; Mollon 1982).

3.2   Color Encoding at Photoreceptors

Newton presumably did the famous experiment where he showed that a beam of white light is really a mixture of photons at different wavelengths, and each wavelength gives a different color percept. Color is very much our subjective sensation. What is the physical reality is the spectral power distribution of light. In Newton's words: "*rays of Light in falling upon the bottom of the eye excite vibrations in the retina. Which vibrations, being propagated along the solid fibres of the optick Nerves into the Brain, cause the sense of seeing.*" (Newton 1704).

3.2.1   From Light Spectrum to Cone Responses

As we have seen before, there are three classes of cones, each with a different spectral sensitivity function or a cone fundamental. We will now see how the cone fundamentals encode wavelength information that eventually gives rise to color vision.

The cone fundamentals we have seen in Fig. 3.3 are absolute sensitivities. It is customary to normalize the cone fundamentals to peak at unity. This normalization eliminates the differences at peak across photoreceptor types, but retains the relative spectral sensitivity within a particular type. Thus, this normalization is useful when we care only about com-

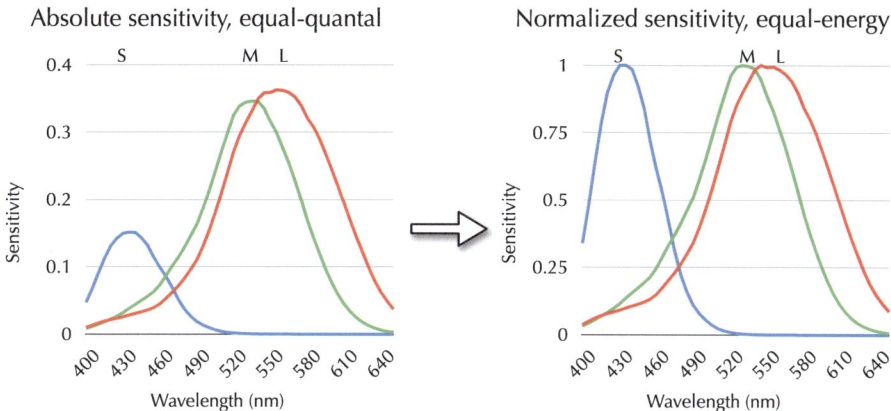

Fig. 3.4 Physiological measurements give us absolute spectral sensitivities on an equal-quantal basis (left), but in color science each cone fundamental function is usually normalized to peak at unity and then converted to an equal-energy form (right)

paring the sensitivity of different wavelengths of a particular type of photoreceptor, but not across different types of photoreceptor.

In addition, the cone fundamentals in Fig. 3.3 are defined on an "equal-quantal" basis: the sensitivities at different wavelengths are given assuming each wavelength has the same amount of photons. Sometimes, especially in CIE standards, the cone fundamentals (and other functions related to cone fundamentals, such as luminous efficiency function and color matching functions, both of which we will discuss later) are defined based on "equal-energy", assuming each wavelength has the same energy/power, not the same amount of photons. As we will see shortly, the equal-energy definition is practically useful since the spectrum of a light is defined as power/energy distribution, rather than quantal distribution, over wavelength.

Figure 3.4 compares the absolute, equal-quantal cone fundamentals with the normalized, equal-energy cone fundamentals. A normalized, equal-energy sensitivity function tells us the relative amount of photon absorption given a unit power at each wavelength. For instance, the normalized L cone response is 1 at 570 nm and 0.4 at 630 nm. This means that given two lights that have the same power/energy, one with photons only at 570 nm and the other with photons only at 630 nm, the fraction of photons absorbed in the 630 nm light is about 40% of that in the 570 nm light.

Critically, this also means if we have a 570 nm light at 1 W and a 630 nm light at 2.5 W, the two lights would cause the same amount of pigment excitations in L cones. If we had only L cones, these two lights would be seen as the exact same light, because the HVS will receive the exact amount of electrical responses—according to the Principle of Univariance. This explains why we could not see colors at night, when only rods are functioning.

In reality, of course, most humans have three classes of cones, so what *is* the signal we receive? Given the Spectral Power Distribution (SPD) of a light $\Phi(\lambda)$, we can calculate the total number of photon absorptions for each cone type, given by:

$$L = \int_\lambda L(\lambda)\Phi(\lambda)d\lambda \tag{3.6a}$$

$$M = \int_\lambda M(\lambda)\Phi(\lambda)d\lambda \tag{3.6b}$$

$$S = \int_\lambda S(\lambda)\Phi(\lambda)d\lambda \tag{3.6c}$$

where $L(\lambda)$, $M(\lambda)$ and $S(\lambda)$ represent the cone sensitivity functions. The fact that we can directly multiply $\Phi(\lambda)$ with, say, $L(\lambda)$ is a result of defining $L(\lambda)$ on an equal-energy/power basis. The L/M/S values we calculate represent the total number of photon absorptions given an incident light. You would know why we care about photon absorption: it is equivalent to pigment excitation up to a constant scaling factor, and pigment excitations produce electrical signals that our brain actually receives. We sometimes simply call the L/M/S value the **cone responses** or **tristimulus values** of a light, but you should know that they do not represent the actual magnitude of the electrical responses of the cones, since the magnitude is not linearly proportional to absorption as we have discussed before.

In actual computation we discretize the spectra and perform summation rather than integration. We also limit the summation to within the [380 nm, 780 nm] range, since the cone fundamentals are practically 0 beyond that range. Assuming that we are quantizing the spectra at a 1-nm interval, the cone responses are linearly related to the light spectrum by:

$$\begin{bmatrix} L(380), L(381), \cdots, L(780) \\ M(380), M(381), \cdots, M(780) \\ S(380), S(381), \cdots, S(780) \end{bmatrix} \times \begin{bmatrix} \Phi(380) \\ \Phi(381) \\ \vdots \\ \Phi(780) \end{bmatrix} = \begin{bmatrix} L \\ M \\ S \end{bmatrix} \tag{3.7}$$

We can see that this is a huge dimensionality reduction. That is, our brain receives only the three-dimensional cone responses, not the actual spectrum of the light, which is of a much higher dimension. This is the basis of the **trichromatic theory of color vision**: color is a three-dimensional system. The theory was first proposed by Young (1802), who conjectured that there are three types of receptors, and later rediscovered, popularized, and extended by Hermann von Helmholtz in the later part of the nineteenth century.

The huge dimensionality reduction also means there are infinitely many lights (with different SPDs) that will be seen as having the same color, as long as they cause the same cone responses. One way to understand this is if we try to solve the system of linear equations in Eq. (3.7) given $[L, M, S]^T$, with the constraint that the Φ vector must be non-negative everywhere (since power cannot be negative), we would generally end up with infinitely many solutions, since it is an *under-determined* system. The fact that multiple physically different lights can end up having the same color is called **metamerism**, and these lights are called **metamers** of each other.

3.2.2 Cone Excitation Space, Spectral Locus, and HVS Gamut

The cone fundamentals essentially give us a color space, which we call the **LMS cone space** or **cone excitation space**. A color space allows us to geometrically interpret a color as a point in the coordinate system. In the cone space, the color of a light is interpreted as the amount of responses in each of the three cone classes produced by the light (as calculated by Eq. (3.7)).

The **spectral locus** is a curve on which each point represents the color of a spectral light at a wavelength. Figure 3.5 shows the spectral locus in the LMS cone space on the right and the cone fundamentals on the left. The L, M, and S cone responses of a spectral light at, for instance, 605 nm are 0.775, 0.265, and 0, which corresponds to the point [0.775, 0.265, 0] in the cone space. Connecting these points for all the spectral lights gets us the spectral locus in the LMS space.

We know a color corresponds to a point in the cone space, but does an arbitrary point in the cone space correspond to a real color? *No.* For instance, if a point has a negative coordinate it obviously could not be a color of a real light, since that a negative cone response would require negative power in the light. Also, [1, 0, 0] is also not a real color, since there is no real light that can produce only L cone response but no responses from M and S cones—if you examine the cone fundamentals carefully. We call these colors **imaginary colors**, since they cannot be produced by physically realizable lights, where the power must be non-negative at any wavelength.

In principle, an [L, M, S] point corresponds to a real color if Eq. (3.7) has a non-negative solution for Φ. The total set of [L, M, S] points that have a non-negative Φ solution corre-

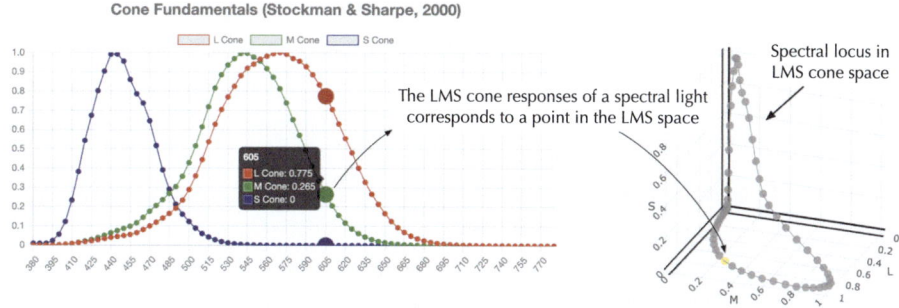

Fig. 3.5 Spectral locus in LMS cone space. From the interactive tutorial in Zhu (2022a)

sponds to all the colors that humans can see, which is called the **gamut** of the human visual system. Geometrically, if a point in the cone space cannot be constructed through a *positive*, linear combination of the points on the spectral locus, it then is not a real color, since the SPD of a real light must be a positive, linear combination of the SPDs of the spectral lights.

For instance, the line segment connecting two points on the spectral locus contains real colors that can be produced by mixing some amount (i.e., positive linear combinations) of the two spectral lights. Of course we can apply this iteratively: once you get a real color through combining spectral colors, the color itself can then be used as a basic color to create other colors. Zhu (2022c) is an interactive tutorial that visualizes the HVS gamut in the cone space (and others), which you are invited to go through.

3.3   Metamerism and Color Matching Experiments

Perhaps the main implication of the trichromatic theory of color is that one can, in theory, produce the color of any light by mixing three other colors. We will take a linear system perspective to give a mathematical explanation of this, and show a famous experiment that empirically confirmed this.

3.3.1   Trichromatic Color Matching

We can produce, in theory, any color by mixing three other colors, which we call the **primary colors**. Here is the mathematical intuition. Let's say the SPDs of the three primary lights are $R(\lambda)$, $G(\lambda)$, $B(\lambda)$. What is the power of each of the primary lights we need to produce the color of a target light $\Phi(\lambda)$? For the color of the mixed light to match that of the target light, their corresponding cone responses must match:

$$\begin{bmatrix} \sum R(\lambda)L(\lambda), & \sum G(\lambda)L(\lambda), & \sum B(\lambda)L(\lambda) \\ \sum R(\lambda)M(\lambda), & \sum G(\lambda)M(\lambda), & \sum B(\lambda)M(\lambda) \\ \sum R(\lambda)S(\lambda), & \sum G(\lambda)S(\lambda), & \sum B(\lambda)S(\lambda) \end{bmatrix} \times \begin{bmatrix} r \\ g \\ b \end{bmatrix} = \begin{bmatrix} \sum \Phi(\lambda)L(\lambda) \\ \sum \Phi(\lambda)M(\lambda) \\ \sum \Phi(\lambda)S(\lambda) \end{bmatrix}, \quad (3.8)$$

where r, g, b represent the power of the three primary lights, respectively. This system in general has one unique solution because we have the same number of unknowns (r, g, b) as the number of equations. Each of the three equations constrains the cone-response matching of one class of cones. This means there is a single unique way to mix three primary lights to produce the color of an arbitrary target light.

What if we have more than three primary lights? We would end up with an *underdetermined* system (e.g., three equations but four unknowns if given four primary lights), which means there are infinitely many ways to mix the primaries to produce the target color.

If we have only two primaries, we end up with an *over-determined* system, where there is in general no solution.

3.3.2 Color Matching Experiments and Color Matching Functions

Equation (3.8) gives a mathematical explanation for trichromatic color matching, but it requires knowing the cone fundamentals, which, as we have seen before in Sect. 3.1.2, were not experimentally measured until the mid 20th century, first through microspectrophotometry (Brown and Wald 1964; Dartnall et al. 1983; Marks et al. 1964) and then through suction electrode (Schnapf et al. 1987). But even without the cone fundamentals, nothing prevents us from performing an actual experiment to find the amount of primaries for producing a color. Thomas Young apparently had no interest in such an experiment (Mollon 2003). Maxwell (1857) is believed to be the first to undertake an actual color matching experiment in the 19th century, but he did the experiments using rotating discs painted with different colors, relying on the temporal integration of the HVS.

Modern color matching experiments started with Wright (Wright 1928, 1929, 1930) and Guild (Guild 1931). International Commission on Illumination (CIE) in 1931 standardized the color matching experiment and synthesized Wright's and Guild's data (without any additional experiments) to obtain what is now known as the CIE 1931 RGB Color Matching Functions. This process is discussed in detail in Broadbent (2004, 2008), Service (2016), Zhu (2020). We summarize the key elements here; the experimental setup is illustrated in Fig. 3.6.

Observers are presented with a 2° visual field. They are given three primary lights, which in the CIE 1931 standard are **spectral lights** (lights that have photons at only one single wavelength; also called monochromatic lights) at wavelengths 435.8, 546.1, and 700 nm.

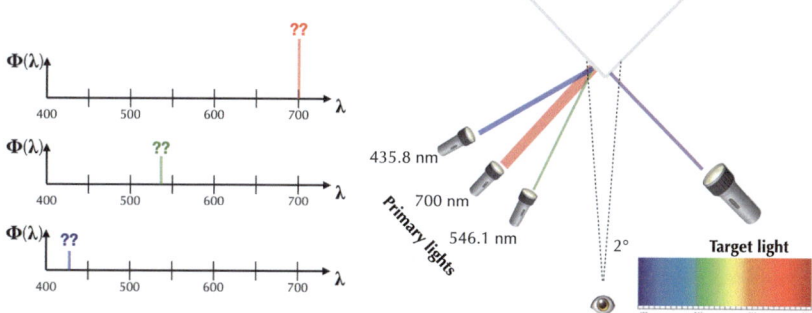

Fig. 3.6 Color matching experiment setup. In CIE 1931 standardization of the experiment, the primary lights are spectral lights at 435.8, 546.1, and 700 nm, and they swept the visible spectrum [380 nm, 780 nm] at a 5-nm interval as the target light. Note that CIE 1931 did not do any actual experiments; they synthesized the data from Wright and Guild

The three primary lights are pointed at the same point on one side of the visual field. On the other side of the visual field is the target light. Their goal is to adjust the power of each of the three primary lights so that the colors from the two sides of the visual field match. CIE 1931 swept the entire visible spectrum for the target light at a 5-nm interval.

3.3.2.1 Color Matching Functions Require a Unit System and a White Point

The results obtained through the color matching experiments are shown in Fig. 3.7 (left panel). The three curves are collectively called the CIE 1931 RGB **Color Matching Functions** (CMFs). Intuitively, the CMFs tell us the amount of primaries needed to match the color at each wavelength. But the devil is in the details. Let's carefully walk through what this plot actually shows.

The y-axis represents the number of units required of each primary so that the mixture matches the color at a given wavelength at x-axis. What is a unit? The unit system is so defined that mixing the three primaries in equal units produces the color of the Equal-Energy White (EEW), whose SPD is a constant across the spectrum.

There are two judgment calls here. First, CIE 1931 decided that EEW was going to be the "white" color in their RGB color space. In general, however, there is no single color that we universally define as white, so if you were to design a color space you get to pick whatever color that you think is white in the color space. That said, an intuitive choice of white is one that is **achromatic** (colorless), a color that, subjectively, can only be described as having a certain level of gray but that has no apparent hue. Daylights at different times of a day are perceptually achromatic and could be used as the white point in a color space.

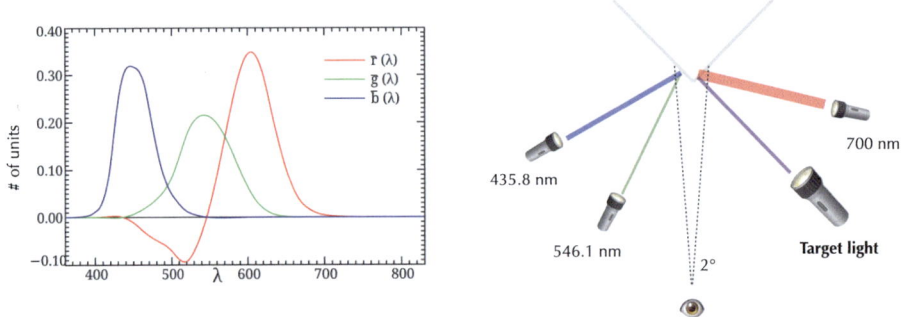

Fig. 3.7 Left: CIE 1931 RGB Color Matching Functions (CMFs); from Marco Polo (2007). The y-axis shows the number of units needed of each primary so that the mixture matches the color at each wavelength (x-axis) on an equal-energy basis. The unit system is so defined that mixing equal amounts (the number of units) of the three primaries produces the color of the equal-energy white, whose SPD is constant over the entire spectrum. Right: the negative values in the CMFs indicate that the corresponding primary light is to be mixed with the target light in order to match the color of the mixture of the other primaries

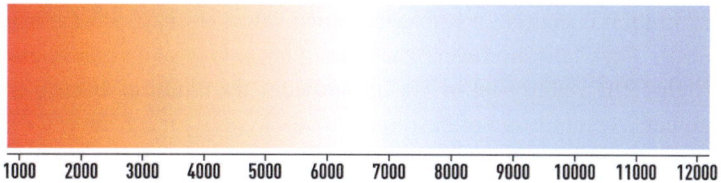

Fig. 3.8 Color from black-body radiation at different temperatures (*x*-axis; unit: Kelvin). CIE Standard Illuminant D65 approximates the SPD of a noon daylight; its color is similar to that of a 6500 K black-body radiation. From Bhutajata (2015)

The daylight colors are shown to be very similar to the colors of black-body radiation at different temperatures (Judd et al. 1964), shown in Fig. 3.8.

You probably do not perceive most of the colors in Fig. 3.8 as achromatic on the display right now, but when you are in an environment illuminated by one of these colors, e.g., outdoors at noon, you do perceive the illuminant as achromatic; this is because of **chromatic adaptation**, a topic we will discuss later in Sect. 4.6.3. Briefly, the human visual system is evolved to adapt to different daylight colors so that when you spend enough time under such an illuminant, you will see the illuminant as achromatic. The adaptation to other colors, however, is weak (or "incomplete" in chromatic adaptation parlance),[3] so it probably does not make much sense to pick other colors as the white point if you want your user to see your white as achromatic. CIE has standardized a set of what they call Standard Illuminants (D series), each of which approximates a different daylight color. For instance, the D65 standard illuminant approximates noon daylight and is similar to the color of a black-body radiation at a temperature of 6500 K. Many common color spaces, such as the sRGB color space, use D65 as the white point.

Second, CIE 1931 RGB space, and virtually all color spaces, define units so that white, however defined, must be produced by an equal-unit mixture of the primaries. This, again, is a judgment call. One could totally design a color space where white is produced by mixing, say, 2 units of red and 1 unit of green and blue each—nothing wrong with that. It is just more intuitive for most people that white is produced by equal amounts of the primaries.

The *x*-axis in Fig. 3.7 is defined on an equal-energy/power basis. That is, the CMFs are interpreted as showing the amount (units) of the primaries needed to produce spectral lights of equal power. So if we actually mix the three primaries at each wavelength as indicated by the CMFs, we will get a set of spectral lights that have the same power.

3.3.2.2 What Does a Negative Unit Mean?

If you observe Fig. 3.7 carefully, you will see that some CMFs are negative over certain ranges. For instance, the red CMF is negative at 500 nm. This is perhaps a bit surprising,

---

[3] After all, artificial lights are a very recent thing in the scale of evolution, so our HVS has not had a chance to adapt to non-daylight colors yet, if ever.

but mathematically it is entirely possible that some values in $[r, g, b]^T$ are negative when solving Eq. (3.8). Physically, however, what does it mean to have a negative amount/power of primary light? The right panel in Fig. 3.7 provides the intuition. It turns out that it is impossible to find a combination of the three primary lights to match the color of a spectral light at 500 nm. What does provide a match is to add a little red primary to the target light, and then we can find a combination of the primaries such as the blue and green mixture has the same color as the target light and red primary mixture.

In fact, if you examine the CMFs, you will see that there is a negative contribution from a primary at all but three wavelengths—the only three exceptions are the wavelengths of the three primaries (where two of the primary contributions are zero and the other is positive). This means that no spectral light color (except the three special cases) can be physically produced by mixing the three primaries.

3.3.2.3 Representing Colors Using CMFs

Given a set of CMFs, we can describe the color of a light with a SPD $\Phi(\lambda)$ using the following equation:

$$
\begin{bmatrix} \bar{r}(380), \bar{r}(381), \cdots, \bar{r}(780) \\ \bar{g}(380), \bar{g}(381), \cdots, \bar{g}(780) \\ \bar{b}(380), \bar{b}(381), \cdots, \bar{b}(780) \end{bmatrix} \times \begin{bmatrix} \Phi(380) \\ \Phi(381) \\ \vdots \\ \Phi(780) \end{bmatrix} = \begin{bmatrix} R \\ G \\ B \end{bmatrix} \tag{3.9}
$$

where $\bar{r}(\lambda)$, $\bar{g}(\lambda)$, and $\bar{b}(\lambda)$ are the CMFs, and R, G, and B are the amounts of the three primaries needed to match the color of $\Phi(\lambda)$.

The CMFs give us another color space, where the color of a light is interpreted as the amount of primary lights needed to match the color of the light. Of course, if we choose a different set of primary lights, we might end up with a new set of CMFs and a new RGB color space.

3.3.3   Connecting Color Matching Functions and Cone Fundamentals

CMFs and cone fundamentals both yield trichromatic color vision, so they must be inherently related, as they are just different ways of describing the same thing. We show the two are linearly related in theory, and the measurement data of the two match well, too.

3.3.3.1 Deriving Color Matching Functions From Cone Fundamentals

Given the cone fundamentals, we can derive the CMFs based on the linear system shown in Eq. (3.8). The interactive tutorial by Zhu (2022a) walks through the process, which you are invited to go over, and we will describe the main steps here.

In order to construct the CMFs, we have to match the colors of all the spectral lights, which means we have to specify cone-response matching at each wavelength. Using the basic idea of Eq. (3.8), we have:

$$
\begin{bmatrix}
\sum R(\lambda)L(\lambda), & \sum G(\lambda)L(\lambda), & \sum B(\lambda)L(\lambda) \\
\sum R(\lambda)M(\lambda), & \sum G(\lambda)M(\lambda), & \sum B(\lambda)M(\lambda) \\
\sum R(\lambda)S(\lambda), & \sum G(\lambda)S(\lambda), & \sum B(\lambda)S(\lambda)
\end{bmatrix}
\times
\begin{bmatrix}
r(380), & \cdots, & r(780) \\
g(380), & \cdots, & g(780) \\
b(380), & \cdots, & b(780)
\end{bmatrix}
=
\begin{bmatrix}
L(380), & \cdots, & L(780) \\
M(380), & \cdots, & M(780) \\
S(380), & \cdots, & S(780)
\end{bmatrix},
\tag{3.10}
$$

where $L(\lambda)$, $M(\lambda)$, and $S(\lambda)$ are the cone fundamentals; $L(\lambda_0)$ is the L cone response of the spectral light at a particular wavelength λ_0; $[r(\lambda_0), g(\lambda_0), b(\lambda_0)]^T$ represents the (to-be-solved-for) power of each primary needed to match the color of the spectral light at λ_0; $R(\lambda)$, $G(\lambda)$, and $B(\lambda)$ are the SPDs of the primary lights used in the CIE 1931 Color Matching Experiment. The first matrix is a constant matrix given a particular set of CMFs, and we will denote it as the **M** matrix. We can solve the system of equations by inverting the first matrix:

$$
\begin{bmatrix}
r(380), & \cdots, & r(780) \\
g(380), & \cdots, & g(780) \\
b(380), & \cdots, & b(780)
\end{bmatrix}
= \mathbf{M}^{-1} \times
\begin{bmatrix}
L(380), & \cdots, & L(780) \\
M(380), & \cdots, & M(780) \\
S(380), & \cdots, & S(780)
\end{bmatrix}.
\tag{3.11}
$$

To get the CMFs, however, we need to turn the power measure into a unit measure. Recall the requirement that white must be produced by equal units of the primaries. We calculate the power of each primary needed to produce the EEW; let's denote the solution $[r_w, g_w, b_w]^T$:

$$
\begin{bmatrix}
r_w \\
g_w \\
b_w
\end{bmatrix}
= \mathbf{M}^{-1} \times
\begin{bmatrix}
L_w \\
M_w \\
S_w
\end{bmatrix},
\tag{3.12}
$$

where $[L_w, M_w, S_w]^T$ denotes the total L, M, and S cone responses of EEW. For the so-calculated $[r_w, g_w, b_w]$ to represent equal units, the last step is to scale $[\bar{r}(\lambda), \bar{g}(\lambda), \bar{b}(\lambda)]^T$ at each λ by $[r_w, g_w, b_w]$:

$$\begin{bmatrix} \bar{r}(380), \cdots, \bar{r}(780) \\ \bar{g}(380), \cdots, \bar{g}(780) \\ \bar{b}(380), \cdots, \bar{b}(780) \end{bmatrix} = \begin{bmatrix} r_w, & 0, & 0 \\ 0, & g_w, & 0 \\ 0, & 0, & b_w \end{bmatrix} \times \begin{bmatrix} r(380), \cdots, r(780) \\ g(380), \cdots, g(780) \\ b(380), \cdots, b(780) \end{bmatrix} \tag{3.13a}$$

$$= \begin{bmatrix} r_w, & 0, & 0 \\ 0, & g_w, & 0 \\ 0, & 0, & b_w \end{bmatrix} \times \mathbf{M}^{-1} \times \begin{bmatrix} L(380), \cdots, L(780) \\ M(380), \cdots, M(780) \\ S(380), \cdots, S(780) \end{bmatrix} \tag{3.13b}$$

$$= \mathbf{T}_{lms2rgb} \times \begin{bmatrix} L(380), \cdots, L(780) \\ M(380), \cdots, M(780) \\ S(380), \cdots, S(780) \end{bmatrix}, \tag{3.13c}$$

where $[\bar{r}(\lambda), \bar{g}(\lambda), \bar{b}(\lambda)]^T$ gives us the unit measure, i.e., the values of the CMFs, at each λ.

3.3.3.2 Cone Space and RGB Space are Related by a Linear Transformation

The rightmost matrix in Eq. (3.13c) is the cone fundamentals written out in the matrix form, and the leftmost matrix in Eq. (3.13c) is the CMFs written out at discrete wavelengths. So Eq. (3.13c) essentially describes a linear transformation from the cone fundamentals to the RGB CMFs, where the transformation is dictated by $\mathbf{T}_{lms2rgb}$. We can look at this in two ways. One, we can think of the cone fundamentals as the CMFs in the cone space: they tell us how much of each cone response we need to match the color of a spectral light. Two, just like how we can construct the spectral locus from cone fundamentals, the RGB CMFs also give us a way to construct the spectral locus—in the RGB space. $\mathbf{T}_{lms2rgb}$ essentially transforms these two representations of the spectral locus, and this is visualized in Fig. 3.9.

There is something deeper: $\mathbf{T}_{lms2rgb}$ not only transforms the spectral locus, it transforms the entire coordinate system from the cone space to the RGB space. In other words, it transforms every single color in the LMS space to its corresponding coordinates in the CIE 1931 RGB space. The way to think about this is to ask: given that the cone space and the CIE

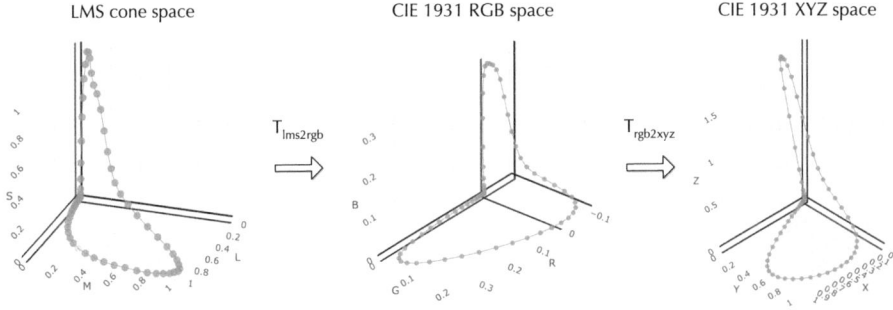

Fig. 3.9 The spectral locus in the LMS cone space, CIE 1931 RGB space, and CIE 1931 XYZ space. The color spaces are a linear transformation away from each other. From the interactive tutorials in Zhu (2022a, b)

1931 RGB space provide two ways to represent the color of a light Φ, how are the cone-space representation $[L_c, M_c, S_c]$ and the RGB-space representation $[R_c, G_c, B_c]$ related? Using Eqs. (3.7), (3.9), and (3.13c), it is easy to see that they are related by a linear transformation through $\mathbf{T}_{lms2rgb}$:

$$
\begin{bmatrix} R_c \\ G_c \\ B_c \end{bmatrix} = \mathbf{T}_{lms2rgb} \times \begin{bmatrix} L_c \\ M_c \\ S_c \end{bmatrix}.
\tag{3.14}
$$

Of course, nothing prevents us from applying an arbitrary linear transformation to the LMS cone space (or the RGB space) to get to another color space. As we will see in Sect. 4.3, if you choose a different set of primaries and/or white light, you will end up with a color space that is one linear transformation away from the cone space. The right panel in Fig. 3.9 shows one such space, called the CIE 1931 XYZ space. There are good reasons why we need the XYZ space, which we will discuss later. For now, just observe how the spectral locus in the XYZ space is transformed from that in the cone space.

3.3.3.3 Cone Responses Fully Explain Psychophysical Color Matching

The CMFs can be both experimentally measured and calculated if we know the cone fundamentals (through a linear transformation), but do the mathematical estimation and the measurement data match? If so, we can say that the physiological process of encoding light power as cone responses can fully account for the color matching experiments in psychophysics.

Baylor et al. (1987) performed one such comparison and showed the two sets of data matched very well. In fact, the modern versions of the cone fundamentals are constructed so that they are precisely a linear transformation away from some RGB CMFs. For instance, the CIE 2006 "physiologically-relevant" LMS functions (based on Stockman et al. (1999) and Stockman and Sharpe (2000)) are constructed by (1) first experimentally measuring the cone fundamentals in psychophysics (from color-vision deficient observers), (2) calibrating the results with a set of RGB CMFs in Stiles and Burch (1959) (which uses a different set of primary lights from the CIE 1931 RGB CMFs) to derive a best-fit linear transformation, and (3) applying the linear transformation to the CMFs to derive a "clean" set of cone fundamentals.

3.4 Post-receptoral Color Encoding: Opponent Processes

Cone-response encoding can perfectly explain the trichromatic theory of color vision, where any color can be mixed from three other colors. The trichromatic theory of color has a perfect neural basis: the human visual system has three classes of cones, so color is a three-dimensional system. But the trichromatic theory is not concerned with our subjective experience of color that we encounter on a daily basis. Here are two examples that highlight the difference between perceptual color experience and physical color mixing.

First, when we see an orange color, we feel that it has a little bit of yellow in it and a little bit of red in it. Even though there are many ways to produce orange, some of which do not require mixing yellow and red lights, we cannot help but perceptually feel that orange combines yellow and red. Second, when we mix a red light with a green light, we get yellow, but perceptually, if we stare at yellow, most people would not say that yellow has contributions from red or green.

Hering (1878, 1964) hypothesized that, perceptually, there are four primary hues, which form two opposing pairs. Opposing hues cannot co-exist, perceptually, in a color. Any hue can be produced by combining two non-opposing hues. The four hues are: the Yellow and Blue opposing hues and the Red and Green opposing hues. Hering also considered light-dark as another opposing pair: no color can be simultaneously light and dark. In his theory, color vision is still a three-dimensional system, where the three axes are: Yellow-Blue axis, Red-Green axis, and light-dark axis. Any color, a point in this 3D space, is produced by mixing some amount of Red *or* Green, some amount of Yellow *or* Blue, and some level of lightness.

The opponent theory seems to contradict the trichromatic theory, which was dominant for the most part of the history—because it has both a solid psychophysical and neural basis. First, the color matching experiment quantitatively shows that, behaviorally, humans could match a color by mixing three other colors. In contrast, Hering had only a qualitative description of perceptual mixing. His description was something like "*after this blue comes blue of increasing redness...(blue violet, red violet, purple red), until the last trace of blueness vanishes in a true red*" (Hering 1964, p. 41). To Hering's theory's rescue, Jameson and Hurvish performed an experiment, called the **hue cancellation experiment**, providing the first quantitative, psychophysical evidence of the opponent processes (Hurvich and Jameson 1957; Jameson and Hurvich 1955).

Second, the trichromatic theory has a clear neural and physiological basis (i.e., wavelength encoding by cone responses), and the physiological data match the behavioral data very well, as shown before. So a natural question is: are there neural mechanisms that can account for the opponent processes and, if so, how does that mechanism relate to the encoding mechanisms by the cone photoreceptors?

It turns out that we do need a set of new neural mechanisms to start accounting for the opponent processes. Not only do these new mechanisms *not* contradict the cone encoding mechanisms, they build on top of the cone encodings and operate post-receptorally. Schrödinger (1925, 1994) synthesized the earlier *zone theory* by von Kries (1905) and argued that the trichromatic theory and the opponent processes were nothing more than different stages of color encoding in the visual system. That said, while these new neural mechanisms seem to have what it takes to form the basis for the behavioral opponent observations, they do not fully explain those observations yet; the link between the two is still very much an open research question.

The rest of this section will discuss the hue cancellation experiment and the quest for a neural and physiological basis in more detail.

3.4.1 Hue Cancellation Experiment

In a landmark study, Jameson and Hurvich (1955) (while working for Eastman Kodak in Rochester) quantitatively measured the perceptual color opponency using a behavioral experiment. The participant is given a test light and is asked to first judge whether the light appeared blue-ish or yellow-ish. If the test light is judged to be blue-ish, the participant is then given a yellow-ish *cancellation light* (e.g., a spectral light at 588 nm) and is asked to adjust the intensity of the cancellation light so that the mixture of the test and cancellation light perceptually appears neither blue nor yellow. If the test light is judged to be yellow-ish, the participant is then asked to adjust the power of a blue-ish cancellation light (e.g., a spectral light at 467 nm) so that the test-cancellation mixture is again neither blue nor yellow. We sweep the spectrum from about 400 to 700 nm for the test light of equal energy, and record the energy of yellow or blue cancellation light needed at each step.

The result for one subject is shown in Fig. 3.10a, where the y-axis is showing the intensity of the yellow and blue cancellation light, i.e., the strength of blue-ness and yellow-ness of the test light. For the reference, we attached a colorbar showing roughly the color of the test light between 400 and 700 nm, but take this color visualization as a huge grain of salt, since it is almost certain that your display will not be able to actually render the colors of the spectral lights.

Unsurprisingly, we get two peaks, one in the blue range and the other in the yellow range, indicating, respectively, that the participant needs a lot of the yellow and blue cancellation lights in those two regions. The test light at about 500 nm requires no cancellation light, indicating light there, which roughly has a green-ish color is yellow-blue neutral: it naturally looks neither blue nor yellow.

Jameson and Hurvich then repeated the same experiment, but this time measuring the red-green opponent process, where the two cancellation lights are a 700 nm red-ish light and a 490 nm green-ish light. The results are in Fig. 3.10b, where the y-axis indicates the amount of red-ness and green-ness in the test light. Two observations are worth noting. First, while it is unsurprising that long-wavelength lights have a strong red component, it is perhaps surprising that short-wavelength lights appear red-ish too. That, however, becomes less surprising when we realize that short-wavelength lights (shorter than pure blue) appear violet, which perceptually is a red-ish blue. Second, because of the two red-ish regions over the spectrum, the entire red-green curve has two zero-crossings, one at about 470 nm and the other near 570 nm: pure blue and pure yellow look neither green nor red.

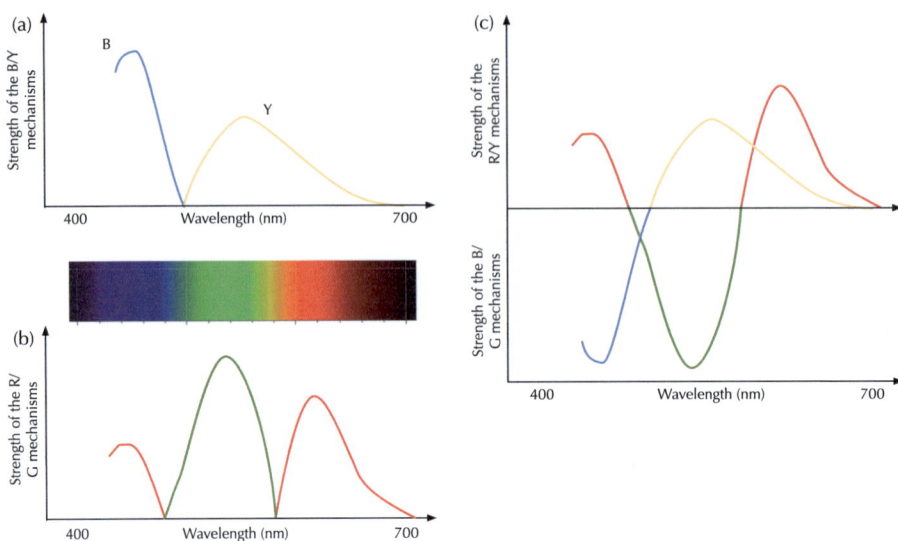

Fig. 3.10 Measurements from the hue cancellation experiment in Jameson and Hurvich (1955). **a** the Blue-Yellow measurement; the *y*-axis shows the intensity of the Yellow/Blue cancellation light, i.e., the relative strength of the "Blue-ness" and "Yellow-ness" in the test light. **b** the Red-Green measurement; notice the two zero-crossings for Green. **c** The same data as A and B except we invert the Blue and Green curves so the *y*-axis is interpreted as the strength of Red-ness and Yellow-ness. The colorbar is generated using the Colour Python package (NumFOCUS 2025)

Figure 3.10c summarizes the two sets of data by inverting the blur section of the curve in (a) and the green section of the curve in (b). That way, the *y*-axis can be simply interpreted as the relative strength of red-ness and yellow-ness over the spectrum.

3.4.2   Light-Dark Mechanism and Luminous Efficiency Function

Hurvich and Jameson (1957) also performed a measurement of the white-black (light-dark) opponent process, asking participants to assess the "whiteness" of spectral lights between 400 and 700 nm of equal power. A more modern method to measure the luminance mechanism is heterochromatic flicker photometry, where we alternate between a test light and a fixed reference light at a frequency of, say, 25 Hz. We adjust the intensity of the test light so that the alternation produces no visual flickering, at which point we say the two lights produce the same level of luminance (Sharpe et al. 2005, 2011). We again sweep the entire visible spectrum for the test light and record the relative intensity at each step. The so-obtained function is called the **luminance efficiency function** (LEF). The dashed gray

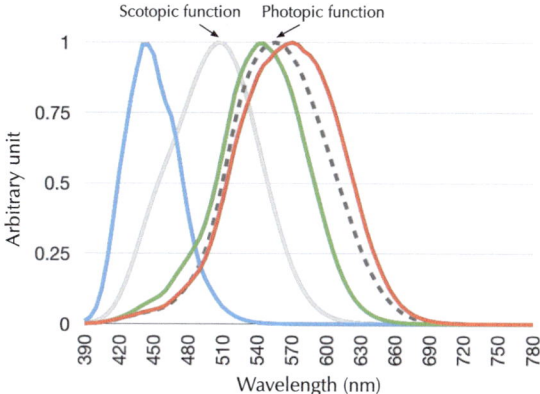

Fig. 3.11 The grey solid curve is the scotopic luminous efficiency function (CIE 1951 standard; based on Wald 1945 and Crawford 1949). The grey dashed curve is the photopic luminous efficiency function (CIE 2008 "physiologically-relevant" 2-deg function; based on Sharpe et al. 2005, 2011) The other three curves are the cone fundamentals, shown for the reference

curve in Fig. 3.11 shows a modern version of the photopic LEF (the so-called CIE 2008 "physiologically-relevant" 2-deg function).[4]

The way to interpret the LEF is that the y-axis is inversely proportional to the light power at each wavelength needed to produce the same level of perceptual brightness. The photopic LEF at 509 nm is about 0.5, half of that at 555 nm. It means we need twice as much power at 509 nm to produce the same level of brightness as that at 555 nm. It also explains the word "efficiency" in the name: if a wavelength needs less power to produce a criterion level of brightness, the wavelength is more efficient in its use of power. The way LEF is obtained, however, does *not* permit us to interpret the result as the relative brightness at different wavelengths. That is, 555 nm is not twice as bright as 509 nm. This is similar to our interpretation of the cone fundamentals.

For comparison, the gray curve in Fig. 3.11 is the scotopic LEF. The CIE 1951 scotopic LEF synthesizes the psychophysical measurements from Wald (1945) and Crawford (1949). Both used a threshold method where they measured the light intensity at each wavelength needed to produce a just detectable flash. Note that the photopic LEF peaks at about 555 nm and the scotopic LEF peaks at about 507 nm.

As a result, the relative brightness of longer-wavelength colors and shorter-wavelength colors is inverted when our vision transitions from the cone-mediated photopic vision to the

---

[4] In later research by Jameson and Hurvich, their white-black function was made equal to the CIE 1924 luminous efficiency function (Hurvich and Jameson 1955, p. 604), which is known to have severe flaws at low wavelengths and which is later corrected by Judd (1951) and Vos (1978). Compared to the Judd and Vos corrections, the function shown here has the advantage of being "physiologically relevant" in that the LEF is a linear combination of the cone fundamentals, whereas both the CIE 1924 LEF and its later corrections are not intentionally designed to be linear combinations of anything.

rod-mediated scotopic vision. This phenomenon is called the **Purkinje shift**. In the words of Glassner (1995, p. 21), "*When the sun is still above the horizon, your cones are active, and the yellow flower will appear lighter than the leaves because yellow is closer to peak of the photopic sensitivity curve than dark green. When the sun has set and light levels are lower, your rods are the principal sensors. The scotopic sensitivity curve is more responsive in the shorter wavelengths, so the green leaves will now appear relatively lighter than the yellow flower, though both will of course be much darker due to the lower amount of incident light.*"

Combining the light-dark (luminance efficiency) curve with the two opponent curves in Fig. 3.10c, we again have three spectral sensitivity functions. Once again, a light with its SPD can be reduced to three-dimensional point, using Eq. (3.6), except (1) instead of the three cone fundamentals we use the three opponent functions, and (2) instead of getting the three cone responses we get the strength of the three opponent mechanisms. Effectively, the hue cancellation curves and the light-dark curve construct a new three-dimensional color space. We call this the **hue-opponent** space, and we will discuss a model for this space shortly on Sect. 3.4.3.3.

3.4.3 Neural and Physiological Basis

The hue cancellation experiment solidifies Hering's opponent theory at the level of psychophysics. But recall Fig. 1.2; any behavioral responses measured through psychophysics are fundamentally the result of the underlying neural and physiological mechanisms. So the next natural step in the scientific quest is to understand what underlying neural and physiological mechanisms can account for the behavioral opponent processes.

3.4.3.1 There are Both Spectrally-Opponent and Non-opponent Neurons

There are RGC and LGN neurons that show opponent properties. Svaetichin (1953, 1956) and Svaetichin and MacNichol (1958) are the first to identify opponent neurons in a fish retina; they recorded from horizontal cells. De Valois et al. (1958, 1966) measured the responses of LGN neurons in macaques using monochromatic lights, and found spectral opponent neurons, which get excited or inhibited depending on the wavelengths.

De Valois et al. (1966) also identified non-opponent cells, whose responses are universally inhibited or excited across the spectrum, respectively. These neurons are still wavelength-sensitive, but their responses are either universally excited or universally inhibited across the spectrum, unlike the spectrally-opponent neurons whose responses change polarity across the spectrum.

3.4.3.2 There are Both Spectrally-Opponent and Non-opponent Neurons

What are some of the underlying visual pathways that could potentially give rise to these spectral tuning curves? Recall that LGN cells/RGCs have antagonistic receptive fields (RFs), and the antagonism seems to be a perfect mechanism to implement the opponent process. This suggests that in order to understand the opponent cells we must study their RF structures.

We will not go into too many details but will use the Y-B opponent cells as an example to describe the general idea. The visual pathway for the Y-B opponent cells seems to be mostly clear. Derrington et al. (1984) showed that some LGN cells receive antagonistic inputs from S cone versus L and M cones. Dacey and Lee (1994) later identified that the small bistratified RGCs (which project to the K cells in the LGN) are responsible for carrying such signals. The small bistratified RGCs are excited by S cone responses and inhibited by L and M cone responses (or vice versa). Since blue-ish lights produce strong S cone responses and red/green lights produce strong L/M cone responses (recall red + green is yellow), it stands to reason that if a cell is excited by S cones and inhibited by L and M cones, it would give a vigorous on-response under blue lights and a vigorous off-response under yellow lights, producing some sort of yellow-ON/blue-OFF spectral tuning curve.

3.4.3.3 A Cone-Opponent Model for Color-Opponent Mechanisms

It is clear that there are cells that receive opponent cone signals; the spectral tuning curves of these cells seem to largely account for the perceptual opponent mechanisms. Based on these observations, Derrington et al. (1984) proposed a *cone-opponent* color space, which is now commonly used (in color science and, to a large extent, visual neuroscience) to give a first-order approximation of the perceptual color-opponent processes. The color space is now famously known as the DKL color space (named after the three authors; the L is Peter Lennie, who was twice on the faculty at University of Rochester and served as the provost).

- The Y-B channel is given by aS-(bL+cM), where a, b, and c are all positive values representing the contributions of the S, L, and M cones to the Y-B opponent process. It is generally said that this signal is delivered by the Koniocellular pathway.
- The R-G channel is given by dL-eM, where d and e are all positive values representing the contributions of the L and M cones to the R-G opponent process. This opponent signal is generally said to be delivered by the Parvocellular pathway.
- The Light-Dark or luminance channel is given by fL+gM, where f and g are all positive values representing the contributions of the L and M cones to the luminance channel. This luminance channel is meant to represent the LEF (Sect. 3.4.2), which generally is believed to be delivered by the Magnocellular pathway.

The DKL space operates not on raw cone responses but on response *contrasts* with respect to a perceptually neutral/achromatic color. The inherent assumption is that the achromatic color should have no strength in any of the three cone-opponent channels and be the origin in the cone-opponent space. The achromatic color depends on an observer's state of chromatic adaptation, a topic we will discuss later in Sect. 4.6.3. People usually fit data to regress the values of the free parameters, and the exact values depend on which cone fundamentals are used and the normalization convention. Brainard (1996) describes one such procedure.

Since the cone-opponent model operates on (contrast of) cone responses, a common theory of color vision is that it is a two-stage process: the wavelength encoding by cone photoreceptors followed by opponent encoding of cone responses post-receptorally. While the cone response encoding can perfectly explain the color matching experiments as we have seen earlier, the cone opponent encoding is only an approximation of the hue cancellation experiments.

References

Baylor DA, Fuortes M (1970) Electrical responses of single cones in the retina of the turtle. J Physiol 207(1):77–92

Baylor DA, Hodgkin A, Lamb T (1974) The electrical response of turtle cones to flashes and steps of light. J Physiol 242(3):685–727

Baylor DA, Lamb T, Yau K (1979) The membrane current of single rod outer segments. J Physiol 288(1):589–611

Baylor DA, Nunn B, Schnapf J (1984) The photocurrent, noise and spectral sensitivity of rods of the monkey macaca fascicularis. J Physiol 357(1):575–607

Baylor DA, Nunn B, Schnapf J (1987) Spectral sensitivity of cones of the monkey macaca fascicularis. J Physiol 390(1):145–160

Bhutajata (2015) Color temperature black body; CC BY-SA 4.0 license. https://commons.wikimedia.org/wiki/File:Color_temperature_black_body_800-12200K.svg

Boettner EA, Wolter JR (1962) Transmission of the ocular media. Invest Ophthalmol & Vis Sci 1(6):776–783

Bowmaker J (1984) Microspectrophotometry of vertebrate photoreceptors: a brief review. Vis Res 24(11):1641–1650

Bowmaker JK, Dartnall H (1980) Visual pigments of rods and cones in a human retina. J Physiol 298(1):501–511

Bowmaker J, Dartnall H, Lythgoe J, Mollon J (1978) The visual pigments of rods and cones in the rhesus monkey, macaca mulatta. J Physiol 274(1):329–348

Brainard D (1996) Cone contrast and opponent modulation color spaces. In: Human Color Vision, 2nd edn, Optical Society of America, pp 563–579

Broadbent AD (2004) A critical review of the development of the cie1931 rgb color-matching functions. Color Res & Appl 29(4):267–272

Broadbent A (2008) Calculation from the original experimental data of the cie 1931 rgb standard observer spectral chromaticity coordinates and color matching functions. Département de génie chimique, Université de Sherbrooke, Québec, Canada, pp 1–17

Brown PK, Wald G (1964) Visual pigments in single rods and cones of the human retina. Science 144(3614):45–52

Crawford B (1949) The scotopic visibility function. Proc Phys Soc Sect B 62(5):321

Crescitelli F, Dartnall HJ (1953) Human visual purple. Nature 172(4370):195–197

CVRL (n.d.) Photopigment curves based on the Stockman & Sharpe (2000) cone fundamentals. http://www.cvrl.org/database/text/pigments/ssabance.htm

Dacey DM, Lee BB (1994) The'blue-on'opponent pathway in primate retina originates from a distinct bistratified ganglion cell type. Nature 367(6465):731–735

Dartnall HJ (1972) Photosensitivity. In: Dartnall HJ (ed) Photochemistry of vision. Springer, Berlin Heidelberg, pp 122–145

Dartnall HJ, Bowmaker JK, Mollon JD (1983) Human visual pigments: microspectrophotometric results from the eyes of seven persons. Proc R Soc Lond Ser B Biolog Sci 220(1218):115–130

De Valois R, Smith C, Kitai S, Karoly A (1958) Response of single cells in monkey lateral geniculate nucleus to monochromatic light. Science 127(3292):238–239

De Valois RL, Abramov I, Jacobs GH (1966) Analysis of response patterns of lgn cells. JOSA 56(7):966–977

Derrington AM, Krauskopf J, Lennie P (1984) Chromatic mechanisms in lateral geniculate nucleus of macaque. J Physiol 357(1):241–265

Fain GL (1976) Sensitivity of toad rods: Dependence on wave-length and background illumination. J Physiol 261(1):71–101

Fu Y (2010) Phototransduction in rods and cones. In: Kolb H, Fernandez E, Nelson R (eds) WebVision: the organization of the retina and visual system

Glassner AS (1995) Principles of digital image synthesis. Elsevier

Granit R (1941) The retinal mechanism of color reception. J Opt Soc Amer 31(9):570–580

Granit R (1943) A physiological theory of colour perception. Nature 151(3818):11–14

Granit R (1945a) The colour receptors of the mammalian retina. J Neurophysiol 8(3):195–210

Granit R (1945b) The electrophysiological analysis of the fundamental problem of colour reception. Proc Phys Soc 57(6):447–463

Guild J (1931) The colorimetric properties of the spectrum. Philosoph Trans R Soc Lond Ser A, Contain Pap Math Phys Char 230(681–693):149–187

Hering E (1878) Zur Lehre vom Lichtsinne: sechs Mittheilungen an die Kaiser. der Wissenschaften in Wien. C. Gerold's Sohn, Akad

Hering E (1964) Outlines of a theory of the light sense (Translation by Jameson and Hurvish; originally published in 1878). Harvard University Press

Hurvich LM, Jameson D (1955) Some quantitative aspects of an opponent-colors theory. ii. brightness, saturation, and hue in normal and dichromatic vision. JOSA 45(8):602–616

Hurvich LM, Jameson D (1957) An opponent-process theory of color vision. Psychol Rev 64(6p1):384

Ingram NT, Sampath AP, Fain GL (2016) Why are rods more sensitive than cones? J Physiol 594(19):5415–5426

Ivo Kruusam gi (2010) Cone cell anatomy; CC BY-SA 3.0 license. https://commons.wikimedia.org/wiki/File:Cone_cell_en.png

Jameson D, Hurvich LM (1955) Some quantitative aspects of an opponent-colors theory. i. chromatic responses and spectral saturation. JOSA 45(7):546–552

Judd DB (1951) Report of us secretariat committee on colorimetry and artificial daylight. CIE Proc 1951(1):11

Judd DB, MacAdam DL, Wyszecki G, Budde H, Condit H, Henderson S, Simonds J (1964) Spectral distribution of typical daylight as a function of correlated color temperature. Josa 54(8):1031–1040

Kosigrim (2007) Rod cell anatomy; released into the public domain by the copyright holder. https://commons.wikimedia.org/wiki/File:Rod%26Cone.jpg

Kraft T, Schneeweis D, Schnapf J (1993) Visual transduction in human rod photoreceptors. J Physiol 464(1):747–765

Kropf A (1982) Photosensitivity and quantum efficiency of photoisomerization in rhodopsin and retinal. In: Methods in enzymology, vol 81, Elsevier, pp 384–392

Lamb T, McNaughton P, Yau KW (1981) Spatial spread of activation and background desensitization in toad rod outer segments. J Physiol 319(1):463–496

Marco Polo (2007) CIE1931 RGB CMF; released into the public domain by the copyright holder. https://commons.wikimedia.org/wiki/File:CIE1931_RGBCMF.svg

Marks W, Dobelle WH, MacNichol EF Jr (1964) Visual pigments of single primate cones. Science 143(3611):1181–1183

Maxwell JC (1857) Xviii.–experiments on colour, as perceived by the eye, with remarks on colour-blindness. Earth Environ Sci Trans R Soc Edinburgh 21(2):275–298

Milo R, Phillips R (2015) Cell biology by the numbers. Garland Science

Mollon JD (1982) Colour vision and colour blindness. In: Mollon JD, Barlow HB (ed) The Senses, Cambridge University Press, pp 165–191

Mollon JD (2003) Introduction: Thomas young and the trichromatic theory of colour vision. In: Pokorny J, Knoblauch K, Mollon JD (eds) Normal & defective colour vision, Oxford University Press, pp 19–34

Naka K, Rushton WA (1966) S-potentials from colour units in the retina of fish (cyprinidae). J Physiol 185(3):536–555

Nathans J (1992) Rhodopsin: structure, function, and genetics. Biochemistry 31(21):4923–4931

Newton I (1704) Opticks, or, a treatise of the reflections, refractions, inflections & colours of light. London: Smith and Walford

Normann RA, Perlman I (1979) The effects of background illumination on the photoresponses of red and green cones. J Physiol 286(1):491–507

Norren DV, Vos JJ (1974) Spectral transmission of the human ocular media. Vis Res 14(11):1237–1244

NumFOCUS (n.d.) Colour: open-source Python package for colour science. https://github.com/colour-science/colour

Polyak SL (1941) The retina. University of Chicago Press

Rodieck RW (1998) The first steps in seeing. Oxford University Press

Rushton WA (1972a) Visual pigments in man. In: Dartnall HJ (ed) Photochemistry of vision. Springer, Berlin Heidelberg, pp 364–394

Rushton WH (1972b) Review lecture. pigments and signals in colour vision. J Physiol 220(3):1P

Schnapf J, Kraft T, Baylor DA (1987) Spectral sensitivity of human cone photoreceptors. Nature 325(6103):439–441

Schneeweis DM, Schnapf JL (1995) Photovoltage of rods and cones in the macaque retina. Science 268(5213):1053–1056

Schrödinger E (1925) Über das verhältnis der vierfarben-zur dreifarbentheorie. Sitzungberichte Abt 2a, Mathematik, Astronomie, Physik, Meteorologie und Mechanik Akademie der Wissenschaften in Wien, Mathematisch-Naturwissenschaftliche Klasse 134:471–490

Schrödinger E (1994) On the relationship of four-color theory to three-color theory (translation by national translation center; originally published in 1925). Color Res Appl 19(1):37

Service P (2016) The wright – guild experiments and the development of the cie 1931 rgb and xyz color spaces

Sharpe LT, Stockman A, Jagla W, Jägle H (2005) A luminous efficiency function, v*(λ), for daylight adaptation. J Vis 5(11):3–3

Sharpe LT, Stockman A, Jagla W, Jägle H (2011) A luminous efficiency function, vd65*(λ), for daylight adaptation: a correction. Color Res & Appl 36(1):42–46

Smith VC, Pokorny J (1975) Spectral sensitivity of the foveal cone photopigments between 400 and 500 nm. Vis Res 15(2):161–171

Snodderly D, Brown P, Delori F, Auran J (1984) The macular pigment. i. absorbance spectra, local-ization, and discrimination from other yellow pigments in primate retinas. Invest Ophthalmol & Vis Sci 25(6):660–673

Stiles W (1939) The directional sensitivity of the retina and the spectral sensitivities of the rods and cones. Proc R Soc Lond Ser B-Biolog Sci 127(846):64–105

Stiles W (1959) Color vision: the approach through increment-threshold sensitivity. Proc Natl Acad Sci 45(1):100–114

Stiles W (1964) Appendix by ws stiles: foveal threshold sensitivity on fields of different colors. Science 145(3636):1016–1017

Stiles WS, Burch JM (1959) Npl colour-matching investigation: final report (1958). Optica Acta: Int J Opt 6(1):1–26

Stockman A, Sharpe LT (2000) The spectral sensitivities of the middle-and long-wavelength-sensitive cones derived from measurements in observers of known genotype. Vis Res 40(13):1711–1737

Stockman A, Sharpe LT, Fach C (1999) The spectral sensitivity of the human short-wavelength sensitive cones derived from thresholds and color matches. Vis Res 39(17):2901–2927

Svaetichin G (1953) The cone action potential. Acta Physiol Scand 29(29):565–600

Svaetichin G (1956) Spectral response curves from single cones. Acta Physiol Scand 39:17–46

Svaetichin G, MacNichol EF (1958) Retinal mechanisms for chromatic and achromatic vision. Ann New York Acad Sci 74(2):385–404

von Kries J (1905) Übersicht der tatsachen, ergebnisse für die theoretische auffassung des sehorgans: Zonentheorie. In: Nagel W (ed) Handbuch der Physiologie des Menschen, Dritter Band: Physiologie der Sinne, 3rd edn. Vieweg und Sohn, Braunschweig, pp 269–274

Vos JJ (1978) Colorimetric and photometric properties of a 2 fundamental observer. Color Res & Appl 3(3):125–128

Wald G (1945) Human vision and the spectrum. Science 101(2635):653–658

Wald G (1964) The receptors of human color vision: action spectra of three visual pigments in human cones account for normal color vision and color-blindness. Science 145(3636):1007–1016

Wright W (1928) A trichromatic colorimeter with spectral primaries. Trans Opt Soc 29(5):225

Wright WD (1929) A re-determination of the trichromatic coefficients of the spectral colours. Trans Opt Soc 30(4):141

Wright W (1930) A re-determination of the mixture curves of the spectrum. Trans Opt Soc 31(4):201

Young T (1802) II. The Bakerian lecture. On the theory of light and colours. Philosoph Trans R Soc Lond 92:12–48

Zhu Y (2020) How the CIE 1931 RGB color matching functions were developed from the initial color matching experiments. https://yuhaozhu.com/blog/cmf.html

Zhu Y (2022a) Interative tutorial: building a color space from cone fundamentals. https://horizon-lab.org/colorvis/cone2cmf.html

Zhu Y (2022b) Interative Tutorial: CIE 1931 XYZ Color Space. https://horizon-lab.org/colorvis/xyz.html

Zhu Y (2022c) Interative tutorial: visualizing human visual gamut. https://horizon-lab.org/colorvis/gamutvis.html

Colorimetry

4

4.1 CIE 1931 XYZ Space

There are two slight inconveniences with the CIE 1931 RGB color space. First, it depends on the exact primary colors (and reference white) you choose. Second, there are also inevitably going to be colors that can be "produced" only by using negative amounts of the primaries, no matter what primaries you choose. While mathematically and physically rigorous, it is not quite intuitive. So CIE in 1931 wanted to standardize a color space that (1) can be used as a "common language" (without having to laboriously specify what the primaries are used every time you say "the RGB color space") and that (2) all the human-visible colors are produced by mixing non-negative amounts of the primaries. That color space is called the **CIE 1931 XYZ** color space, sometimes referred to simply as the XYZ color space.

You might be wondering: isn't the LMS cone space already a color space that satisfies the two conditions above, and if so, why do we have to invent a new XYZ space? The cone space is tied intrinsically to the HVS, so it does not vary (significantly) in population. It is also a color space where all the colors are expressed using positive amounts of the primaries (cone responses). These are all true, but remember the cone fundamentals were not reliably available back in 1931 (Sect. 3.1).

Fairman et al. (1997), Brill (1998), and Service (2016, Sect. 4) describe the process and the (sometimes rather arbitrary) design decisions that went into turning the CIE 1931 RGB space into the 1931 XYZ space. Zhu (2022c) is an interactive tutorial that walks through the math.

The bottom line is that the transformation from the CIE RGB to the XYZ space is *constructed* to be a linear transformation. Figure 4.1 shows how the spectral locus is transformed from the RGB to the XYZ space, governed by the matrix $\mathbf{T}_{rgb2xyz}$. We can see that in the RGB space the spectral locus enters negative octants, but it stays entirely within the all-positive, first octant in the XYZ space. The transformation also gives a new set of CMFs in the XYZ space. The Y CMF is intentionally designed to match the CIE 1924 Luminous

Y. Zhu, *Visual Computing For Architects*, Synthesis Lectures on Computer Architecture, https://doi.org/10.1007/978-3-032-05018-2_4

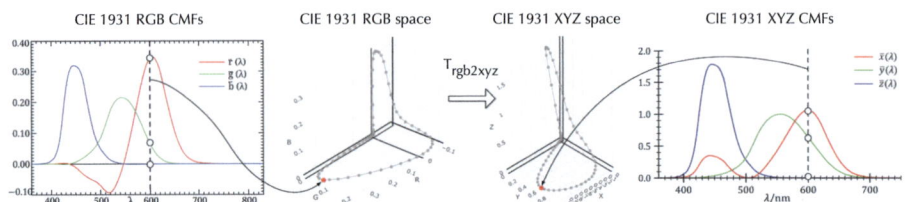

Fig. 4.1 The CIE 1931 XYZ color space (right) is constructed to be a linear transformation from the CIE 1931 RGB color space (left). Notice how a color, say, 600 nm spectral light is represented differently in the two color spaces. This figure visualizes how the spectral locus and the CMFs are transformed. The exact coefficients of the transformation matrix $T_{rgb2xyz}$ are omitted here but are widely available online. The CIE 1931 RGB CMFs figure is adapted from Marco Polo (2007), and the XYZ CMFs figure is adapted from ACDX (2009)

Efficiency Function (LEF), so that by looking at the Y value of a color, we can tell what its luminance is (refer to Sect. 3.4.2 for the definition of the LEF and its various caveats).

4.2   Chromaticity Diagram and Its Interpretation

How do a color that is mixed from 1:2:4 units of RGB primaries and a color that is mixed from 2:4:8 units of the primaries relate? The amount of a primary is directly proportional to the power of that primary, so the second color can be obtained by doubling the power of each primary in the first color. Similarly, halving the power of each primary in the second color gets us the first color. Intuitively, lights that have the same primary quantity ratio have the same "objective color quality" while differing in the intensity.

4.2.1   Chromaticity Is the Result of a Perspective Projection

More formally, we can calculate the primary ratio $r : g : b$ of a color and then normalize the ratio such that $r + g + b = 1$ (100%). The so-calculated r, g, b values of a color are called the (RGB) **chromaticity** values of that color. Mathematically, the chromaticity of a color defined in an RGB space is calculated from its absolute quantity by:

$$r = \frac{R}{R + G + B} \tag{4.1a}$$

$$g = \frac{G}{R + G + B} \tag{4.1b}$$

$$b = \frac{B}{R + G + B} \tag{4.1c}$$

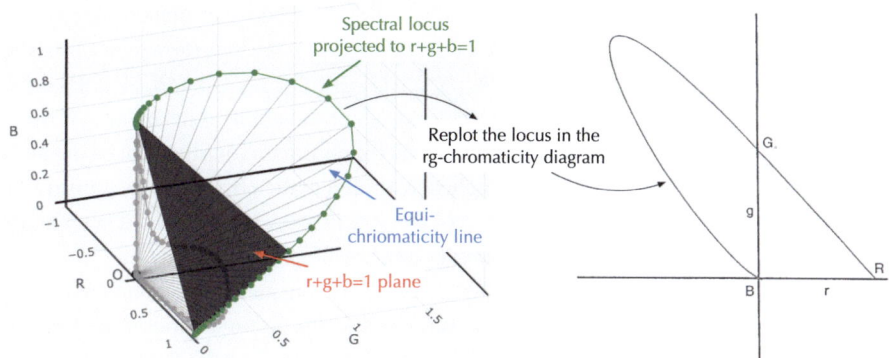

Fig. 4.2 Visualization of the CIE 1931 RGB space and its rg-chromaticity diagram. Left: the transformation from an [R, G, B] color to its [r, g, b] chromaticity is a perspective projection to the $r + g + b = 1$ plane. Each line that goes through the origin is an "equi-chromaticity" line, in that all the colors on that line have the same chromaticity. We use the CIE 1931 RGB color space for illustration here, but the same idea applies to other color spaces as well, e.g., the CIE 1931 XYZ space. From the interactive tutorial in Zhu (2022b). Right: visualization of the spectral locus in CIE 1931 RGB space; from Fairman et al. (1997, Fig. 2)

Geometrically, going from the RGB values of a color to the rgb chromaticity is equivalent to a *perspective projection*, where we project an [R, G, B] point through the origin to the $r + g + b = 1$ plane. The left panel in Fig. 4.2 visualizes this projection. Each line that goes through the origin is an "equi-chromaticity" line, in that all the colors on that line have the same chromaticity. The spectral locus is so projected to the $r + g + b = 1$ plane. Since there are only two degrees of freedom in chromaticity, we can visualize the chromaticity in a two-dimensional space, and usually the r and g coordinates are used. The right panel in Fig. 4.2 shows the spectral locus in the rg-chromaticity diagram.

4.2.2   xy-Chromaticity Diagram and Its Interpretation

Of course we can do the same if a color is defined in the XYZ space or the LMS cone space, and we omit the trivial math here. The left panel in Fig. 4.3 shows the xy-chromaticity diagram. It is obtained by first converting from the XYZ space to the xyz space and then plotting only the x and y axes (z is implicit in that $x + y + z = 1$). The horseshoe curve is the spectral locus. For the reference, we also show the three primary lights and the white point of the CIE 1931 RGB color space as well as the Planckian locus, which shows the chromaticities of the black-body radiation at different temperatures (Fig. 3.8).

We can make a few general observations. First, the triangle in the diagram represents the chromaticity values of all the colors that can be produced by mixing different amounts of the three colors whose chromaticities are the vertices of the triangle. That is, given three colors $[R_1, G_1, B_1]$, $[R_2, G_2, B_2]$, $[R_3, G_3, B_3]$ and their chromaticity coordinates $\mathbf{c_1} = [\frac{R_1}{R_1+G_1+B_1}]$, $\mathbf{c_2} = [\frac{R_2}{R_2+G_2+B_2}]$, and $\mathbf{c_3} = [\frac{R_3}{R_3+G_3+B_3}]$, we can show if we mix these colors to form a color C, $[\alpha R_1 + \beta R_2 + \gamma R_3, \alpha G_1 + \beta G_2 + \gamma G_3, \alpha B_1 + \beta B_2 + \gamma B_3]$ (α, β, γ are the contributions of the primary colors), C's chromaticity is necessarily inside the triangle $\triangle \mathbf{c_1 c_2 c_3}$. So the triangle $\triangle \mathbf{RGB}$ represents the chromaticities that can be physically produced by the CIE 1931 RGB primary lights. We call that the **chromaticity gamut** of the color space, or sometimes simply the gamut of the color space, but we should keep in mind that the actual gamut of a color space is always a three-dimensional concept.

Second, we can extend from mixing three colors to mixing an arbitrary number of colors and show that the interior of the spectral locus represents the chromaticities of all the colors that humans can see, i.e., the gamut of the HVS. This is true because the shape of the spectral locus is convex, so connecting any two points (i.e., mixing two colors) on or inside the locus will never go beyond the locus. By extension, a positive linear combination of any points on or inside the locus will always stay inside the locus. A natural implication is that any point outside the spectral locus represents an imaginary color, since that point can never be constructed by a positive linear combination of points on or inside the spectral locus.

Third, the right panel in Fig. 4.3 shows the gamut of a few common color spaces. The sRGB color space is the most commonly used color space; virtually every single display supports it, and images, by default, are encoded in the sRGB format. We will have more to say about displays and image encoding later. Observe how small the sRGB gamut is: it

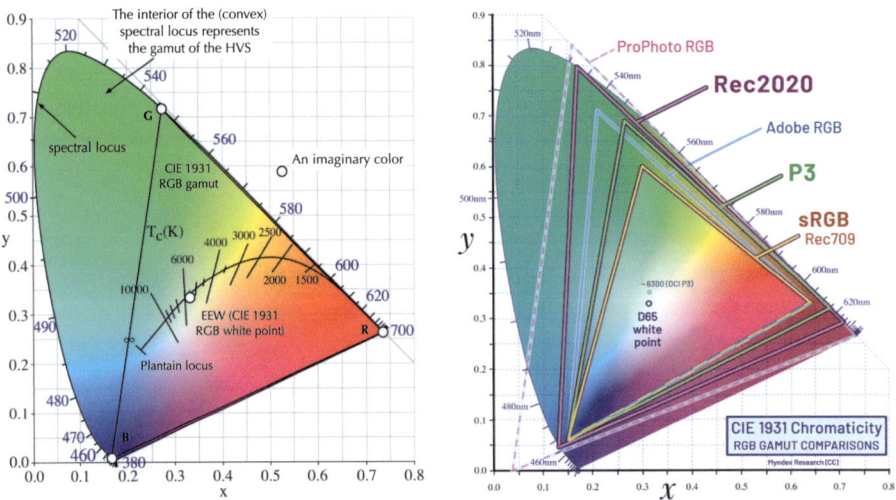

Fig. 4.3 Left: The gamut and spectral locus of the CIE 1931 RGB space visualized in the xy-chromaticity diagram; adapted from PAR (2012). The Planckian locus is shown for the reference too. A point outside the (convex) spectral locus is an imaginary color. Right: comparison of different color spaces in the xy-chromaticity diagram; from Myndex (2022). A color space's chromaticity gamut is a triangle; a color outside the triangle cannot be physically produced in that color space

covers about 35% of the HVS gamut. P3 is a more wider gamut that is supported in many new displays. Rec.2020 is an even wider gamut that is yet to be widely supported; it is 72% larger than the sRGB gamut and 37% larger than the P3 gamut. ProPhotoRGB contains colors that are beyond the HVS gamut, so to produce all the real colors in the ProPhotoRGB space we will need more than three primary lights. It is mostly used in Adobe Lightroom and Adobe Camera RAW software. They both deal with RAW images before they are encoded in a format that is displayable. We will talk about RAW imaging and processing later in Sect. 9.6.

Finally, no display can produce all the colors that humans can see. No matter where you choose to place the primary colors in the chromaticity diagram and how many primaries you choose, the resulting gamut will never completely cover the entire HVS gamut as long as the primary colors are real colors (i.e., on or inside the spectral locus) and you have a finite number of them. This is again because the spectral locus is convex. For this reason, do not trust the colors in any xy-chromaticity diagram: the undisplayable colors are approximated by in-gamut, displayable colors. This is called gamut mapping, which we will discuss in Sect. 4.6.2.

4.2.3 HVS Gamut

We can systematically sample the chromaticities in the chromaticity diagram to visualize how the HVS gamut looks like. Figure 4.4 visualizes the HVS gamut in both the XYZ space and the xy-chromaticity diagram. Comparing the two, you can see how a selected set of colors in the highlighted XYZ space map to a curve in the xy-chromaticity diagram.

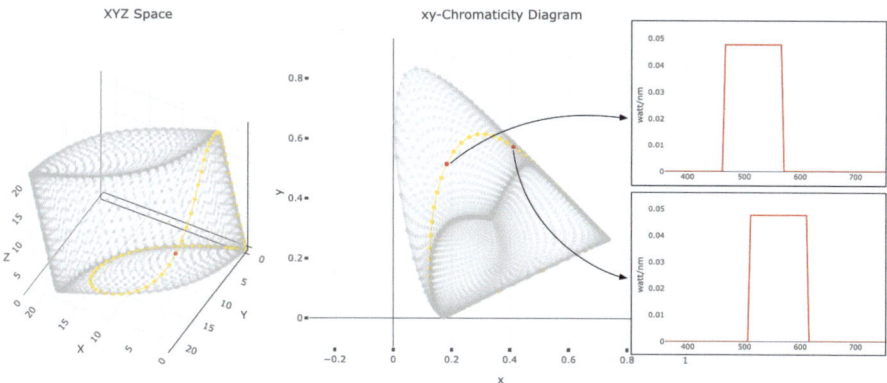

Fig. 4.4 HVS gamut visualized in the XYZ space and in the xy-chromaticity diagram. We systematically sample the chromaticities in the chromaticity diagram using square pulses as the light SPDs (insets on the right). From the interactive tutorial in Zhu (2022d)

There are, of course, many ways you can sample the chromaticities to get good coverage of the HVS gamut, and Zhu (2022d) is an interactive tutorial that talks about this in detail (you can also see what the HVS gamut looks like in different color spaces). A common way seems to be to generate SPDs that are square pulses with equal peaks (see the insets on the right), which will guarantee that you do not repeatedly sample the same chromaticity point. This is what the popular Python package Colour (NumFOCUS 2025) does, but nothing prevents you from using a different method, as explored in Zhu (2022d). Of course, the actual HVS gamut has no boundary: we can indefinitely grow the gamut by simply scaling up the light power.

4.3   Color Cube

The various color spaces we have been discussing are great, but they do not seem to be the sort of color spaces we use in everyday software when specifying colors. By far the most common way in practical applications to specify colors is by using a **color cube**, where you can specify the primary values (usually R, G, and B) of a color, each an integer between 0 and 255. What exactly are the colors that can be represented by such a color cube? How is it related to the color gamut we have discussed, and how do we construct a color cube? These are questions explored in the interactive tutorial (Zhu 2022d), which you are invited to go through. Figure 4.5 illustrates the idea, and we will give a brief summary of the main steps.

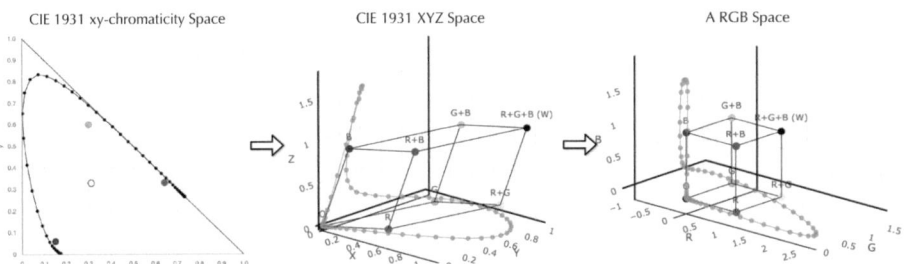

Fig. 4.5 Pick the primary colors (which usually are termed R, G, and B, because they usually are red-ish, green-ish, and blue-ish) and the white point in the xy-chromaticity space (left panel) and then construct a color cube from them (right panel). Note how the spectral locus is now positioned in the constructed RGB space. From the interactive tutorial in Zhu (2022a), which we invite you to study, you can see that as you change the primary colors and/or the white point, the resulting color gamut and the color cube will change accordingly

4.3.1   Step 1: A Linear Transformation From the XYZ Space

- We know that a color space is defined by its three primary colors *and* the white point, which you get to choose when building your own color cube. The left panel shows one such choice, which happens to be what is used by the sRGB color space.
- Knowing these four points uniquely defines the shape of a parallelepiped in the XYZ space (middle panel). The space inside the parallelepiped corresponds to actual colors that can be produced by using the primary colors.
  Note that at this point we know only the relative shape, but not the absolute scale, of the parallelepiped: we can uniformly scale the power of the primary colors and white point, which will not change their chromaticity values but will expand or shrink the parallelepiped. The convention is to set the Y value of white to be 1 and normalize everything else accordingly, but of course the actual luminance of white (and any other color) depends on the actual device used.
- Now we turn the parallelepiped to a cube that is positioned between [0, 1] in all three directions (right panel). The white point in the XYZ space will be [1, 1, 1] in the color cube, signifying that white is produced from equal units of the three primary colors. This amounts to a linear transformation from the XYZ space.
  Note also how the spectral locus is now positioned in the RGB space: part of the locus (and by extension the HVS gamut) is now outside the RGB cube, showing that there exist real colors (i.e., inside the HVS gamut) that cannot be produced by the choice of the primary colors. This is consistent with our gamut interpretation in the chromaticity diagram (Fig. 4.3).

What we have done so far is to construct a linear transformation matrix, $T_{xyz2rgb}$, which transforms the parallelepiped (middle panel in Fig. 4.5) to a cube (right panel in Fig. 4.5). This transformation matrix will change if we change any primary color or the white point of our color space (the interactive tutorial in Zhu (2022a) will allow you to do exactly that). Either way, the color cube we have built so far is luminance-linear: if we double the power of a light whose color is [R, G, B], we will get a color [2R, 2G, 2B]. This is because the XYZ space is luminance-linear, and the RGB cube we have so far is a linear transformation from the XYZ space.

4.3.2   Step 2: Color Quantization and Gamma

We get a cube now, but we are not done yet. The cube is a continuous solid between [0, 0, 0] and [1, 1, 1], but the digital representation of a color is discrete and finite, so we have to quantize the solid. Assuming we have, say, 8 bits (i.e., 256 discrete levels) to represent the contribution of each primary color, the question is how to allocate the 256 levels to the [0, 1] range.

So far the contribution of a primary color is linearly correlated with the power of the primary: doubling the contribution of a primary requires doubling the power of the corresponding light. Therefore, a uniform allocation of the bits would mean uniformly quantizing the light power range. As we have seen in Sect. 3.1.3, the electrical response of a photoreceptor is not linearly proportional to the light power (even though the amount of photon absorption and pigment excitation are!); the response incrementally saturates as the light power increases. As a result, the perceptual brightness level also gradually saturates with the light power. Therefore, uniformly quantizing the power range would lead to a *non-uniform* quantization of the brightness range, which is what we ideally want in order to best use the limited bit budget.

To uniformly quantize the brightness levels, a common method is to first model the brightness level (B) as a power-law function of the raw channel value ($v \in [0, 1]$) by $B = v^{1/2.2}$ and then quantize B uniformly. The constant factor 2.2 is called the **gamma** of the system. For instance, a red-channel value of 0.5 would translate to $\lfloor 0.5^{1/2.2} \times 255 \rfloor = 186$ in an 8-bit encoding. The relationship between B and v is called the Opto-Electronic Transfer Function (**OETF**). OETF is usually performed by an imaging system such as a camera, which turns optical signals (luminance) into electrical signals (bits in a color space).

Note that the gamma-based OETF does not model the actual relationship between perceived brightness and light luminance, but it is a close engineering hack. The behavioral brightness perception is largely accounted for by the photoreceptor/RGC response to light intensity. As we discussed in Sect. 3.1.3, the relationship between the electrical response of a photoreceptor and the light intensity is usually modeled by a (generalized) Michaelis equation, which incrementally saturates and exhibits a diminishing return, just like a power-law function using a gamma.

The sRGB color space (Anderson et al. 1996) slightly modifies this OETF to avoid numerical issues when v is small. The sRGB standard uses a linear scaling when v is very small[1] and adjusts the gamma to be 2.4 so that the overall quantization function approximates a uniform power-law function with a gamma of 2.2.

There are two caveats here. First, v is *proportional* to luminance L, but is *not* exactly L, so the same v will result in different Ls on different displays that differ in their peak luminance. So encoding B as a power-law function of v does not mean the OETF actually models the correct relationship between B and L. That is why the sRGB standard specifies the peak luminance of the display (white point) as $80\,cd/m^2$. Presumably this means that at this particular luminance range (0 to $80\,cd/m^2$), the relationship between B and L roughly follows the power law. Second, light adaptation (a later topic) will also play a role, since the HVS responds to contrasts over the mean illuminance, rather than absolute illuminance, and the mean illuminance varies largely across viewing environments. The sRGB standard also

---

[1] This makes sense given our understanding in Sect. 3.1.3 that the receptor's electrical response is approximately linear against the light luminance when the luminance is very low.

specifies that the mean illuminance level of the viewing environment to be 64 lux. When actually viewing an sRGB image, both conditions are rarely met, so take all these with a huge grain of salt.

4.3.3 RGB Color Spaces are Linearly Related in Luminance

By "RGB color space", we mean a color space that is defined by its three primary colors (and critically also the white point), which we call R, G, and B for simplicity, but they certainly do not have to look like red-ish, green-ish, and blue-ish. Different RGB color spaces might use different gammas and quantization schemes. In the end, the discrete RGB values are usually not linearly related to luminance. We can go back to a luminance-linear space from the discrete RGB values by inverting the gamma encoding process described above. For instance, in sRGB space, 186 would translate to 0.5 in the luminance-linear sRGB space.

Once in a luminance-linear space, different color spaces are simply a linear transformation away from each other. The transformation matrix can be calculated based on the primary colors and the white point of the two color spaces. We will omit the math here, but to get an idea just go back to Fig. 4.5. Two color spaces having different primary colors and white points will end up being two different parallelepipeds that are related by a transformation matrix. Another way to think about this is that each luminance-linear RGB color space is a linear transformation away from the XYZ space, so these RGB spaces must be linearly related too.

4.4 HSB/HSL/HSV Space

A color cube is one way to represent an RGB color space. Another common way to represent an RGB color space is to use a cylindrical-coordinate representation. There are two such representations, HSL (Hue, Saturation, and Lightness) and HSV (Hue, Saturation, and Value), which is also called HSB (B for Brightness). These are not new color spaces; their gamut is identical to that of the corresponding RGB color space. They are just different ways to organize colors in a color space; instead of using three-dimensional coordinates to represent a color as in a color cube, they use cylindrical coordinates.

Figure 4.6 compares a typical color cube (left) and its HSL representation (right). We omit the transformation math here, but one can imagine how we turn the white point in a color cube to the top plane, the black point to the bottom plane, and expand everything else so that a cube surface morphs into a cylindrical surface. The three dimensions in an HLS space are hue, saturation, and lightness. Very informally, hue represents subjectively different colors (red, orange, yellow, etc.), saturation represents how much white a color has (a color with a higher saturation means it is more "pure"), and lightness represents the brightness. In this sense, hue and saturation also find their interpretations in the CIE 1931 xy-chromaticity

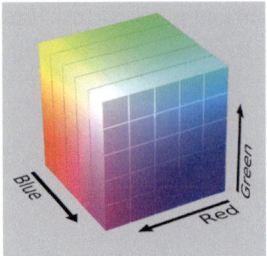 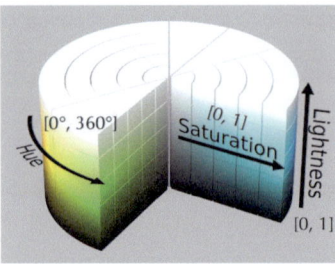 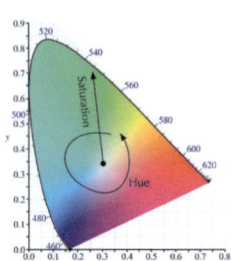

Fig. 4.6 We can represent an RGB color cube (left) using cylindrical coordinates. One such representation is the HSL color space (right), where hue, saturation, and lightness have intuitive interpretations. Hue and saturation also have intuitive interpretations in the CIE 1931 xy-chromaticity diagram, which normalizes luminance so lightness information is absent. Left: from SharkD (2010b). Middle: adapted from SharkD (2010a). Right: from BenRG (2009)

diagram (right), where a color closer to the spectral locus has a higher saturation (and colors closer to white-ish colors are *desaturated*), and the spectral locus cycles through different hues. Lightness is not concerned with in the chromaticity diagram, which normalizes the color intensity.

You can imagine what the benefit of using an HSL/HSB color space is. It is more intuitive to pick colors in these color representations since the three dimensions have intuitive interpretations that better align with how we describe colors in our everyday language. So we can more easily reason about how a color will change if we vary a dimension. In contrast, it is sometimes hard to predict how a color will change when we, say, increase the red channel by 10. I almost exclusively use the HSL/HSB space when picking colors in graphing software.

4.5   Display Native Gamut

The display has a native color space. Each display pixel is implemented by (usually) three sub-pixels, each of which has an implementation-specific SPD and acts as a primary light. The retina then spatially integrates the lights from the three sub-pixels, i.e., mixing the three primary colors. We can individually control the luminance of each sub-pixel and, by extension, the actual color of the mixed pixel. The luminance can be controlled by (1) the duty cycle of a pixel through Pulse Width Modulation (PWM), (2) the current supply to each sub-pixel, or (3) the voltage supply to each sub-pixel. The luminance is strictly linear with respect to the drive signal in the first case, approximately linear in the second case, and non-linear in the third case (Miller 2019, p. 112). The mapping from the electrical drive signal strength to the luminance level is usually called the Electro-Optical Transfer Function (**EOTF**).

The display's native color space is most likely not exactly sRGB or any standard color space. The primary colors (and the white point) depend on the emission spectrum of each sub-pixel, which in turn depends on the material used. For instance, inorganic LEDs have a narrower emission spectra than the organic LEDs (Huang et al. 2020), so they tend to be able to generate more saturated colors and, thus, the resulting display gamut is wider. One has to balance multiple trade-offs in a display design, such as invariance of chromaticity versus luminance, lifetime, power consumption, and cost, so it is difficult to tune the pixel spectra *just* so that the colors precisely match that of a standard.

Field Sequential Displays (FSD) rely on the temporal integration of our visual system to create different colors. The most common example of an FSD is modern Digital Light Processing (DLP) projectors. We will not discuss specific display implementations; instead, we will focus on the color space of a display regardless of how the colors are produced.

As an example, Fig. 4.7 shows the the sub-pixels images of the green primary colors in the P3 and sRGB color space as displayed on a 4th-generation iPad Pro. We can make a few observations. First, the emission patterns of P3 green and sRGB green are different. The P3 green is more "pure", where the red and blue sub-pixels are contributing very little, whereas the sRGB green requires noticeable contribution from the red sub-pixels. This is not surprising because the P3 green is much more saturated (closer to spectral colors) than the sRGB green, as shown in the right figure in Fig. 4.3. The actual contributions of red sub-pixels in sRGB green as seen by my eye are not as strong as seen in this iPhone-taken image; the image signal processing pipeline in the iPhone definitely has introduced its artifacts.

Second, even for the P3 green, there are still some contributions from the red sub-pixels. This suggests that the native display gamut is different from (and larger than) P3. This makes sense: for a display to support a particular color space, say, the P3 space, the display's native color space must be no smaller than the P3 space.

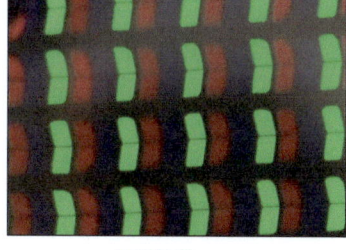

P3 Green   sRGB Green

Fig. 4.7 Microscope-magnified subpixel images of P3 green and sRGB green primary (both are [0, 255, 0] in their respective color spaces) on a 4th-generation iPad Pro taken from an iPhone 12 Pro (whose image signal processing chain introduces color inaccuracies; the red sub-pixel contributions to the sRGB green are not as strong when seen by naked eye). As a side note, you can also see that when the image is focused on the green sub-pixels, the red (and blue) sub-pixels are out of focus, a result of chromatic aberration

4.6   Color Management

An end-to-end workflow might involve multiple output media (e.g., displays, prints), and it is important to correctly translate colors between them to accurately reproduce the color appearance. There are a few issues that need our attention.

First, you might edit a photo encoded in the P3 color space, save the photo in a file, and share it with your friend, who will view the image on a display that supports only the sRGB color space. Multiple color spaces are involved here. The image is first encoded in the P3 space and then will have to be reinterpreted in the sRGB space. A color, say, [10, 20, 30] encoded in the P3 color space is not the same color as the sRGB color [10, 20, 30], so we must correctly translate a color encoded in the source color space to the destination color space.

Second, a potential issue in this transformation is that the P3 color space has a larger gamut than that of sRGB, so there will necessarily be colors in the photon that will never be accurately reproduced on your friend's display—what do we do with these colors? Each display also has its own native color space, and an sRGB/P3 image will have to be transformed to the display's native space. Fundamentally, if we want to display, say, a P3-encoded image, the display's native gamut must be no smaller than P3.

Finally, the viewer might be under a different viewing condition than the condition under which the photo was originally edited. The viewing condition could affect the actual appearance of a color, so we must account for this shift in viewing condition.

Taking care of all these is part of **color management**, whose goal is to maintain a consistent color appearance throughout the workflow that might involve wildly different devices. It requires a collaboration between every single piece that touches color in the workflow: the image file must come with a *profile* that specifies what color space its pixel colors are encoded in and (an estimation of) the viewing condition under which the image was originally edited/viewed, the software that manipulates image content must correctly read and interpret the profile and perform the necessary transformation, potentially through APIs exposed by the Operating System (OS), and the display firmware and drive must communicate with the OS a similar profile of the display itself. Giorgianni and Madden (2009) and Sharma (2018) are two excellent references for color management. We will describe the key issues here.

4.6.1   Color Space Transformation

When opening and viewing an image encoded in, say, sRGB on a display, a few transformations have to happen (Miller 2019, Sect. 7.1). The display's native color space is most likely not exactly sRGB or any standard color space; we must correctly translate a color encoded in the sRGB space to the display's space. A color [10, 20, 30] encoded in sRGB is not the same color as [10, 20, 30] in the display's color space. This transformation is done in two steps.

First, the image file ideally has metadata that tells us what color space its pixel colors are encoded in or, better, the transformation matrix from the image's color space to a device-independent color space, say the CIE XYZ space. The way to describe such information has been standardized by International Color Consortium (ICC) in what is called the *ICC profile* (International Color Consortium 2019). We can embed an ICC profile in common image file formats such as JPEG. Second, the display itself also has to report its native color space. To do that, modern displays usually come with an ICC profile that describes how to transform from the CIE XYZ space to the display's native space. Now when the Operating System gets the image file, it would first transform the sRGB colors to the XYZ space using the ICC profile in the image and then transform the colors in the XYZ to the display's native space using the display profile.[2] You can see that the XYZ space here serves to connect the input color space and the output color space. ICC calls such a space a Profile Connection Space (PCS).

The transformation from the XYZ space to the display's native space is necessarily linear. To calculate the transformation matrix, we will first measure the chromaticity values of the display's native primary colors and the white point offline (Balasubramanian 2003). Then we take the exact the same steps as described in Sect. 4.3.1: we are essentially creating a color cube for the display ([1, 1, 1] represents the display white point, i.e., when all the sub-pixels emit maximum luminance, etc.).

4.6.1.1 Converting Pixel Colors to Drive Signals

After this transformation, we have obtained a set of luminance-linear, analog (between [0, 1]) color values in the display's native color space. The next step is to turn the real-valued colors into discrete values (drive signals) that can be sent to the display to control the luminance of each sub-pixel. Ideally, we want 255 (assuming 8 bits) to produce maximum luminance and 0 to produce minimum luminance. Depending on how the display adjusts its luminance (by PWM, current, or voltage), the drive signal versus luminance relationship, i.e., EOTF, may or may not be linear. Either way, we can offline calibrate an EOTF look-up table (or regress a function), from which we can then map a desired luminance level to a discrete value.

What is the desired luminance level for a pixel? It would be *amazing* if your display could reproduce the scene luminance, but that is unlikely, because the real world has a much higher, orders of magnitude higher, dynamic range (DR) than that of a display. A main challenge in imaging and display, thus, is **tone mapping**, which is concerned with mapping a high-dynamic-range scene to a low-dynamic-range display. This mapping can be described by an Opto-Optical Transfer Function (**OOTF**). Both the OETF of an imaging system and

---

[2] While in the XYZ space, we usually perform an additional transformation so that sRGB white becomes the white point in the display space. This is called *chromatic adaptation*, which we will discuss later in Sect. 4.6.3.

the EOTF of a display participate in the OOTF, and if the product of OETF and EOTF is not the desired OOTF, one would need to implement an Electro-Electrical Transfer Function (**EETF**) as part of the image processing pipeline to reach the desired OOTF. Tone mapping is the focus of extensive research (Mantiuk et al. 2015, Reinhard 2010).

4.6.2   Gamut Mapping

When viewing a P3-encoded image on a display whose gamut is smaller, e.g., similar to that of sRGB, the colors might not be accurately reproduced. The best thing we can do is to approximate an out-of-gamut color with an in-gamut color to minimize the color error. This is called **gamut mapping**. Morovič (2008) and Glassner (1995, Sect. 3.6) describe the basic algorithms, with the former being more recent and comprehensive.

The simplest strategy would be to simply clamp out-of-range values, so a color of [12, 200, 300] would become [12, 200, 255]. Clearly, other than being extremely simple to implement, this strategy would introduce large color reproduction errors. ICC has defined four **rendering intents**, each of which corresponds to a gamut mapping algorithm (vaguely worded, and the implementation detail might vary). For instance, the *Absolute* rendering intent leaves all the in-gamut colors unchanged but maps the out-of-gamut colors to the boundary of the color gamut. The *Perceptual* rendering intent can be implemented by uniformly projecting all the colors to the white point so that all the colors are in-gamut. You can imagine that while this maintains the relative color appearance between colors (which the Absolute rendering intent fails at), but it would also change in-gamut colors that could have been accurately rendered!

4.6.3   Chromatic Adaptation

The final step is to account for the difference in viewing conditions between when the image was originally created and when it will be viewed. This is through **chromatic adaptation**. The specific element of viewing condition that chromatic adaptation accounts for is the color of the illuminant. We will provide the intuition behind chromatic adaptation here, and a more detailed discussion can be found in Zhu (2021). Additional, Fairchild (2013, Chaps. 7–8) is a comprehensive reference; MacAdam (1982, Chap. 11) and Wandell (1995, Chap. 9) provide more psychophysical and neural contexts; Shirley and Marschner (2021, Chpt 18.3) succinctly describes the mathematics relevant to computer graphics.

Throughout the day, we encounter a variety of lighting conditions, from incandescent bulbs to natural sunlight, yet our color perception remains relatively stable. This constancy arises because our visual system adapts to differing illuminant colors through a process known as chromatic adaptation.

Johannes von Kries (Kries 1902, 1905) hypothesized that (in modern interpretations) we adapt by scaling the spectral sensitivities of individual classes of cone photoreceptors under different illuminants.[3] The sensitivities scale such that the cone responses of a neutral point remain constant under different illuminants as if the color of the illuminant is "discounted." A neutral point reflects light uniformly across its wavelength, so its color is the color of the illuminant itself. Since common illuminants (e.g., daylights) appear white-ish, the color of the illuminant or the color of a neutral point is also called the "**white point**" or "reference white" of the scene.

An important concept in chromatic adaptation is the user's **adaptation state**, or the "internal white point", which refers to the color that the user endogenously regards as white. When a user is exposed to a natural illuminant (e.g., daylight) S for a sufficiently long time, the user has fully adapted to the illuminant, at which point the user's adaptation state *is* S.

Adaptation state must be considered during color management (and rendering and imaging[4]). If an image is initially presented to a user adapted to illuminant S but then later presented to the same user, now adapted to a different illuminant T, the colors in the image will appear differently than they do under S, as cone sensitivity scaling depends on the adaptation state.

To compensate for the change of adaptation state, we must transform a color c_S in the original image rendered under S to c_T such that c_T, viewed under T, appears to be the same color as c_S, viewed under S. This conversion is done via a linear Chromatic Adaptation Transform (CAT) function, whose details are omitted (but can be found in the texts referenced above) and is denoted as $f_{S \to T}(\cdot)$ here:

$$c_T = f_{S \to T}(c_S). \tag{4.2}$$

In practice, the CAT is applied in conjunction with the color space transformation (Sect. 4.6.1), since both are linear. Gamut mapping is then applied to the transformed colors. The real challenge in practice is to estimate the adaptation state S during creation and T during viewing. A simple assumption that is often made is that humans adapt to the white of the color space in which they create/view an image. This is perhaps not a bad assumption when there is a large amount of white on the display (e.g., UI elements), but it will obviously fail otherwise. In Mark Fairchild's words, determining the state of adaptation is the "biggest unsolved problem."

Finally, it is worth noting that the full color appearance modeling goes beyond just chromatic adaptation, which accounts for a specific aspect of viewing conditions: the color of the illuminant. Fairchild (2013) provides a detailed survey of other factors influencing the viewing condition and phenomena that simply could not be explained by viewing condition alone.

---

[3] This is a phenomenological model in that sensitivity scaling in other retinal cells is also almost certainly involved (Webster 2011) and that cognitive (top-down) influences can be substantial (Smithson 2005).

[4] In fact, the white balancing algorithm in raw image post-processing (Sect. 9.6) is a computational simulation of the chromatic adaptation process in the HVS.

4.7   Color Differences and "Perceptually Uniform" Color Spaces

In many practical applications, we need to calculate color differences. For instance, an image synthesis algorithm might want to be minimize the color difference in the synthesized image and some form of "ground truth"; a display's color reproduction might not be 100% accurate, so we want to quantitatively compare the quality of different displays by measuring the color difference (compared to the colors to be reproduced) each introduces. Fortunately, once we put colors into a three-dimensional coordinate system, calculating color differences becomes natural: the distance between two colors gives a measure of the difference between the two colors.

However, for the Euclidean distance to be a good measure, we must be sure that the distance is proportional to the perceptual color difference. How do we quantify the perceptual color difference? Practically there are not many cases where we need to quantify large color differences. What is more important is to quantify small color differences. So a typical approach is to estimate the **Just Noticeable Difference** (JND) threshold of a color. For a given reference color, we can use a threshold-detection psychophysical paradigm such as the one described in Duinkharjav et al. (2022) to estimate the set of colors that are just noticeably different from the reference color. These experiments are called *color discrimination* tests.

A color space is said to be "perceptually uniform" if the JND measure is the same regardless of where the reference color is in the color space. If so, the Euclidean distance is a good measure of perceptual color differences. Unfortunately, the common CIE XYZ space is not perceptually uniform. This is demonstrated in the seminar work by MacAdam (1942, 1943) (MacAdam did the work while working for Eastman Kodak at Rochester and he later was an adjunct professor at University of Rochester).[5] He measured the thresholds in the CIE 1931 xy-chromaticity space for a set of colors. He found that the thresholds for a reference color fit an ellipse-shaped contour. Within an iso-discrimination ellipse, all the colors are non-discriminable with respect to the center, reference color. A modern rendition of his results is shown in Fig. 4.8 (left); the ellipse sizes are magnified ten times to be visible. Of course the actual iso-discrimination contour would be a 3D solid (ellipsoid) in the XYZ space; the ellipses in the xy-chromaticity diagram are projections of the ellipsoids.

We can see that the not only the iso-discrimination contours (ellipses) are not circles, their shapes also vary significantly across the gamut, indicating that the XYZ space is not perceptually uniform. Quite a few attempts have been made to transform the XYZ space into a more perceptually uniform space. The two common ones are the CIE 1976 L*u*v* (CIELUV) space and the (more widely used) CIE 1976 L*a*b* (CIELAB) space, both of which are non-linear transformations from the XYZ space.

The so-called CIE Delta E 1976 color difference metric (ΔE_{ab}^*) is defined as the Euclidean distance in the CIELAB space. If CIELAB is truly perceptually uniform (as far as color discrimination is concerned), ΔE_{ab}^* being 1.0 would mean a JND. However, this

---

[5] He did not use a direct threshold-detection strategy but indirectly estimated the thresholds using variations in color matching experiments.

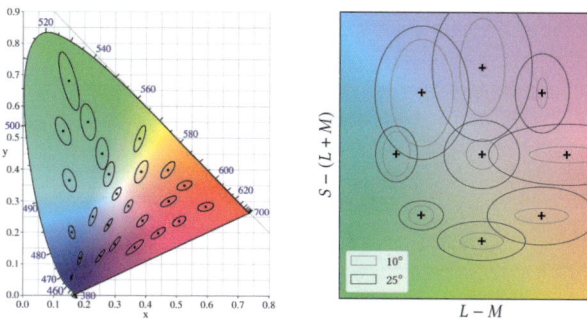

Fig. 4.8 Left: MacAdam ellipses (measured at 2° eccentricity) plotted in the xy-chromaticity diagram (the ellipse sizes are magnified 10 times to be more visible); from Anonymous (2009). Each ellipse is an iso-discrimination contour, within which all the colors are non-discriminable from the center, reference color. Right: A set of MacAdam ellipses in the (chromatic plane of the) DKL space (Derrington et al. 1984) (also see Sect. 3.4) under two eccentricities; from Duinkharjav et al. (2022, Fig. 4a)

is not true either (Sharma 2003, Fig. 1.18). CIE has since recommended a new, much more involved, and non-Euclidean measure in the CIELAB space, called the Delta E 2000 metric (ΔE_{00}), to better achieve better perceptual uniformity (Sharma et al. 2005). The Delta E 2000 metric is still not perfect, but it is a significant improvement and is widely used in practice.

MacAdam's original data were collected at 2° eccentricity. Given that the visual acuity reduces as the eccentricity increases, it is only natural that the iso-discrimination ellipses expand in size as the eccentricity. Duinkharjav et al. (2022) measures the ellipses under different eccentricities. The right panel in Fig. 4.8 compares the results between 10° and 25°. Not surprisingly, the ellipses are larger in the latter.

References

ACDX (2009) CIE 1931 XYZ Color Matching Functions; CC BY-SA 4.0. https://commons.wikimedia.org/wiki/File:CIE_1931_XYZ_Color_Matching_Functions.svg

Anderson M, Motta R, Chandrasekar S, Stokes M (1996) Proposal for a standard default color space for the internet-sRGB. In: Color and imaging conference, Society of imaging science and technology, vol 4, pp 238–245

Anonymous (2009) MacAdam Ellipses in the CIE1931 xy chromaticity diagram; CC BY-SA 3.0 license. https://commons.wikimedia.org/wiki/File:CIExy1931_MacAdam.png

Balasubramanian R (2003) Device characterization. In: Sharma G (ed) Digital color imaging handbook. CRC Press, pp 269–384

BenRG (2009) CIE1931 xy chromaticity plot; released into the public domain by the copyright holder. https://commons.wikimedia.org/wiki/File:CIE1931xy_blank.svg

Brill MH (1998) Erratum: how the CIE 1931 color-matching functions were derived from wright-guild data. Color Res Appl 23(4):259–259

Derrington AM, Krauskopf J, Lennie P (1984) Chromatic mechanisms in lateral geniculate nucleus of macaque. J Physiol 357(1):241–265

Duinkharjav B, Chen K, Tyagi A, He J, Zhu Y, Sun Q (2022) Color-perception-guided display power reduction for virtual reality. ACM Trans Graph (TOG) 41(6):1–16

Fairchild MD (2013) Color appearance models, 3rd edn. Wiley

Fairman HS, Brill MH, Hemmendinger H (1997) How the CIE 1931 color-matching functions were derived from wright-guild data. Color Res Appl 22(1):11–23

Giorgianni EJ, Madden TE (2009) Digital color management: encoding solutions, vol 13. Wiley

Glassner AS (1995) Principles of digital image synthesis. Elsevier

Huang Y, Hsiang EL, Deng MY, Wu ST (2020) Mini-LED, micro-LED and OLED displays: present status and future perspectives. Light: Sci Appl 9(1):105

International Color Consortium (2019) Specification ICC.2:2019 (Profile version 5.0.0 - iccMAX). https://color.org/specification/ICC.2-2019.pdf

Kries V (1902) Chromatic adaptation. Festschrift der Albrecht-Ludwigs-Universit t pp 145–158

Kries V (1905) Influence of adaptation on the effects produced by luminous stimuli. Handbuch der Physiologie des Menschen 3:109–282

MacAdam DL (1942) Visual sensitivities to color differences in daylight. JOSA 32(5):247–274

MacAdam DL (1943) Specification of small chromaticity differences. JOSA 33(1):18–26

MacAdam DL (1982) Color measurement: theme and variations. Springer, Berlin, Heidelberg

Mantiuk R, Krawczyk G, Zdrojewska D, Mantiuk R, Myszkowski K, Seidel HP (2015) High dynamic range imaging. In: Wiley encyclopedia of electrical and electronics engineering, Wiley

Marco Polo (2007) CIE1931 RGB CMF; released into the public domain by the copyright holder. https://commons.wikimedia.org/wiki/File:CIE1931_RGBCMF.svg

Miller ME (2019) Color in electronic display systems. Springer, Berlin

Morovič J (2008) Color gamut mapping, 2nd edn. Wiley

Myndex (2022) A comparison of RGB gamuts of sRGB, P3, Rec2020, etc. using the CIE1931 chromaticity diagram; CC BY-SA 4.0 license. https://commons.wikimedia.org/wiki/File:CIE1931xy_gamut_comparison_of_sRGB_P3_Rec2020.svg

NumFOCUS (n.d.) Colour: open-source Python package for colour science. https://github.com/colour-science/colour

PAR (2012) Plankian locus; released into the public domain by the copyright holder. https://commons.wikimedia.org/wiki/File:PlanckianLocus.png

Reinhard E (2010) High dynamic range imaging acquisition, display, and image-based lighting, 2nd edn. Morgan Kaufmann Publishers

Service P (2016) The wright – guild experiments and the development of the CIE 1931 RGB and XYZ color spaces

SharkD (2010a) HSL color solid cylinder; CC BY-SA 3.0 license. https://commons.wikimedia.org/wiki/File:HSL_color_solid_cylinder_saturation_gray.png

SharkD (2010b) RGB color cube; CC BY-SA 3.0 license. https://commons.wikimedia.org/wiki/File:RGB_Cube_Show_lowgamma_cutout_a.png

Sharma A (2018) Understanding color management. Wiley

Sharma G (2003) Color fundamentals for digital imaging. In: Sharma G (ed) Digital color imaging handbook. CRC Press, pp 14–127

Sharma G, Wu W, Dalal EN (2005) The CIEDE2000 color-difference formula: implementation notes, supplementary test data, and mathematical observations. Color Res Appl 30(1):21–30

Shirley P, Marschner S (2021) Fundamentals of computer graphics, 5th edn. AK Peters/CRC Press

Smithson HE (2005) Sensory, computational and cognitive components of human colour constancy. Philos Trans R Soc B: Biol Sci 360(1458):1329–1346

Wandell BA (1995) Foundations of vision. Sinauer Associates

Webster MA (2011) Adaptation and visual coding. J Vis 11(5):3–3

Zhu Y (2021) Principles and practices of chromatic adaptation. https://yuhaozhu.com/blog/chromatic-adaptation.html

Zhu Y (2022a) Interative tutorial: building a color cube. https://horizon-lab.org/colorvis/colorcube.html

Zhu Y (2022b) Interative tutorial: chromaticity, gamut, and the scary world of imaginary colors. https://horizon-lab.org/colorvis/chromaticity.html

Zhu Y (2022c) Interative tutorial: CIE 1931 XYZ color space. https://horizon-lab.org/colorvis/xyz.html

Zhu Y (2022d) Interative tutorial: visualizing human visual gamut. https://horizon-lab.org/colorvis/gamutvis.html

So far in our discussion of color, our focus has been on howour visual system encodes light spectrum coming from an object into color perception. We have, however, not cared much about how an object produces light in the first place. An object could, of course, emit light itself. In the real world, however, the vast majority of objects have colors not because they emit light but because they interact with light that impinges upon them. The light-matter interaction modifies the energy spectrum of the incident light, and the modified light is scattered back to our eyes, giving rise to (color) vision.

Agreat deal of computer graphics is concerned with *rendering* the color of objects, and the name of the game is to model the light-matter interactions in a physically accurate manner so that the colors in the generated imagery look real. This part of the book is concerned with the physical principles that govern light-matter interactions insofar as they are used in rendering photorealistic color images. We will not cover implementation-specific topics such as how these principles can be implemented in graphics pipelines (e.g., OpenGL, Vulkan, and OptiX); nor will we cover how these pipelines are implemented on modern GPU hardware correctly and efficiently.

Any coverage of physics in rendering is necessarily an approximation—based on phenomenological models that abstract away unimportant details of the underlying physics while maintaining what is relevant for image synthesis. Deep learning and AI techniques push this kind of approximation to the extreme.With these techniques, rendering is re-branded as *novel view synthesis*, the prime example of which is the increasingly popular class of (neural) radiance-field rendering methods such asNeRF and 3DGS.

These methods are fundamentally image-based rendering (Sect. 5.3.7): they sample, reconstruct, and re-sample the light field—using modern learning methods such as (stochastic) gradient descent. Interestingly, even though they do not exactly model the physics governing the light-matter interactions, their learning model is parameterized with physics-inspired formulations, i.e., a simplified form of the volume rendering equation, which we will analyze carefully. By understanding the governing physics, we can better interpret these learning-based methods, understand their limits, and reason about potential opportunities for improvement.

The Basics

5

5.1   Overview

When a beam of photons hits a material surface, some of the photons will be scattered directly back to your eyes, and others will penetrate into the material. These surface phenomena are governed by **surface scattering**. We use the word "scattering" here to generally refer to lights coming back from the surface. Depending on the material, some of the scattered photons are along the perfect mirror-reflection directions, and others might be more diffuse. You might sometimes see the word "reflection" used. Reflection is sometimes used in the same way as scattering, which will be our use, but other times is reserved for the perfect, mirror-like reflection. Usually what the word means is self-evident given the context, but we will err on the side of verbosity when we want to mean a specific form of reflection.

Photons that penetrate the surface will further interact with particles in the material, which absorb, scatter, or might even emit photons. This is called **subsurface scattering** (SSS) in computer graphics. Even though we use the term "scattering", you should know that the actual SSS processes involve not only scattering but also absorption and emission. It turns out that the principles that govern SSS are exactly the same as those that govern the interactions between photons and particles in the so-called "participating media", such as clouds, fogs, and smokes. In computer graphics, light transport in participating media is called **volume scattering**, and again, even though we use the term "scattering", absorption and emission are usually involved in the most general cases.

The way to model SSS/volume scattering is different from the way to model surface scattering: we no longer consider the material as a continuous surface and the light-matter interaction as photons bouncing off of the surface; instead, we break a material down into small particles and model how photons interact with individual particles.

Very importantly, the difference in the modeling methodology does *not* imply that there somehow is a fundamental difference between surface scattering and volume scattering. Ultimately, both are caused by the light, an oscillating electromagnetic field, exciting discrete

97
Y. Zhu, *Visual Computing For Architects*, Synthesis Lectures on Computer Architecture,
https://doi.org/10.1007/978-3-032-05018-2_5

electric charges. The differences lie in how the charges are arranged in space and in relation to one another. The laws that govern how photons interact with the charges are described by the electromagnetic theories in the classical regime and, in the quantum regime, by the quantum electrodynamics (QED).[1] In fact, using the electromagnetic theories, we can show that surface reflection/refraction is nothing more than the coherent scattering of incident light waves by the surface particles.

Since there is no fundamental differences in the underlying physics, the only meaningful distinction is one between different phenomenological approximations, or "models", of the same underlying physics. We totally could invoke the electromagnetic theories or QED, and if we did, we would have one single unified model that explains both surface scattering (reflection and refraction) and volume scattering. Doing so, however, is not only unnecessary (because many, not all, real-world material color phenomena could be modeled without them) and too computationally expensive, but also, perhaps more importantly, blinds us from the relatively simple intuitions in each scenario. Instead, each phenomenological model is based on a set of high-level guiding principles, which are approximations of the underlying physical process but are sufficient to quantitatively describe light-matter interactions in each scenario.

Johnsen (2012) is a great reference, which has some equations but generally focuses on building intuitions and mostly uses the electromagnetic language rather than the quantum language. If you want to get to the nuts and bolts of the mathematical modeling, Bohren and Clothiaux (2006) is a phenomenal text whose models are also built in the electromagnetic land. Feynman (1985) has an accessible and breathtaking introduction to QED that I highly recommend.

Dorsey et al. (2010) is a classic text on material appearance modeling in graphics that covers a range of topics, including modeling, measurements, and various implementation issues in practice. Johnston-Feller (2001) is specifically concerned with paintings; it has many interesting discussions of pigments and pigment mixtures and has many real-world data and insights that are rarely found elsewhere.

5.2   Observed Reflection and Transmission

Regardless of the details of surface scattering and volume scattering, a material appears to have some color because some photons leaving the material enter our eye. If we observe the material from the same side of the light source, it is the lights reflected from the material that matter. If we observe the material from the other side of the light source, it is the light transmitted through the material that matter. At the highest level of abstraction, we can model the material color in the real world by modeling the *observed* reflection and transmission

---

[1] The electromagnetic theories do not explain everything in light-matter interactions. Famously, they do not explain how the interference pattern in the double-slit experiment still arises even if the photons are delivered sequentially.

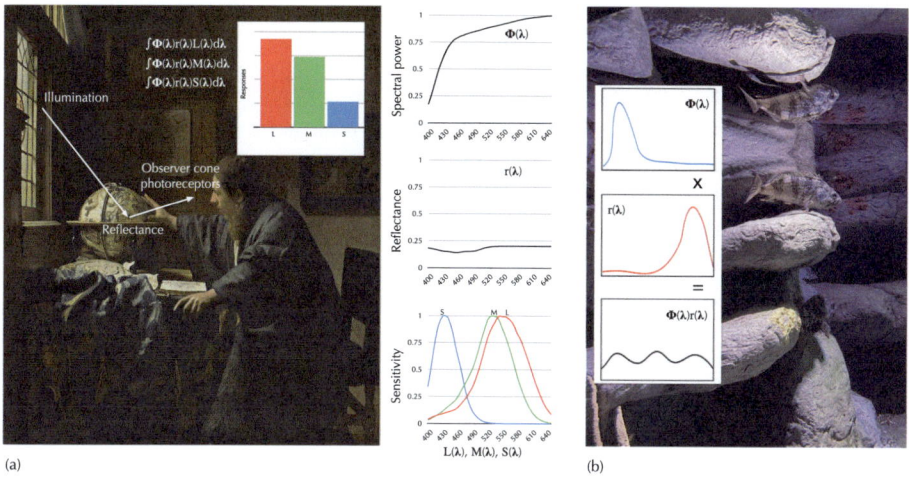

Fig. 5.1   a: Apparent spectral reflectance modifies the illumination spectrum and dictates the observed color; adapted from The Astronomer by Johannes Vermeer (1668). **b**: A photo of Acadia Redfish I took in the Ripley's Aquarium of Canada. The fish ordinarily looks red-ish under a white-ish light, but appears colorless in the aquarium, which simulates the lighting environment in the deep sea where lights are predominately blue/violet. The spectral data are not accurate and for the illustration purpose only

apparent to an outside observer: how much of the incident power is reflected/transmitted back to the eye?

We can quantify the observed reflection and transmission using the **spectral reflectance function** $r(\lambda)$ and the **spectral transmittance function** $t(\lambda)$, respectively. These two functions spare us the details of how lights interact with a material but describe, at each wavelength λ, the percentage of optical power that is reflected back to the eye or transmitted through the material and enters the eye, respectively.

Figure 5.1a illustrates this modeling at work using the famous The Astronomer by Johannes Vermeer. We will proceed with our discussion using reflectance, but the case idea can be easily extended to transmittance. Vermeer paints an astronomer looking at a globe. Given the illumination coming from the window $\Phi(\lambda)$ and the spectral reflectance of the point on the globe under gaze $r(\lambda)$, the light reflected toward the eye is then $\Phi(\lambda)r(\lambda)$. We can then calculate the color of these lights using the cone fundamentals or some set of CMFs, the same way as if the lights were directly emitted from the globe.

As another example, Fig. 5.1b is a photo of Acadia Redfish I took in the Ripley's Aquarium of Canada. The fish ordinarily looks red-ish under a white-ish light, which suggests that its spectral reflectance $r(\lambda)$ peaks at longer wavelengths: it scatters more long-wavelength, i.e., red-ish, lights than short-wavelength lights. But the fish appears colorless in the aquarium, which simulates the lighting environment in the deep sea where lights $\Phi(\lambda)$ are predominately blue/violet.[2] As a result, the scattered lights have a rather uniform spectral power distribution, resulting in a gray-ish appearance.

Figure 5.1 makes an important simplification: the reflectance of a point p on the material is simplified to only a single spectrum. In reality, the reflectance of a point p depends on both ω_i, the direction of the light incident on p, and ω_s, the outgoing direction (leaving p) through which one observes the material. In certain materials where SSS contributes to the material appearance (e.g., translucent materials like jade), the reflectance can also depend on light incident on *other* points of the material surface. So when we use a single reflectance spectrum to model material colors, what we have implicitly assumed is that the reflectance spectrum has been calculated in such a way that when you multiply it with the incident illumination, you get the scattered light power that is actually observed.

The reflectance is a "quick-and-dirty" abstraction that we often use to give a rough estimation/explanation of a material's color, but it is so high-level that it hides lots of the low-level details: what exactly are the light-matter interactions that cause the surface and subsurface scattering behaviors that eventually give rise to the apparent reflectance and transmittance spectra? The remaining chapters in this part essentially answer this question.

5.3   A Little Bit of Radiometry and Photometry

To be more formal about surface and volume scattering, we need to scientifically define a few physical properties pertaining to light propagation spatially and angularly. This is called **radiometry**, which operates completely at the geometric optics level, so we will be describing light as a collection of photons, each of which can travel along a particular direction with certain energy associated with it. [Reinhard et al. (2008), Chap. 6] and [Bohren and Clothiaux (2006), Chap. 4] have more rigorous treatments of radiometry, and we will here just introduce the language and a few important radiometric quantities that are relevant to our discussion.

5.3.1   Energy and Power

Each photon carries a certain amount of energy that is determined by its wavelength governed by:

$$Q = \frac{hc}{\lambda},\tag{5.1}$$

where c is the speed of light, λ is the photon wavelength, and h is the Planck's constant.

---

[2] Which results from a combination of water selectively absorbing medium-to-long wavelengths of light and increasing scattering of short wavelengths in the Rayleigh regime (Sect. 7.3.3).

Power, or more formally in radiometry, **radiant flux** is the total amount of energy passing through some surface in space per unit time. Or, taking a calculus perspective, power Φ is defined as:

$$\Phi = \lim_{\Delta t \to 0} \frac{\Delta Q}{\Delta t} = \frac{dQ}{dt}. \tag{5.2}$$

The way to think about this is that each photon carries a certain amount of energy so if you monitor photons passing across a surface over a period of time Δt, you can calculate the average power of that period by dividing the total energy passed by Δt. As Δt approaches 0, we get the instantaneous power.

Of course, energy/power is a function of wavelength, so more rigorously we should be talking about *spectral* power $\Phi(\lambda)$, which has a unit of W/nm:

$$\Phi(\lambda) = \lim_{\Delta \lambda \to 0} \frac{\Delta \Phi}{\Delta \lambda} = \frac{d\Phi}{d\lambda}, \tag{5.3}$$

where $\Delta \Phi$ is the total power within a wavelength interval $\Delta \lambda$.

5.3.2   Irradiance

Our power calculation is done with respect to a surface area, but how about the power at each point on the surface area? You can imagine that some points get more photons and others get fewer, so it is useful to characterize the power at any given point. Technically, the answer to the question "how many photons hit a particular point" is *zero*, since the area of a single point is 0.[3] The meaningful question is: what is the power *density* of a particular point p? **Irradiance** is such a quantity.

Imagine again that you are monitoring photons crossing a surface for a period Δt; you can calculate the average power received per unit area by dividing the average power by the surface area, and when you shrink the surface area to an infinitesimal point p, we can calculate the power density, i.e., the irradiance, of p by:

$$E(p) = \lim_{\Delta A \to 0} \frac{\Delta \Phi(p)}{\Delta A} = \frac{d\Phi(p)}{dA}. \tag{5.4}$$

Irradiance is a more primitive measure than power, because we can derive the power of a surface by integrating the irradiance over the surface area:

$$\Phi = \int^A E(p) dA. \tag{5.5}$$

---

[3] A similar question is: imagine you are throwing darts at a wall; what is the probability of hitting a particular point p? The answer is 0. The meaningful question to ask is: what is the probability density of hitting p?.

Irradiance has a unit of $W\,m^{-2}$, and *spectral* irradiance has a unit of $W\,m^{-2}nm^{-1}$.

5.3.3 Solid Angle

Irradiance is concerned with the power of all the photons incident on a point, but photons hit a point from all directions, so how do we quantify the amount of light coming from a direction?

A direction is a vector, which is invariant to translational transformations, so the two parallel "arrows" r_1 and r_2 in Fig. 5.2 (left) represent the same vector/direction. Therefore, conceptually it is easier if we translate all the arrows so that they start from the same origin when we want to reason about a collection of directions.

How do we count the number of directions? In 2D, we use a *planar angle* to measure the amount of directions. Given an origin O and a vector, we rotate it to generate an arc. The angle subtended by the arc and O is a measure of the amount of directions we have just covered. The angle can also be mathematically given by the ratio s/r, where s is the arc length and r is the radius of the circle. This matches our intuition that if we increase the radius of the circle, we would get a longer arc but the same angle. A full circle has a planar angle of 2π.

We can similarly define the size of a set of directions in 3D. We draw a sphere around O, and imagine that we have some area on the spherical surface. Connecting O to every point on that area represents a direction in 3D. So the spherical surface area is a measure of the amount of 3D directions. Like in the 2D case, we want the measure to be invariant to the spherical radius, so we define **solid angle**, a measure of the size of a set of 3D directions, as:

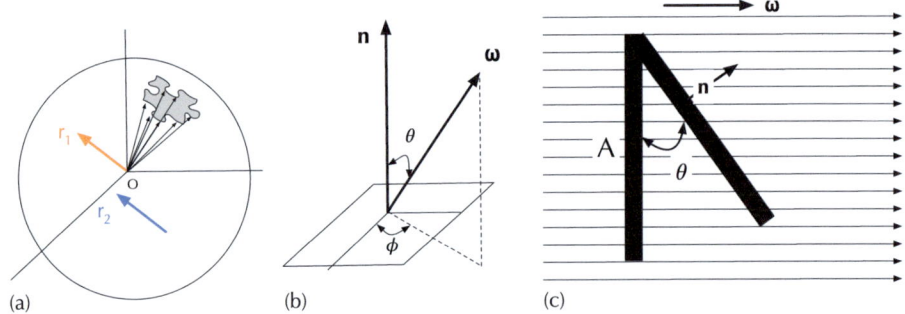

(a)   (b)   (c)

Fig. 5.2 a: A solid angle is a measure of the size of a collection of directions in 3D. A direction is a vector, which is translationally invariant, so r_1 and r_2 refer to the same direction. **b**: In spherical coordinate systems, a 3D direction can be parameterized by two angles, a polar angle θ and an azimuthal angle ϕ. **c**: Radiance is an intrinsic property of the radiation field, but we can measure it differently

$$\Omega = \frac{A}{r^2}, \tag{5.6}$$

where A is an area on a spherical surface and r is the radius. The unit of a solid angle is the **steradian** (sr), and the entire sphere subtends a solid angle of 4π.

Sometimes we want to know the size of the set of directions from a point O to an arbitrary surface. We would project that surface to a sphere and get a projected spherical area A, using which we can invoke Eq. 5.6 to estimate the solid angle subtended by the surface. One useful trick that might help sometimes is to project the surface to the unit sphere (i.e., $r = 1$), and the solid angle is mathematically equivalent to the projected area on the unit sphere. But the most useful intuition I use whenever I am confused about what a particular solid angle means is to always think of the set of directions/vectors that are represented by that solid angle.

5.3.4 Radiance

We can now ask, what is the amount of flux received by a point from a particular direction? Photons travel in all sorts of directions. Let's consider an imaginary detector with an area A that is able to receive light from only one direction ω, as illustrated in Fig. 5.2 (right). We can measure the total flux received by the detector Φ, from which we know that the power per unit area along the direction ω is simply $\frac{\Phi}{A}$.

Now imagine that we place the detector so that its normal subtends an angle θ with respect to the light direction ω. Figure 5.2b explicitly illustrates this angle, where the tilted detector lies in the xy-plane, and the z direction is the normal n. In a spherical coordinate system, a direction ω can be parameterized by two angles: a polar angle θ and an azimuthal angle ϕ.

The total flux received by the detector has changed to $\Phi \cos\theta$, because the area that is available to receive photons is now $A\cos\theta$. We call this the "effective area". As a result, the power per area at the direction ω remains the same, i.e., $\frac{\Phi}{A}$. This is not surprising, because we are not changing the radiation field, only how we measure it. When the effective area reaches 0 (i.e., the detector is completely parallel to the light direction), the detector collects no photons, but it certainly does not mean that there is no light in the field.

If we now want to measure light power coming from another direction, we would change the detector so that it receives light from only that direction. In reality, this is, of course, not possible. No detector can screen lights only from one direction. If we place a detector in a radiation field, it is going to receive photons from all sorts of directions. We can limit the directions of photons that the detector collects by placing a baffle that allows only certain directions to hit the detector.

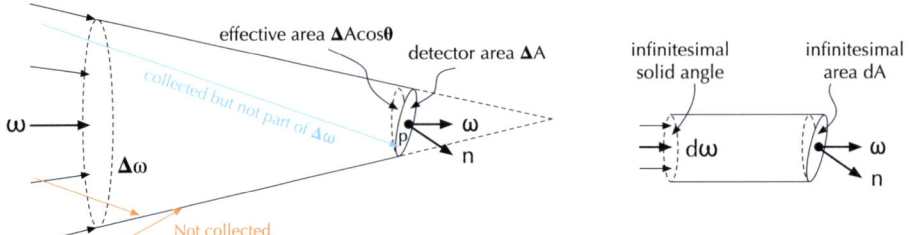

Fig. 5.3 Left: the baffle limits the directions through which incident photons can be collected by the detector. As we reduce the solid angle of the baffle $\Delta\omega$ and the detector ΔA, the average power per unit "effective area" per unit solid angle approaches $L(p, \omega)$, the radiance at position p along direction ω. Right: intuitively we can think of a point (an infinitesimal area) receiving lights from a single direction (an infinitesimal solid angle) as just a tiny area intercepting a tiny cylinder

This setup is illustrated in Fig. 5.3 (left). The total flux collected by the detector is $\Delta\Phi$, the detector size is ΔA, and the solid angle subtended by the baffle is $\Delta\omega$. The average power collected per unit "effective area" per unit direction by the detector is then:

$$\frac{\Delta\Phi}{\Delta A \cos\theta \, \Delta\omega}. \tag{5.7}$$

The baffle does a good job of rejecting many directions that are outside $\Delta\omega$, but unless it is infinitely long, the detector will still collect some photons traveling through directions outside $\Delta\omega$. But as we reduce the detector size and the baffle size, the baffle becomes a very thin cylinder over a very small detector, which collects light from a very small area along a very small solid angle, visualized in Fig. 5.3 (right).[4] In calculus terms, when we let the detector size and baffle's solid angle approach 0, we obtain the quantity called **radiance**:

$$L(p, \omega) = \lim_{\Delta\omega \to 0} \lim_{\Delta A \to 0} \frac{\Delta\Phi}{\Delta A \cos\theta \, \Delta\omega} \tag{5.8a}$$

$$= \frac{d}{d\omega} \frac{d\Phi(p)}{dA \cos\theta} = \frac{d^2\Phi(p)}{d\omega dA \cos\theta} \tag{5.8b}$$

$$= \frac{dE(p)}{d\omega \cos\theta} \tag{5.8c}$$

$$= \frac{dE_\perp(p)}{d\omega} \tag{5.8d}$$

Equation 5.8b is the definition of radiance, and it can be rewritten to Eq. 5.8c given the definition of irradiance (see Eq. 5.4). Radiance is an intrinsic property of the radiation field, and the reason we have the $\cos\theta$ term in the definition is merely due to the way we have

---

[4] It is just a visualization convention, but visualizing $d\omega$ as a cylinder rather than a cone makes it easier to imagine what $dA \cos\theta$ is like.

chosen to measure the property (using a detector that is θ-oriented). Radiance has a unit of $W \, m^2 \, sr^{-1}$, and *spectral* radiance has a unit of $W \, m^2 \, sr^{-1} nm^{-1}$.

Radiance is a density function: the density of power at a point along a direction. As with any density function, it is useful when it gets integrated to compute some other quantities. For instance, given the radiance $L(p, \omega)$, the irradiance at p is given by:

$$E(p, \Omega) = \int^{\Omega} L(p, \omega) \cos \theta d\omega. \tag{5.9}$$

Here we write the irradiance as $E(p, \Omega)$ to explicitly mean that the irradiance depends not only on the specific position p and the solid angle Ω over which the lights are coming.

Looking at the effective area in Fig. 5.3, if the irradiance at the infinitesimal area p is $dE(p)$, the irradiance at the (infinitesimal) effective area, which is projected from dA along ω, is $\frac{dE(p)}{\cos \theta}$. Combining this with Eq. 5.8c, we can interpret the radiance $L(p, \omega)$ differently: it is the ratio between $dE_{\perp}(p)$, the infinitesimal irradiance defined at the surface perpendicular to the light direction, and the infinitesimal solid angle. This is shown in Eq. 5.8d.

Using this interpretation of radiance, we can also give a more operational interpretation of Eq. 5.9: we first calculate the infinitesimal irradiance $dE_{\perp}(p) = L(p, \omega)d\omega$ made by lights at the direction ω, then "transfer" that to the infinitesimal irradiance at the detector surface through the $\cos \theta$ factor, and then repeat this for all the directions and accumulate the contributions.

5.3.5   Lambertian Emitter, Radiant Intensity, and Lambert's Cosine Law

A **Lambertian emitter** or an ideal *diffuse emitter* is a flux-emitting point whose emitted radiance is constant regardless of the outgoing direction. A related concept is a **Lambertian scatterer** or an ideal *diffuse surface*, which is a surface point where the scattered radiance is independent of the scattering direction.

It might come as a surprise that the flux emitted by a Lambertian emitter through a fixed solid angle is different for different emission directions. Consider a setup where a Lambertian emitter has an infinitesimal area dA. The power emitted by dA toward its normal direction in an infinitesimal solid angle of $d\omega$ is $d\Phi_0 = L dA$, where L is the radiance. The power emitted toward an oblique direction ω through the same solid angle is $d\Phi_{\theta} = L d\omega \cos \theta dA$.

In radiometry, the ratio of infinitesimal power and infinitesimal solid angle is called the **radiant intensity**,[5] denoted I:

$$I(\omega) = \frac{d\Phi}{d\omega}. \tag{5.10}$$

---

[5] Or simply, the "intensity", which is an extremely overloaded term, so we will be verbose and use "radiant intensity.".

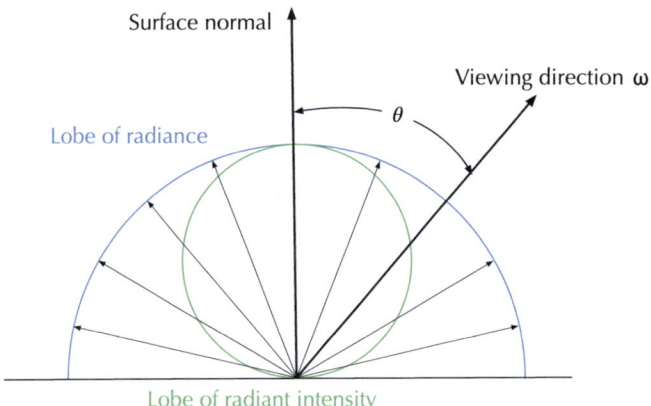

Fig. 5.4 Comparison between the radiance distribution (constant w.r.t. viewing direction ω) and radiant intensity distribution (weakens by a factor of $\cos\theta$) of a Lambertian emitter/scatterer

I is a meaningful measure only for a point source (e.g., our infinitesimal Lambertian emitter here). We can see that for a Lambertian emitter, the radiant intensity decays by a factor of $\cos\theta$: $\frac{d\Phi_\theta}{d\omega} = \frac{d\Phi_0}{d\omega}\cos\theta$. This is usually called the **Lambert's cosine law**, named after Johann Heinrich Lambert, from his Photometria (Lambert 1760). Similarly, if we have a Lambertian scatterer, its scattered radiant intensity will also decay by $\cos\theta$ as the polar angle θ of the viewing direction ω increases.

Figure 5.4 compares the radiance distribution and radiant intensity distribution of a Lambertian emitter/scatterer. Both distributions are over the entire hemisphere, but we show only a cross section. The distributions are visualized as two lobes, and the distance of a point on the lobe to the origin is proportional to the value at that point. The radiance distribution is constant regardless of ω but the radiant intensity is proportional to $\cos\theta$. This difference stems from the fact that intensity is defined with respect to the power at the detector/emission area (dA) while radiance is defined with respect to power at the effective area (d$A\cos\theta$).

5.3.6   The Measurement Equation in Camera Imaging

We will study this more carefully in the imaging lecture, but given that we have the basic understanding of radiometry, it is probably a good time to show you how radiometry is of fundamental importance to camera imaging. For simplicity, let's just consider one single pixel.

Each pixel is very small, but it has a finite area, say A_p. Each pixel is constantly being bombarded by lights that enter the aperture, which has a size V. The raw pixel value is roughly proportional to the energy it receives during the exposure time.[6] So using the basic radiometry, we can write the total energy received by a pixel during the exposure time T as:

$$Q = \int^T \int^{A_p} \int^{\Omega(p,V)} L(p, \omega) \cos \theta \; d\omega \; dp \; dt, \tag{5.11}$$

where $\Omega(p, V)$ explicitly expresses that a solid angle is determined by the aperture V and a point p on the pixel surface. Of course this quantity changes with p. We sometimes omit p and V when it is clear what Ω refers to, but here, since the solid angle changes with the dummy variable p in the integral equation, we express it explicitly. This equation is sometimes called the **measurement equation** of an image sensor in computer graphics (see (Kolb et al. 1995; Reinhard et al. 2008, Sect. 6.8.1) and (Pharr et al. 2023, Sect. 5.4)). Usually the inner integral over the solid angle is expressed as a spatial integral over the aperture; the derivation is available in standard texts and is omitted here.

We can see, again, that radiance is the most fundamental quantity. Knowing the radiance distribution in the camera, we can, in theory, synthesize the value of any pixel and, thus, an entire image. How do we know the radiance distribution inside a camera? We can calculate it if we know (1) the distribution of the radiance impinging on the camera optics and (2) the material properties of the camera optics (e.g., lenses, filters, etc.). The effects of the camera optics are nothing more than surface scattering and volume scattering, so using the principles we will introduce in this Part of the book, we can convert the radiance distribution outside the camera (in the scene) to that inside the camera.

5.3.7   Light Field

There is a name for the distribution of the radiance in the space—it is called the **light field**, which refers to the complete set of all the possible radiances flowing through every possible direction. Knowing the light field of a scene, we can in theory synthesize any image captured by any camera—limited only by the limitations of geometric optics. This is fundamentally because, given the light field information, we can estimate the irradiance, power, and energy of anything at any time at will.

The field of **light-field imaging** is concerned with capturing the light field of a scene. **Light-field display** is a 3D display technology that attempts to reproduce the light field of a scene, which is usually captured beforehand by some sort of light-field imaging technique. Reproducing the light field provides the depth information of a scene that is missing in conventional 2D displays, and is one of the technologies for an immersive experience (other technologies include varifocal displays, multi-focal displays, and holographic displays).

Light-field rendering is concerned with rendering a new image/photo at a novel perspective given a set of photons taken at other perspectives. It is a form of **image-based**

---

[6] Assuming there is no noise and there is no quantization error in converting analog signals to digital signals.

rendering. The idea is that each image capture is a sample of the light field followed by a low-pass filter (i.e., the integration in Eq. 5.11). Rendering an image at a new perspective is a classic signal sampling and reconstruction problem, where the new image is nothing more than another sample of the light field. In this sense, many familiar tasks such as interpolating between video frames, panoramic photography, and (stereoscopic) 360° video rendering are all light-field rendering in disguise.

As with any signal resampling task, the ideal solution to light-field rendering is to first estimate the underlying light field from a set of samples and then re-sample the light field given the new perspective. Signal filtering is necessary for both signal reconstruction and anti-aliasing, and the name of the game is to design good filters that are practically useful and computationally tractable. Of course, modern-day image-based rendering, known under the name (neural) radiance-field rendering (Mildenhall et al. 2021; Kerbl et al. 2023), treats the whole problem as a learning problem and learns to reconstruct from massive amounts of data.

5.3.8 Photometric Quantities

Spectral radiant flux (power), irradiance, radiant intensity, and radiance are all radiometric quantities. They all have a **photometric** counterpart, which weighs the radiometric quantity by the luminous efficiency function (LEF). The LEF, as we have discussed in Sect. 3.4.2, at a particular wavelength is inversely proportional to the radiometric quantity at each wavelength needed to produce the same level of perceptual brightness.

For instance, given a spectral radiant flux $\Phi(\lambda)$, the corresponding photometric counterpart is then:

$$\Phi_v(\lambda) = K\Phi(\lambda)V(\lambda), \tag{5.12}$$

where $\Phi_v(\lambda)$ is the spectral **luminous flux**, $V(\lambda)$ is the LEF, and K is a constant that, for historical reasons, takes the value of 683.002. The total luminous flux is then:

$$\Phi_v = \int_\lambda K\Phi(\lambda)V(\lambda)\mathrm{d}\lambda. \tag{5.13}$$

Luminous flux has a unit of **lumen** (lm), so K has a unit of lm/W. We can also weigh the radiant power by the scotopic LEF, in which case K = 1700 (lm/W).

Other radiometric quantities can be similarly converted to the photometric counterparts. Specifically,

- the photometric counterpart of irradiance is **illumination**, which has a unit of lx = $\mathrm{lm/m^2}$, which is also called the **lux**;
- the photometric counterpart of radiance intensity is **luminous intensity**, which has a unit of cd = lm/sr, which is called the **candela**;

- the photometric counterpart of radiance is **luminance**, which has a unit of $lm/(m^2sr) = cd/(m^2)$, which is also called the **nit**.

Sometimes radiometric vs. photometric quantities are also called the radiant versus luminous quantities. The way to interpret the photometric quantities is that they take into account the spectral sensitivity of a particular photodetector, which in our case is the photoreceptors on the retina. But if we use other detectors, such as an image sensor, we will have a different spectral sensitivity, and the corresponding photometric measurements will be different. We will study the spectral sensitivity of image sensors in later chapters.

References

Bohren CF, Clothiaux EE (2006) Fundamentals of atmospheric radiation: an introduction with 400 problems. Wiley

Dorsey J, Rushmeier H, Sillion F (2010) Digital modeling of material appearance. Elsevier

Feynman R (1985) QED: the strange theory of light and matter by Richard Feynman. Princeton University Press

Johnsen S (2012) The optics of life: a biologist's guide to light in nature. Princeton University Press

Johnston-Feller R (2001) Color science in the examination of museum objects: nondestructive procedures. Getty Publications

Kerbl B, Kopanas G, Leimkühler T, Drettakis G (2023) 3d gaussian splatting for real-time radiance field rendering. ACM Trans Graph 42(4):139-1

Kolb C, Mitchell D, Hanrahan P (1995) A realistic camera model for computer graphics. In: Proceedings of the 22nd annual conference on Computer graphics and interactive techniques, pp 317–324

Lambert JH (1760) Photometria sive de mensura et gradibus luminis, colorum et umbrae. Sumptibus viduae Eberhardi Klett, typis Christophori Petri Detleffsen

Mildenhall B, Srinivasan PP, Tancik M, Barron JT, Ramamoorthi R, Ng R (2021) NeRF: representing scenes as neural radiance fields for view synthesis. Commun ACM 65(1):99–106

Pharr M, Jakob W, Humphreys G (2023) Physically based rendering: from theory to implementation, 4th edn. MIT Press

Reinhard E, Khan EA, Akyuz AO, Johnson G (2008) Color imaging: fundamentals and applications. CRC Press

Vermeer J (1668) The astronomer; released into the public domain. https://en.wikipedia.org/wiki/File:Johannes_Vermeer_-_The_Astronomer_-_1668.jpg

Surface Scattering

6.1   BRDF

Generally, the energy distribution of the surface scattering is captured by the Bidirectional Reflectance Distribution Function (**BRDF**) (Nicodemus et al. 1977). Informally, it tells us how the incident energy from a particular direction is distributed to different exiting directions. The BRDF is parameterized by three parameters: a surface point p, the direction of light incident on p, denoted ω_i, and the direction of light leaving p, denoted ω_s. So the BRDF is usually written as $f_r(p, \omega_s, \omega_i)$.

The way to understand BRDF $f_r(p, \omega_s, \omega_i)$ is to consider the following. $L(p, \omega_s)$, i.e., the radiance leaving p toward ω_s, is dependent on the light incident on p. When the incident light on p comes from only the direction ω_i, the irradiance at p is zero, since the solid angle of a single direction ω_i is zero, so naturally $L(p, \omega_s)$ is 0 (assuming there is no other light hitting p). When p receives light from a non-zero solid angle of directions $\Delta\omega_i$ (centered around ω_i), the irradiance of p is increased by $\Delta E(p, \omega_i)$. At the same time, due to this increase in incident light, $L(p, \omega_s)$ is no longer zero; the increase in the radiance leaving p over ω_s is denoted $\Delta L(p, \omega_s)$.

As we increase $\Delta\omega_i$, both $\Delta E(p, \omega_i)$ and $\Delta L(p, \omega_s)$ increase. BRDF is defined as the ratio of the two *increments* when $\Delta\omega_i$ approaches 0 (when the radiance along all directions in $\Delta\omega_i$ can be thought of as a constant):

$$f_r(p, \omega_s, \omega_i) = \lim_{\Delta\omega_i \to 0} \frac{\Delta L(p, \omega_s)}{\Delta E(p, \omega_i)} = \frac{dL(p, \omega_s)}{dE(p, \omega_i)} = \frac{dL(p, \omega_s)}{L(p, \omega_i)\cos\theta_i\,d\omega_i}. \tag{6.1}$$

A Useful Approximation

Now assume that we illuminate p through a finite, but small, solid angle Ω_i. Turning the differential equation into an integral equation:

Y. Zhu, *Visual Computing For Architects*, Synthesis Lectures on Computer Architecture, https://doi.org/10.1007/978-3-032-05018-2_6

$$L(p, \omega_s) = \int^{\Omega_i} f_r(p, \omega_s, \omega_i) dE(p, \omega_i) \tag{6.2a}$$

$$= \int^{\Omega_i} f_r(p, \omega_s, \omega_i) L(p, \omega_i) \cos \theta_i d\omega_i \tag{6.2b}$$

$$\approx f_r(p, \omega_s, \omega_i) \int^{\Omega_i} L(p, \omega_i) \cos \theta_i d\omega_i \tag{6.2c}$$

$$= f_r(p, \omega_s, \omega_i) E(p, \Omega_i), \tag{6.2d}$$

$$f_r(p, \omega_s, \omega_i) \approx \frac{L(p, \omega_s)}{E(p, \Omega_i)}. \tag{6.2e}$$

The derivation proceeds as follows:

- The simplification from Eqs. 6.2b to 6.2c assumes that the BRDF is a constant over all the directions in Ω_i.
- The integration in Eq. 6.2c has no analytical solution, since we do not know the analytical form of $L(p, \omega_i)$, but we know the integration is just another way of expressing the total irradiance incident upon p over Ω_i, which is denoted as $E(p, \Omega_i)$. This gets us to Eq. 6.2d.
- To be more rigorous, the integration in Eq. 6.2c evaluates to $E(p, \Omega_i) + C$, where C is a constant. Given the boundary condition that $L(p, \omega_s) = 0$ when $E(p, \Omega_i) = 0$, we know $C = 0$, so C is omitted.

Ultimately, we can see from Eq. 6.2e that the BRDF $f_r(p, \omega_s, \omega_i)$ can also be calculated as the ratio between the *absolute* radiance $L(p, \omega_i)$ and the absolute irradiance $E(p, \Omega_i)$ illuminated from a very small, but finite solid angle Ω_i. Another way to interpret this is that the so-calculated BRDF is the average BRDF over Ω_i.

Isotropic Material

A 3D direction ω expressed in the Cartesian coordinate system can also be expressed by two 2D planar angles in the spherical coordinate system: the polar angle θ and the azimuthal angle ϕ. So BRDF can also be parameterized as $f_r(p, \theta_s, \phi_s, \theta_i, \phi_i)$. A material is **isotropic** if its BRDF satisfies $f_r(p, \theta_s, \phi_s, \theta_i, \phi_i) = f_r(p, \theta_s, \phi_s + x, \theta_i, \phi_i + x)$ for any x. An intuitive way to think of an isotropic material is this: if you pick a point p and rotate the material about the normal vector at p, the color of p does not change. This is because rotation about the normal vector keeps θ_i and θ_s unchanged and varies ϕ_i and ϕ_s by the same amount.

The nice thing about an isotropic BRDF is it can be parameterized with one fewer degree of freedom: $f_r(p, \theta_s, \phi_s - \phi_i, \theta_i)$. This is because it is $(\phi_i - \phi_s)$ rather than the specific values of ϕ_s or ϕ_i that matter.

6.2 Reflectance and Albedo

The BRDF does not have to be a value between 0 and 1. Let's say that there is 100 J of energy incident on a point coming from a solid angle $\Delta\omega_i$. That amount of energy is distributed across all the outgoing directions in the hemisphere, which forms a solid angle of $4\pi/2 = 2\pi$. So on average the energy exiting per direction is $\frac{100}{2\pi} J$, which clearly is greater than 1. This is not surprising, since BRDF is ultimately a *density* measure, a *distribution*, which is most meaningful when it is integrated to calculate some quantity. Integrating the BRDF gives a percentage/fraction measure between 0 and 1, i.e., reflectance, which we will discuss next.

For the energy to be conserved, the total outgoing energy at any point must not exceed that of the incident energy received by that point. Assume that a point p receives an irradiance dE_i from a direction ω_i over an infinitesimal solid angle $d\omega_i$, and the outgoing radiance along the direction ω_s due to that irradiance is $f_r(p, \omega_s, \omega_i)dE_i$. Then the outgoing irradiance leaving p over an infinitesimal solid angle $d\omega_s$ around ω_s would be $f_r(p, \omega_s, \omega_i)dE_i \cos\theta_s d\omega_s$. If we integrate all the outgoing directions, we get the total outgoing irradiance dE_o, which must not exceed the incident irradiance dE_i:

$$dE_o = \int^{\Omega} dE_i f_r(p, \omega_s, \omega_i) \cos\theta_s d\omega_s \tag{6.3a}$$

$$\Rightarrow \int^{\Omega} f_r(p, \omega_s, \omega_i) \cos\theta_s d\omega_s = \frac{dE_o}{dE_i} = \rho_{dh}(p, \omega_i) \leq 1. \tag{6.3b}$$

dE_i is independent of ω_s, so it can be hoisted out of the integration, which gets us Eq. 6.3b, which holds for any arbitrary incident direction ω_i. ρ_{dh} is defined as the ratio between dE_o and dE_i. When Ω is the hemisphere, ρ_{dh} is called the **directional-hemispherical reflectance** in the computer vision and graphics literature, and is interpreted as the percentage of energy scattered by a point over the entire hemisphere given the incident light from a particular direction. Clearly, ρ_{dh} is a function of both p and ω_i and takes a value between 0 and 1.

Since we are dealing with geometric optics, the Helmholtz reciprocity holds:

$$f_r(p, \omega_s, \omega_i) = f_r(p, \omega_i, \omega_s), \tag{6.4}$$

which means the energy conservation can also be expressed as:

$$\int^{\Omega} f_r(p, \omega_s, \omega_i) \cos\theta_i d\omega_i = \rho_{hd}(p, \omega_s) \leq 1, \tag{6.5}$$

where ρ_{hd} is called the **hemispherical-directional reflectance** when Ω is the hemisphere. ρ_{hd}, a function of p and ω_s, is interpreted as the percentage of energy reflected toward a particular direction ω_s given the incident energy over the entire hemisphere.

Equation 6.5 can be derived by first rewriting Eq. 6.3b as $\int^{\Omega} f_r(p, \omega_i, \omega_s) \cos \theta_s d\omega_s \leq 1$ (using the reciprocity) followed by switching ω_s and ω_i (simply a change of notation). This derivation suggests that $\rho_{hd}(p, \omega_i) = \rho_{dh}(p, \omega_s)$, a natural consequence of the reciprocity.[1]

We can also describe the relationship between all the outgoing irradiance E_o of a point over a solid angle Ω_s due to all the incident irradiance E_i over a solid angle Ω_i:

$$E_o = \int^{\Omega_s} \left(\int^{\Omega_i} f_r(p, \omega_s, \omega_i) L(p, \omega_i) \cos \theta_i d\omega_i \right) \cos \theta_s d\omega_s \leq E_i = \int^{\Omega_i} L(p, \omega_i) \cos \theta_i d\omega_i.$$

$$(6.6a)$$

$$\rho_{hh}(p) = \frac{E_o}{E_i} \leq 1.$$

$$(6.6b)$$

Equation 6.6b defines ρ_{hh}, which is called the **hemispherical-hemispherical reflectance** when both Ω_1 and Ω_2 are hemispheres. ρ_{hh} has another name: **albedo**. When $f_r(p, \omega_s, \omega_i)$ is independent of (invariant to) ω_i and ω_s, i.e., when p is an ideal **Lambertian** surface (see Sect. 6.4), Eq. 6.6a can be re-written as:

$$E_o = E_i \rho_{hh}(p) = \int^{\Omega_s} f_r(p, \omega_s, \omega_i) \left(\int^{\Omega_i} L(p, \omega_i) \cos \theta_i d\omega_i \right) \cos \theta_s d\omega_s \qquad (6.7a)$$

$$= \int^{\Omega_s} f_r(p, \omega_s, \omega_i) E_i \cos \theta_s d\omega_s \qquad (6.7b)$$

$$= E_i \int^{\Omega_s} f_r(p, \omega_s, \omega_i) \cos \theta_s d\omega_s \qquad (6.7c)$$

$$= E_i \rho_{dh}(p, \omega_i), \qquad (6.7d)$$

where Eq. 6.7b is derived using the definition of E_i in Eqs. 6.6a and 6.7c is derived since E_i is independent of ω_s, and Eq. 6.7d is derived by using the definition of ρ_{dh} in Eq. 6.3b.

We can see that for a Lambertian surface the albedo (ρ_{hh}) is equivalent to ρ_{dh} and ρ_{hd}, but this relationship is not true in general. We can also show that for a Lambertian surface, the BRDF is the constant $\frac{\rho_{hh}}{\pi}$. Starting from Eq. 6.7c:

$$E_i \rho_{hh} = E_i \int^{\Omega_s} f_r(p, \omega_s, \omega_i) \cos \theta_s d\omega_s = E_i f_r(p, \omega_s, \omega_i) \int^{\Omega_s} \cos \theta_s d\omega_s = E_i f_r(p, \omega_s, \omega_i) \pi$$

$$(6.8a)$$

$$\Rightarrow f_r(p, \omega_s, \omega_i) = \frac{\rho_{hh}}{\pi} \qquad (6.8b)$$

The derivation uses the integral results that:

---

[1] For instance, if $\rho_{hd}(p, \omega_i) = \frac{1}{1+\omega_i^2}$, then $\rho_{dh}(p, \omega_s)$ must take the form $\rho_{dh}(p, \omega_s) = \frac{1}{1+\omega_s^2}$.

$$d\omega = \sin\theta d\theta d\phi, \tag{6.9a}$$

$$\int^{\Omega=2\pi} \cos\theta d\omega = \int_0^{2\pi}\int_0^{\pi/2} \cos\theta \sin\theta d\theta d\phi$$

$$= 2\pi \int_0^{\pi/2} \cos\theta \sin\theta d\theta$$

$$= \pi, \tag{6.9b}$$

when Ω is the hemisphere.

You might be thinking that, mathematically, for Eq. 6.7a to hold, f_r just needs to be independent of ω_i, but not ω_s, so do we really need to assume a Lambertian surface here? It turns out that if f_r is independent of ω_i, it must also be independent of ω_s (can you prove this?[2]) and, thus, must be a constant (i.e., $\frac{\rho_{hh}}{\pi}$ in Eq. 6.8b) for a given p.

Finally, one can also define the **directional-directional reflectance**, which is naturally a function of both the incident direction and outgoing direction and can be defined as the ratio between the incident irradiance and the outgoing irradiance when both the incident and outgoing solid angles approach 0.

To compare the BRDF and directional-directional reflectance, both are sensitive to both the incident and outgoing directions. But the former is a density measure, whereas the latter is a fraction/percentage measure. Integrating BRDF over a finite set of directions gives us some measure reflectance. This is why the BRDF is defined as the radiance/ irradiance ratio rather than radiance/radiance or irradiance/irradiance ratio; it is to reflect the fact that the energy of a small cone of incident directions is distributed over all the directions over the hemisphere, and what we care to characterize is the *distribution* of the incident energy over all outgoing directions.

6.3   The Rendering Equation

Given the BRDF, we can estimate the outgoing radiance of a point given its illumination using the well-known **Rendering Equation**.

The setup is that we have a surface on which there is a point p that is receiving light from a solid angle Ω. We are interested in calculating the exiting radiance leaving p toward an arbitrary direction ω_s. The rendering equation formulates this calculation by:

$$L(p, \omega_s) = \int^{\Omega} f_r(p, \omega_s, \omega_i)L(p, \omega_i)\cos\theta_i d\omega_i, \tag{6.10}$$

---

[2] One informal way to do so is the following. Since $f_r(p, \omega_s, \omega_i)$ is independent of ω_i, let's rewrite it as $g(p, \omega_s)$. Now we invoke the reciprocity and rewrite $f_r(p, \omega_s, \omega_i)$ as $g(p, \omega_i)$. The only way for $g(p, \omega_s) = g(p, \omega_i)$ is for g to be dependent only on p.

where $L(p, \omega_s)$ is the outgoing radiance from p toward the direction ω_s; Ω is usually a hemisphere in surface scattering, since lights hitting a surface point can come from anywhere in the hemisphere, in which case Eq. 6.10 is also called the *reflection equation*, indicating the fact that the equation governs surface reflection/scattering.

The rendering equation is exactly the same equation in Eq. 6.2b, so there is nothing more profound about the rendering equation than the definition of the BRDF: we are simply following the BRDF's definition and turning the differential equation into an integral one. Intuitively, the way to understand this equation is that every ray that hits p makes some contribution toward the outgoing radiance $L(p, \omega_s)$, and the integration just accumulates all the contributions. In particular:

- $L(p, \omega_i)\mathrm{d}\omega_i$ is the incident irradiance of a differential solid angle $\mathrm{d}\omega_i$; note that the irradiance calculated here is defined with respect to a surface perpendicular to the direction of ω_i.
- $L(p, \omega_i)\cos\theta\mathrm{d}\omega_i$ applies the Lambert's cosine law and calculates the irradiance at the surface where p lies.
- $f_r(p, \omega_s, \omega_i)L(p, \omega_i)\cos\theta\mathrm{d}\omega_i$ "transfers" the differential incident irradiance to the differential outgoing radiance toward ω_s through the BRDF function.
- The integration over all the incident directions calculates the total outgoing radiance given all the incident lights.

The rendering equation in theory allows us to calculate the entire light field, i.e., the radiance distribution in space, given an arbitrary p and ω_s. Why is knowing the light field important? Recall Eq. 5.11: knowing the light field allows us to synthesize any image or calculate the color of any object from any perspective.

It is, of course, much easier said than done when it comes to solving the rendering equation, which itself is worth multiple chapters in a computer graphics textbook. We will not get into it here; let's just consider the following challenges. First, the integrand in Eq. 6.10 generally has no analytical form, so we will not be able to get an analytical solution to the integral equation. A common method is Monte-Carlo integration, which samples the integrand at different points and estimates the integral from the samples.

Second, in a realistic environment, we need to solve the rendering equation *recursively*. Note how the radiance function shows up on both sides of the equation. Put it in another way, when using Monte-Carlo integration to solve Eq. 6.10 we need to sample the value of $L(p, \omega_i)$ for a specific ω_i—how? We evaluate Eq. 6.10 again, but this time treating ω_i as the ω_s, which means we invoke Monte Carlo integration again. You can see how this can quickly blow up the computation: the number of rays whose radiances we need to calculate exponentially increases as long as we need to sample more than one ray at each point. A big chunk of physically-based graphics is devoted to addressing this issue; the most commonly used strategy is called **path tracing**, for which (Pharr et al. (2023), Chap. 13) is a great reference.

Another way to think of this is that there are infinitely many paths through which light can propagate and be incident on a point. A **global illumination** method for rendering would attempt to track all these paths (e.g., through Monte Carlo methods). In contrast, a **local illumination** method is concerned with only a small subset of these paths, in which case we might be able to evaluate the rendering equation as a single-pass integration while avoiding recursion. For instance, we might consider lights only from direct light sources. We will see the counterpart of this exact situation in surface scattering/volume rendering in Sect. 7.4. For this reason, the rendering equation is sometimes called the **light transport equation** (LTE), because it in principle captures how light is transported in space.[3]

An interesting, and approximate, global illumination method that avoids path tracing is the idea of **environment map** (Ramamoorthi (2009), Chap. 3). It assumes that the light sources are so distant from the objects in the scene that all points in the scene receive the same incident radiance distribution. That is, $L(p, \omega_i)$ in Eq. 6.10 is a function of only ω_i but not p. We can then pre-compute (through path tracing for instance) or directly measure $L(\omega_i)$ offline and store them in a data structure. For instance, we can use the equirectangular projection to store a discretized form of $L(\omega_i)$, or use spherical harmonics to (approximately) store a parameterized form of $L(\omega_i)$. Either way, the data structure that stores pre-computed $L(\omega_i)$ is called an environment map, which we can load at rendering time, plug it into the rendering equation, and calculate the outgoing radiance by simply evaluating the integral.

Finally, we also need to somehow know the BRDF of the material. There are generally two methods of going about it. We can, of course, measure it, but we have no realistic way of measuring the complete BRDF for a material, because we would have to measure infinitely many points and, for each point, infinitely many incident and outgoing directions. We can only sample the BRDF using something called a *goniospectroreflectometer* or a *goniospec-trophotometer* (Judd and Wyszecki (1975), pp. 402–410), but there is still a massive amount of samples we need to take and to store. Lots of prior work goes into efficiently sampling, measuring, and deriving BRDFs (Marschner et al. (2000), Matusik (2003), Pharr et al. (2023), Sect. 9.8).

Another approach is to parameterize the BRDF so that we can evaluate the BRDF on demand rather than storing all the BRDF data, and this is what we will discuss next.

6.4   Specular Versus Glossy Versus Diffuse Materials

In everyday life, material surfaces are usually classified as being specular, glossy, or diffuse. Figure 6.1 shows examples of the three materials. We can now give a more rigorous treatment of these material types using BRDF, which will, in turn, give us some inspiration for parameterizing the BRDF.

---

[3] To be exact, the LTE sometimes has an emission term at the right-hand side to denote the spontaneous emission from a surface point.

Perfectly Specular Material

If a surface is perfectly smooth, like a mirror, it is called a **perfectly specular** material. Such materials follow the **Snell's law**, which governs the angles of reflection and refraction, and the **Fresnel equations**, which govern the energy of reflection and refraction.

In the plane of incidence (the plane uniquely determined by the incident direction and the surface normal), the reflection direction is symmetric about the surface normal as the incident direction. More precisely, if the incident direction is ω_i (parameterized by the polar angle θ_i and azimuthal angle ϕ_i) and the reflection direction is ω_s (θ_s, ϕ_s), we have:

$$\theta_s = \theta_i, \tag{6.11a}$$

$$\phi_s = \phi_i + \pi. \tag{6.11b}$$

The refraction/transmitted direction ω_t (θ_t, ϕ_t) follows:

$$n_1 \sin \theta_i = n_2 \sin \theta_t, \tag{6.12a}$$

$$\phi_t = \phi_i + \pi, \tag{6.12b}$$

where n_1 is the refractive index of the medium where light comes from and n_2 is that of the medium that reflects/refracts the lights.

The energy of the reflected and refracted light is governed by the Fresnel equations. We will spare you the details, but it suffices to say that the fractions of reflected/refracted light are dependent on the incident angle, refractive indices of the two interface media, and the polarization states of the light. If you work out the math and assume that the incident light is unpolarized, the percentage of reflected energy $F_r(\omega_i)$ for an incident direction ω_i is given by:

$$F_r(\omega_i) = \frac{r_a + r_e}{2}, \tag{6.13a}$$

$$r_a = \left(\frac{n_2 \cos \theta_i - n_1 \cos \theta_t}{n_2 \cos \theta_i + n_1 \cos \theta_t} \right)^2, \tag{6.13b}$$

$$r_e = \left(\frac{n_1 \cos \theta_i - n_2 \cos \theta_t}{n_1 \cos \theta_i + n_2 \cos \theta_t} \right)^2. \tag{6.13c}$$

We call $F_r(\omega_i)$ the **specular reflectance**, which not only varies with ω_i but also is also a spectral term; we omit the wavelength for simplicity. Assuming no loss of energy, the specular transmittance, i.e., the fraction of the transmitted energy, is given by $1 - F_r$.

Fresnel's equations are best understood in the context of the electromagnetic theory and are derived by treating light as waves in an *electric field* (the fact that we need to consider polarization states of a light is a giveaway). While F_r cannot be derived from radiometry, it is fundamentally about the energy transfer of surface scattering, which radiometry is also concerned with. So F_r can be integrated into the radiometry framework. One good example is to express the BRDF of a specular material using F_r:

$$f_r(p, \omega_s, \omega_i) = F_r(\omega_i) \frac{\delta(\theta_s - \theta_i)\delta(\phi_s - \phi_i - \pi)}{\cos \theta_i}, \tag{6.14}$$

where $\delta(x)$ is the Dirac delta function, which is 0 everywhere except when $x = 0$ and has the property $\int \delta(x)dx = 1$.

We can verify that this BRDF makes sense. First, the BRDF is non-zero only when Eq. 6.11 holds because of the double-delta term. Second, the energy conservation is followed. For instance, if we calculate the directional-hemispherical reflectance by plugging the BRDF into Eq. 6.3b and assuming Ω is a hemisphere, we get:

$$\frac{E_o}{E_i} = \rho_{dh}(p, \omega_i) = \int^{\Omega} F_r(\omega_i) \frac{\delta(\theta_s - \theta_i)\delta(\phi_s - \phi_i - \pi)}{\cos \theta_i} \cos \theta_s d\omega_s \tag{6.15a}$$

$$= F_r(\omega_i) \int^{\Omega} \frac{\delta(\theta_s - \theta_i)\delta(\phi_s - \phi_i - \pi)}{\cos \theta_i} \cos \theta_s d\omega_s \tag{6.15b}$$

$$= F_r(\omega_i). \tag{6.15c}$$

Since $F_r(\omega_i)$ is independent of ω_s, Eq. 6.15a evaluates to Eq. 6.15b. The integration in Eq. 6.15b evaluates to 1. This is because, informally, the integrand is non-zero only when Eq. 6.11 holds, at which point $\theta_s = \theta_i$, so the cosine terms cancel out. So the integration is just sort of a hugely complicated way of writing $\int \delta(x)dx$, which is 1.

We can see that the specular reflectance F_r is equivalent to ρ_{dh}, the directional-hemispherical reflectance. This makes sense, because in specular materials the scattering is directional if the incident light is directional. So the directional-hemispherical reflectance reduces to the "directional-directional" reflectance, which is essentially the specular reflectance.

The specular reflectance is also equivalent to the hemispherical-directional reflectance ρ_{hd}. We can show this either by simply invoking the reciprocity that $\rho_{hd} = \rho_{dh}$ or by plugging the BRDF into Eq. 6.5 and obtaining (assuming Ω is hemisphere):

$$\rho_{hd}(p, \omega_s) = \int^{\Omega} F_r(\omega_i) \frac{\delta(\theta_s - \theta_i)\delta(\phi_s - \phi_i - \pi)}{\cos \theta_i} \cos \theta_i d\omega_i \tag{6.16a}$$

$$= F_r(\hat{\omega}_s) = F_r(\omega_s), \tag{6.16b}$$

where $\hat{\omega}_s(\theta_s, \phi_s - \pi)$ is the mirror-reflection direction of $\omega_s(\theta_s, \phi_s)$. The integral evaluates to $F_r(\hat{\omega}_s)$ because, informally, the integrand is non-zero only when Eq. 6.11 holds, at which point $\omega_i = \hat{\omega}_s$ so $F_r(\omega_i) = F_r(\hat{\omega}_s)$; the integral is a complicated way of writing $\int F_r(\omega_i)\delta(\hat{\omega}_s - \omega_i)d\omega_i$, which evaluates to $F_r(\hat{\omega}_s)$. The result has an intuitive explanation: for a specular surface, the scattered energy along ω_s given a hemispherical illumination is the same as when the illumination comes only from $\hat{\omega}_s$. We can then show that $F_r(\hat{\omega}_s) = F_r(\omega_s)$, which is not surprising given reciprocity; you can also verify it by going through the equations in Eq. 6.13.

Interestingly, the specular reflectance F_r in general is *not* equivalent to the hemispherical-hemispherical reflectance ρ_{hh}. To see this, plug the specular BRDF into Eq. 6.6a (assuming Ω_i and Ω_s are hemispheres):

$$E_o = \int^{\Omega_s} \left(\int^{\Omega_i} f_r(p, \omega_s, \omega_i) L(p, \omega_i) \cos \theta_i d\omega_i \right) \cos \theta_s d\omega_s \qquad (6.17a)$$

$$= \int^{\Omega_s} \left(F_r(\omega_s) L(p, \omega_s) \right) \cos \theta_s d\omega_s \qquad (6.17b)$$

$$= \int^{\Omega_i} F_r(\omega_i) L(p, \omega_i) \cos \theta_i d\omega_i, \qquad (6.17c)$$

$$E_i = \int^{\Omega_i} L(p, \omega_i) \cos \theta_i d\omega_i. \qquad (6.17d)$$

We can see that only when $F_r(\omega_i)$ is a constant do we get $F_r(\omega_i) = \frac{E_o}{E_i} = \rho_{hh}$. Interestingly, when $F_r(\omega_i)$ is constant, the specular material is isotropic (can you prove it?). Since $F_r(\omega_i)$ does not have to be a constant, specular materials could be anisotropic. That is, it is theoretically possible that a material always reflects specularly, but the reflected energy depends on the incident direction.

Diffuse Material

When the surface is rough, the energy of surface reflection deviates away from the perfect mirror-like reflection and, instead, distributes across the hemisphere. When the surface becomes rough enough, the distribution of outgoing energy can become uniform across all outgoing directions over the entire hemisphere. Such a surface is called a **diffuse** or an ideal **Lambertian** surface. The perfect Lambertian surface does not exist, but many things in the real world come close, such as paper, marble, or wood.

The BRDF is a Lambertian surface is a uniform function. As we have seen in Eq. 6.8b, $f_r(p, \omega_s, \omega_i) = \frac{\rho_{hh}}{\pi}$ when ρ_{hh} is the surface albedo and is between 0 and 1. It is easy to see that diffuse materials are always isotropic.

Glossy Material

The surface scattering in most materials is in-between being perfectly specular and perfectly diffuse. These materials scatter light to a small cone of directions, usually centered around the direction of a perfect reflection. These materials are usually called **glossy** or sometimes, confusingly, "specular", too. The energy distribution of a glossy material is neither a Delta function (as in the perfectly specular case) nor a uniform function (as in the diffuse case). It is usually a function that peaks at the mirror-reflection direction and gradually decays as we move away from that direction.

| Specular | Diffuse | Glossy |

Fig. 6.1 Left: a specular material and its BRDF. Middle: a diffuse material and its BRDF. Right: a glossy material and its BRDF. From Daderot (2012), Fareham (2007), Prabhu B Doss (2007), VonHaarberg (2018a, b, c)

The bottom figures in Fig. 6.1 illustrate an example of the BRDF for each of the three surface types under a given incident direction. An actual BRDF (for a given surface point and a given incident direction) would be a 3D shape, and what we are showing here is the cross section. The shape of the locus is drawn to be proportional to the magnitude of the BRDF; the locus in graphics literature is sometimes called the *specular lobe*.

The spectral-lobe visualization gives us a hint: we can parameterize a BRDF by mathematically describing the shape of the specular lobe. In fact, the BRDFs for the Lambertian surface and for the specular materials are two such examples; see Eqs. 6.14 and 6.15. A glossy BRDF is more difficult to parameterize. Many BRDF parameterizations have been proposed; some are empirical, while others attempt to be physically plausible. The most popular and widely used is based on the microfacet model, which we will discuss next.

6.5   BRDF Parameterization with Microfacet Models

The assumption of the microfacet model is that the surface scattering behavior of a point depends on its local roughness: the rougher the surface, the more diffuse the surface scattering becomes. To model the roughness, the surface is modeled as a collection of small microfacets, each of which acts like a perfect mirror. A specular surface is one where all the microfacets have the exact same orientation. As the surface becomes rougher, the mirrors become more randomly oriented. When the mirrors are completely randomly oriented, the resulting surface scattering becomes diffuse.

To derive a microfacet model, we need to first define the orientation of each microfacet. Given a beam of incident lights from a particular direction, we can then trace, following the laws governing specular reflection, how the lights are scattered by the collection of the microfacets given their orientations. In the end, we obtain the collection of outgoing directions, from which we can derive the BRDF.

There are many variants of the microfacet model. They have one thing in common: they do not explicitly model the scattering of each ray at each microfacet but, rather, model the scattering of the microfacets *statistically* given the *distribution* of the microfacet orientations. In the end, they can either have an analytical form of the BRDF (Lambertian surface being an extreme example), have a close approximation of the analytical form, or can numerically estimate the BRDF efficiently (mostly through sampling).

Without going into the details, we will refer you to (Pharr et al. (2023), Sect. 9.6) for a mathematical treatment of the general idea and to Cook and Torrance (1982), Oren and Nayar (1995), Torrance and Sparrow (1967), Walter et al. (2007), Ward (1992) for the classical models.

Microfacets Models are Discrete Models Applied to a Continuous Domain

If the microfacet theory does not sound weird to you, it should!

In a microfacet model, we are still modeling surface scattering using discrete objects (microfacets) and events (perfect mirror-like reflection on each microfacet). Is it surprising that we can use the discrete microfacet model to reason about the behavior of a *continuous* surface? Given any point p on a surface, wouldn't p correspond to one single microfacet, and the behavior of p simply be the result of a perfect mirror reflection there? If so, how can the microfacet model describe non-specular surface scattering of glossy and diffuse materials?

An intermediate answer is that the microfacet theory is just a modeling methodology. We use a set of discrete microfacets to derive the surface-scattering statistics of that set of microfacets, but then simply assume that the so-derived statistics apply anywhere on a continuous surface of interest. Still, does this methodology reflect the physical reality?

Well, the physical world is fundamentally not continuous; when we break down the surface into finer and finer scales, we eventually get to molecules and atoms, so the surface property undergoes wild fluctuations depending on whether a small area contains molecules or not. If that is the level of detail you want to get into, you have to model things at the molecular and atomic levels (or even lower). Figure 6.2 illustrates this idea.

Fortunately for many real-world use-cases, we do not have to go there. Our eyes have a resolution limit, so we cannot resolve the details of a tiny surface area anyway; image sensors also have a resolution limit. The just-resolvable area δA, set by the spatial resolution limit of our visual system, is more than large enough that it contains many microfacets, so the aggregated behavior of those microfacets can effectively model the observed scattering

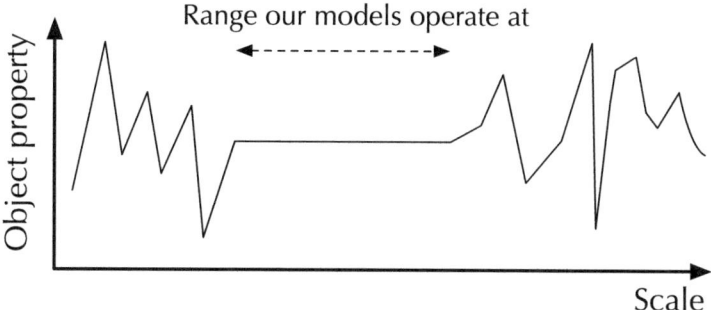

Fig. 6.2 Triphasic profile of object property. Object property at both the macroscopic scale and at the atomic/molecular scale fluctuates wildly, but at there is a scale where the property does not very much. Models based on radiometry operate at this scale. This scale is sufficiently small (smaller than the spatial resolution of human vision and typical cameras) so our calculus machinery can be applied, but still larger than individual molecules and atoms so that we do not have to worry about the wild fluctuations at that scale

of δA, which is all that matters to our vision (and to computer graphics and imaging, which is concerned only with satisfying human vision). So effectively what the microfacet theory does is to assume that the small δA (which contains a distribution of microfacets) is just within the range where the surface scattering property is stable. When the microfacet theory says something about a particular point p, it is really saying something about δA.

This way of modeling and thinking is pervasive in radiometry, which uses differential and integral equations and thus has inherently assumed that the radiation field under modeling is continuous. That is not true. Take irradiance as an example. The average irradiance of a surface changes dramatically at the microscopic level when we initially reduce the surface area, because the photon distribution over a large area is likely very non-uniform. When the surface area is sufficiently small, the number of photons hitting the surface will change proportionally with the surface area, because at that scale the photon distribution is roughly uniform. This is the scale at which irradiance is defined. But if we keep reducing the area smaller and smaller, the amount of photons hitting a tiny area will, again, undergo wild fluctuations depending on whether there are photons in the area of not—photons are discrete packets of energy. We will see another example shortly in volume scattering, where we use a small volume of discrete particles to build a model for radiative energy transfer, which we then apply to any given point in a continuous volume.

Orthogonal to the discussion above is the limitation that microfacet models do not account for the surface roughness on the scale of the light wavelength. In the regime where the length of each microfacet is comparable with the light wavelength, diffraction takes place. As a result, reflection does not follow the Snell's law and is wavelength dependent. In fact, this is how we get iridescence; in engineering, people make diffraction gratings that take advantage of the wavelength dependency to disperse lights of different wavelengths.

References

Cook RL, Torrance KE (1982) A reflectance model for computer graphics. ACM Trans Graph (ToG) 1(1):7–24

Daderot (2012) Kongens have, Copenhagen, Denmark; CC0 1.0 license. https://commons.wikimedia. org/wiki/File:Marble_ball_-_Kongens_Have_-_Copenhagen_-_DSC07898.JPG

Fareham S (2007) Heart of the city water feature Sheffield; CC BY-SA 2.0 license. https:// commons.wikimedia.org/wiki/File:Heart_of_the_City_water_feature_Sheffield_-_geograph.org. uk_-_618552.jpg

Judd DB, Wyszecki G (1975) Color in business, science, and industry, 3rd edn. Wiley

Marschner SR, Westin SH, Lafortune EP, Torrance KE (2000) Image-based bidirectional reflectance distribution function measurement. Appl Opt 39(16):2592–2600

Matusik W (2003) A data-driven reflectance model. Ph.D. thesis, Massachusetts Institute of Technology

Nicodemus F, Richmond J, Hsia J, Ginsberg I, Limperis T (1977) Geometrical considerations and nomenclature for reflectance, vol 160. US Department of Commerce, National Bureau of Standards Washington, DC, USA

Oren M, Nayar SK (1995) Generalization of the Lambertian model and implications for machine vision. Int J Comput Vis 14:227–251

Pharr M, Jakob W, Humphreys G (2023) Physically based rendering: From theory to implementation, 4th edn. MIT Press

Prabhu B Doss (2007) Tso Kiagar Lake Ladakh; CC BY 2.0 license. https://commons.wikimedia. org/wiki/File:Tso_Kiagar_Lake_Ladakh.jpg

Ramamoorthi R (2009) Precomputation-based rendering. Found Trends® Comput Graph Vis 3(4):281–369

Torrance KE, Sparrow EM (1967) Theory for off-specular reflection from roughened surfaces. JOSA 57(9):1105–1114

VonHaarberg (2018a) Illustration of a diffuse BRDF; CC0 1.0 license. https://commons.wikimedia. org/wiki/File:BRDF_diffuse.svg

VonHaarberg (2018b) Illustration of a glossy BRDF; CC0 1.0 license. https://commons.wikimedia. org/wiki/File:BRDF_glossy.svg

VonHaarberg (2018c) Illustration of a mirror BRDF; CC0 1.0 license. https://commons.wikimedia. org/wiki/File:BRDF_mirror.svg

Walter B, Marschner SR, Li H, Torrance KE (2007) Microfacet models for refraction through rough surfaces. Rendering techniques 2007:18th

Ward GJ (1992) Measuring and modeling anisotropic reflection. In: Proceedings of the 19th annual conference on computer graphics and interactive techniques, pp 265–272

Subsurface and Volume Scattering

7

7.1 An Informal Discussion to Build Intuition

Once inside the material (through surface refraction), a photon roams about until it meets a particle. The interactions between photons and particles are governed by the subsurface scattering (SSS) or volume scattering processes. As noted before, photon emission, absorption, and scattering all take place during the SSS/volume scattering processes, not just scattering, even though the names suggest otherwise. We will generally ignore emission in our discussion unless otherwise noted, but just note that emission does happen and is correlated with absorption, since emission is the result of absorbed photons having (e.g., chemical) reactions with the particles.

Also a reminder that SSS and volume scattering are governed by exactly the same principles, because they are exactly the same thing. In computer vision and graphics literature they might be used to refer to superficially different phenomena. Volume scattering is concerned with materials that can be modeled as a volume of particles, like fog, clouds, and smoke; they are given the name **participating media** in computer graphics. SSS is, instead, more commonly used to refer to solids where subsurface-scattered photons contribute to their observed colors.

Subsurface scattering is so termed to distinguish itself from surface scattering, but what is beneath the surface is nothing more than a volume of particles. In fact, what is above the surface is also a volume of particles. Looking at Fig. 7.1, the air, Material 1, and Material 2 can all be thought of as participating media. We usually model the air as a vacuum so photons traverse in straight lines undisturbedly, but if we were to be exact, we would want to model the particles in the air, which becomes a participating medium. So "above-surface scattering" is as different from as surface scattering as is subsurface scattering.

© The Author(s), under exclusive license to Springer Nature Switzerland AG 2026 125
Y. Zhu, *Visual Computing For Architects*, Synthesis Lectures on Computer Architecture,
https://doi.org/10.1007/978-3-032-05018-2_7

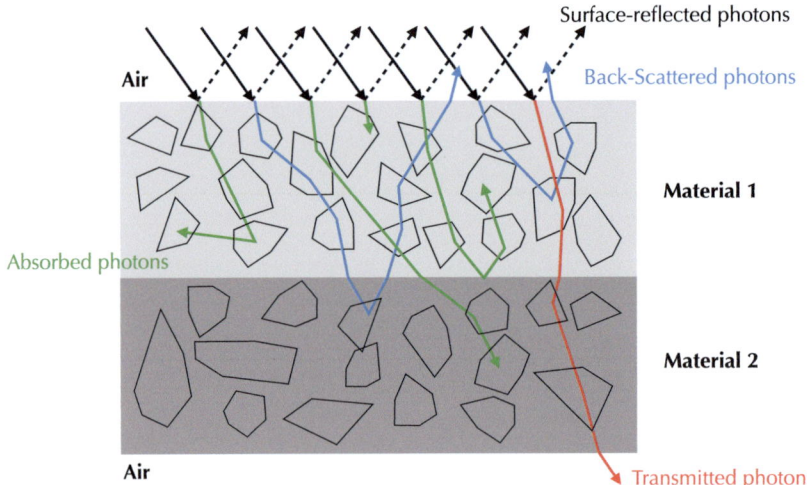

Fig. 7.1 At the Air-Material 1 interface, photons are either reflected directly back or penetrate into the material through refraction. The refracted photons interact with the material particles through the volume scattering processes, where some photons are absorbed and others penetrate into Material 2. For someone observing from the outside, a portion of the photons would eventually leave the material composite altogether and re-enter the air. Some of these leaving photons are called the back-scattered photons that contribute to the apparent surface reflectance; others transmit through the materials and contribute to the apparent transmittance of the material composite

7.1.1   General Intuitions

We will use Fig. 7.1 as a running example to discuss the life of photons inside the material. At the Air-Material 1 interface, photons are either reflected directly back or penetrate into the material through refraction. When a refracted photon meets a particle, the particle might absorb the photon or scatter it away. If absorbed, the photon is "dead" and can be removed from the discussion. If scattered, the photon might appear to change its direction and continue to travel on a straight line until it meets another particle, so in principle a photon can be scattered multiple times.

There are three fates a photon eventually has to accept: (1) it might be absorbed along the way, (2) it might re-emerge from Material 1 back to the air, or (3) it might emerge to the air from the bottom of Material 2. Absorption is easy to understand: a photon has a certain probability of being absorbed when it meets a particle, so the longer it travels, the more likely it will be absorbed. Let's examine the other two cases where a photon escapes the media.

- After multiple scattering, some of the initial photons that enter Material 1 from the air will reach the Material 1-air boundary again, but this time from the material side. At that point, the photons necessarily go through another round of reflection-refraction governed by the surface scattering processes. The refracted photons will re-emerge from Material 1. This is called **back-scattering**, because these photons are scattered back to where they come. As a consequence, when we observe the material from the same side of the illumination, the lights that enter our eye come from two sources: the initial surface scattering and the back-scattering.

• Some photons might leave Material 1 from the other side and enter Material 2, in which photons go through the same volume scattering processes, where some are absorbed, some can be turned back to Material 1, and some, critically, can hit the Air-Material 2 interface. Just like what happens at the Air-Material 1 interface, some of the photons will eventually emerge from Material 2. These photons essentially survive the absorption of all the particles in the media. When you observe the material from the opposite side of the illumination, it is these transmitted photons that dictate the color of the material.

Sometimes people will also say, "sub-surface scattering is caused by photons exiting at a point different from the incident point." It points to the fact that a photon can re-emerge anywhere from the material after SSS, whereas surface scattering is *modeled* to be taking place only at the incident point (although we will see later that this is just a useful macroscopic abstraction or, rather, modeling strategy).

7.1.2   Transparent Versus Opaque Versus Translucent Materials

We often hear materials being described as opaque, translucent, and transparent. We can now more scientifically approach these terms given the intuitions we have built so far.

Transparent Materials

Transparent materials either scatter light predominantly in forward directions or they scatter very little light (other than surface scattering). As a result, most photons traveling through the material are either absorbed or go through without changing much of their the directions. So if you hold a transparent material against a light source, you can clearly see through the material and see the light on the other side. This does not mean transparent materials always have the same color as the light source—absorption could be wavelength-selective. An example is aqueous/dye solutions where dye molecules are very small ($\sim$ nm range) and, thus, scatter little light so they look transparent, but depending on the absorption spectrum (which depends on how the dye molecules interact with molecules in the solvent), most dye solutions are not colorless.

Opaque Materials

In many materials, photons arriving at the material surface are either reflected right away at the surface or, for those that do penetrate into the materials, are all absorbed by the subsurface particles. Examples include conductors like metals, whose subsurface absorption is very strong, or sufficiently thick dielectrics. These materials are **opaque** in two senses. First, their transmittance is practically 0. Because of strong absorption, no photon re-emerges at the other side of the material. If you hold, say, a brick (dielectric) against a light bulb, the brick would completely block the light. Second, their reflectance is independent of the substrate or the material beneath them, so they completely hide the color of the substrate.[1] Painters know that if they want to cover a layer in their painting, they will need to apply a very thick layer of paint on top.

Translucent Materials

Translucent materials such as jade, wax, and human skin are neither opaque nor transparent. If you hold wax against a light bulb, the wax will not completely block the light, so you will see some light, but you will not be able to see clearly the other side through the wax, since photons from the light bulb are very much volume-scattered after passing through the wax. Clearly modeling SSS is critical for accurately estimating the color of translucent materials. In fact, in graphics literature we sometimes see things like "modeling translucent material must consider sub-surface scattering." In this sense, we might be tempted to classify participating media as translucent materials, because their colors certainly very much depend on volume scattering. While it is technically correct, people rarely do that, perhaps just because of the weirdness of calling, say, smokes, a material rather than a medium?

It is *not* true that SSS is important only in modeling translucency. Modeling SSS can be important for opaque materials. Consider the wax case: what if we make the wax very thick? The thick wax will eventually become opaque in that it will completely hide the material behind it. But that does not mean volume scattering does not matter here; the back-scattered photons do contribute to the apparent color of a thick wax.

Oil Painting Example

To put things together, consider a painting. One way paintings are characterized is by how they were painted, and we might see things like "oil on canvas". Oil means the paint is oil paint, where paint pigments are dispersed into (usually linseed) oil, which is usually called the binder or the vehicle. Canvas is the substrate, which is nothing more than another material that is right beneath the painting.

The oil itself is somewhat transparent, especially when you just apply a thin layer on the canvas. But with the paint pigments, the entire oil paint becomes a translucent material. When photons leave the oil paints, they immediately interact with the canvas. If the paint layer is thick enough, virtually no photon can ever reach the canvas. But if the paint is

---

[1] Technically speaking, having a zero transmittance requires the material to have a stronger absorption than hiding the substrate, because in the latter case photons have to make a round trip, so they have more opportunities to be absorbed.

relatively thin, the property of the substrate will contribute to the overall color of the paint. For instance, if the canvas is white-ish, a good percentage of the photons will be reflected back. The same paint would look much darker if the canvas is black, which absorbs a lot of photons.

7.1.3 Equilibrium

We can view the light-material interaction as a dynamical system under an equilibrium. To appreciate this, consider again Fig. 7.1. Some photons entering Material 1 are back-scattered and hit the Air-Material 1 interface and some of those photons will re-enter Material 1 through internal reflection. Those photons will then go through multiple scattering, and as a result some will be back-scattered again and hit the Air-Material 1 interface. The cycle goes on. The secondary back-scattering is weaker in power than the first back-scattering, and the third-order back-scattering is even weaker, and so on. So eventually you can imagine that the total number of photons back-scattered at the surface will reach a constant.

In fact, this sort of dynamics takes place everywhere inside the material along every direction. If you pick a point $\mathbf{p}$ in the material (or at the surface) and a direction ω starting at the point, the radiance at $(\mathbf{p}, \omega)$ is a constant under equilibrium. In other words, the spatial radiance distribution (a.k.a., the light field) is not changing over time.

The equilibrium is reached almost instantaneously, since light propagates incredibly fast. So the equilibrium discussion is probably of no practical impact in modeling or actual measurement, but it is still important to keep this in mind. The (spectral) reflectance/BRDF modeling/measurement is done assuming equilibrium, and later when we model volume scattering, we will set up the differential equations under the equilibrium assumption, too.

7.2   Absorption

We will focus on modeling absorption in this chapter, and the way we build the models is fundamental to how scattering will be dealt with later.

7.2.1   A Simple Case: Collimated Illumination on Uniform Medium

Imagine that a beam of light hits a volume of particles. The light is **collimated** in that all photons travel along the same direction. We take a slice of the material perpendicular to the incident direction. The slice is so thin that no particles in that material cover each other from the direction of the incident light. This is shown in Fig. 7.2 (left). We also, for now, assume that the medium is *uniform* in that the **number concentration** c (i.e., the number of particles per unit volume) of each slice is exactly the same.

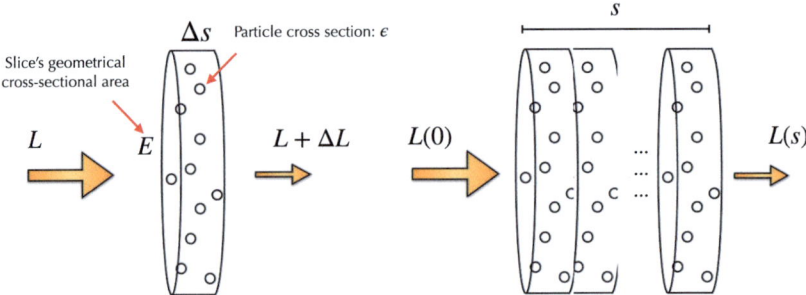

Fig. 7.2 Conceptual model to help reason about photon absorption; see text

Say the slice has a depth of Δs and a geometrical cross-sectional area of E. All the particles have the same geometrical cross-sectional area of ϵ_g. In the simplest model, a photon is absorbed whenever it hits a particle. In reality, the chance of absorption can be higher or lower. The *effective* area available for absorption is

$$\epsilon = \epsilon_g Q_a, \tag{7.1}$$

where Q_a is called the **absorption efficiency** and is usually smaller than 1 for molecules (which have small ϵ_g) and greater than 1 for large particles (whose ϵ_g can be large). Q_a is wavelength dependent, so we should have written it as $Q_a(\lambda)$, but we will omit the wavelength in our notations for simplicity's sake. In physics, ϵ is called the **absorption cross section** of the particle; it characterizes the intrinsic capability of a particle to absorb photons. Mind the subtle but important difference between the geometrical cross-sectional area and the cross section of a particle.

The question we are interested in is, if the incident radiance is L, what is the radiance leaving the slice $L + \Delta L$? By convention, the difference between the exitant and incident radiance is always ΔL, which in this case has to be negative. The percentage of photons that are absorbed by this slice of particles $(-\frac{\Delta L}{L})$ is equivalent to the cross-sectional area of the slice that is covered by the total cross sections of the particles:

$$-\frac{\Delta L}{L} = \frac{cE\,\Delta s\epsilon}{E}, \tag{7.2a}$$

$$\frac{\Delta L}{\Delta s} = -c\epsilon L = -\sigma_a L, \tag{7.2b}$$

where c is the particle concentration of the slice, and $E\,\Delta s$ is the total volume of the slice. So $cE\,\Delta s$ is the number of particles in this thin slice, and $cE\,\Delta s\epsilon$ is the total cross section of all the particles. Given the assumption that no particles are covering each other, $\frac{cE\,\Delta l\epsilon}{E}$ is then the percentage of the thin slice's cross-sectional area that is available for photon absorption and, thus, the percentage of the incident photons that are absorbed. The negative sign on the left-hand side of Eq. (7.2a) signals the fact that ΔL is negative.

We rewrite Eq. (7.2a) as (7.2b), which shows that the amount of photon absorption per unit length ($\frac{\Delta L}{\Delta s}$) is proportional to the current amount of photons up to a scaling factor $c\epsilon$. In the computer graphics literature, $c\epsilon$ is called the **absorption coefficient**, denoted σ_a.

When Δs approaches infinity, we can rewrite Eq. (7.2b) as a differential equation in Eq. (7.3a). This equation is a classic case of exponential decay, and its solution is given by Eq. (7.3b), which allows us to calculate the remaining radiance after the light travels a length s:

$$\frac{dL}{ds} = \lim_{\Delta s \to 0} \frac{\Delta L}{\Delta s} = -\sigma_a L, \tag{7.3a}$$

$$L(s) = L_0 e^{-\sigma_a s}, \tag{7.3b}$$

where $L_0 = L(0)$ is the initial radiance of the light before interacting with the particles, as visualized in Fig. 7.2 (right), $L(s)$ denotes the radiance at a particular length s.

Equation (7.3b) is called the **Bouguer-Beer-Lambert's law** (BBL), which is a geometrical optics' simplification of the electromagnetic theory of light-matter interaction where the matter is purely absorptive (Mayerhöfer et al. 2020).

Absorption Coefficient

The absorption coefficient is an important measure of the medium's ability to absorb photons. It has a unit of m^{-11}, which means it is not bound by 0 and 1. One way to interpret the absorption coefficient is to observe that $\sigma_a ds = dL/L$, which is the fraction of the radiance absorbed or the probability of light absorption by an infinitesimal slice. So $\sigma_a = (dL/L)/ds$ can be interpreted as the probability *density* of photon absorption, i.e., the probability of absorption per unit length traveled:

$$\sigma_a = \lim_{\Delta s \to 0} \frac{\Delta L}{L} / \Delta s = \frac{dL}{L ds}. \tag{7.4}$$

Like any density measure, absorption coefficient is most useful when it is integrated: when we integrate σ_a over the length that light travels, we get the fraction/percentage of the light absorbed. One can also show that $1/\sigma_a$ is the expected value of the distance a photon can travel before being absorbed (Bohren and Clothiaux 2006, Sect. 5.1.3); this quantity is given the name **mean free path** (l). To derive l, observe that the probability that a photon is absorbed after traveling a distance s is $1 - e^{-\sigma_a s}$. So the probability *density* of absorption as a function of the distance s is:

$$f(s) = \frac{d(1 - e^{-\sigma_a s})}{ds} = \sigma_a e^{-\sigma_a s}. \tag{7.5}$$

So the expected value of s, which we can interpret as the distance a photon can travel on average before being absorbed, is:

$$l = \int_0^\infty sf(s)\mathrm{d}s = 1/\sigma_a. \tag{7.6}$$

An Alternative Derivation

An equivalent way of deriving the BBL law is the following. We divide the entire volume (with a total length of s) into N thin slices, each with a length of Δs. After the first slice, the surviving portion of the initial radiance is $L = L_0(1 - \sigma_a \Delta s)$, so after going through all the N slices, the remaining radiance is given by Eq. (7.7a):

$$L_N = L_0(1 - \sigma_a \Delta s)^N = L_0(1 - \sigma_a \frac{s}{N})^N, \tag{7.7a}$$

$$L(s) = \lim_{N \to \infty} L_0(1 - \sigma_a \frac{s}{N})^N = L_0 e^{-\sigma_a s}. \tag{7.7b}$$

Now when $\mathrm{d}s$ becomes infinitesimally small, N approaches infinity, so the limit of the remaining radiance as a function of the total length s is given in Eq. (7.7b), which is the same as Eq. (7.3b).

7.2.2   A Few Important Quantities

We can now define a few other commonly used quantities (omitting the wavelength dependence for simplicity). The **transmittance** T of a volume with a total thickness of s is defined as the percentage of the transmitted/unabsorbed photons after traveling the length of s (Eq. 7.8a). The **absorbance** A is the product of $\sigma_a s$. The **absorptance** a of a volume is defined as the percentage of the absorbed photons by the volume, which relates to T and A by Eq. (7.8b).

$$T = \frac{L(s)}{L_0} = e^{-\sigma_a s}, \tag{7.8a}$$

$$A = -\ln T = \ln \frac{L(s)}{L_0} = \sigma_a s, \tag{7.8b}$$

$$a = 1 - T = 1 - e^{-A}. \tag{7.8c}$$

We have seen these definitions in Sect. 3.1.2. One very nice thing about the absorbance A is that it is approximately equivalent to absorptance a when A is small (which would be true when, e.g., the length s is very small, as is the case when discussing how a photoreceptor absorbs photons when illuminated transversely).

Another nice thing about absorbance is that absorbances add, because *absorption coefficients add*. Imagine you have n kinds of particles mixed up in a medium, each with a different absorption coefficient σ_a^i. The overall absorbance of the medium is the sum of the individual absorbance A^i derived as if the medium is made up of only one kind of particles. That is:

$$A = \sum_i^n A^i = s \sum_i^n \sigma_a^i = s \sum_i^n c^i \epsilon^i, \tag{7.9}$$

where c^i and ϵ^i are the concentration and absorption cross section of the ith particles. Specifically, c^i is defined as:

$$c^i = \frac{n_i}{V}, \tag{7.10}$$

where n_i is the number of the ith kind of particles in the material, and V is the material volume.

This is not a surprising result. As long as particles in a thin slice of this new heterogeneous medium do not cover each other, we can easily extend Eq. (7.2a) and the rest of the derivation to consider multiple kinds of particles; eventually Eq. (7.9) would be a natural conclusion. We will omit the derivation here for simplicity sake.

Equation (7.9) is a nice conclusion to have, because usually we *are* dealing with hybrid media. For instance, paint is a mixture of binder particles and pigment particles, and a mist is a mixture of water droplets and air particles. If we do not want to model individual matters, we can use a single absorption coefficient to describe the aggregate behavior of the mixture. That absorption coefficient does have a physical meaning: it is the concentration-weighted sum of the individual absorption coefficients.

There are a bunch of other quantities defined in the literature. The state of the definitions is a bit of a mess, largely because different communities use different definitions.

- In visual neuroscience people sometimes use a quantity called **specific absorbance** (see, e.g., Bowmaker and Dartnall 1980), which is the absorbance per unit length $\frac{A}{s}$. Whenever you see a quantity that starts with the word "specific", chances are that the quantity is defined per unit length. You can see that specific absorbance is actually just our absorption coefficient.
- In scientific communities, especially chemistry and spectroscopy, people define ϵ, rather than $c\epsilon$, to be the absorption coefficient. You can see the appeal of doing that—ϵ is a more fundamental measure of a medium's ability to absorb photons, independent of the particle concentration c (and certainly independent of the traversal length s).
- The absorbance defined in Eq. (7.8b) is technically called the **Naperian absorbance**, because we take the natural logarithm of T. Sometimes people also use the **decadic absorbance**, which is defined as $-\log T$. This quantity is also called the **optical density**.
- Finally, the number concentration c here is defined in terms of the absolute quantity per unit volume, but sometimes people want to define c as the **molar concentration**, which is the number of moles per unit volume. If so, all other derived quantities are then prefixed with "molar". Next time when you see something like the **molar decadic absorption coefficient**, you know what it is!

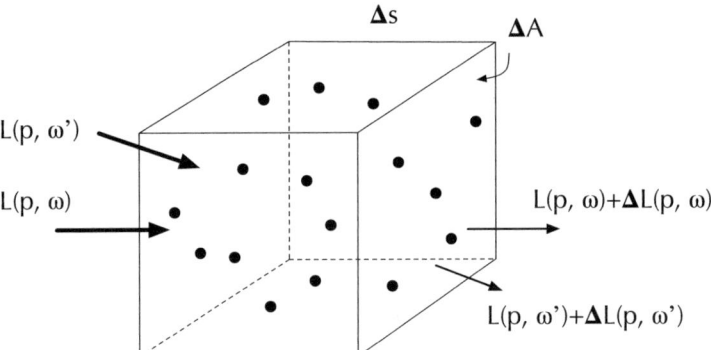

Fig. 7.3 A conceptual model to help reason about photon absorption in the general case, where the absorption coefficient can vary spatially and directionally. The medium is divided into many tiny elemental volumes, each of which is so small that particles do not cover each from any direction

The annoying thing is that people do not always tell you which definition they use. The plea I have to you is to be specific about which definition *you* use in your writing and tell me when I am being vague!

7.2.3   General Case

So far we have assumed that the absorption coefficient $\sigma_a = c\epsilon$ is a constant regardless of the position p in the medium and along any direction ω. The former property assumes that the medium is uniform, and the latter property is called **isotropic**[2] in that the medium's ability to absorb photons is independent of the light direction.

Both assumptions are problematic in practice. The concentration can change spatially and should be denoted $c(p)$, where p is an arbitrary position in space. ϵ can also change with p and, more importantly, change with the direction of light incidence ω. For instance, the particles might not be spherical, so their geometrical cross-sectional area and, thus, the cross section ϵ available for absorbing photons can depend on ω. As a result, the absorption coefficient should generally be denoted $\sigma_a(p, \omega)$.

Effectively, our conceptual model, shown in Fig. 7.3, has to be changed to one where the entire body of particles is divided into many equally-sized volumes (with a length Δs and an area ΔA), each of which is so small that particles do not cover each other from any direction. The radiance reduction per unit length in a small volume is then expressed as:

---

[2] "Isotropic" is a very overloaded term; it just means some physical property is invariant when measured from different directions. So depending on what physical property you care about, "isotropic" can mean different things. The property we care about here is a volume's ability to absorb photons, which is different from our earlier use of isotropy, which is concerned with the ability of a surface to scatter photons.

$$\frac{\Delta L(p, \omega)}{\Delta s} = -\sigma_a(p, \omega)L. \tag{7.11}$$

Given this model, we can calculate the exitant radiance after light travels a length s through the medium:

$$L(p + s\omega, \omega) = L(p, \omega)e^{-\int_0^s \sigma_a(p+t\omega, \omega)dt}, \tag{7.12}$$

where ω is the (unit) direction of the incident radiance, $L(p, \omega)$ is the incident radiance, and $L(p + s\omega, \omega)$ is the exitance radiance (radiance toward ω leaving the entire medium after traveling s).

You would notice that for a beam with an oblique incident direction, the distance traveled, say $\Delta s'$, can be different (longer or shorter than) from Δs. Our model can account for this by folding the factor $\Delta s'/\Delta s$ specific to a particular direction ω' into the absorption coefficient $\sigma_a(p, \omega')$. Note that the $\Delta s'/\Delta s$ factor should be the average for all the incident photons with the same direction ω' across the entire ΔA.

7.2.4 Nature and Applicability of the Model

The absorption model (the BBL law) derived before (Eqs. 7.3b and 7.12) is a continuous one, but it is derived based on modeling discrete particles and events. It is another example of the modeling methodology discussed on Sect. 6.5.

Equation (7.12) seems to suggest that absorption coefficient $\sigma_a(p, \omega)$ is continuously defined at any position p in the medium along any direction ω. It is not true. For starters, concentration c is not continuous. Rather, it exhibits the triphasic profile shown in Fig. 6.2. As we keep shrinking the size of the volume to the molecular scale, eventually the concentration depends on whether the tiny volume contains any molecules or not, so it becomes wildly discontinuous, not to mention the headache of dealing with a partial molecule in a volume—should it be counted or not? In general, the absorption coefficient can be an arbitrary discontinuous function that is not integrable.

What about Eq. (7.3b) where the absorption coefficient is uniform so we do not have to take the integral? Well, that is a lie too: concentration is not continuous, so it cannot be uniform everywhere, and, by extension, the absorption coefficient cannot be a constant everywhere either. So Eq. (7.3a) is technically wrong when we let $\Delta s \to 0$ (i.e., $N \to \infty$), which is necessary for us to construct the differential equation (or take the limit in Eq. 7.7b). For Eq. (7.3a) to be true, the concentration/absorption coefficient must be a constant everywhere, which can be true only if the volume is continuous.

What has to happen is that the limit of Δs cannot be literally 0 and the limit of N cannot be infinity. What we do is to keep reducing Δs to the point where the concentration (and thus absorption coefficient) is insensitive to slight perturbation of Δs (i.e., operating in the stable range in Fig. 6.2), and call it the concentration/absorption coefficient of that specific

Δs. And we repeat this for all the Δs. This certainly applies to the general-case models in Eqs. (7.11) and (7.12), where we iterate over not the thin slices Δs but all the tiny volumes ($\Delta A \times \Delta s$). So all the integral symbols are secretly summing over an extremely fine-grained grid.

How big of an error are we introducing here? Technically, we should sum all N slices across the total traversal length s in Eq. (7.7a). If we assume Δs to be very small (even though not infinitesimal) compared to s, N would be large, so taking the integration (equivalent to letting $N \to \infty$) would be very close to summing over N. Similarly, the integral in Eq. (7.12) should have been a summation of the concentration in each of the N slices. If you want to be pedantic, however, the integration there is exact: we can model c as a piece-wise function, where the value at each piece is the concentration of the corresponding volume. Integrating over a piece-wise function is the same as summing all the pieces. Only the exponential expression in Eq. (7.12) is inexact.

The discontinuity of the medium is, of course, orthogonal to the discontinuity and non-uniformity in the light field itself. For instance, the fact that we use $\frac{cE\Delta l\epsilon}{E}$ as the percentage of photon absorption in Eq. (7.2a) (and implicitly in Eq. 7.3b) assumes that the irradiance of the incident illumination is continuous and uniform in the small volume. This is technically not true because photons are discrete packets of energy. But in practice this is not a concern because we can assume that there is an enormous amount of photons incident on the small volume, and these photons are randomly distributed.

In essence, we are using the aggregated behavior of many photons to model the behavior of a small volume. This is similar to the microfacet models, where we use the aggregated behavior of many microfacets to statistically model the behavior of a small macro-surface.

This sort of modeling strategy is a weird case where the discrete model provides the "ground truth", which is approximated by a continuous model. I say ground truth—to the extent that the geometrical optics can approximate the electromagnetic theory of light-matter interaction. The BBL law fails when the wave nature of photons has to be considered (Mayerhöfer et al. 2020).

7.3   Scattering

Scattering is much more difficult to reason about than absorption, primarily because a scattered photon is not "dead" and continues to participate in light-matter interaction. The way to study scattering is to first understand the behavior of a single scattering event and then consider the overall behavior of a large of collection of particles.

This chapter focuses on discussing a single scattering event (Sect. 7.3.2), and the next chapter discusses the general case where a large collection of particles interacts with photons. Before all these, though, it is useful to first build some intuitions as to why there is a distinction between a single scattering event and scattering by a particle collection and explicitly lay out the assumptions made for the rest of our discussions (Sect. 7.3.1).

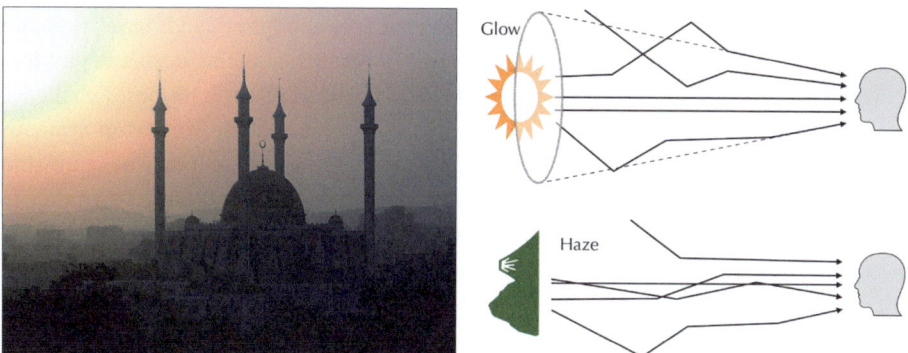

Fig. 7.4 Left: The atmospheric scattering of the sand coming from the Sahara during Harmattan glows in the sun and gives a hazy view of the remote mountains. Nigeria's National Mosque is in the foreground; from Jones (2005). Right: illustrations of the glow of the sun and the haze. Both are due to scattering, and the difference is purely visual but not fundamental

7.3.1 Scattering by a Particle Versus a Collection of Particles

In geometric optics terms, scattering can be thought of as an event that takes place between a photon and a particle. In the real world, however, objects and media are usually made of a large collection of particles, which introduces two complications: multiple scattering and interference.

Multiple Scattering

First, it is possible that a scattered photon, after traveling a certain distance, meets another particle and gets scattered again. This makes it considerably more difficult to analyze the effect of scattering by a medium than does the scattering of a single particle.

Look at Fig. 7.4 (left) taken during Harmattan, where the atmosphere is full of sand and dust blown from the Sahara. The large collection of particles in the atmosphere scatters light, glowing the sun and giving the remote mountains a hazy view. The right panel illustrates the scattering events that give rise to the glow and the haze.

Without scattering, sunlight enters the eye directly. With scattering, some photons from the sun are first knocked out of the view and could potentially be then scattered again back to the eye. Some photons that enter the eye might even come from nearby objects other than the sun. The scattering creates a glow around the sun, and, for the observer, the sun appears larger than it actually is. The hazy view of the mountains is created by exactly the same scattering processes. The photons that enter the eyes are mixed up from different parts of the mountains and from other objects. The mountains appear hazy rather than glowing as the sun does simply because the sun has a higher brightness contrast against the background than does a region on the mountain. So the distinction between "glow" and "haze" is nothing more than a visual difference at a superficial level rather than anything deeper in physics.

You can see why multiple scattering by large collections of particles poses challenges to our analysis. If a photon is scattered once in the medium, the only effect of scattering would be to knock photons out of our line of sight, and thus, remote objects would only look dimmer rather than hazy. In this case, scattering would function exactly like absorption, for modeling purposes at least. With multiple scattering, we have to track not only photons that are scattered out but also photons that are scattered into the rays that enter our eyes.[3] This is a daunting task considering that we are usually dealing with millions of particles and billions of photons, if not more.

If you want to be absolutely pedantic, we can distinguish the following cases:

1. a single scattering event, where a photon meets a particle and is scattered away;
2. single scattering, where a photon is scattered *once* by a medium (a large collection of photons), which is under

   a. a collimated illumination, so the radiance of a ray can only be weakened because photons are scattered to other directions,
   b. an arbitrary illumination, so the radiance of a ray can be both weakened and augmented (by photons scattered from other directions);

3. multiple scattering, where a photon is scattered *multiple times* by a medium, so the radiance of a ray can both be weakened and augmented.

Section 7.3.2 studies Case 1 and Case 2(a) together, because the latter is the statistical consequence of the former. Section 7.4 studies Case 2(b) and Case 3 together because they have the same observable effects and, thus, are modeled in the same way.

Interference and Coherence

Second, when there is a large collection of particles, the scattered radiation fields of individual particles can interfere with each other. The exact impact of interference can only be calculated by considering the wave nature of the light. But to the first order, the inference depends on how densely packed the particles are.

In fact, the specular surface scattering we discussed in Sect. 6.4 is just a macroscopic approximation of the microscopic volume scattering where particles interfere non-randomly. In a mirror or a glass of water, the particles/molecules are very densely packed to the point that the distance between two particles is smaller than the wavelength of the light. As a result, the scattering is *coherent*, which gives rise to the *illusion* of a specular surface. One

---

[3] Technically photons from other objects can enter our eye through a single-scattering event; see the discussion at the end.

can show that the Fresnel equations are the solution to the Maxwell's equations when surface particles are densely packed.

Why would the particle density matter? If particles are very close to each other, their radiation fields are close too, so the interference is stronger and cannot be ignored. More importantly, when particles are close to each other, their spatial positions can no longer be treated as random, so the interference can become coherent. Imagine you drop particles into a vast empty space; the particle sizes are much smaller relative to the space, so their spatial distribution can be roughly described as random. But if the particles are very densely packed, where the next particle can be is very much restrained, so their positions are highly correlated, leading to coherent scattering.

We will generally assume **incoherent scattering** unless otherwise noted, where individual scattering events interfere each other in random ways, so we are spared of the complication of thinking of the wave nature of the photons. Under this assumption, the total power scattered by a collection of particles is the same as the sum of the power scattered by the individual particles. This happens when the particles are sufficient sufficiently distant (separated by more than multiple wavelengths) and their spatial arrangements are uncorrelated.

7.3.2 A Single Scattering Event

Scattering Efficiency and Coefficient

Intuitively, scattering has a similar effect as absorption: it weakens the radiance by taking photons away from a beam of light. The difference is that scattered photons are not dead; they are re-directed to other directions. We can define two important quantities, one to characterize a *particle*'s ability to scatter photons and the other to characterize a *medium*'s ability to scatter photons.

Similar to the situation in absorption, the intrinsic capability of a particle to scatter photons is defined by the particle's **scattering cross section** ϵ_s, which itself is the product of the geometrical cross-sectional area of the particle ϵ_g and the **scattering efficiency** Q_s. We can then define the **scattering coefficient** σ_s of a medium (a large collection of particles), which characterizes the ability of the medium to scatter photons away from its incident radiance. σ_s is the product of the particle concentration of the medium c and the particle's scattering cross section ϵ_s. Again, σ_s has a unit m^{-1} and is not bound by 0 and 1; it is best interpreted as the probability density (i.e., probability per unit length) of light being scattered away. Of course, both the scattering efficiency and scattering coefficient can vary spatially, angularly, and spectrally.

The effects of scattering and absorption add up, because they both weaken a radiance. We can extend Eq. (7.12) to consider scattering (again omitting the wavelength from the equations):

$$L(p + s\omega, \omega) = L(p, \omega)e^{-\int_0^s (\sigma_a(p+t\omega,\omega)+\sigma_s(p+t\omega,\omega))dt}, \tag{7.13a}$$

$$T(p \to p + s\omega) = \frac{L(p + s\omega, \omega)}{L(p, \omega)} = e^{-\int_0^s (\sigma_a(p+t\omega,\omega)+\sigma_s(p+t\omega,\omega))dt}, \tag{7.13b}$$

where $\sigma_s(p, \omega)$ is the scattering coefficient at p toward the direction ω, and $T(p \to p + s\omega)$ is defined as the **transmittance** between p and $p + s\omega$ along the direction ω.

Equation (7.13a) can be derived using the same idea as that used for deriving the absorption equation in Sect. 7.2.1 by modeling a thin layer Δx—with an additional assumption that Δx is so thin that a photon is scattered at most once before leaving Δx. Therefore, scattering by a single particle has the same effect as absorption: they both take the photon out of the radiance, and that is why the absorption equation (Eq. 7.12) can be directly extended here.

Think of the applicability of Eq. (7.13a): it says that the radiance of a ray can only be weakened. If the incident light has only one direction (e.g., a collimated beam), Eq. (7.13a) is true when a photon is scattered at most once in the medium. This is because a scattered photon will not have a chance to get back to the ray. If the incident light is not monodirectional, e.g., diffuse illumination, Eq. (7.13a) in general does not apply—even if we consider only single scattering. This is because photons originally not along the direction ω can be scattered toward it through just one single scattering event. We can see how limited Eq. (7.13a) is: it applies only when the illumination is collimated and we assume only single scattering. We will relax this constraint later.

Just like the absorption case (Eq. 7.9), if a medium is mixed with different particles, each with a different scattering coefficient, the overall scattering coefficient is the sum of the individual scattering coefficients as if the medium is made up of a particular kind of particles.

The sum of the scattering coefficient and absorption coefficient is called the **extinction coefficient** or **attenuation coefficient**, denoted $\sigma_t(p, \omega)$:

$$\sigma_t(p, \omega) = \sigma_a(p, \omega) + \sigma_s(p, \omega). \tag{7.14}$$

The ratio between the scattering coefficient and the attenuation coefficient is called the **single-scattering albedo** of the medium:

$$\rho = \frac{\sigma_s(p, \omega)}{\sigma_t(p, \omega)}. \tag{7.15}$$

This albedo can be seen as the volumetric counterpart of the surface albedo discussed in Eq. (6.6). The two forms of albedo have the same physical meaning: the fraction of the incident energy that is scattered away (i.e., not absorbed). A dark medium (e.g., smoke) has a lower albedo, and a bright medium (e.g., mist) has a higher albedo.

The sum of the scattering and absorption cross sections is called the **extinction cross section** or **attenuation cross section**, denoted $\epsilon_t = \epsilon_a + \epsilon_s$. And of course $1/\sigma_t$ is the mean free path in a medium where both absorption and scattering take place, i.e., the mean distance a photon can travel without being absorbed or scattered away.

Scattering Direction Distribution: Phase Function

While the scattering efficiency (coefficient) characterizes how well a particle (medium) is able to scatter photons, it tells us nothing about the *direction* of scattering. The direction of a single scattering event is characterized by the **phase function** $f_p(p, \omega_s, \omega_i)$, which can be interpreted as the probability *density* function that a photon incident from a direction ω_i is scattered toward a direction ω_s. We will omit p and write the phase function as $f_p(\omega_s, \omega_i)$ when the discussion is unconcerned of p.

$f_p(\omega_s, \omega_i)$ is defined as the fraction of the irradiance incident from an infinitesimal solid angle $d\omega_i$ that is scattered toward an infinitesimal solid angle $d\omega_s$ per unit solid angle:

$$f_p(\omega_s, \omega_i) = \lim_{\Delta\omega_s \to 0} \lim_{\Delta\omega_i \to 0} \frac{\Delta E_o(\omega_s)}{\Delta E_i(\omega_i)} / \Delta\omega_s = \frac{d^2 E_o(\omega_s)}{d E_i(\omega_i) d\omega_s} = \frac{d^2 E_o(\omega_s)}{L(\omega_i) d\omega_i d\omega_s}. \quad (7.16)$$

$\Delta E_i(\omega_i)$ is the incident irradiance over a small solid angle $\Delta\omega_i$ and scatters in all directions. $\Delta E_o(\omega_i)$ is the outgoing irradiance over a small solid angle $\Delta\omega_s$, so $\frac{\Delta E_o(\omega_s)}{\Delta E_i(\omega_i)}$ is the fraction of the photons incident from $\Delta\omega_i$ that are scattered over $\Delta\omega_s$ or, alternatively, the probability that a photon incident from $\Delta\omega_i$ is scattered toward $\Delta\omega_s$; this ratio/fraction is clearly a value between 0 and 1. Dividing that fraction by $\Delta\omega_s$ gets us the probability per unit solid angle. When both the incident solid angle $\Delta\omega_i$ and the outgoing solid angle $\Delta\omega_s$ approach 0, the fraction can be interpreted as the directional-directional reflectance (Sect. 6.2), and the probability per solid angle within $\Delta\omega_s$ becomes the probability *density* toward ω_s.

Like all density functions, the meaning of a phase function is most clear when it is integrated to compute some other quantity. Integrating Eq. (7.16) over all the outgoing directions ω_s:

$$dE_o = \int^{\Omega=4\pi} f_p(\omega_s, \omega_i) L(\omega_i) d\omega_i d\omega_s \quad (7.17a)$$

$$= L(\omega_i) d\omega_i \int^{\Omega=4\pi} f_p(\omega_s, \omega_i) d\omega_s \quad (7.17b)$$

$$= dE_i \int^{\Omega=4\pi} f_p(\omega_s, \omega_i) d\omega_s. \quad (7.17c)$$

To interpret this integration, consider a point that receives an incident radiance of $L(\omega_i)$ over an infinitesimal solid angle $d\omega_i$. The point receives a total irradiance of $dE_i = L(\omega_i) d\omega_i$, which is scattered in all directions. The density of the irradiance scattered toward a particular direction ω_s is $f_p(\omega_s, \omega_i) L(\omega_i) d\omega_i$,[4] which when multiplied by $d\omega_s$ gives us the actual irradiance scattered over a small solid angle $d\omega_s$ around ω_s. Integrating all outgoing directions over the entire sphere (4π) we have Eq. (7.17a).

---

[4] A direction ω_s has a solid angle of 0, so its associated irradiance is technically 0, too. What $f_p(\omega_s, \omega_i) L(\omega_i) d\omega_i$ represents is the irradiance per solid angle.

Now, of course, some of the photons in dE_i might not be scattered; they could be absorbed, or they could simply not hit the cross section of any particle. So technically $dE_o \leq dE_i$ in Eq. (7.17c), just like how energy conservation is expressed in surface scattering in Eq. (6.3b). By the convention in the volume scattering literature, however, the phase function is defined such that dE_i refers to only the portion of the incident irradiance that does get scattered. Therefore, $dE_o = dE_i$, so we have:

$$\int^{\Omega=4\pi} f_p(\omega_s, \omega_i)d\omega_s = \int^{\Omega=4\pi} f_p(\omega_s, \omega_i)d\omega_i = 1. \tag{7.18}$$

That is, the phase function integrates to 1; the second integral can be derived using the Helmholtz reciprocity (since we are still dealing with geometrical optics):

$$f_p(\omega_i, \omega_s) = f_p(\omega_s, \omega_i). \tag{7.19}$$

One way to interpret the fact that the phase function integrates to 1 is that the phase function is the *conditional* probability density function of scattering: given that a photon is scattered, what is the probability (density) of scattering to a particular direction?

Phase Function Versus BRDF

The phase function can be seen as the volumetric counterpart (in the sense that we are talking about volume scattering) of BRDF (Sect. 6.1)—with two differences. First, the definition of the BRDF accounts for absorption, so the BRDF integrates to *at most* 1, whereas the integral of the phase function is normalized to 1. This difference in definition is born purely of convention.

The second difference is more fundamental. There is no $\cos\theta$ term when using the phase function; see, e.g., Eq. (7.17), unlike how the BRDF is used to turn irradiance into radiance (e.g., Eq. 6.3b). In fact, from Eq. (7.17) we can see that given a radiance $L(\omega_i)$ and a solid angle $d\omega_i$, the irradiance is simply $L(\omega_i)d\omega_i$ rather than $L(\omega_i)\cos\theta_i d\omega_i$. Didn't we say that there is a cosine fall-off between radiance and irradiance (Sect. 5.3.4)?

One intuition that might help is that in volume scattering we are dealing with points, which can receive flux from the entire sphere and have no definition of a normal (because points are dimensionless and shapeless) or, perhaps more conveniently, have a "flexible" normal that changes with the illumination direction and is always facing directly at the illumination. Entertain this thought experiment. We set up a small surface detector at a point and measure the power of the detector; if the incident light is parallel to the surface, the detector would receive no power, but would you say that the *point* does not receive any light and that the radiation field has no power? Of course not.

The fact that a parallel surface would receive no photons absolutely does not mean the illumination has no power; the radiation field is the same whether it is illuminating a surface or illuminating a point. But if we are modeling a surface, we *want* our model to say that the power received by the surface is 0, because it matches our phenomenological observation (that a detector arranged that way would receive no recording); when we are modeling a point in volume scattering, we *want* the point to receive a power as if the point has a "normal" that is directly facing the illumination because, again, this matches our phenomenological observation.

Ultimately, the difference is a conscious choice of modeling strategy even though the underlying physics is exactly the same. That is why models based on BRDF and phase function are phenomenological models. If you deal with electromagnetic theories and QED, you would not have to have this distinction between modeling surface and volume scattering.

With the understanding that there is no cosine fall-off in volume scattering, Eq. (7.16) can be re-written as:

$$f_p(\omega_s, \omega_i) = \frac{d^2 E_o(\omega_s)}{dE_i(\omega_i)d\omega_s} = \frac{d}{dE_i(\omega_i)} \frac{dE_o(\omega_s)}{d\omega_s} = \frac{dL_o(\omega_s)}{dE_i(\omega_i)} = \frac{dL_o(\omega_s)}{L_i(\omega_i)d\omega_i}, \qquad (7.20)$$

where $dL_o(\omega_s)$ is the infinitesimal outgoing radiance toward ω_s. In this sense, the phase function operates in exactly the same way as the BRDF (Eq. 6.1): they both operate on irradiance and turn infinitesimal irradiance into infinitesimal radiance.

Isotropic Medium and Isotropic Scatters

Given the normalization in the phase function, the scattering efficiency should actually be parameterized as $\bar{Q}_s(p, \omega_s, \omega_i)$:

$$\bar{Q}_s(p, \omega_s, \omega_i) = Q_s(p, \omega_i) f_p(p, \omega_s, \omega_i), \qquad (7.21)$$

where $Q_s(p, \omega_i)$ should be be interpreted as the *total* scattering efficiency at p over all outgoing directions for a given incident direction ω_i. Similarly, the scattering coefficient would be expressed as:

$$\bar{\sigma}_s(p, \omega_s, \omega_i) = \sigma_s(p, \omega_i) f_p(p, \omega_s, \omega_i), \qquad (7.22)$$

where $\sigma_s(p, \omega_i)$ is interpreted as the *total* scattering coefficient at p over all outgoing directions for a given incident direction ω_i.

While $f_p(\cdot)$ is technically a 4D function parameterized by ω_s and ω_i, the phase function of many natural media is 1D and depends only on the angle θ subtended by ω_s and ω_i. Consider under what conditions this simplification can be true.

- First, it says that the phase function does not depend on the absolute incident direction ω_i but the relative angle between ω_i and ω_s. To get a visual intuition, see Fig. 7.5; if the phase function is invariant to the photon incident direction ω_i, we can, without losing any generality, assign ω_i to the z-axis; the scattered direction ω_s is parameterized by θ and ϕ.

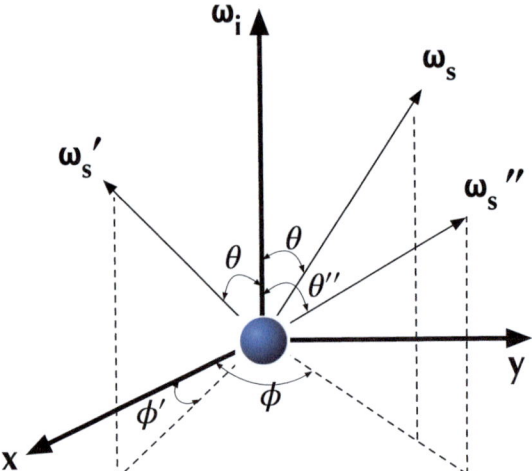

Fig. 7.5 The phase function of a spherical particle is (1) invariant to the incident direction ω_i, which, without losing generality, is taken to be the z-axis here, and (2) also invariant to the azimuthal angle ϕ of the outgoing direction ω_s but depends on the polar angle θ. So $f_p(\omega_s, \omega_i) = f_p(\omega_s', \omega_i) \neq f_p(\omega_s'', \omega_i)$. Media consisting of such particles are called isotropic media, but it does not mean the particle itself is an isotropic scatterer, which does not exist, but if it did, its phase function would be a constant (invariant to both θ and ϕ)

- Second, it also says the phase function depends on only θ but not ϕ. That is, the phase function is rotationally symmetric about the incident direction ω_i. So $f_p(\omega_s, \omega_i) = f_p(\omega_s', \omega_i) \neq f_p(\omega_s'', \omega_i)$.

Intuitively, the phase function has the following two properties:

- If you fix the incident direction, no matter how you rotate the particle, the phase function distribution is the same. Alternatively, if you change the incident direction, the phase function distribution moves along with the incident direction.
- Given an incident direction, the phase function distribution is axially symmetric about the incident direction.

The two conditions above are met only when the medium consists of randomly distributed spherically symmetric particles,[5] in which case (1) there is no reason to think that any incident direction is special, so the phase function certainly is invariant to ω_i, and (2) there is no reason to think ω_s and ω_s' are any different since one should not expect the scattering behavior to change if we rotate the sphere about the incident direction (z-axis).

---

[5] Or when the medium consists of randomly distributed and oriented spherically asymmetric particles, in which case the medium is *statistically* spherically symmetric.

A medium consisting of spherically symmetric particles is called a *symmetric* or an **isotropic medium**. Usually when we refer to an isotropic medium, not only is the phase function but also the total scattering coefficient $\sigma_s(p, \omega_i)$ (Eq. 7.22) rotationally invariant to the incident direction.[6]

As we said earlier, "isotropic" is an unbelievably overloaded term. People also call a particle an **isotropic scatterer** if its phase function is a constant, i.e., invariant to ω_s; such a phase function is sometimes called an *isotropic phase function*. An isotropic scatterer does not exist; it is a purely theoretical construction, and if it existed, its phase function would take the value of $\frac{1}{4\pi}$ given Eq. (7.18).

7.3.3 Common Models and General "Rules"

There are many factors that determine the exact scattering efficiency and scattering direction, which can be calculated by solving the Maxwell's equations. We will talk about a few common models here; we focus on the intuitions while omitting the exact mathematical expressions, which can be found in standard texts. From the models, we can identify a few general "rules" or, rather, approximations under certain assumptions.

The main theory or model for a single scattering event is called the **Mie scattering** theory, which, strictly speaking, applies only when the particle is spherical; see Sharma (2003, Sect. 3.5.2), Bohren and Clothiaux (2006, Sect. 3.5), and Melbourne (2004, Chap. 3). Mie scattering is *not* somehow a different scattering process from any other scattering, and the Mie theory is nothing more than the solution to the Maxwell's equations under certain conditions.[7]

The Mie theory predicts that the overall scattering efficiency Q_s is:

$$Q_s = \frac{8}{3}\gamma^4 \left(\frac{m^2 - 1}{m^2 + 2} \right) \left[1 + \frac{6}{5} \left(\frac{m^2 - 1}{m^2 + 2} \right) \gamma^2 + \cdots \right], \tag{7.23a}$$

$$\gamma = \frac{r}{\lambda_m}, \tag{7.23b}$$

$$m = \frac{n}{n_m}, \tag{7.23c}$$

where m is the the relative refractive index between the particle and the medium surrounding the particle, and γ is the ratio between the particle radius r and the incident light wavelength in the surrounding medium λ_m. The notion of surrounding media might come across as a little surprising: doesn't the material consist merely of its particles? Hardly. For instance, in paints, pigments are surrounded by binders (e.g., linseed oil in oil paints, egg yolk in

---

[6] In theory, it is certainly possible to have a medium whose total scattering coefficient/efficiency varies with the incident direction but not the angular distribution/probability of the scattered photons.

[7] The modern form of the solution is summarized, not invented, by Gustav Mie but the solution had been developed by many predecessors such as Ludvig Lorenz.

tempera paints, and beeswax in encaustic paints) and usually some amount of water (except oil paints). When paint dries, some water might be evaporated, leaving pockets of air, which also contributes to the surrounding media.

We can draw a few general conclusions from the model.

Small-Particle (Rayleigh) Scattering

For small particles where $\gamma \ll 1$ (generally when the radius is ten times smaller than the wavelength of the incident light), only the first term in Eq. (7.23a)'s bracket matters, so the scattering efficiency is inversely proportional to λ_m^{-4}. The inverse proportionality to λ_m^{-4} *largely* (but apparently not entirely) explains why the sky is blue and why the sun is red (Bohren and Clothiaux 2006, Sect. 8.1). Why? First, recognize that individual molecules, such as air molecules, are usually sub-nm in size, so they scatter in this small-particle regime. Short wavelength lights from the sun are scattered by the atmospheric molecules more toward the sky and eventually enter your eyes, so if you look at the sky (against the sun) it would appear blue; when you look at the sun directly, the photons entering your eyes are mostly those unscattered ones that transmit directly through the atmosphere, and they are mostly longer-wavelength photons.

By then water molecules are also similarly small, so why would water look so different from the air? It is because water molecules are very densely packed, so their scatterings are coherent. In fact, the end result of such coherent scatterings by a collection of water molecules is that water appears specular.

The photopigments in a photoreceptor are very small in size compared to the wavelengths of visible light (each rhodopsin has a cross-section area of about $1 \times 10^{-2}\,nm^2$ (Milo and Phillips 2015, p. 144)), so they almost do not scatter lights at all, only absorption. That is why we could use microspectrophotometry (MSP) to measure a photoreceptor's (transverse) absorption rate (Sect. 3.1.2): MSP measures the amount of light transmitted through a photoreceptor, and if there is little scattering, then all the photons that are not measured must be absorbed by the photoreceptor.

Scattering in the small-particle regime is also called **Rayleigh scattering**, which, again, is *not* somehow a fundamentally different scattering process, and the Rayleigh scattering theory (worked out by Lord Rayleigh, who won the Nobel Prize in Physics in 1904) is nothing more than a special case of the Mie scattering theory; see Sharma (2003, Sect. 3.5.1) and Bohren and Clothiaux (2006, Sect. 3.2).

The phase function in the Rayleigh regime is proportional to $1 + \cos^2 \theta$, so the backward and forward scatterings are roughly equally probable. Taking the phase function into account, the scattering efficiency (in the form defined in Eq. 7.21) in Rayleigh scattering is proportional to:

$$Q_s \propto \left(\frac{r}{\lambda_m}\right)^4 \frac{m^2 - 1}{m^2 + 2}(1 + \cos^2 \theta). \tag{7.24}$$

Impact of Particle Size

When the particle size increases, the scattering efficiency increases, initially very quickly, but eventually saturates. In fact, the Mie theory predicts that when the particle size is much larger than the wavelength (e.g., more than 100 times larger), the scattering efficiency approaches a constant 2 regardless of m and λ_m (Johnsen 2012, Fig. 5.4).

The particle size also affects the phase function. As we have discussed above, small particles in the Rayleigh regime tend to scatter photons equally in the forward and backward directions, while large particles primarily scatter photons in the forward directions. The forward fraction increases as the particle size increases.

Consider the scenario in Fig. 7.1, where Material 1 sits on top of Material 2, and our goal is to hide Material 2 so that the color of Material 1 is dependent only on the illumination (not the property of Material 2). There is an interesting trade-off between scattering efficiency and scattering direction here. If we want Material 1 to hide Material 2, we want the particles in Material 1 to scatter a lot of light (high scattering efficiency) backwards. If the scattering efficiency is low (so photons march on and are hindered only by absorption) or the scattering is heavy in the forward directions, photons penetrate through Material 1 and reach Material 2, which would then contribute to the overall color.

Now, to scatter a lot of light, we need the particles to be large, but then the scattering will be mostly in the forward directions. So there exists a sweet spot of the particle size that provides the highest "hiding power" for a material per unit volume. If we work out the math, we will see that the sweet spot falls roughly in the visible wavelength range. That is why most paint pigments have a diameter between 100 nm and 1 μm (have a diameter between 2015). Of course, no matter how poor the hiding power is for a particular paint, if you apply enough of it, it will eventually hide whatever is behind it. Dye pigments are rather small in size (nm range), so they scatter few photons and that is why dye solutions look relatively transparent.

Impact of Refractive Index

Generally, the scattering efficiency increases with m at all particle sizes until when the particles are so large that the scattering efficiency becomes a constant. This is supported by Eq. (7.23a), too ($\frac{m^2-1}{m^2+2}$ monotonically increases and has a limit of 1).

For large particles, while m does not affect the scattering efficiency, it influences the scattering directions. When m is small, the scattering tends to be more forward, whereas when m is large, the scattering tends to be toward large angles (i.e., more photons will be back-scattered). This is why wet objects look darker (recall the unpleasant experience of accidentally spilling water on your pants). In dry paints, the medium surrounding the textile particles is air, and in wet paints it is water. m becomes smaller when the material is wet (i.e., the relative refractive-index difference becomes smaller between the textile particles and water), so most of the scattering will be forward, increasing the traversal length of photons and essentially giving photons more opportunities to be absorbed.

Aspherical Particles

What if the particle is not spherical? The Mie theory does not apply. Analytical or even numerical solutions to the Maxwell's equations would be difficult, so perhaps a better approach is just to parameterize a model and fit it with the experimental data.

One popular one-parameter parameterization of the phase function is the **Henyey–Greenstein** phase function; see Pharr et al. (2018, Sect. 11.3.1) and Bohren and Clothiaux (2006, Sect. 6.3.2), which takes the form:

$$p(\theta) = \frac{1}{4\pi} \frac{1 - g^2}{(1 + g^2 - 2g \cos\theta)^{3/2}}, \tag{7.25}$$

where g is the free parameter and is usually called the **asymmetry parameter**.

We hasten to emphasize that the Henyey–Greenstein function has absolutely zero physical meaning; it is designed for fitting experimental phase function data, so in the modern deep learning era, you might as well try a deep neural network.

7.4   Radiative Transfer Equation and Volume Rendering

So far we have assumed that a ray can only be attenuated, which can happen only when the illumination is collimated and we assume single scattering. Under this assumption, Eq. (7.13a) allows us to calculate any radiance in the medium (by weakening the initial radiance). General media are much more complicated: illumination can be from anywhere, and multiple scattering must be accounted for. As a result, external photons can be scattered into a ray of interest, as we have intuitively discussed in Sect. 7.3.1.

In the realm of geometric optics and radiometry, the general way to model lights going through a material/medium amounts to solving the so-called **Radiative Transfer Equation** (RTE), whose modern version was established by Chandrasekhar (1960), who won the Nobel Prize in physics in 1983 (not for the RTE). The RTE provides a mathematical way to express an arbitrary radiance in a medium.

7.4.1   Radiative Transfer Equation

The basic idea is to set up a differential equation to describe the (rate) of the radiance *change*. Given an incident radiance $L(p, \omega_s)$, we are interested in $L(p + \Delta s\omega_s, \omega_s)$, the radiance after the ray has gone a small distance Δs. The radiance can be:

- attenuated by the medium because of absorption;
- attenuated by the medium because photons are scattered out into other directions; this is called **out-scattering** in graphics;

- augmented by photons that are scattered into the ray direction from all other directions— because of multiple scattering[8]; this is called **in-scattering** in graphics;
- augmented because particles can emit photons.

The attenuation (reduction) of the radiance over Δs is:

$$- L(p, \omega_s)\sigma_t(p, \omega_s)\Delta s. \tag{7.26}$$

The radiance augmentation due to in-scattering is given by:

$$\int^{\Omega=4\pi} f_p(p, \omega_s, \omega_i)\sigma_s(p, \omega_s)\Delta s L(\omega_i)d\omega_i$$
$$= \sigma_s(p, \omega_s)\Delta s \int^{\Omega=4\pi} L(p, \omega_i)f_p(p, \omega_s, \omega_i)d\omega_i. \tag{7.27}$$

The way to interpret Eq. (7.30) is the following. $L(p, \omega_i)$ is the incident radiance from a direction ω_i, $L(p, \omega_i)d\omega_i$ is the irradiance received from $d\omega_i$, of which $\sigma_s(p, \omega_i)\Delta s L(p, \omega_s)$ $d\omega_i$ is the irradiance scattered in all directions after traveling a distance Δs. That portion of the scattered irradiance is multiplied by $f_p(\omega_s, \omega_i)$ to give us the radiance toward ω_s (see Eq. 7.20). We then integrate over the entire sphere, accounting for the fact that lights can come from anywhere over the space, to obtain the total augmented radiance toward ω_s.

If we consider emission, the total radiance augmentation is:

$$\sigma_a(p, \omega_s)\Delta s L_e(p, \omega_s) + \sigma_s(p, \omega_s)\Delta s \int^{\Omega=4\pi} L(p, \omega_i)f_p(p, \omega_s, \omega_i), d\omega_i. \tag{7.28}$$

where $L_e(p, \omega_s)$ is the emitted radiance at p toward ω_s, so the first term represents the total emission over Δs. If we let:

$$L_s(p, \omega_s) = \sigma_a(p, \omega_s)L_e(p, \omega_s) + \sigma_s(p, \omega_s) \int^{\Omega=4\pi} L(p, \omega_i)f_p(p, \omega_s, \omega_i)d\omega_i, \tag{7.29}$$

the total augmentation can be simplified to:

$$L_s(p, \omega_s)\Delta s, \tag{7.30}$$

where the L_s term is sometimes called the **source term** or **source function** in computer graphics, because it is the source of power at p.[9]

---

[8] Technically, even single scattering can lead to augmentation if there is illumination coming from anywhere outside the ray direction.

[9] Some definitions do not include emission in the source term, while in other definitions the source term is what is defined here divided by σ_t.

Combining Eqs. (7.26) and (7.30), the net radiance change is[10]:

$$\Delta L(p, \omega_s) = L(p + \Delta s \omega_s, \omega_s) - L(p, \omega_s) \tag{7.31a}$$
$$= -L(p, \omega_s)\sigma_t(p, \omega_s)\Delta s + L_s(p, \omega_s)\Delta s. \tag{7.31b}$$

As Δs approaches 0, we get (assuming ω_s is a unit vector as in Eqs. (7.12) and 7.13a):

$$\omega_s \cdot \nabla_p L(p, \omega_s) = \frac{dL(p, \omega_s)}{ds} = \lim_{\Delta s \to 0} \frac{L(p + \Delta s \omega_s, \omega_s) - L(p, \omega_s)}{\Delta s}$$
$$= -\sigma_t(p, \omega_s)L(p, \omega_s) + L_s(p, \omega_s), \tag{7.32}$$

where ∇_p denotes the gradient of L with respect to p, and $\omega_s \cdot \nabla_p$ denotes the directional derivative, which is used because technically p and ω_s are both defined in a three-dimensional space, so what we are really calculating is the rate of radiance change at p along ω_s.

Equation (7.32) is the RTE, which is an integro-differential equation, because it is a differential equation with an integral embedded. The RTE has an intuitive interpretation: if we think of radiance as the power of a ray, as a ray propagates, its power is attenuated by the medium but also augmented by "stray photons" from other rays. The latter is given by $L_s(p, \omega_s)$, which can be thought of as the augmentation of the radiance per unit length.

The RTE describes the rate of change of an arbitrary radiance $L(p, \omega_s)$. But our ultimate goal is to calculate the radiance itself? Generally the RTE has no analytical solution. There are two strategies to solve it. First, we can derive analytical solutions under certain certain assumptions and simplifications.

- For instance, the integral in Eq. (7.32) can be approximated by a summation along N directions; then we can turn Eq. (7.32) into a system of N differential equations to be solved. This is sometimes called the **N-flux theory**. We will omit a formal treatment but refer you to Bohren and Clothiaux (2006, Sect. 6.1), Volz and Simon (2001, Sect. 3.1.2), and Klein (2010, Sect. 5.5) for details. You might have heard of the famous Kubelka-Munk model (Kubelka and Munk 1931a, b; Kubelka 1948) widely used in modeling the color of pigment mixture; it is essentially a special case of the N-flux theory where $N = 2$.
- Another assumption people make is to assume that volume scattering is isotropic and can be approximated as a *diffusion* process. This is called the **diffusion approximation** (Ishimaru 1977; Ishimaru et al. 1978), which is widely used in both scientific modeling (Farrell et al. 1992; Eason et al. 1978; Schweiger et al. 1995; Boas et al. 2001) and in render-

---

[10] A subtlety you might have noticed is that not all the out-scattering of $L(p, \omega_s)$ attenuates the radiance; some of the scattering could be toward ω_s so should augment the radiance. This is not a concern since our augmentation term Eq. (7.30) integrates over the entire sphere, so it considers $L(p, \omega_s)$ again as part of in-scattering and accounts for the forward-scattered portion of $L(p, \omega_s)$.

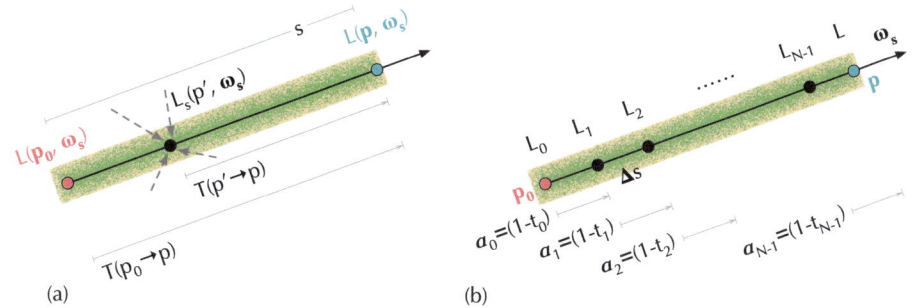

Fig. 7.6 a Illustration of the continuous VRE (Eq. 7.33). **b** Illustration of a discrete VRE (Eq. 7.35a), where the integral in the continuous VRE is replaced by a summation between p_0 and p at an interval of Δs; t_i is the total transmittance between p_i and p_{i+1}; L_i is a shorthand for $L_s(p_i, \omega_s)$, the source term of at p_i toward ω_s

ing (Stam 1995; Jensen et al. 2001; Dong et al. 2013, Chap. 7); see Bohren and Clothiaux (2006, Sect. 6.2) for a theoretical treatment.

The second approach deserves its own section.

7.4.2 Volume Rendering Equation

The second approach, which is particularly popular in computer graphics, is to first turn the RTE into a purely integral equation and then *numerically* (rather than analytically) estimate the integral using Monte Carlo integration, very similar to how the rendering equation is dealt with for surface scattering (Sect. 6.3).

The way to think of this is that in order to calculate any given radiance $L(p, \omega_s)$, we need to integrate all the changes along the direction ω_s up until p. Where do we start the integration? We can start anywhere. Figure 7.6a visualizes the integration process. Let's say we want to start from a point p_0, whose initial radiance toward ω_s is $L_0(p_0, \omega_s)$. Let $p = p_0 + s\omega_s$, where ω_s is a unit vector and s is the distance between p_0 and p. An arbitrary point p' between p_0 and p would then be $p' = p_0 + s'\omega_s$.[11]

Now we need to integrate from p_0 to p by running s' from 0 to s. Observe that the RTE is a form of a *non-homogeneous* linear differential equation, whose solution is firmly established in calculus. Without going through the derivations, its solution is:

---

[11] There are two alternative parameterizations, both of which are common in graphics literature. The first (Pharr et al. 2023) is to express $p_0 = p + s\omega_s$ (s being positive), but then the initial radiance would have to be expressed as $L(p_0, -\omega_s)$, since ω_s now points from p to p_0. The other is to express $p_0 = p - s\omega_s$ (s again being positive) (Fong et al. 2017); this avoids the need to switch directions but uses a negative sign. It is a matter of taste which one to use, but be alert to the different conventions.

$$L(p, \omega_s) = T(p_0 \to p)L_0(p_0, \omega_s) + \int_0^s T(p' \to p)L_s(p', \omega_s)\mathrm{d}s', \qquad (7.33)$$

where $T(p_0 \to p)$ is the transmittance between p_0 and p along ω_s, and $T(p' \to p)$ is the transmittance between p' and p along ω_s. Recall the definition of transmittance in Eq. (7.13b): it is the remaining fraction of the radiance after attenuation by the medium after traveling the distance between two points. In our case here:

$$T(p' \to p) = \frac{L(p + s\omega_s, \omega_s)}{L(p + s'\omega_s, \omega_s)} = e^{-\int_{s'}^s \sigma_t(p + t\omega, \omega)\mathrm{d}t}, \qquad (7.34a)$$

$$T(p_0 \to p) = \frac{L(p + s\omega_s, \omega_s)}{L(p, \omega_s)} = e^{-\int_0^s \sigma_t(p + t\omega, \omega)\mathrm{d}t}, \qquad (7.34b)$$

This integral equation in the graphics literature is called the **volume rendering equation** (VRE) or the **volumetric light transport equation**—the counterpart of the surface LTE (Sect. 6.3). Looking at the visualization in Fig. 7.6a, the VRE has an intuitive interpretation: the radiance at p along ω_s is the the contribution of p_0 plus and contribution of every single point between p_0 and p.

- The contribution of p_0 is given by its initial radiance L_0 weakened by the transmittance between p_0 and p;
- Why would a point p' between p_0 and p make any contribution? It is because of the source term (Eq. 7.29): p' might emit lights, and some of the in-scattered photons at p' will be scattered toward ω_s. The contribution of p' is thus given by the source term L_s weakened by the transmittance between p' and p.

The form of the VRE might appear to suggest that it is enough to accumulate along only the *direct* path between p_0 and p, which is surprising given that there are infinitely many scattering paths between p_0 and p (due to multiple scattering). For instance, it appears that we consider only the outgoing radiance toward ω_s from p_0, but p_0 might have outgoing radiances over other directions, which might eventually contribute to $L(p, \omega_s)$ through multiple scattering. Are we ignoring them?

The answer is that the VRE *implicitly* accounts for all the potential paths between p_0 and p because of the L_s term, which expands to Eq. (7.29). That is, every time we accumulate the contribution of a point between p_0 and p, we have to consider the in-scattering from all the directions at that point. Another way to interpret this is to observe that the radiance term L appears on both sides of the equation. Therefore, the VRE must be solved recursively by evaluating it everywhere in space.

Does this remind you of the rendering equation (Eq. 6.10)? Indeed, the VRE can be thought of as the volumetric counterpart of the rendering equation. Similarly, we can use Monte Carlo integration to estimate it, just like how the rendering equation is dealt with— with an extra complication: the VRE has two integrals: the outer integral runs from p_0 to p

and, for any intermediate point p', there is an inner integral that runs from p' to p to evaluate the transmittance $T(p' \to p)$. Therefore, we have to sample both integrands.

Similar to the situation of the rendering equation, sampling recursively would exponentially increase the number of rays to be tracked. Put it another way, since there are infinitely many paths from which a ray gains its energy due to multiple scattering, we have to integrate infinitely many paths. Again, a common solution is path tracing, for which (Pharr et al. (2023), Sect. 14) is a great reference.

A simplification that is commonly used is to assume that there is only single scattering directly from the light source. In this way, the L_s term does not have to integrate infinitely many incident rays over the sphere but only a fixed amount of rays emitted from the light source *non-recursively*. This strategy is sometimes called **local illumination** in volume rendering, as opposed to **global illumination**, where one needs to consider all the possible paths of light transport. The distinction is similar to that in modeling surface scattering (Sect. 6.3).

7.4.3 Discrete VRE and Scientific Volume Visualization

Sometimes the VRE takes the following discrete form:

$$L = \sum_{i=0}^{N-1} \left(L_i \Delta s \prod_{j=i+1}^{N-1} t_j \right) \tag{7.35a}$$

$$= \sum_{i=0}^{N-1} \left(L_i \Delta s \prod_{j=i+1}^{N-1} (1 - \alpha_j) \right) \tag{7.35b}$$

$$= L_{N-1}\Delta s + L_{N-2}\Delta s(1 - \alpha_{N-1}) + L_{N-3}\Delta s(1 - \alpha_{N-1})(1 - \alpha_{N-2}) + \cdots$$

$$+ L_1 \Delta s \prod_{j=2}^{N-1}(1 - \alpha_j) + L_0 \Delta s \prod_{j=1}^{N-1}(1 - \alpha_j). \tag{7.35c}$$

Equation (7.35a) looks very much like Eq. (7.33): the former turns the two integrals in the latter, both the outer integral and the inner one carried by $T(\cdot)$, to discrete summations using the Riemann sum over N discrete points along the ray between p_0 and p at an interval of $\Delta s = \frac{s}{N}$.

The notations are slightly different; Fig. 7.6b visualizes how this discrete VRE is expressed with the new notations.

- L is $L(p, \omega_s)$, the quantity to be calculated;
- L_i is a shorthand for $L_s(p_i, \omega_s)$, i.e., the source term (Eq. 7.29) for the ith point between p_0 and p toward ω_s; by definition, p_0 is the 0th point (so L_0 is the initial radiance $L_0(p_0, \omega_s)$ in Eq. 7.33) and p is the Nth point;

- t_i represents the total transmittance between the ith and the $(i+1)$th point and is given by $e^{-\sigma_t(p_i,\omega_s)\Delta s}$ (notice the integral in continuous transmittance Eq. (7.13b) is gone, because we assume the transmittance between to adjacent points is a constant in the Reimann sum);
- α_i is the **opacity** between the ith and the $(i+1)$th point, which is defined as the residual of the transmittance between the two points: $1 - t_i$.

See Max (1995, Sect. 4) or Kaufman and Mueller (2003, Sect. 6.1) for a relatively straight-forward derivation, but hopefully this form of the VRE is equally intuitive to interpret from Fig. 7.6b. It is nothing more than accumulating the contribution of each point[12] along the ray, but now we also need to accumulate the attenuation along the way just because of how opacity is defined by convention (per step), hence the product of a sequence of the opacity residuals.

This way of computing the VRE is usually used in the scientific visualization literature, where people are interested in visualizing data obtained from, e.g., computer tomography (CT) scans or magnetic resonance imaging (MRI). There, it is the relative color that people usually care about, not the physical quantity such as the radiance, so people sometimes lump $L_i \Delta s$ together as C_i and call it the "color" of the ith point. The VRE is then written as:

$$C = \sum_{i=0}^{N-1} \left(C_i \prod_{j=i+1}^{N-1} (1 - \alpha_j) \right). \tag{7.36}$$

The C terms are defined in a three-dimensional RGB space, and Eq. (7.36) is evaluated for the three channels separately, similar to how Eqs. (7.35a) and (7.33) are meant to be evaluated for each wavelength independently. Since color is a linear projection from the spectral radiance, the so-calculated C (all three channels) is indeed proportional to the true color, although in visualization one usually does not care about the true colors anyway (Sect. 7.4.3).

This formulation is also called the *back-to-front* compositing formula in volume render-ing, since it starts from p_0, the farthest point on the ray to p. We can easily turn the order around to start from p and end at p_0 in a *front-to-back* fashion (C_{N-1} now corresponds to p_0):

$$C = \sum_{i=0}^{N-1} \left(C_i \prod_{j=0}^{i-1} t_j \right). \tag{7.37}$$

While theoretically equivalent, the latter is better in practice because it allows us to opportunistically terminate the integration early when, for instance, the accumulated opacity is high enough (transmittance is low enough), at which point integrating further makes little numerical contribution to the result.

---

[12] Technically the contribution of each small segment between two discrete points because of the Reimann sum.

Another Discrete Form of VRE

A perhaps more common way to express the discrete VRE is to approximate the average transmittance t using the first two terms of its Taylor series expansion and further assume that the medium has a low albedo, i.e., $\sigma_t \approx \sigma_a$ and $\sigma_s \approx 0$ (that is, the medium emits and absorbs *only*); we have:

$$1 - \alpha_i = t_i = t(p_i \rightarrow p_{i+1})$$

$$= e^{-\sigma_t(p_i,\omega_s)\Delta s} = 1 - \sigma_t(p_i, \omega_s)\Delta s + \frac{(\sigma_t(p_i, \omega_s)\Delta s)^2}{2} - \cdots \quad (7.38a)$$

$$\approx 1 - \sigma_t(p_i, \omega_s)\Delta s \quad (7.38b)$$

$$\approx 1 - \sigma_a(p_i, \omega_s)\Delta s. \quad (7.38c)$$

$$\Rightarrow \alpha_i \approx \sigma_a(p_i, \omega_s)\Delta s. \quad (7.38d)$$

Now, observe that the L_i term in Eq. (7.35a) is the source term in Eq. (7.29), which under the low albedo assumption has only the emission term, so:

$$L = \sum_{i=0}^{N-1} \left(L_i \Delta s \prod_{j=i+1}^{N-1} (1 - \alpha_j) \right) \quad (7.39a)$$

$$= \sum_{i=0}^{N-1} \left(\sigma_a(p_i, \omega_s) L_e(p_i, \omega_s)\Delta s \prod_{j=i+1}^{N-1} (1 - \alpha_j) \right), \quad (7.39b)$$

$$= \sum_{i=0}^{N-1} \left(L_e(p_i, \omega_s)\alpha_i \prod_{j=i+1}^{N-1} (1 - \alpha_j) \right). \quad (7.39c)$$

If we let $C_i = L_e(p_i, \omega_s)$, the discrete VRE is then expressed as Levoy (1988):

$$C = \sum_{i=0}^{N-1} \left(C_i \alpha_i \prod_{j=i+1}^{N-1} (1 - \alpha_j) \right). \quad (7.40)$$

This can be interpreted as a form of **alpha blending** (Smith 1995), a typical trick in graphics to render transparent materials. It makes sense for our discrete VRE to reduce to alpha blending: our derivation assumes that the volume does not scatter lights, so translucent materials become transparent.

Again, Eq. (7.40) is the back-to-front equation, and the front-to-back counterpart looks like:

$$C = \sum_{i=0}^{N-1} \left(C_i \alpha_i \prod_{j=0}^{i-1} t_j \right). \quad (7.41)$$

If you compare the two discrete forms in Eqs. (7.36) and (7.40), it would appear that the two are not mutually consistent! Of course we know why: (1) Eq. (7.40) applies two further approximations (low albedo and Taylor series expansion) *and* (2) the two C terms in the two equations refer to different physical quantities (compare Eqs. 7.35b with 7.39c).

The Second Form Is More Flexible

What is the benefit of this new discrete form, comparing Eqs. (7.37) and (7.41)? Both equations can be interpreted as a form of weighted sum, where C_i is weighted by a weight w_i, which is $\prod_{j=0}^{i-1} t_j$ in the first case and $\alpha_i \prod_{j=0}^{i-1} t_j$ in the second case. The most obvious difference is that the weights in the first case are correlated but less so in the second case. The weights are strictly decreasing as i increases in the first case, since $t_i < 1$.

In the second case, the weights are technically independent. One way to understand this is to observe, in the second case, that $w_0 = \alpha_0$ and $w_{i+1} = w_i \frac{\alpha_{i+1}(1-\alpha_i)}{\alpha_i}$, so there is generally a unique assignment of the α values for a given weight combination. This "flexibility" will come in handy when we can manually assign (Sect. 7.4.3) or learn the weights (Sect. 7.4.4). Note, however, that if we impose the constraint that $\alpha \in [0, 1]$, we are effectively constraining the weights too.

Visualization Is Not (Necessarily) Physically-Based Rendering!

These discrete VRE forms might give you the false impression that we have avoided the need to integrate infinitely many paths, because, computationally, the evaluation of the VRE comes down to a *single-path* summation along the ray trajectory. Not really. Calculating the C_i terms in the new formulations still requires recursion if the results are meant to be physically accurate. Of course we can sidestep this by, e.g., applying the local-illumination approximation, as mentioned before, to avoid recursion.

Scientific visualization offers another opportunity: we can simply *assign* values to the Cs and even the αs without regard to physics. The goal of visualization is to discover/highlight interesting objects and structures while de-emphasizing things that are irrelevant. So the actual colors are not as important, which gives us great latitude to determine VRE parameters.

Figure 7.7 compares volume-rendered images for scientific visualization (a) and for photorealistic rendering (b). In the case of visualization, the data were from CT scans. In both scans, the outer surface is not transparent but is rendered so just because we are interested in seeing the inner structures that are otherwise occluded. The user makes an executive call to assign a very low transparency to the bones in the knee model 0 but a very high transparency value to the skin and other tissues: this is not physically accurate but a good choice for this particular visualization. Photorealistic rendering, in contrast, has to be physically based and does not usually have this flexibility. See figures in Wrenninge and Bin Zafar (2011) and Fong et al. (2017) for more examples.

There is volume rendering software that would allow the users to make such an assignment depending on what the user wants to highlight and visualize. With certain constraints and

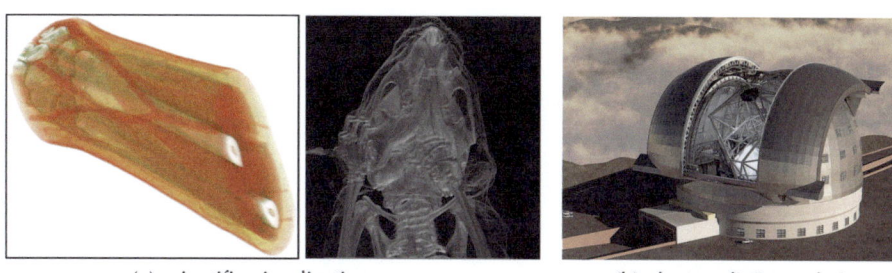

(a) scientific visualization   (b) photorealistic rendering

Fig. 7.7 Comparing visualization and rendering. **a** Two examples of scientific visualization (of CT data) using volume rendering; from MathiasRav (2009), Sjschen (2025). **b** Photorealistic volume rendering; adapted from Gnash (2017)

heuristics, one can also procedurally assign the α and C values from the raw measurement data, usually a density field (see below) acquired from whatever measurement device is used (e.g., CT scanners or MRI machines), using what is called the *transfer functions* in the literature.[13] Making an assignment usually is tied to a *classification* problem: voxels/points of different classes should have different assignments.

Density Fields

Physically speaking, the medium in RTE/VRE is parameterized by its absorption and scattering coefficients, which are a product of cross section and concentration, which is sometimes also called the density. In physically-based volume rendering, this is indeed how the density is used from the very beginning (Kajiya and Von Herzen 1984; Blinn 1982).

In visualization where being physically accurate or photorealistic is unimportant, the notion of an attenuation coefficient[14] loses its physical meaning; it is just a number that controls how the brightness of a point weakens. People simply call the attenuation coefficient the density (Kaufman and Mueller 2003), presumably because, intuitively, if the particle density is high the color should be dimmer. If you want to be pedantic, you might say that the attenuation coefficient depends not only on the density/concentration but also on the cross section (Eq. 7.2b), so how can we do that? Remember in visualization one gets to make an executive call and *assign* the density value (and thus control α), so it does not really matter if the value itself means the physical quantity of density/concentration. This is apparent in early work that uses volume rendering for scientific visualization (Sabella 1988; Williams and Max 1992), where attenuation coefficients are nowhere to be found.

---

[13] Some (color) transfer functions could have physical underpinnings, such as applying a single-scattering shading algorithms (i.e., local illumination); see, e.g., Levoy (1988, Sect. 3) or Max (1995, Sect. 5), but the goal there is not to precisely model physics but for better, subjective visualization.

[14] Which is the only coefficient needed and which participates in calculating α (Eq. 7.36).

For this reason, the raw volume data obtained from raw measurement device for scientific (medical) visualization are most often called the density field, even though what is being measured is almost certainly not the density field but a field of optical properties that are related to, but certainly do not equate, density. For instance, the raw data you get from a CT scanner is actually a grid of attenuation coefficients (Bharath 2009, Chap. 3).

7.4.4   Discrete VRE in (Neural) Radiance-Field Rendering

There is another field where the discrete VRE (especially our second form Eq. 7.40) is becoming incredibly popular: (neural) radiance-field rendering. The two most representative examples are NeRF (Mildenhall et al. 2021) and 3DGS (Kerbl et al. 2023). They are fundamentally image-based rendering or light-field rendering (Sect. 5.3.7), where they sample the light field of the scene by taking a set of images at different camera poses and learn to reconstruct the underlying light field, from which they can then re-sample a new camera pose and, thus, render the corresponding image as if it was taken at that new camera pose. This is re-branded in the modern era as "novel view synthesis".

We will assume that you have read the two papers above so that we can focus on interpreting these radiance-field methods within the fundamental framework of physically-based rendering. Such a re-interpretation would allow us to better understand where these methods come from, how they have introduced new tweaks to physically-based rendering, and what their limitations might be.

The first thing to notice is that NeRF and 3DGS, being essentially a sampling and reconstruction method, use the discrete form of the VRE (mostly Eq. 7.40) as the reconstruction function. This means they assume that the radiance is calculated by a single-path summation along the ray trajectory without the need for path tracing and solving the actual RTE/VRE. The reason they can reduce infinite paths to a single-path evaluation is very similar to that in scientific visualization, except now instead of assigning the "color" values C and opacity values α (or equivalently the density field as discussed above), they train a neural network to directly learn these values.

VRE for Surface Rendering?

It is interesting to observe that both NeRF and 3DGS (and the vast majority of their later developments) use the discrete VRE form in Eq. (7.40) as their forward model and can evidently do a very good job at rendering opaque surfaces. Is this surprising? Isn't Eq. (7.40) designed to render transparent materials/volumes (alpha blending)?

For opaque surfaces, the "ground truth" is the surface rendering equation (Sect. 6.3), which can be seen as a form of weighted sum, where the BRDF $f_r(p, \omega_s, \omega_i)$ weighs the incident light irradiance $L(p, \omega_i) \cos \theta_i d\omega_i$. In theory, the weights are independent of each other: the value of $f_r(p, \omega_s, \omega_i)$ at different ω_i can technically be completely uncorrelated.

But in reality they are most likely somewhat correlated for real materials: the appearance of a material does not change dramatically when the incident light direction changes slightly. For volumes/translucent materials, the "ground truth" is the VRE, which you could also say is a weighted sum, although the weights are constrained if the α values are constrained (e.g., between 0 and 1), which is the case in NeRF and 3DGS training (Sect. 7.4.3).

So effectively, when rendering opaque surfaces, we are using a form of (theoretically) constrained weighted sum to approximate another (practically) constrained weighted sum, and we hope that we can learn the approximation from a large amount of offline samples. The learned parameters (color and opacity of each point) should not be interpreted literally in the physical sense. One advantage of this parameterization is that it *could* be used to render volumes or translucent materials if needed, where the ground truth *is* VRE, in which case the learned parameters might be more amenable to physical interpretations.

Volume Graphics Versus Point-Based Graphics

Related to volume graphics, there is also a subtly different branch of graphics called **point-based graphics** (PBG) (Levoy and Whitted 1985; Gross and Pfister 2011). The boundary is somewhat blurred, but given the way the two terms are usually used, we can observe a few similarities and distinctions. Both volume graphics and PBG use discrete points as the rendering primitives (as opposed to continuous surfaces such as a mesh), although the input points in volume graphics are usually placed on uniform grids (Engel et al. 2006, Sect. 1.5.2) whereas points in PBG can be spatially arbitrary.

Traditionally, PBG is almost exclusively used for photorealistic rendering of surfaces. In fact, the points used in PBG are usually acquired as samples on continuous surfaces (Gross and Pfister 2011, Chap. 3). PBG usually uses object-order rendering through splatting, although ray casting is used too, but RTE/VRE is not involved in the rendering process (Gross and Pfister 2011, Chap. 6).

In contrast, the use of volume graphics is much broader. Volume rendering can be used for photorealistic rendering of participating media and translucent surfaces (by solving the RTE/VRE), or it can be used for non-photorealistic data visualization (by evaluating the single-path, discrete VRE), at which point whether the object to be rendered is called a participating medium, a translucent surface, or anything else is irrelevant, because visualization does not care much about being physically accurate.

3DGS is a somewhat interesting case. It is largely a form of PBG because the rendering primitives are unaligned surface samples, and its splatting technique (which we will discuss shortly) resembles that developed in the PBG literature (Gross and Pfister 2011, Sect. 6.1). However, 3DGS does use the discrete VRE as the forward model. Again, as discussed just above, VRE is just a way for 3DGS to parameterize its forward mode, so the comparison with traditional volume graphics and PBG should not be taken literally.

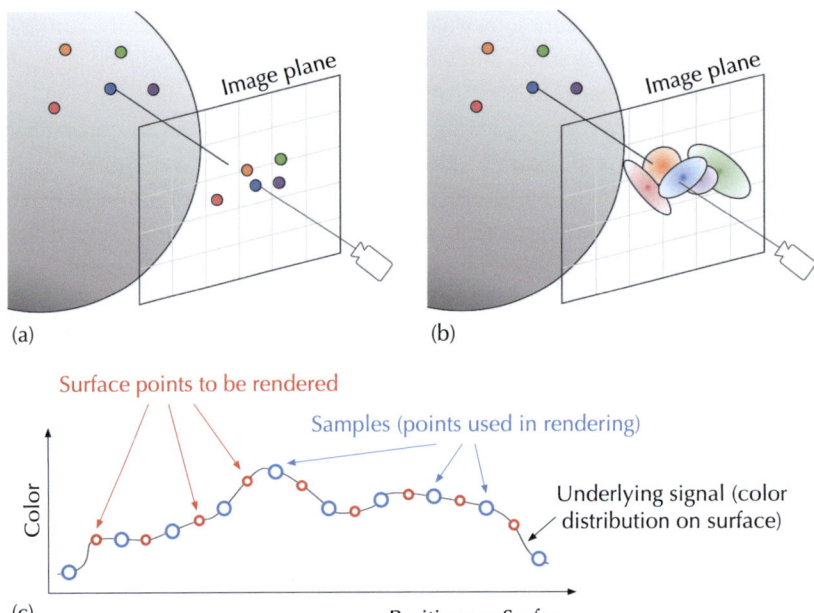

(a)   (b)

(c)   Position on Surface

Fig. 7.8 a Directly projecting discrete points to the image plane would create holes in the rendered image. **b** In splatting, each point is associated with a splat or a footprint function, which can distribute the color of the point to a spatial region on the image plane; **c** Splatting essentially allows signal interpolation, which amounts to first reconstructing the underlying signal from the samples (with potential anti-aliasing filtering) followed by re-sampling at new, desired positions

Splatting Is Signal Filtering

Splatting, initially proposed by Westover (1990) for visualizing volume data, is a common rendering technique used in PBG and 3DGS-family models. We discuss what splatting is, why it works, and how it is used in NeRF and 3DGS. We start by asking: how can we render continuous surfaces from discrete points? If we directly project the points to the sensor plane, we obviously will get holes, as shown in Fig. 7.8a. This is, of course, not an issue if the rendering primitives are meshes (or procedurally-generated surfaces).

The key is to realize that "meshless" does not mean surfaceless: the fact that we do not have a mesh as the rendering primitives does not mean the surface does not exist. Recall that the points used by PBG are actually samples on the surface. To render an image pixel is essentially to estimate the color of a surface point that projects to the pixel (ignoring supersampling for now). From a signal processing perspective, this is a classic problem of signal filtering: reconstruction and resampling.

That is, ideally what we need to do is to reconstruct the underlying signal, i.e., the color distribution of the continuous surface[15] (combined with an anti-aliasing pre-filter[16]) and then resample the reconstructed/filtered signal at positions corresponding to pixels in an image. This is shown in Fig. 7.8c. The name of the game is to design proper filters. The issue of signal sampling, reconstruction, and resampling is absolutely fundamental to all forms of photorealistic rendering and not limited to PBG; Pharr et al. (2023, Chap. 8) and Glassner (1995, Unit II) are great references.

Another way to think of this is that the color of a surface point is very likely related to its nearby points that have been sampled as part of the rendering input, so one straightforward thing to do is to interpolate from those samples to calculate colors of new surface points. Signal interpolation is essentially signal filtering/convolution.

There is one catch. In classic signal sampling theories (think of the Nyquist-Shannon sampling theorem), samples are uniformly taken and, as a result, we can use a single reconstruction filter. But in PBG the surface samples are non-uniformly taken, so a single reconstruction filter would not work. Instead, we need a different filter for each point. The filter in the PBG parlance is called a *splat*, or a *footprint function*; it is associated with each point (surface sample) and essentially distributes the point color to a local region, enabling signal interpolation. This is shown in Fig. 7.8b. The exact forms of the footprint functions would determine the exact forms of the signal filters. Gaussian filters are particularly common, and Gaussian splatting is a splatting method that uses Gaussian filters (Greene and Heckbert 1986; Heckbert 1989; Zwicker et al. 2001b).

From a 3D modeling perspective, instead of having a continuous mesh, the scene is now represented by a set of discrete points, each of which is represented by a 2D Gaussian distribution, which is called a surface element or a surfel (Pfister et al. 2000). Each surfel is then projected to the screen space to generate a splat as the corresponding reconstruction kernel of that surface point; the reconstruction kernel, after projection, is another Gaussian filter (which can be cascaded with an anti-aliasing pre-filter). The color of each screen space point is then calculated by summing over all the splats (each of which is, of course, scaled by the color of the sample), essentially taking a weighted sum of the colors of the neighboring surface samples (see Zwicker et al. (2001b, Fig. 3) for a visualization) or, in signal processing parlance, resampling the reconstructed signal with the reconstruction kernels.

This rendering process is traditionally called surface splatting (Zwicker et al. 2001b). Yifan et al. (2019) is an early attempt to learn the surfels through a differential surface splatting process. Surface splatting is a reasonable rendering model in PBG: the "ground truth" in rendering surfaces is the rendering equation, which can also be interpreted as a weighted sum.

---

[15] Assuming a diffuse surface so we care to reconstruct the color of each point, not the radiance of each ray.

[16] The compound filter combining reconstruction and anti-aliasing filters is sometimes also called a resampling filter, because the compound filter is used during resampling to calculate the new sample values.

One can also apply the same splatting idea to volume rendering. In this case, each point in the scene is represented by a 3D Gaussian distribution, which is projected to a 2D splat in the screen space. The color of a pixel is then calculated through, critically, alpha blending the corresponding splats, not weighted sum. This is called volume splatting (Zwicker et al. 2001a). 3DGS can be seen as a differential variant of traditional volume splatting, even though it is also very effective in rendering opaque surfaces (and we have discussed the reason on Sect. 7.4.4).

7.4.5   Integrating Surface Scattering with Volume Scattering

The rendering equation governs the surface scattering or light transport in space, and the RTE/VRE governs the volume/subsurface scattering or light transport in a medium. Both processes can be involved in a real-life scene. For instance, the appearance of a translucent material like a paint or a wax is a combination of both forms of scattering/light transport (Fig. 7.1). Another example would be rendering smoke against a wall.

Conceptually nothing new needs to be introduced to deal with the two forms of light transport together. Say we have an opaque surface (a wall) located with a volume (smoke) in the scene. If we want to calculate the radiance of a ray leaving a point on the wall, we would evaluate the rendering equation there, and for each incident ray, we might have to evaluate the VRE since that ray might come from the volume. In practice it amounts to extending the path tracing algorithm to account for the fact that a path might go through a volume and bounce off between surface points. See Pharr et al. (2023, Sect. 14.2) and Fong et al. (2017, Sect. 3) for detailed discussions.

Another approach, which is perhaps more common when dealing with translucent materials (whose appearance, of course, depends on both the surface and subsurface scattering), is through a phenomenological model based on the notion of Bidirectional Scattering Surface Reflectance Distribution Function (**BSSRDF**) (Nicodemus et al. 1977). The BSSRDF is parameterized as $f_s(p_s, \omega_s, p_i, \omega_i)$, describing the infinitesimal outgoing radiance at p_s toward ω_s given the infinitesimal power incident on p_i from the direction ω_i:

$$f_s(p_s, \omega_s, p_i, \omega_i) = \frac{\mathrm{d}L(p_s, \omega_s)}{\mathrm{d}\Phi(p_i, \omega_i)}. \tag{7.42}$$

BSSRDF can be seen as an extension of BRDF in that it considers the possibility that the radiance of a ray leaving p_s could be influenced by a ray incident on another point p_i due to SSS/volume scattering. Given the BSSRDF, the rendering equation can be generalized to:

$$L(p_o, \omega_s) = \int^A \int^{\Omega=2\pi} f_s(p_s, \omega_s, p_i, \omega_i) L(p_i, \omega_i) \cos\theta_i \, \mathrm{d}\omega_i \, \mathrm{d}A, \tag{7.43}$$

where $L(p_o, \omega_s)$ is the outgoing radiance at p_o toward ω_s, $L(p_i, \omega_i)$ is the incident radiance at p_i from ω_i, A in the outer integral is the surface area that is under illumination, and $\Omega = 2\pi$ means that each surface point receives illumination from the entire hemisphere.

We can again use path tracing and Monte Carlo integration to evaluate Eq. (7.43) if we know the BSSRDF, which can, again, either be analytically derived given certain constraints and assumptions or measured (Frisvad et al. 2020). To analytically derive it, one has to consider the fact that the transfer of energy from an incident ray to an outgoing ray is the consequence of a cascade of three factors: two surface scattering (refraction) factors, one entering the material surface p_i from ω_i and the other leaving the material surface at p_i toward p_o, and a volume scattering factor that accounts for the subsurface scattering between the incident ray at p_i and the exiting ray at p_o (Pharr et al. 2018, Sect. 11.4). If all three factors have an analytical form, the final BSSRDF has an analytical form too. This is the approach that, for instance, Jensen et al. (2001) takes.

References

Bharath A (2009) Introductory medical imaging. Morgan & Claypool

Blinn JF (1982) Light reflection functions for simulation of clouds and dusty surfaces. ACM SIG-GRAPH Comput Graph 16(3):21–29

Boas DA, Brooks DH, Miller EL, DiMarzio CA, Kilmer M, Gaudette RJ, Zhang Q (2001) Imaging the body with diffuse optical tomography. IEEE Signal Process Mag 18(6):57–75

Bohren CF, Clothiaux EE (2006) Fundamentals of atmospheric radiation: an introduction with 400 problems. Wiley

Bowmaker JK, Dartnall H (1980) Visual pigments of rods and cones in a human retina. J Physiol 298(1):501–511

Chandrasekhar S (1960) Radiative transfer. Courier Corporation

Dong Y, Lin S, Guo B, et al. (2013) Material appearance modeling: a data-coherent approach. Springer

Eason G, Veitch A, Nisbet R, Turnbull F (1978) The theory of the back-scattering of light by blood. J Phys D: Appl Phys 11(10):1463

Engel K, Hadwiger M, Kniss JM, Rezk-Salama C, Weiskopf D (2006) Real-time volume graphics. A K Peters, Ltd

Farrell TJ, Patterson MS, Wilson B (1992) A diffusion theory model of spatially resolved, steady-state diffuse reflectance for the noninvasive determination of tissue optical properties in vivo. Med Phys 19(4):879–888

Fong J, Wrenninge M, Kulla C, Habel R (2017) Production volume rendering: Siggraph 2017 course. In: ACM SIGGRAPH 2017 courses, pp 1–97

Frisvad JR, Jensen SA, Madsen JS, Correia A, Yang L, Gregersen SKS, Meuret Y, Hansen PE (2020) Survey of models for acquiring the optical properties of translucent materials. Comput Graph Forum. Wiley Online Library 39:729–755

Glassner AS (1995) Principles of digital image synthesis. Elsevier

Gnash (2017) Rendering of the extremely large telescope from 2009; CC BY-SA 4.0 license. https://commons.wikimedia.org/wiki/File:Latest_Rendering_of_the_E-ELT.jpg

Greene N, Heckbert PS (1986) Creating raster omnimax images from multiple perspective views using the elliptical weighted average filter. IEEE Comput Graph Appl 6(6):21–27

Gross M, Pfister H (2011) Point-based graphics. Elsevier

Heckbert PS (1989) Fundamentals of texture mapping and image warping. master's thesis. University of California, Berkeley

Ishimaru A et al (1978) Wave propagation and scattering in random media, vol 2. Academic Press, New York

Ishimaru A (1977) Theory and application of wave propagation and scattering in random media. Proc IEEE 65(7):1030–1061

Jensen HW, Marschner SR, Levoy M, Hanrahan P (2001) A practical model for subsurface light transport. In: ACM SIGGRAPH computer graphics, pp 511–518

Johnsen S (2012) The optics of life: a biologist's guide to light in nature. Princeton University Press

Jones K (2005) The sand/dust from the harmattan coming from the Sahara gives the Nigeria's National Mosque in Abuja, a nice glow; CC BY-SA 2.0 license. https://commons.wikimedia.org/wiki/File: MosqueinAbuja.jpg

Kajiya JT, Von Herzen BP (1984) Ray tracing volume densities. ACM SIGGRAPH Comput Graph 18(3):165–174

Kaufman A, Mueller K (2003) Volume visualization and, volume graphics. Technical Report, Stony Brook University

Kerbl B, Kopanas G, Leimkühler T, Drettakis G (2023) 3D Gaussian splatting for real-time radiance field rendering. ACM Trans Graph 42(4), Article ID 139, pp 1–14

Klein G (2010) Industrial color physics

Kubelka P (1948) New contributions to the optics of intensely light-scattering materials. Part I. Josa 38(5):448–457

Kubelka P, Munk F (1931a) An article on optics of paint layers (translated by SH Westin). Z Tech Phys 12(593–601):259–274

Kubelka P, Munk F (1931b) Ein beitrag zur optik der farbanstriche. Z tech Phys 12:593–601

Levoy M (1988) Display of surfaces from volume data. IEEE Comput Graph Appl 8(3):29–37

Levoy M, Whitted T (1985) The use of points as a display primitive. Technical Report, University of North Carolina at Chapel Hill

MacEvoy B (2015) The material attributes of paints. https://www.handprint.com/HP/WCL/pigmt3.html#particlesize

MathiasRav (2009) Volume rendering of a mouse skull (CT) using shear warp algorithm; CC BY-SA 3.0 license. https://en.wikipedia.org/wiki/File:VolRenderShearWarp.gif

Max N (1995) Optical models for direct volume rendering. IEEE transactions on visualization and computer graphics 1(2):99–108

Mayerhöfer TG, Pahlow S, Popp J (2020) The bouguer-beer-lambert law: shining light on the obscure. ChemPhysChem 21(18):2029–2046

Melbourne WG (2004) Radio occultations using earth satellites: a wave theory treatment, 1st edn. Wiley

Mildenhall B, Srinivasan PP, Tancik M, Barron JT, Ramamoorthi R, Ng R (2021) Nerf: representing scenes as neural radiance fields for view synthesis. Commun ACM 65(1):99–106

Milo R, Phillips R (2015) Cell biology by the numbers. Garland Science

Nicodemus F, Richmond J, Hsia J, Ginsberg I, Limperis T (1977) Geometrical considerations and nomenclature for reflectance, vol 160. US Department of Commerce, National Bureau of Standards Washington, DC, USA

Pfister H, Zwicker M, Van Baar J, Gross M (2000) Surfels: surface elements as rendering primitives. In: Proceedings of the 27th annual conference on computer graphics and interactive techniques, pp 335–342

Pharr M, Jakob W, Humphreys G (2018) Physically based rendering: from theory to implementation, 3rd edn. MIT Press

Pharr M, Jakob W, Humphreys G (2023) Physically based rendering: from theory to implementation, 4th edn. MIT Press

Sabella P (1988) A rendering algorithm for visualizing 3D scalar fields. ACM SIGGRAPH Comput Graph 22(4):51–58

Schweiger M, Arridge S, Hiraoka M, Delpy D (1995) The finite element method for the propagation of light in scattering media: boundary and source conditions. Med Phys 22(11):1779–1792

Sharma G (2003) Color fundamentals for digital imaging. In: Sharma G (ed) Digital color imaging handbook. CRC Press, pp 14–127

Sjschen (2025) Volume rendered CT scan of a forearm with different color schemes for muscle, fat, bone, and blood; released into the public domain by the copyright holder. https://commons.wikimedia.org/wiki/File:CTWristImage.png

Smith AR (1995) Alpha and the history of digital compositing. Technical report, Citeseer

Stam J (1995) Multiple scattering as a diffusion process. In: Rendering techniques'95: proceedings of the Eurographics workshop in Dublin, Ireland, June 12–14, 1995, vol 6. Springer, pp 41–50

Volz HG, Simon FT (2001) Industrial color testing, vol 2. Wiley-VCH New York

Westover L (1990) Footprint evaluation for volume rendering. In: Proceedings of the 17th annual conference on Computer graphics and interactive techniques, pp 367–376

Williams PL, Max N (1992) A volume density optical model. In: Proceedings of the 1992 workshop on volume visualization, pp 61–68

Wrenninge M, Bin Zafar N (2011) Production volume rendering: Siggraph 2011 course. In: ACM SIGGRAPH 2011 courses, pp 1–71

Yifan W, Serena F, Wu S, Öztireli C, Sorkine-Hornung O (2019) Differentiable surface splatting for point-based geometry processing. ACM Trans Graph (TOG) 38(6):1–14

Zwicker M, Pfister H, Van Baar J, Gross M (2001a) EWA volume splatting. In: Proceedings visualization, VIS'01. IEEE, pp 29–538

Zwicker M, Pfister H, Van Baar J, Gross M (2001b) Surface splatting. In: Proceedings of the 28th annual conference on Computer graphics and interactive techniques, pp 371–378

Part III
Imaging

Part III of the book will discuss imaging, the transduction of optical signals to electrical systems. Our discussion will center on the two fundamental components of any imaging system: optics and the image sensor. We begin with an overview of optics in imaging systems, covering core concepts such as the pinhole model, lenses, aberrations, and diffraction limits. We also explain key photographic concepts, including depth of field, magnification, and field of view, and introduce computational models of imaging through the lens of linear system theory. We then turn to image sensors, examining the basic principles by which optical signals are converted to electrical charges and then to digital values. We will introduce hardware implementations of these processes for both monochromatic and color sensing. Finally, we will discuss how the raw sensor signals are processed to yield images that can be consumed by human or machine vision systems.

Imaging Optics

8

8.1   Overview

This chapter focuses on the first stage in an imaging system: the optics, i.e., optics that are used for image formation. The goal of this chapter is to build a good understanding of the image formation process in optics. Optics manipulates/transforms optical signals, so the signal after optics is still in the optical domain. In later chapters, we will discuss how the optical signals are transformed into electrical signals (first to analog and then to digital signals) and how such electrical signals are further processed.

Imaging optics is important for human vision (because the ocular media of our eyes form an image on the retina), cameras (almost all of which have some form of optics), and graphics (where modeling optics is important for photorealistic rendering). Optics can also be used for ostensibly non-imaging purposes such as communication and computation. But of course the distinction is not black and white. You can argue that imaging is simultaneous communication (transferring signals from one side of the imaging system to the other side) and computation (the output signal is the result of a transfer function, usually not an identity function, applied to the input signal).

We will generally assume that the goal of the optics design is to form visually pleasing images as well as possible. The thinking is that if we provide a high-quality image, we are giving the downstream consumer, whether a human observer or a machine vision algorithm, the best chance to extract information from it.

This might not always be necessary. For instance, in machine vision/robotics applications, the consumer of an image is a computer vision algorithm such as object detection; so long as the algorithm can detect the object, the quality of the image itself is of no significance. In fact, one might argue that it is beneficial to design the imaging system so that the output image is obfuscated to protect privacy as long as essential features pertaining to downstream algorithms are preserved—this is an active area of research.

© The Author(s), under exclusive license to Springer Nature Switzerland AG 2026   169
Y. Zhu, *Visual Computing For Architects*, Synthesis Lectures on Computer Architecture,
https://doi.org/10.1007/978-3-032-05018-2_8

There is also a burgeoning area of research, which this chapter is largely unconcerned with, called **computational imaging**, where a significant amount of computation is involved to form a final image (Bhandari et al. 2022). In many cases under such a paradigm, the initial image formed by the optics is rather unintelligible, and the name of the game is to design computational algorithms that can recover the "clean" image. This is usually formulated as an **inverse problem**: the optics (which could be anything, even duct tape (Antipa et al. 2017)) transforms information in the physical world into a set of observations, and the algorithm inverts that forward model to obtain the original physical information from the observations. Even in this case, understanding and modeling the forward image formation process of the optics is crucial: only with that knowledge can we invert that process to obtain the physical information. In fact, one usually *co-designs* the image formation process (e.g., optics) with the inversion algorithm to maximize the overall performance.

In this sense, imaging is a form of sensing, and the ultimate goal of imaging is to obtain information about the physical world. A visually pleasing image is one way such information can be represented, but there are other forms of information we might be interested in: depth, geometry, spectral radiance, polarization, absorption/scattering coefficient of the media, etc. Many imaging systems are designed to obtain such non-visual information, which is beyond our scope. For instance, an X-ray CT scanner is an essentially computational imaging device; it captures a set of raw images, which by themselves are not directly useful. Subsequent computational algorithms are used to obtain the actual information of interest, the absorption/scattering coefficient of the medium, from the raw images. We have actually covered the gist of the forward process in this imaging device when we discuss volume scattering.

We will assume that there is a sensor plane on the other side of the imaging system to capture observations. An actual sensor has many pixels (along with many other components, some of which are optics!), each of which has a small but non-zero size, which plays a role in signal processing. In this chapter, however, we will assume that each pixel is infinitesimal. Therefore, the image formed on the sensor plane, for now, is assumed to be a continuous 2D function: for any (x, y) point on the sensor, there is an irradiance value. A retina is a sensor, and the continuous image on the retina is usually called the **optical image** in vision science. An actual image captured by the sensor, whether biological (retina) or engineered, is necessarily discretized—by pixels or photoreceptors.

8.2   Pinhole Model

We will start by discussing the pinhole system, which is very simple and not commonly used but carries interesting properties and implications for more complex imaging systems that we will turn to later.

8.2.1   (Why) Do We Need Optics in an Imaging System?

What if we just expose the image sensor or our retina to lights? We will get garbage because each pixel/photoreceptor receives light from everywhere in the scene. Figure 8.1 (left) illustrates the geometry of this imaging system.

Each pixel receives light from everywhere in space. Assuming that each point in space is an ideal Lambertian emitter/scatterer, the two highlighted pixels will receive slightly different energy from the same point because of the cosine fall-off as a function of the incident direction. But if the sensor is much smaller relative to the distance to the physical space, the differences in fall-offs between different pixels are small, so we can say that each pixel roughly receives the same energy. In this case, the differences in pixel values are due to noise. So that's why the image looks like a random garbage.

8.2.2   Pinhole Imaging

What we need is for each pixel to receive information only from a small spatial region in the scene. This is what a pinhole camera does, as illustrated in Fig. 8.1 (middle). If the pinhole is infinitesimally small such that it allows only a single ray direction to go through, each pixel (which, again, for now is assumed to be an infinitesimal point on the sensor plane) captures light from only a single point in the scene.

As the pinhole size shrinks, the information captured by two adjacent pixels becomes more distinct, which is desirable, but if the pinhole size is too small, there are two issues. First, a pinhole that is too small requires a long exposure time. We will discuss this in Sect. 9.2, but a pixel is very much like a photoreceptor in that it is a photon collection device. Intuitively, the amount of photons a pixel collects (which we care about because it relates to the brightness of the captured image) is, roughly, proportional to both the pinhole area and the exposure time, so if we reduce the pinhole size, we need to increase the exposure time to maintain the pixel brightness.

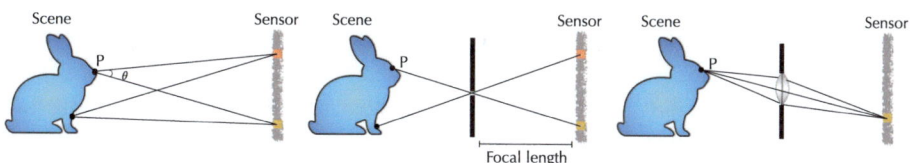

Fig. 8.1 Left: without a pinhole, different pixels get roughly the same signal, and the differences between pixels are due mostly to noise. Middle: with a pinhole, the signal received by each pixel is restricted to a small area in the physical scene. Right: with a lens, the signal received by each pixel is still restricted to a small physical area, but the signal is much stronger

  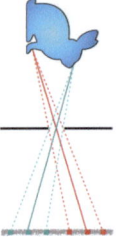 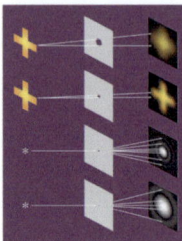

(a) Blur from large aperture   (b) Blur from long exposure   (c) The effect of pinhole size

Fig. 8.2 **a** Blur from large aperture/pinhole (defocus blur); from Königs (2022). **b** Blur from long exposure (motion blur); from Königs (2006). **c** Defocus blur arises from large pinholes, but when the pinhole becomes very small (on the order of light wavelength) diffraction occurs; adapted from Alves (2006)

An excessively long exposure time not only poses challenges to actually taking the photo but also leads to **motion blurs**. Figure 8.2b shows an image captured by a pinhole camera where, during exposure, objects are moving. As a result, each pixel receives light from different points in the scene and, visually, the resulting image carries motion blurs.

Second, as the pinhole size gets smaller and smaller, eventually we get to the diffraction limit, which means we cannot use geometric optics anymore and a single point in the scene does not translate to a single point in the image plane. We will discuss this shortly in Sect. 8.2.3.

What happens if we increase the pinhole size? We get a blurrier image. Figure 8.2a shows one such image captured by a pinhole camera using a pinhole size of 0.5 mm. The blur can be easily explained by the geometry of pinhole imaging, as shown in Fig. 8.2c, where the information of a point in the scene is spread or "smeared" across multiple pixels if the pinhole size is too large, leading to the blurs. For this reason, the blur here is a form of **defocus blur**; we will later see how a lens-based imaging system can also have a defocus blur with the same mechanism: information at a physical point in the scene is spread across multiple pixels even when the point itself is stationary.

Even in a lens-based imaging system, we do not technically have a pinhole, but we usually still have an aperture, which acts like a pinhole in the sense that it limits the amount of light that is allowed into the rest of the system, so the aperture size certainly dictates the imaging quality. Our eye is certainly a lens-based imaging system, and the pupil acts as the aperture. The pupil size changes from roughly 2 mm in relatively high ambient light levels to about 8 mm under low light intensities.

Amazingly, pinhole-only imaging is used in some animals. The most famous one is perhaps Nautilus, which has a pinhole eye without lenses (Zhang et al. 2021). The pinhole size is relatively large; the diameter varies between 0.4 and 2.8 mm (Hurley et al. 1978), so you can imagine the imaging quality is not great.

8.2.3   Diffraction Limit

When the pinhole becomes very small, diffraction becomes visible. The diffraction pattern is called the Airy disk. Figure 8.3 (left) shows a computer-simulated Airy disk, and Fig. 8.3 (rights) shows how the intensity of the Airy disk falls off from the center.

Diffraction is usually thought of as a wave phenomenon, where the light wave propagated from a small pinhole gets expanded spatially and forms the Airy disk pattern But perhaps a more principled way to understand diffraction is through quantum mechanics, which says that the more certain we are of the position of a photon we are less certain of the direction of its travel, and vice versa. When the pinhole is infinitesimal, we know for certain where a photon is, so we are uncertain where it is going to go: the result is the Airy disk pattern. In contrast, when the pinhole is large, we are less certain of the spatial position of a photon, so we are more certain of its direction of travel; as a result, diffraction contributes little to the overall imaging.

Imaging through a small pinhole can be thought of as a "single-slit" experiment. When we have a "double-slit" experiment with two small pinholes, the diffraction patterns from the two pinholes interfere, and we get the beautiful interference pattern that you perhaps have seen in middle-school physics class. Interestingly, there is a sequential version of the double-slit experiment, where photons are sent to the two slits sequentially, one by one. Amazingly, if we wait long enough, we will still see the interference pattern. This firmly establishes the fact that lights do behave like particles, not waves, just in a probabilistic manner.

Theoretical Maximum Resolving Power

Diffraction is a form of blur because the optical power of a power in the scene is spread spatially on the detector plane. Therefore diffraction limits the maximum resolving power of an imaging system. The way to quantify that is to imagine that we have two different

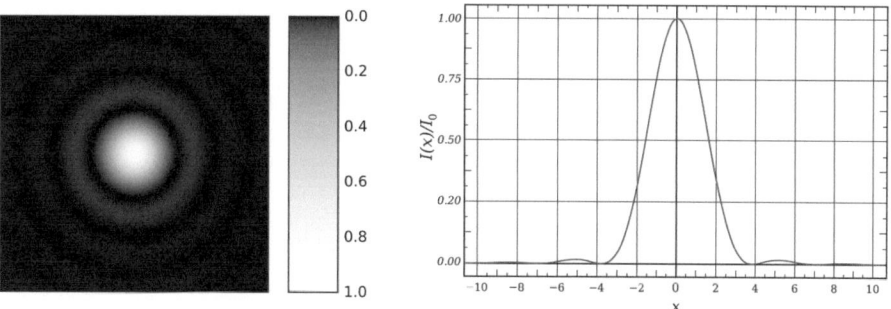

Fig. 8.3 Left: compute-simulated Airy disk (contrast is slightly exaggerated); from Sakurambo (2007). Right: the intensity of an Airy disk pattern as a function of the spatial position (0 being the center); adapted from Inductiveload (2009)

points in space imaged through a pinhole. Each point, of course, will cause a diffraction pattern. The two Airy disks add up linearly in the power domain in the captured image, but when the two points are sufficiently apart spatially, the peaks of the two Airy disks will be sufficiently apart on the detector plane as well, which means we can tell the two points apart from the image (because the power of the Airy disks falls off very quickly with the distance to the center). When the two points are closer, the peaks of the Airy disks are closer; when the two peaks are sufficiently close, the superposition of the two Airy disks will result in an image where we cannot easily tell the two peaks apart, and that is when we know we have reached the resolution limit of the imaging system.

A common criterion used to quantify such a limit is called the **Rayleigh criterion**, first defined by Lord Rayleigh (who won the Nobel Prize in Physics in 1904 and the namesake of the Rayleigh scattering), which says the two points are *regarded* as just resolvable when the center of the airy disk of one point coincides with the first minimum of the other (Rayleigh 1879). If you go through the math, this translates to:

$$\theta \approx 1.22 \frac{\lambda}{D}, \tag{8.1}$$

where λ is the light wavelength, D is the diameter of the pinhole, and θ is the angular resolution of the imaging system, i.e., the angle subtended by the two points and the pinhole. As an example, assuming a 550 nm typical visible light, when the pupil size is about 2 mm, which is a typical size under normal daylight, the resolvable angular resolution between two points is about 0.02 degree.

Note that I italicize "regarded" in the text above. There is no reason why one cannot distinguish between two points separated less than the Rayleigh criterion in a given scenario or train a deep neural network to do so. The Rayleigh criterion for the most part serves as an intuitive criterion that works empirically well with observations.

How do we improve the resolving power of an imaging system? One way is to use shorter wavelength lights, which, according to Eq. (8.1), would allow us to resolve objects that are closer. Optical microscopes use visible light, whereas electron microscopes take advantage of the wave nature of *electrons* to achieve much higher resolution than optical microscopes. The *de Broglie wavelength* of an electron is inversely proportional to its momentum. An electron microscope accelerates electrons to very high speeds, which reduces their wavelengths to below 1 nm (c.f., hundreds of nm for visible light) and increases the overall resolving power of the imaging system.

8.3   Lenses and Aberrations

A convex lens brings many rays from a point together, as shown in Fig. 8.1 (right). If the sensor plane is placed such as the image is in focus (which we will discuss shortly), the captured image is the geometrically the same as the one captured by a pinhole camera, but much brighter given the same exposure time. Both a pinhole imaging system and a convex-lens imaging system perform a perspective projection, which is basically the camera model used in computer vision when a camera needs to be modeled and in simple graphics rendering pipelines.

8.3.1   Image Formation with an Ideal Lens

What is the imaging process of a convex lens? How do we model the behavior of a (convex) lens? We can model this using the basic geometrical optics. Figure 8.4 shows the setup. Assume we have a convex lens, which is made of two spherical surfaces combined together The curvatures of the two surfaces are R_1 (right surface) and R_2 (left surface). The two surfaces are separated by a distance d, which we call the thickness of the lens. The refractive indices of the air and the lens are n_1 and n_2, respectively. The goal is to calculate, for a ray originating from a distance u on the optical axis in the scene and traveling in a direction that subtends an angle θ with the optical axis, what happens when it reaches the other side.

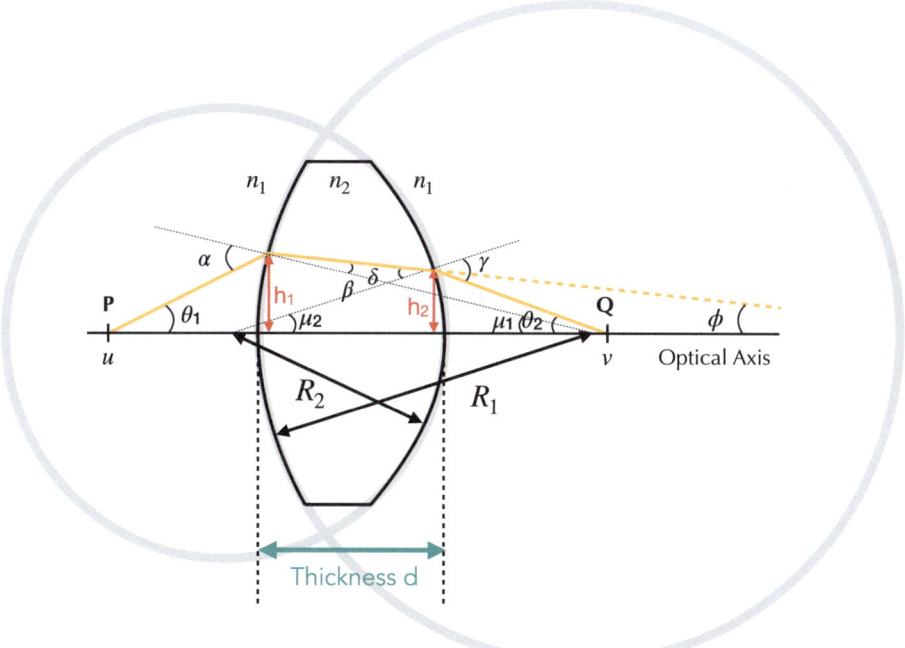

Fig. 8.4 The setup to derive the lens maker's equation, which requires two assumptions: the thin lens assumption and the paraxial assumption

We will apply the Snell's law at the two interfaces, essentially tracing the ray through the lens. At the first interface, we have:

$$n_1 \sin \alpha = n_2 \sin \beta, \tag{8.2a}$$

$$\alpha = \theta_1 + \mu_1, \tag{8.2b}$$

$$\beta = \mu_1 - \phi, \tag{8.2c}$$

$$\sin \mu_1 = \frac{h_1}{R_1}, \tag{8.2d}$$

$$\tan \theta_1 = \frac{h_1}{u}. \tag{8.2e}$$

As the light travels inside the lens and reaches the second interface, we have:

$$n_2 \sin \delta = n_1 \sin \gamma, \tag{8.3a}$$

$$\delta = \mu_2 + \phi, \tag{8.3b}$$

$$\gamma = \mu_2 + \theta_2, \tag{8.3c}$$

$$\sin \mu_2 = \frac{h_2}{R_2}, \tag{8.3d}$$

$$\tan \theta_2 = \frac{h_2}{v}. \tag{8.3e}$$

Now, we are going to make two assumptions. First, we will assume that the lens is very thin; the thickness d is very small. As a result, $h_1 \approx h_2$. This is called the *thin-lens assumption*. Second, we will assume that the ray stays close to the optical axis as it travels. Such rays are **paraxial rays**, and this assumption is called the *paraxial assumption*. That is, $\theta_1, \theta_2, \alpha, \beta, \gamma, \delta, \mu_1$, and μ_2 are very small angles, for which we can apply the usual small-angle approximation in trigonometry, e.g., $\sin(\alpha) \approx \tan(\alpha) \approx \alpha$ and $\cos(\alpha) = 1$.

Using these two assumptions and through a little algebra, we will get:

$$\frac{n_2 - n_1}{n_1} \left(\frac{1}{R_1} + \frac{1}{R_2} \right) = \left(\frac{1}{u} + \frac{1}{v} \right). \tag{8.4}$$

This is called the **Lens Maker's Equation**. Critically, observe that v depends only on u regardless of the path the ray takes (for a given lens with a particular set of n_1, n_2, R_1, and R_2). Therefore, all rays originating from an on-axis point will converge at the same point on the other side of the optical axis. This is crucial, because it means we can place a single detector **Q** (e.g., a pixel) on the imaging side (right side of the lens in this diagram) to capture all the rays from the point **P**. In other words, if we place the detector at **Q**, the point **P** would be *in focus*. In fact, you can show that this is true for all points in space, not just on-axis points: all the rays originating from a point on one side of the lens will converge to another point on the other side of the lens. In reality, of course, only paraxial rays with a thin lens follow this.

Now, if the ray originates from infinity (as if it is parallel to the optical axis), where $u = \infty$, we have

$$\frac{1}{v} = \frac{n_2 - n_1}{n_1}\left(\frac{1}{R_1} + \frac{1}{R_2}\right) := \frac{1}{f}. \tag{8.5}$$

This allows us to derive the position v where a parallel ray intersects with the optical axis. We define that position as the **focal length** f of the imaging system.

Plugging Eq. (8.5) into (8.4) gives us the familiar **Gaussian Lens Equation**:

$$\frac{1}{u} + \frac{1}{v} = \frac{1}{f}. \tag{8.6}$$

Under the ideal thin lens and paraxial approximation, the ray-tracing diagram is simplified to the one depicted in Fig. 8.5, where:

- rays parallel to the optical axis always pass through the focal point (which has a distance f to the optical center) on the other side;
- rays passing through the focal point will be parallel on the other side;
- a ray passing through the optical center does not change its direction if the lens is symmetric; otherwise the incident ray at the first interface is parallel to that leaving the second interface as if the ray has been shifted.

Figure 8.5 shows that if we place an image sensor in the image space (right side of the lens) at v, all the points at the depth u in the world space (left side of the lens) will be in focus. Another important point Fig. 8.5 makes clear is that, if in focus, the captured image is the geometrically the same as the one captured by a pinhole camera (but of course brighter

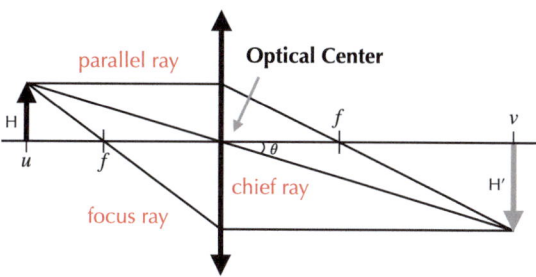

Fig. 8.5 Under an ideal thin lens and paraxial approximation, the ray-tracing diagram can be simplified so that points at the same depth (S) are all in focus at the same depth (S') on the other side of the lens. The chief ray is the ray that passes the center of the aperture, which is assumed to coincide with the optical center (not shown). The magnification of the lens is $M = H'/H$, and the field-of-view (FoV) of the system is 2θ (assuming that H' is half of the sensor, which is symmetric)

given the same exposure time because more rays are captured): the optical center of the lens is the pinhole here *geometrically*.

Accommodation

Let's assume that $R_1 = R_2 = R$; Eq. (8.5) suggests that if we reduce R (increase the curvature of the lens surface), f reduces as well. Then look at Eq. (8.6); if f reduces and we fix the object at the distance u, for that object to be in focus we have to reduce v, i.e., move the sensor plane closer to the lens. That is, if we curve the lens surfaces more, rays focus closer to the optical center as if the lens bends light more, and vice versa.

   Another way to think of this is that if we cannot move the relative distance between the sensor and the lens, to focus on an object (in the world space) closer to the lens (u reduces), the lens focal length f has to reduce too. This is exactly what our eye lens does: to focus on closer objects, the lens curves more to gain more light-bending power. For that to take place, the ciliary muscle would have to contract. Conversely, to focus on farther objects, the ciliary muscle relaxes, which reduces the curvature of the lens, which now bends light less and, thus, allows us to focus on farther objects. Changing the focal length through changing the curvature is called **accommodation**. As one gets older, the ciliary muscle is not as effective in contracting the lens. That is why one uses the reading glasses, which provide additional light-bending power to assist that of the eye lens. Recall, from Sect. 2.2.1, that while the lens is flexible, most of the light refraction was done at the air-cornea interface because of the large difference in the refractive index there.

   In cameras, unless you are using liquid lenses, the curvature of each lens surface stays fixed once fabricated, so how do we focus on objects closer or farther than we are currently focused on? The answer is we move the lens, essentially solving for v given a new u using Eq. (8.6). This is essentially how auto-focus works in cameras. Alternatively, we could also move the sensor, but in practice the sensor stays fixed (e.g., attached to the back of the camera housing), and it is the lens that is movable.

8.3.2 Magnification Versus Field-of-View

Using simple trigonometry in Fig. 8.5, we can relate the size of an object in the world space (H) and that in the image space (H'):

$$M = \frac{H'}{H} = \frac{f}{u - f} = \frac{1}{\frac{u}{f} - 1}, \tag{8.7}$$

where M is the magnification of the imaging system. We can see that M increases as f does. That is why telephoto cameras, those that you see in, for instance, sports broadcasting, are very long: they need to be long to accommodate a large focal length so that they can magnify objects that are very small (far away).

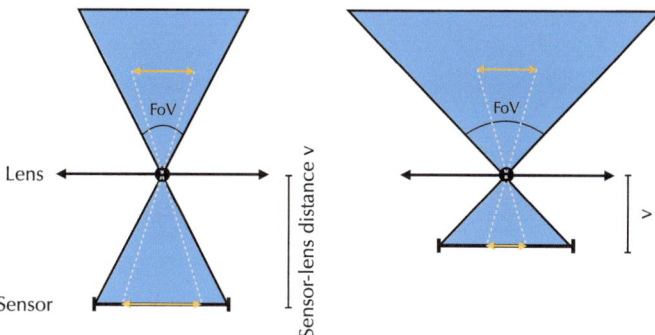

Fig. 8.6 Increasing the focal length increases the magnification but reduces the FoV. For simplicity, we use a pinhole geometry here, but both the pinhole camera and the ideal thin lens (with the paraxial approximation) perform the same perspective projection, leading to the same image formation geometrically

What do we sacrifice when we increase magnification by increasing the focal length? The FoV reduces. The FoV of an imaging system is the extent of the observable world that can be captured by the sensor. Let's use Fig. 8.5 to derive this, and for simplicity's sake, let's just assume that the sensor size is $2H'$ and is symmetric about the optical axis, i.e., the object at u is just fully captured by the sensor. The figure omits the upper half of the sensor. The FoV is defined as $2\theta = 2 \times \arctan(H'/v)$.

Now for the same object at u, if f increases, v has to increase as well for the object to be captured in focus. As a result, θ reduces, so does the FoV. This intuitively makes sense: if an object is magnified more on the sensor, which has a fixed size, the amount of *other* objects that can be captured naturally reduces, hence the reduction of the FoV. As an example, the two imaging systems in Fig. 8.6 differ only in the focal length: the one on the left has a shorter focal length f and hence a shorter sensor-lens distance v (for the same object to be captured in focus), which translates to a larger magnification and narrower FoV.

8.3.3 Magnifying Glasses and Projection Lenses

The Gaussian lens equation also helps us understand the geometry behind magnifying glasses and the projection lenses in AR/VR devices and cinematography.

When $u < f$ in Eq. (8.6), v is negative. As a result, the object does not form a physical image in the image space, because rays from a point on the object do not converge to a point in the image space. Instead, those rays *diverge*, and the extension of those rays actually converge at a point farther away from the lens in the world space. Now, if our eye is at the right place, i.e., the diverging rays converge on the retina after traveling through the eye lens, as is the case in Fig. 8.7 (top), we will see a magnified object. In this case, the lens acts as a magnifying glass.

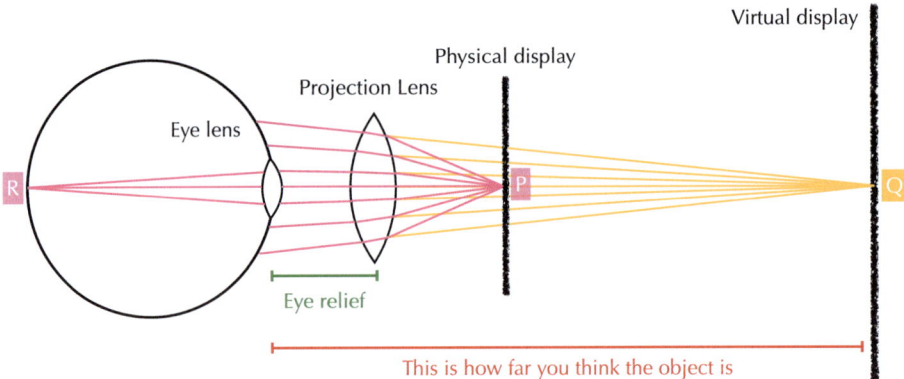

Fig. 8.7 A magnifying glass projects a small and close real image to a larger and farther virtual image. VR devices all have a pair of magnifying glasses to create a virtual display that our eye lenses can focus on

The magnifying glass functionally (1) projects a small physical object to an apparently larger virtual object that is (2) farther away from the eye. These two functionalities are exactly what a project lens in AR/VR need. Figure 8.7 illustrates a projection lens in VR; the optics in AR are much more complicated, but the basic idea of a projection lens applies there too. In AR/VR devices, the actual display is very close to the eye, to the point that no eye lens can actually be accommodated to focus on the display (the lens would have to be curved so unrealistically much). Of course the display itself is very small, so seeing details is hard, too. The solution is to place a convex lens between the display and the eye, and the three components are so positioned that the display is closer to the lens than a focal length. As a result, the actual, physical display is projected to a much larger virtual display that is also farther away, to which our eye lens could actually accommodate. When you watch a movie in a cinema on a large screen or use a home projector, there is a projection lens sitting at the back doing the same thing.

8.3.4 Depth of Field

What if the sensor is not correctly positioned according to the Gaussian lens equation (Eq. 8.6)? The object/point being imaged will be out of focus, and the result is a blur on the image. Figure 8.8 shows three cases, where the sensor (5) and the lens are fixed in position (4), under which objects at plane 2 (with a distance T to the lens) would be in focus, but both object 1 and object 3 would be out of focus because rays originating from them will be spread across a small area on the sensor plane, looking like blurs. The shape of the blur is called the **bokeh**, which is mostly determined by the aperture shape (and also aberrations

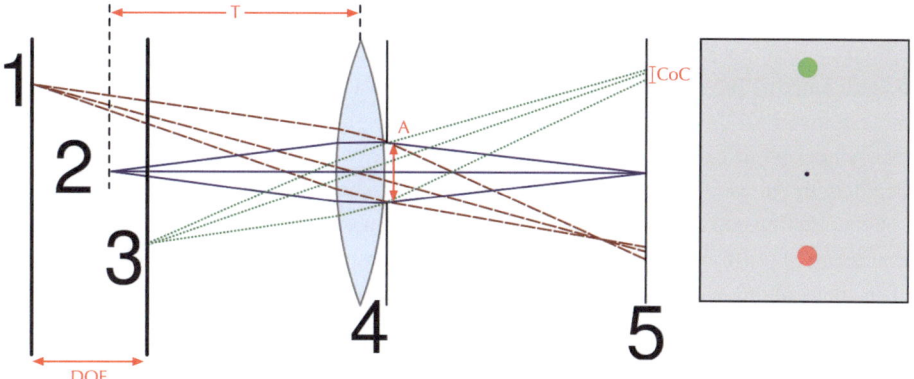

Fig. 8.8 The setup to derive the depth-of-field (DoF) equation; adapted from FrantzDale (2010a). CoC: circle of confusion

introduced by the imaging system, which we will see later). If the aperture is a circle, the bokeh would be one too, and we call such a blur the **circle of confusion** (CoC).

As the CoC increases, eventually it becomes objectionable to the human visual system. Exactly what that CoC threshold depends on a number of factors that we will omit here (e.g., how the image will be scaled when being viewed, the contrast sensitivity of the human visual system, etc.), but let's just use C to denote that threshold for now. You can see that if an object is placed slightly before or after the depth T (where the object is perfectly in focus), as long as the resulting CoC is smaller than C, our visual system would still regard it as in focus. The distance between the nearest and farthest objects whose CoCs are still within C is called the depth-of-field (DoF) of the system.

Using geometrical optics and with a few assumptions, we can show that the DoF is given by:

$$DoF \approx \frac{2CT^2N}{f^2} = \frac{2CT^2}{fA},\tag{8.8}$$

where T is the distance of the object that is perfectly in focus, f is the focal length, and $N = f/A$ is called the **F-number** of the camera, which is defined as the ratio between the focal length and the aperture size (A).

Given Eq. (8.8), there are three ways to increase the DoF. First, we can increase T, i.e., focus on objects that are farther away (e.g., landscape photography). Second, we can decrease the focal length, but just keep in mind that changing the focal length will also affect the magnification and FoV as discussed in Sect. 8.3.1. Finally, we can also reduce the aperture size, which would increase the F-number. Changing the aperture size, however, will have implications on other aspects of the imaging quality. Specifically, a small aperture increases the exposure time and, thus, motion blur.

A larger DoF would mean that objects within a larger depth range could be simultaneously in focus. A shallow DoF, however, is at many times desirable. The "portrait mode" in many modern smartphone cameras essentially captures photos with a shallow DoF. Intuitively, one can invert all three methods above to obtain a shallow DoF, but what if the hardware does not permit us to do that? For instance, what if we cannot increase the aperture size and focal length but want to capture a close object with a shallow DoF?

Computation comes to the rescue. There is a notion of **Synthetic DoF**, which uses post-processing algorithms to emulate a shallow DoF. For instance, one might first capture an all-in-focus photo, estimate the depth for each pixel in the photo (including the pixels that correspond to the object that we do want to have in focus), then selectively blur pixels that are farther or closer than the objects of interest. This is what the portrait mode in Google's Pixel phone does (Wadhwa et al. 2018).

Synthetic DoF is a classic example of computational photography, where the imaging system is largely assisted by computational algorithms (to reduce the design complexities of the imaging hardware). In this case, computation is required mainly to estimate depth. In turns out that auto-focus in cameras is all about depth estimation, which, again, usually involves some form of collaboration between software and hardware.

8.3.5   Aberration

When building an imaging system, we ideally want a point in the physical space to be captured as a single point in the image space. In our derivation of the Gaussian lens equation in Sect. 8.3.1, this is indeed the case, so if the sensor is correctly positioned, we will capture a sharp image of the point. This derivation, however, assumes an ideal thin lens and considers only paraxial rays. It turns out that the equation still holds even if the lens is thick (i.e., the distance between the two surfaces is not negligible), even though the definition of the focal length would have to be slightly more complicated than Eq. (8.5) (Hecht 2016, Sect. 6.1).

The real complication is that in practice we cannot ignore non-paraxial rays (i.e., rays that do not stay close to the optical axis), in which case rays from a single point (or from infinitely far away) will not all converge at a single point in the image space, resulting in a blur. Mathematically, this means we cannot invoke the small angle approximations. For instance, using Taylor expansion, we have:

$$\sin \theta = \theta - \frac{\theta^3}{3!} + \frac{\theta^5}{5!} - \cdots . \tag{8.9}$$

When considering paraxial rays, we can afford to consider only the first term, but when θ is large, we have to include other terms. When considering the second term of Taylor series expansion (compared to considering only the first term), five forms of **aberrations** show up: spherical aberration, coma, astigmatism, field curvature, distortion. Geometrical optics that

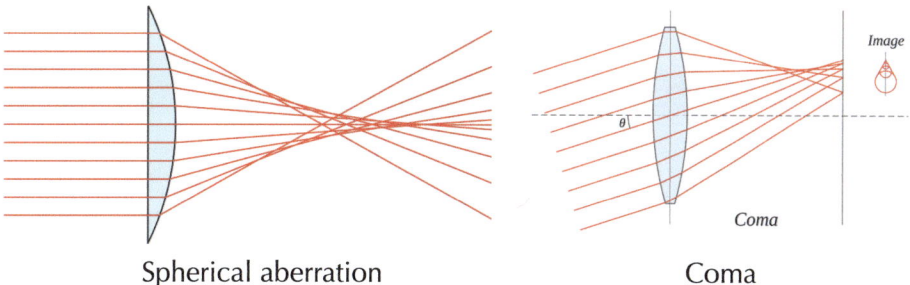

Fig. 8.9 Left: spherical aberration; from Mglg (2008). Right: coma; from Glrx (2018)

consider the second term are called the **third-order theory**, as opposed to the **first-order theory** or **Gaussian optics** that considers only the first term.

Spherical Aberration

It turns out that for a spherical lens, non-paraxial rays originating from a point on the optical axis will not converge at the same point. This can be shown by going through the derivation of the Gaussian lens equation (Sect. 8.3.1) but this time without the small angle approximations. We would then see that v depends not only on u and f but also on the direction of the ray leaving u. By extension, not all rays parallel to the optical axis (especially those that are far away from the optical axis) will focus at the same point. This is called the spherical aberration, which is illustrated in Fig. 8.9 (left).

Mirrors have spherical aberrations too. Perfectly spherically curved mirrors cannot focus parallel lights; parabolic mirrors are free from spherical aberrations. One might venture to guess that's why Archimedes could not have used mirrors to burn Roman ships, because they could not have had the skills to make parabolic mirrors. The burning mirror story is more likely a story than a fact. There are just too many technical reasons why that would have been very hard. For instance, it would have taken a very large mirror given the intensity of sunlight and the distance of the ships, and the ship would have to be perfectly positioned at the focal point (Rorres n.d.; Mills and Clift 1992).

Coma

While spherical aberration is concerned with rays from on-axis points or parallel rays that are also parallel to the optical axis, another aberration called coma or comatic aberration is concerned with rays from off-axis points or, as illustrated in Fig. 8.9 (right), parallel rays that have an oblique incident angle w.r.t. the optical axis. We can show that rays from an off-axis point focus on different points and, by extension, parallel rays that are not parallel to the optical axis do not focus on the same point. This aberration is called coma because the resulting blur looks like a coma.

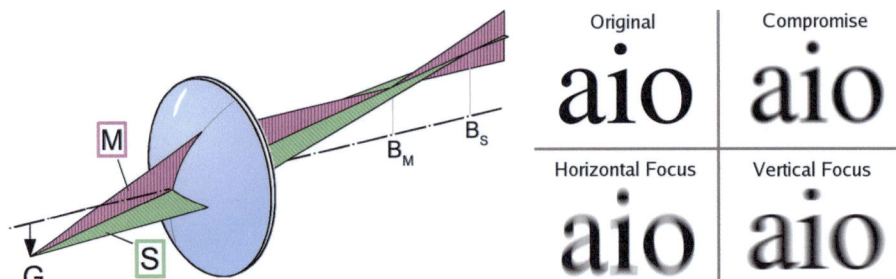

Fig. 8.10 Left: an illustration of astigmatism; adapted from Schmid (2008). Right: the images captured when the sensor plane is placed at different positions; from Tallfred (2005)

Astigmatism

Yet another form of aberration is called astigmatism. It is also concerned with points off the optical axis. In particular, we are concerned with rays propagated in two planes. The first plane is one defined by the object point and the optical axis and is called the **tangential plane** or the **meridional plane**. The other plane is one that is orthogonal to the meridional plane and is called the **sagittal plane**. It turns out that rays from the two planes focus on different points on the optical axis. This is illustrated in Fig. 8.10 (left), where all the rays in the meridional (M) plane focus at B_M and all the rays in the sagittal (S) plane focus at B_S.

The blur we get depends on where we place the sensor plane, and some examples are shown in Fig. 8.10 (right). If we place the sensor at B_M, a single point source gets imaged as a horizontal/lateral "line" due to the spread of the rays in the S plane. We say a line, but it is not actually a line because rays in other planes (other than the M and S planes) will not focus at B_M and still contribute to the image formation, so the resulting image is really a very much elongated ellipse. If the object is not a point but, say, spans a plane (top-left), the resulting image has a somewhat horizontal/lateral blur as if the in-focus image is smeared laterally (bottom-right).

As we move the sensor beyond B_M, the elongated ellipse gradually expands vertically and then becomes circular, and then shrinks laterally; eventually, when the sensor is placed at B_S, we get a vertical "line" (an elongated ellipse along the vertical axis) because, mainly, of the rays in the M plane. The resulting image would appear to have a somewhat vertical blur as if the in-focus area were smeared vertically (bottom-left). The somewhat circular blur when the sensor plane is in-between B_M and B_S means that the resulting image (top-right) appears as if the in-focus image is smeared in all directions.

Field Curvature

If an imaging system is free of all the previous aberrations, a single point in the world space corresponds to a single point in the image space. However, a plane of points in the world space would not correspond to a plane in the image space. In fact, it would correspond to a

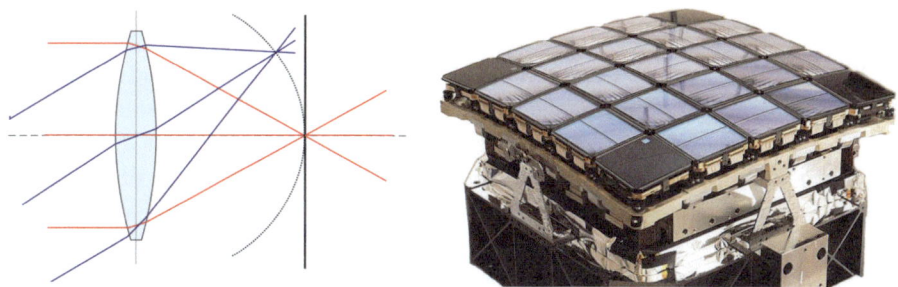

Fig. 8.11 Left: a manifestation of field curvature; from FrantzDale (2010b). Right: focal plane of Kepler space telescope is curved to mitigate field curvature; from HandWiki (2024)

curved surface. If we used a planar sensor for imaging, we would get a blurred image. This form of aberration is called field curvature, as illustrated in Fig. 8.11 (left).

While it might be difficult to build a single curved sensor, it is relatively easy to assemble a set of sensors on a curved surface. The image-sensor array of the Kepler space observatory is curved to compensate for the field curvature, as shown in Fig. 8.11 (right) Interestingly, you might recall that the human retina is not planar either; it is curved. This to some extent helps mitigate the effect of field curvature.

Distortion

Even when all the previous aberrations are somehow corrected, the image would look sharp but distorted. Distortion does not introduce blurs. Rather, it is a result of the variation of magnification as a function of the distance to the optical axis (object height).

Equation (8.7) suggests that magnification depends only on the object distance to the lens u, but in reality the magnification depends also on the object height. We can imagine that for a point that is distant from the optical axis, rays originating from that point will not be paraxial rays. If the magnification increases with the height, we have a positive or **pincushion distortion**; otherwise, we have a negative or **barrel distortion**. The two forms of distortion are illustrated in Fig. 8.12.

Fig. 8.12 A comparison of pincushion (positive) distortion and barrel (negative) distortion; from WolfWings (2008a, b)

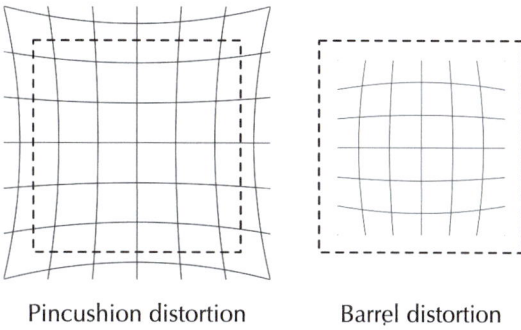

Pincushion distortion   Barrel distortion

Chromatic Aberration

All the aberrations we have discussed before are present even if we consider only a single wavelength; they are called monochromatic aberrations. When we consider lights that comprise a mixture of different wavelengths, **chromatic aberration** shows up. Chromatic aberration arises fundamentally because the refractive index is a function of wavelength; after all, that is how Newton was able to disperse white light and show the spectrum. Figure 8.13 (left) illustrates the issue of chromatic adaptation, which introduces "colorful" blurs. Figure 8.13 (right) shows how the refractive index of BK7 glass (which is commonly used in lenses) changes with wavelength.

As another example, I took a picture of my 4th-gen iPad Pro when it displayed sRGB white. I intentionally focused on the green subpixels. As a result, the other two subpixels are out of focus—due to chromatic aberration.

Correction for Aberrations

One of the main tasks of optical design, especially for imaging lenses, is to correct for aberrations. There are two main approaches: non-spherical (aspherical) lenses and compound lenses.

Optical designers often use multiple (compound) lenses in combination to correct various aberrations. For instance, chromatic doublets or apochromatic triplets are specifically designed to counteract chromatic aberration. One obvious downside of compound lenses is form factor, which becomes an issue for systems like Augmented Reality that need to be very compact.

One promising technology that people are currently investigating is called **freeform optics**. Traditional aspherical lenses, while deviating away from a spherical design and can avoid compound lenses in many cases, are still rotationally symmetric, so they are still limited in what they can do. Freeform optics take this concept further by allowing surfaces that lack rotational symmetry, providing additional degrees of freedom in optical design.

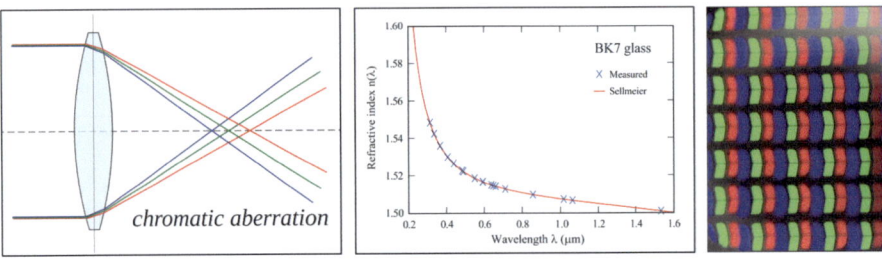

Fig. 8.13 Left: illustration of chromatic adaptation; adapted from Mellish (2006). Middle: refractive index versus wavelength for BK7 glass; from Bob (2007). Right: sRGB white as displayed by a 4th-generation iPad Pro; the image is captured when focusing on the green subpixel, so other subpixels are out of focus

This enables better correction of higher-order aberrations, such as coma and astigmatism, which aspheric lenses alone may not fully eliminate.

8.3.6 Not All Blurs are Created Equal

Ideally a point source in the scene should really be captured as a single point in the image plane, but we have seen a few ways that a blur can occur. But not all blurs are created equal; it is perhaps useful to review the different causes of a blur.

Blurs can result from aberrations, diffraction, defocus, and motion. We have just seen blurs from aberrations, but just note that not all aberrations result in blurs, an example of which would be distortion. Assuming an aberration-free imaging system, if the sensor is not placed as the focal plane, we could get a de-focus blur, as we have seen in the DoF section (Sect. 8.3.4). Note that a pinhole camera would never have defocus blur, because its DoF is infinite (using $A = 0$ in Eq. 8.8).

Even if the sensor is placed as the focal plane, but if the object is motion, we would most likely get motion blur, because the exposure time is finite—unless of course the exposure time is so short that the object motion, when projected on the sensor plane, is within the pixel width. The longer the exposure time, the more pronounced the motion blur becomes.

Finally, we have blurs from diffraction, which, as we have discussed in Sect. 8.2.3, is fundamentally a result of the quantum nature of light. If an imaging system is free from all previous forms of blur,[1] we say it is "diffraction limited", because its imaging capability (the ability to avoid blurs) is limited only by diffraction.

8.3.7 Radiometric Analysis of Lens

What does a convex lens do to the radiance of incident light? We know that the radiance of a ray does not change as the ray propagates through space along a particular direction, but what does a lens do to the radiance? This is an important problem in practice: the lens essentially transforms the light field in the physical scene to the light field inside the camera, which means if we know the latter *and* the radiance transformation done by the lens, we can infer the light field in the scene.

The way to reason about it is to think of a lens as performing a sequence of two refractions at its two surfaces, so we will have to first reason about, at each surface, what happens to the radiance and then consider the composite effect of the two surfaces.

With a little radiometry (which we will omit but refer to Bohren and Clothiaux (2006), Sect. 4.1.6 for the derivation), we can show that the radiance after refraction L_r relates to the incident radiance L_i by:

---

[1] Mostly aberration, because defocus can be easily fixed and motion blur is out of the hands of an imaging system.

$$L_r = n^2 L_i, \tag{8.10}$$

where n is the relative refractive index of the lens/medium to the air. Usually $n > 1$, which means after refraction the radiance increases. This makes sense because after refraction from the air to, say, glass, the set of incident rays maps to a smaller solid angle.

What happens in the second surface? The same thing except the relative refractive index is now $1/n$, since we are now going from the medium to the air:

$$L_o = \frac{1}{n^2} L_r, \tag{8.11}$$

where L_o is the radiance leaving the lens. Combining the two equations above, we can see $L_o = L_i$, meaning the lens does not change the radiance. This is a nice result, because it essentially means we can simply trace rays through a lens and be reasonably sure that the ray radiance does not change.

Intuitively, this conclusion is obviously *wrong*: some energy of incident light is absorbed/reflected away by the lens, so the energy leaving the lens is definitely smaller than that entering the lens. So the derivation above is a bit of a simplification, because we have assumed that no reflection takes place at each surface and no absorption by the lens. That said, this invariance largely still holds if we confine ourselves to near-normal angles of incidence and assume typical materials for lenses (which are mostly transparent with little absorption).

8.4   Computational Modeling Using Linear System Theory

How do we model the image formation process of an image system? We could trace rays out of a point in the world space, but it has many limitations. First, we could afford to sample only a few rays for a point. Second, we could afford to sample only a few points on an object. Third, things like diffraction that go beyond geometrical optics need special treatment if not straight up impossible. How do we effectively model the image formed on the sensor plane?

8.4.1   Basic Idea of a Linear System Theory

A common modeling strategy is to first characterize the response of the imaging system against a *single point source*. If we assume that the system is **linear and shift invariant** (LSI), we can derive how the system responds to an arbitrarily complex object, which is treated as nothing more than a collection of (infinitely many) points, using the linear system theory. Let's unpack this step by step.

Point Spread Function

The response of a single point source is called the **Point Spread Function** (PSF) of the imaging system. How does the PSF look like? Ideally, a single point in the world space would be imaged as a single point in the image plane, so the corresponding PSF would be a Dirac delta function, but as we have discussed in Sect. 8.3.6, in reality the image of a single point would be blurred, whether it is because of diffraction, defocus, or aberration (assuming the point source is stationary).

Figure 8.14 (left) shows a few examples of the PSFs. The bottom-right corner shows a diffraction-limited PSF, which is essentially the Airy disk (but visualized as a 2D grayscale map). As we move vertically up, we add more spherical aberration to the system, and as we move to the right, we add more defocus to the system. Figure 8.14 (middle) shows a PSF of a system with astigmatism; this time the PSF is visualized in 3D rather than a 2D grayscale map. We can see that the PSF is not radially symmetric; rather, it is elongated along one dimension, which matches our intuition of astigmatism (see Fig. 8.10).

Linear System

Informally, if there are two inputs x and y to the system, say two points in the world space, and the responses to these two inputs, i.e., their respective PSFs, are $H(x)$ and $H(y)$, the response of a linear system to a new input $\alpha x + \beta y$ would be $\alpha H(x) + \beta H(y)$. αx means to scale the input x's value (e.g., irradiance of a point) by a factor of α.

A linear system essentially means when we image two points simultaneously, the resulting image is equal to the sum of the individual image of each point. You can imagine how this would simplify our modeling later. In practice, an imaging system is linear when it interrogates non-coherent light, e.g., sunlight or OLEDs, rather than lasers.

Shift-Invariant System

An imaging system is shift invariant if its PSF of a point is invariant to the shifts of the point in the world space. This property allows us to use a single PSF to characterize the system.

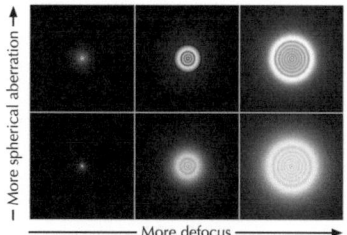 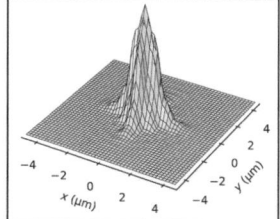 

Fig. 8.14 Left: PSF of a diffraction-limited system (bottom-left), with spherical aberration (vertically) and with defocus (horizontally); adapted from Mdf (2005). Middle: PSF (visualized in 3D) with astigmatism. Right: in a linear and shift-invariant imaging system, image formation is equivalent to a convolution using the PSF; from Mdf (2006)

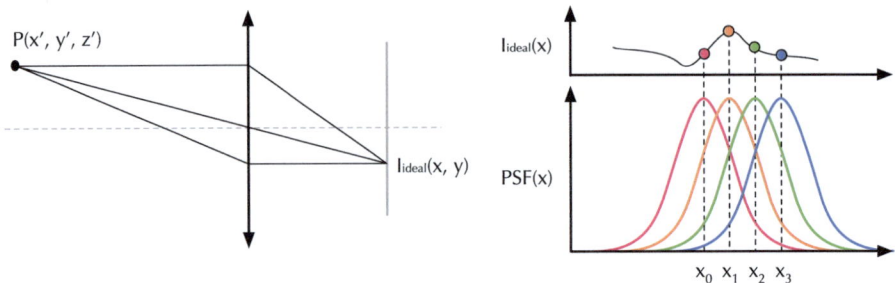

Fig. 8.15 Left: geometrically, the ideal image I_{ideal} is a perspective projection of the scene, and radiometrically $I_{ideal}(x, y)$ corresponds to the irradiance from $P(x', y', z')$ that are captured by the imaging system. Right: the intuition behind why imaging in a LSI system is a convolution with the PSF

Of course, in reality a system is hardly shift-invariant. For instance, if we move a point away from or closer to the lens, we get different kinds of defocus blurs, so the point response depends on depth. Even if we shift a point within a single depth plane, the rays incident on the lens, leaving the lens, and, by extension, hitting the sensor plane would be different. Even ignoring aberrations, different incident angles result in different irradiance captured by the sensor plane (because of the Lambertian cosine law and is a form of "vignetting").

In general, however, shift invariance approximately holds if we assume that the object to be imaged is very far away from the lens (so the depth variation within an object is negligible with respect to the overall distance to the lens) and the imaging system has a relatively small FoV.

8.4.2   Modeling Image Formation in LSI Systems

Under the linear and shift-invariance assumptions, we can derive a simple but incredibly useful computational model for the image formation process, which is decoupled into two conceptual steps.

In the first step, we calculate an ideal image I_{in} formed by the imaging system, assuming the imaging system PSF is a delta function. This in turn assumes that the imaging system has no diffraction/aberration and the sensor plane is properly positioned so every scene point is sharply in focus (no defocus blur).[2] I_{in} is a 2D continuous function.

Geometrically, I_{ideal} is a perspective projection of the 3D scene to the sensor plane. That is, each (x, y) point in this ideal image I_{ideal} corresponds to a point $P(x', y', z')$ in the scene as if that scene point is captured through a pinhole (recall that geometrically an ideal thin lens performs the same projection as a pinhole system). This is shown in Fig. 8.15

---

[2] Which is of course impossible because different scene depths would require different sensor positions to be all in focus.

(left). Radiometrically, the value of $I_{ideal}(x, y)$ is an irradiance quantity, representing the irradiance emitted from $P(x', y', z')$ that is captured at $I_{ideal}(x, y)$. We will discuss in Sect. 9.4.4 exactly how to calculate this irradiance.

In the second step, we then using the PSF function $f(\cdot)$ to convolve I_{ideal}, and the result:

$$I_{actual} = I_{ideal} \star f, \tag{8.12}$$

is the actual image formed by the imaging system. This is illustrated in Fig. 8.14 (right).

The convolution is a natural conclusion once we assume linearity (irradiances add) and shift invariance (constant PSF) of the imaging system. Figure 8.15 (right) illustrates the intuition using an 1D example. $I_{ideal}(x, y)$ is the irradiance at (x, y) with a delta PSF. With a non-delta PSF, the irradiance of $I_{ideal}(x, y)$ is distributed over the sensor plane as defined in the PSF. Each point on the sensor, thus, receives contributions from all the point spreads. Since we assume linearity, the result is a convolution between I_{ideal} and the PSF.

Why? Here is a quick demonstration. Taking a discrete case with four points as an example and assuming we are interested in calculating the actual irradiance $I_{actual}(x_0)$, the contribution from x_0 itself is $I_{ideal}(x_0)f(0)$, the contribution from x_1 is $I_{ideal}(x_1)f(x_0 - x_1)$, and similarly the contributions from x_2 and x_3 are, respectively, $I_{ideal}(x_2)f(x_0 - x_2)$ and $I_{ideal}(x_3)f(x_0 - x_3)$. So the actual irradiance received by x_0 is:

$$I_{actual}(x_0) = I_{ideal}(x_0)f(0) + I_{ideal}(x_1)f(x_0 - x_1)$$
$$+ I_{ideal}(x_2)f(x_0 - x_2) + I_{ideal}(x_3)f(x_0 - x_3). \tag{8.13}$$

You can see when we generalize from four points to a continuous signal I_{ideal}, Eq. (8.13) becomes Eq. (8.12).

In the literature, it is common to see people taking images from a dataset, e.g., ImageNet, and simply convolve a PSF against them. The underlying assumption is that those images are captures of distant objects with an ideal system (with no blurs) and, thus, can be treated as essentially irradiance maps I_{ideal}.

What if the system is not shift invariant? For instance, if we cannot assume that objects are all very far away from the lens, scene points at different depths will have different PSFs. So long as we can still assume linearity, however, we can still relatively easily simulate the image formation process using the exact same principle shown before in Fig. 8.15: "convolving" against spatially varying PSFs is equivalent to summing the PSFs (each of course scaled by the corresponding irradiance). This is a bit similar to surface splatting in PBG (Sect. 7.4.4), where each surface sample has a different reconstruction filter, so reconstruction amounts to summing each reconstruction filter, each scaled by the sample color.

8.4.3   Fourier Perspectives: OTF and MTF

Since we are using convolution to model imaging in LSI systems, it is only natural to take
a Fourier perspective. Recall the convolution theorem:

$$\mathcal{F}(f \star g) = \mathcal{F}(f)\mathcal{F}(g), \tag{8.14a}$$

$$f \star g = \mathcal{F}^{-1}(\mathcal{F}(f)\mathcal{F}(g)), \tag{8.14b}$$

where $\mathcal{F}$ and $\mathcal{F}^{-1}$ denote Fourier transform and inverse Fourier transform. This allows us
to reason about the effect of an imaging system in the frequency domain.

The Fourier transform of a PSF is called the Optical Transfer Function (OTF), which is
necessarily complex-valued, which has a magnitude and a phase component. The magnitude
component of the OTF is called the Modulation Transfer Function (MTF) and the phase
component of the OTF is called the Phase Transfer Function (PTF):

$$OTF(\omega) = MTF(\omega)e^{i\,PTF(\omega)}. \tag{8.15}$$

What is the OTF of an ideal PSF, i.e., a delta function? It is a constant 1 across all
frequencies. This makes sense: an ideal PSF introduces no blur so it does nothing to each
spatial frequency.

Figure 8.16 shows two more examples; the top half shows the OTF, PSF, and the resulting
imaging of a diffraction-limited system (i.e., PSF being an Airy disk), and the bottom half

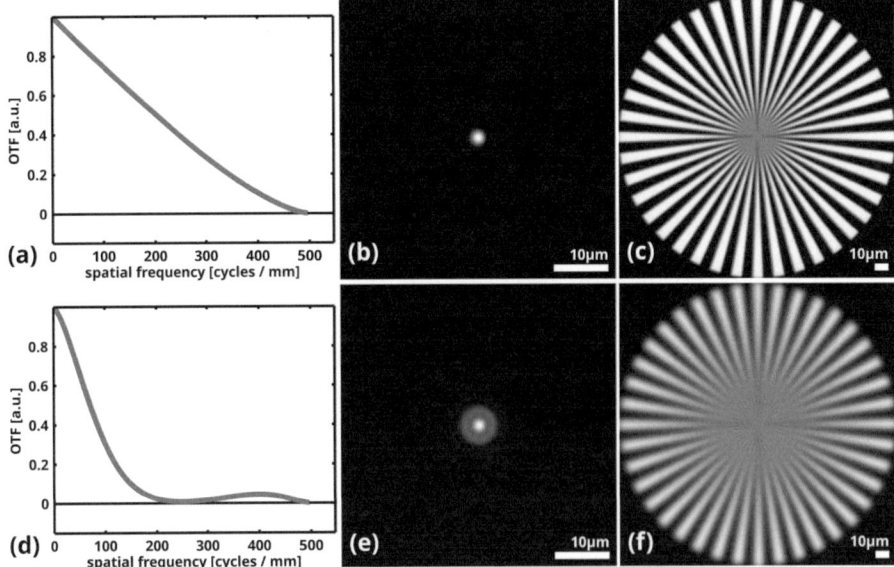

Fig. 8.16 Top: OTF, PSF, and the resulting image of a diffraction-limited system. Bottom: OTF, PSF,
and the resulting image of a diffraction-limited but defocused system. From Tom.vettenburg (2017)

shows the same system with a defocus blur. In both cases, the OTF is the same as the MTF because the Fourier transform of both PSFs have zero phase (PTF is zero at any ω). You can convince yourself of this by taking a Fourier transform of the Airy function and assuming that defocus adds a Gaussian blur to the Airy disk; we will omit the math here. General OTFs do have a phase term because the PSFs of many aberrations, e.g., coma and astigmatism, are not radially symmetric.

We can see that in the diffraction-limited case, the OTF drops to 0 at a frequency of 500, meaning information at any frequency higher than the cut-off is lost. The (first) cut-off for the defocused system is at an even lower frequency (about 200), naturally leading to more blurs in the resulting image.

References

Alves D (2006) Pinhole size chart; CC BY 2.0 license. https://www.flickr.com/photos/dominicspics/4589206921

Antipa N, Kuo G, Heckel R, Mildenhall B, Bostan E, Ng R, Waller L (2017) Diffusercam: lensless single-exposure 3D imaging. Optica 5(1):1–9

Bhandari A, Kadambi A, Raskar R (2022) Computational imaging. MIT Press

Bob (2007) Refractive index vs. wavelength for BK7 glass; CC BY-SA 3.0 license. https://en.wikipedia.org/wiki/File:Sellmeier-equation.svg

Bohren CF, Clothiaux EE (2006) Fundamentals of atmospheric radiation: an introduction with 400 problems. Wiley

FrantzDale B (2010a) Effect of aperture on blur and DOF; CC BY-SA 3.0 license. https://commons.wikimedia.org/wiki/File:Depth_of_field_illustration.svg

FrantzDale B (2010b) Ray diagram showing field curvaure; CC BY-SA 3.0 license. https://commons.wikimedia.org/wiki/File:Field_curvature.svg

Glrx (2018) Ray diagram illustrating a form of coma aberration; CC BY-SA 3.0 license. https://commons.wikimedia.org/wiki/File:Lens-coma.svg

HandWiki (2024) Kepler space telescope focal plane; CC BY-SA 3.0 license. https://handwiki.org/wiki/index.php?curid=2015813

Hecht E (2016) Optics, 5th edn. Pearson

Hurley AC, Lange GD, Hartline PH (1978) The adjustable "pinhole camera eye of nautilus. J Exp Zool 205(1):37–43

Inductiveload (2009) Mathematical function of an airy disk pattern; released into the public domain by the copyright holder. https://commons.wikimedia.org/wiki/File:Airy_Pattern.svg

Königs J (2006) Analog pinhole photography with multiple exposure; CC BY-SA 4.0 license. https://commons.wikimedia.org/wiki/File:1o_Fenstertisch_mit_R%C3%BCChrger%C3%A4t.jpg

Mdf (2005) A simulation of spherical aberration in an optical system with a circular, unobstructed aperture admitting a monochromatic point source; released into the public domain by the copyright holder. https://commons.wikimedia.org/wiki/File:Spherical-aberration-disk.jpg

Mdf (2006) Imaging as a convolution against the PSF; released into the public domain by the copyright holder. https://commons.wikimedia.org/wiki/File:Convolution_Illustrated_eng.png

Mellish B (2006) Chromatic aberration diagram; CC BY-SA 3.0 license. https://commons.wikimedia.org/wiki/File:Chromatic_aberration_lens_diagram.svg

Mglg (2008) Conceptual ray diagrams of spherically aberrated lenses; released into the public domain by the copyright holder. https://commons.wikimedia.org/wiki/File:Spherical_aberration_2.svg

Mills AA, Clift R (1992) Reflections of the 'burning mirrors of archimedes. With a consideration of the geometry and intensity of sunlight reflected from plane mirrors. Eur J Phys 13(6):268

Rayleigh L (1879) XXXI. Investigations in optics, with special reference to the spectroscope. Lond, Edinb, Dublin Philos Mag J Sci 8(49):261–274

Rorres C (n.d.) Burning mirrors: refuting the legend. https://math.nyu.edu/Archimedes/Mirrors/legend/legend.html

Sakurambo (2007) A computer-generated image of an Airy disk (the grayscale intensities have been adjusted to enhance the brightness of the outer rings of the Airy pattern); released into the public domain by the copyright holder. https://commons.wikimedia.org/wiki/File:Airy-pattern.svg

Schmid M (2008) Graphic illustratic the astigmatism phenomenon; CC BY-SA 3.0 license. https://commons.wikimedia.org/wiki/File:Meridional%2BSaggittalEbene_1.svg

Tallfred (2005) Text blurred by different focal positions of an astigmatic lens; 3-clause BSD License. https://commons.wikimedia.org/wiki/File:Astigmatism_text_blur.png

Thycoop/photographs (2022) Small park in logatec made with matchbox pinhole camera on Kodak Portra 400 film; CC BY-SA 4.0 license. https://commons.wikimedia.org/wiki/File:Small_park_in_logatec_matchbox_pinhole_camera.jpg

Tomvettenburg (2017) Illustration of the optical transfer function and its relation to image quality; CC BY-SA 4.0 license. https://en.wikipedia.org/wiki/File:Illustration_of_the_optical_transfer_function_and_its_relation_to_image_quality.svg

Wadhwa N, Garg R, Jacobs DE, Feldman BE, Kanazawa N, Carroll R, Movshovitz-Attias Y, Barron JT, Pritch Y, Levoy M (2018) Synthetic depth-of-field with a single-camera mobile phone. ACM Trans Graph (ToG) 37(4):1–13

WolfWings (2008a) Barrel distortion visual example; released into the public domain by the copyright holder. https://commons.wikimedia.org/wiki/File:Barrel_distortion.svg

WolfWings (2008b) Pincushion distortion visual example; released into the public domain by the copyright holder. https://commons.wikimedia.org/wiki/File:Pincushion_distortion.svg

Zhang Y, Mao F, Mu H, Huang M, Bao Y, Wang L, Wong NK, Xiao S, Dai H, Xiang Z et al (2021) The genome of nautilus pompilius illuminates eye evolution and biomineralization. Nat Ecol Evol 5(7):927–938

Image Sensor Architecture

9

9.1 Overview

The main job of the sensor is to turn optical signals, i.e., the optical image impinging on the sensor plane, into electrical signals, i.e., digital images. This conversion is broken down into two steps, first by converting photons to charges followed by turning charges into digital numbers.

Figure 9.1a shows a cross-sectional view of the sensor hardware, which has three main components.

- First, there is a set of optical elements sitting on the sensor. These optical elements are not the imaging optics we discussed in the previous chapter because their main goal is not to form an image.
- Second, under these optical elements are the photodiodes, which turn optical signals carried in photons to electrical signals in the form of electric charges.
- Third, interleaved with the photodiodes is the circuitry that processes the output of the photodiodes, turning charges into digital values.

From a computational perspective, we can model an image sensor as a signal processing chain, a transfer function f, that transfers the optical signal to the electrical signal. The optical signal itself has noise, and every step in the signal processing chain not only manipulates the signal itself but also introduces/affects the noise:

$$f : (\mu_p, \sigma_p) \mapsto (\mu_y, \sigma_y), \tag{9.1}$$

where μ_p and σ_p are the mean (signal) and standard deviation (noise) of the input optical signal, respectively, and μ_y and σ_y are the mean and standard deviation of the output electrical signal. The key goal of this chapter is to build a quantitative model of f.

© The Author(s), under exclusive license to Springer Nature Switzerland AG 2026   195
Y. Zhu, *Visual Computing For Architects*, Synthesis Lectures on Computer Architecture,
https://doi.org/10.1007/978-3-032-05018-2_9

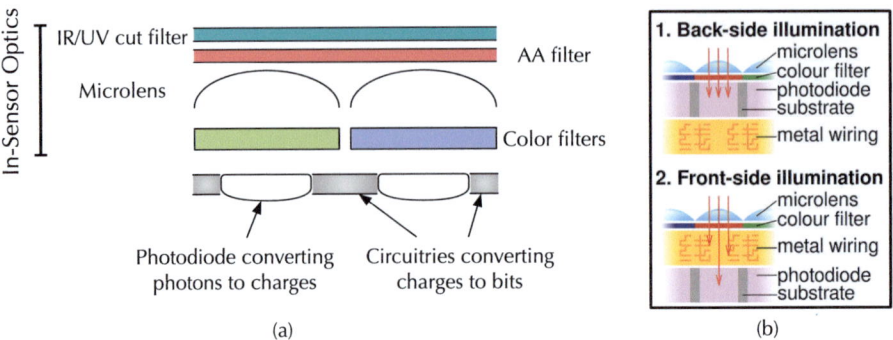

Fig. 9.1 **a** A conceptual, cross-sectional view of the sensor with the optical elements, photodiodes, and the peripheral circuitries. **b** Comparison between (1) front-illuminated sensor, where lights have to first traverse through the peripheral circuitries before reaching the light-sensitive photodiodes, and (2) back-illuminated sensor, where lights can directly reach the photodiodes; from Cmglee (2019)

There are two ways the pixels and the wires that read out the pixel outputs are physically arranged, shown in Fig. 9.1b. In the **back-side illumination** (BSI) arrangement, the wiring of the circuitries is behind the photodiodes, which directly interface with the lights. In the **front-side illumination** (FSI) arrangement, the metal wiring sits between the light and the photodiodes. This means light could be absorbed and scattered through the metal layer before reaching the photodiodes, reducing the chance of a photon being properly captured. While earlier image sensors used FSI because it is easier to manufacture, almost all commercial image sensors use BSI now (Swain and Cheskis 2008).

FSI is actually quite similar to the structure of human eyes, where, if you recall, the photoreceptors are "hiding" behind other retinal neurons such as the retinal ganglion cells, which are functionally the last layer of retinal processing but anatomically sitting at the first layer on the retina. Different from the FSI sensor, however, the non-photoreceptor neurons on the retina do very little to light: they do not absorb or scatter light much and can be generally thought of as transparent. Metal wires, of course, disrupt incident photons significantly.

9.2   From Photons to Charges and Digital Numbers

We will talk about how optical signals are first converted to electrical signals in the form of charges, and then talk about how the charges are detected, at which point the electrical signals are manifested as voltage potentials. The voltage potentials are then quantized as digital numbers, which are the raw pixel values. We will focus on the basic building blocks that enable these conversions and leave it to Sect. 9.3 to discuss how these building blocks are connected in a global sensor architecture. The discussion here assumes monochromatic sensing without noise. We will talk about color sensing and the noise issue later.

9.2.1   Photons to Charges

What turns optical signals to electrical signals is the light-sensitive photodiode in a pixel. A photodiode is a p-n junction made of silicon, a semiconductor material. When a photon hits silicon and is absorbed, an electron from the silicon *might* be freed/emitted, transforming optical signals to electrical signals. This is called the **photoelectric effect** (Einstein 1905a, b), the discovery of which won Albert Einstein his Nobel Prize.

In particular, when a photon is absorbed, if its energy is greater than or equal to the **work function** ϕ of the material, which is the minimum energy needed to free an electron from the surface of the material, the photon can transfer its energy to an electron and free the electron. A photon's energy is given by the **Planck's relation**:

$$\mathcal{E} = hf = \frac{hc}{\lambda}, \tag{9.2}$$

where h is the Planck constant, f is the photon frequency, and c is the speed of light. So if $hf > \phi$, an absorbed photon can free an electron. Interestingly, the residual energy $hf - \phi$ becomes the kinetic energy of the electron, so a photon with a shorter wavelength (i.e., higher frequency) would allow the emitted electron to move faster.

It is clear that there is a frequency threshold ϕ/h, lower than which a photon would never be able to free an electron. Higher than the threshold, there is generally a one-to-one mapping between an absorbed photon and an emitted electron: an absorbed photon always frees an electron. Since the work function of silicon is about 1.1 eV (electron volt), absorption of photons with wavelengths longer than 1100 nm would not emit any electron.

Quantum Efficiency

A key figure of merit in image sensing is the notion of **quantum efficiency** (QE), which is the ratio between the number of electrons collected and the number of incident photons:

$$QE = \frac{\text{\# of electrons collected}}{\text{\# of incident photons}}. \tag{9.3}$$

Figure 9.2a shows the QE spectrum of an image sensor in the Hubble Space Telescope. It might come as a surprise that QE is lower than 1 (even for wavelengths well within the 1000 nm threshold) and is actually wavelength dependent: shouldn't every absorbed photon (within the wavelength threshold) always free an electron? There are two reasons.

First, the denominator in the QE definition is the number of *incident* photons, not the number of absorbed photons. Not all photons that hit the photodetector will be absorbed. Figure 9.2b shows the spectral absorption coefficient σ (unit 1/cm) of silicon on the left y-axis, and the right y-axis shows the corresponding mean free path l (i.e., the expected length a photon can travel within silicon before being absorbed) at different wavelengths; recall from Eq. (7.6) that $l = 1/\sigma$. We can see that absorption is strongest for the blueish lights but decays very rapidly toward the longer wavelengths. This definition of QE is

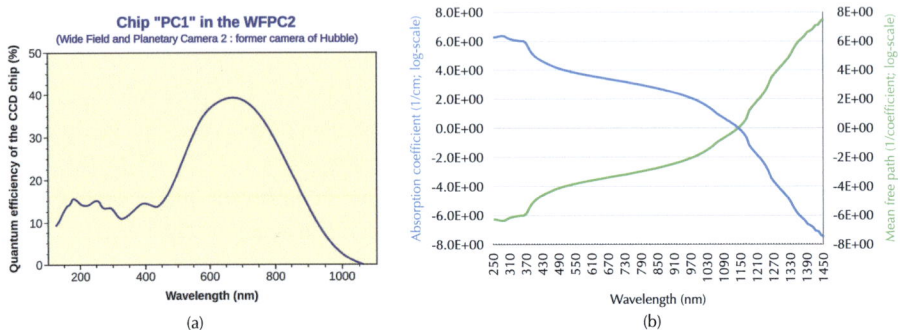

Fig. 9.2 a Quantum efficiency of a sensor on the Hubble Space Telescope; from Eric Bajart (2010) with data from Biretta and McMaster (2008, Fig. 4.2). **b** Silicon absorption coefficient (left axis) and mean free path (right axis) as a function of wavelength; data from Green and Keevers (1995)

different from how QE is defined in human vision. Recall from Sect. 3.1.1; there, QE is the probability of pigment excitation once the pigment actually absorbs a photon; there, the QE of photopigment is roughly two-thirds and is not wavelength-sensitive.

Second, the nominator in the QE definition is the number of *collected*, not emitted, electrons: even if an electron is freed by an absorbed photon, that electron might not actually be collected and contribute to the electrical signal. Depending on where the electrons are freed, some of them need to go through a random walk (think of it as Brownian motion) before being collected, and you can imagine some electrons can be recombined with the holes during the walk.

Given QE, the total number of emitted electrons after an exposure time T is given by:

$$N = \int_\lambda QE(\lambda) Y(\lambda) \mathrm{d}\lambda \tag{9.4a}$$

$$= \int_\lambda QE(\lambda) \frac{\Phi(\lambda) T \lambda}{hc} \mathrm{d}\lambda, \tag{9.4b}$$

where $Y(\lambda)$ is the number of photons incident on a photodiode at a particular wavelength λ during the exposure time T (assuming Y is invariant during T here). $Y(\lambda)$ is related to the spectral power distribution (SPD) of the incident light $\Phi(\lambda)$ by: $Y(\lambda) = \frac{\Phi(\lambda) T \lambda}{hc}$, where $\Phi(\lambda)T$ is spectral energy distribution. Using the Planck's relation (Eq. 9.2), we can turn the spectral energy distribution into the spectral quantity distribution: $\frac{\Phi(\lambda) T \lambda}{hc}$.

Note that we define QE for the photodiode itself: the denominator in Eq. (9.3) refers to the number of photons incident on the photodiode, not those that enter the camera system. This is an important distinction, because many photons that enter the camera would not even make their way to the photodiode; some of them are reflected at the lens surfaces, and others are absorbed by the various filters (Sect. 9.4). In many contexts, the QE is reported with respect to the entire camera system, where the denominator *is* the number of photons entering the camera. Always ask what the precise definition of a QE is when reading the literature.

Pixel Well and Dynamic Range

We can intuitively think of each pixel as a well (a pixel well) that collects electrons. Equation (9.4) indicates that there are two main factors that determine the number of electrons going into a particular pixel well: the incident light power and the exposure time. A pixel cannot indefinitely collect electrons. The **full-well capacity** (FWC) is the max amount of electrons that can be held by a pixel. More electrons than the FWC would *saturate* the well, at which point no charges will be stored by the pixel. When a pixel well is saturated, photographers call that pixel "over-exposed". This is illustrated in Fig. 9.3, where, ordinarily, the number of charges collected is proportional to the incident light luminance until the pixel well is full.

A larger FWC leads to a higher sensor **dynamic range**, which, informally, refers to the range of scene luminance that a sensor can capture. Formally, the dynamic range is defined as the ratio between the highest and the lowest luminance level that can be *faithfully* captured. The highest level is the FWC, but what about the lowest level? Wouldn't that simply be 0 and, if so, wouldn't the dynamic range of any image sensor be infinity?

The answer is that at very low light levels the charges collected by a pixel are dominated by noise. We call the charges collected when there is no incident light the "noise floor", which can be measured by taking an image when the camera is in dark. The dynamic range is thus the ratio between the FWC and the noise floor (Nakamura 2006, Sect. 3.4.2.1). We will not get into too much detail, but the noise floor is dominated by "dark noise", which is caused by the thermally dislodged electrons, and the "read noise", which is the noise introduced by the read-out circuitry. We refer you to Boukhayma (2018), Nakamura (2006, Sect. 3.3), and Rowlands (2020b, Sects. 3.8 and 3.9) for detailed discussions on noise.

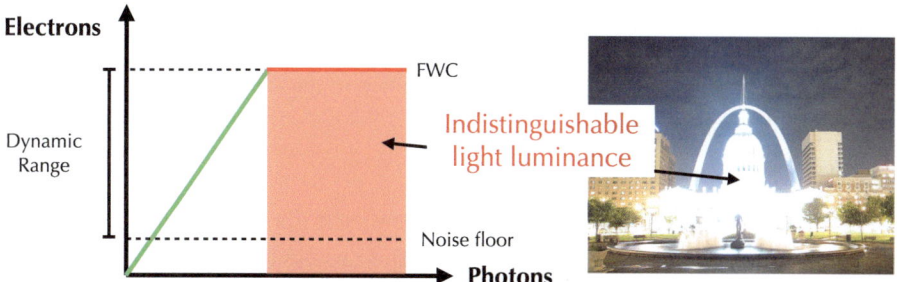

Fig. 9.3 Illustration of dynamic range, which is the ratio of the FWC and the noise floor; adapted from Kevin McCoy (2009). Incident luminance higher than the FWC saturates a pixel, leading to over-exposure

9.2.2   Measuring Charges

Basic Principle

Now that we have turned photons to charges—the freed electrons move to the n region and the holes move to the p region of the p-n junction—the next step is to measure the charges. The basic principle of doing so is using a capacitor: we use the electrons to discharge a capacitor with a known capacitance; by measuring the voltage difference before and after the discharge, we can then estimate the number of emitted electrons:

$$\Delta V = \frac{Q_{SIG}}{C_{FD}} \times g = \frac{Nq}{C_{FD}} \times g, \tag{9.5}$$

where Q_{SIG} is the charge in the signal stored in the capacitor, C_{FD} is the capacitance, and g is the voltage gain of whatever device is used to read out the voltage (usually a source follower; see later). Q_{SIG} itself is the product of N, the number of charges in the signal, and q, the elementary charge.

We can see that once we can measure ΔV, we can get an estimate of N. Why do we care about N? Intuitively, the incident light luminance is positively related to N: more incident photons means higher luminance. Luminance L, if we are interested in only grayscale, monochromatic imaging, is ultimately what we want to estimate.

It is important to realize that the actual relationship between L and N is not linear. We know that luminance is defined as:

$$L = \int_{\lambda} V(\lambda)\Phi(\lambda)d\lambda, \tag{9.6}$$

where $V(\lambda)$ is the luminance efficiency function (LEF) and $\Phi(\lambda)$ is the SPD of the incident light. Taking Eqs. (9.6) and (9.4b) together, we can see that given N, we cannot quite estimate L, because L depends on $\Phi(\lambda)$, but estimating $\Phi(\lambda)$ from N is an under-determined problem, as Eq. (9.4b) shows. To be exact, L does not necessarily scale linearly with N—it does not even necessarily scale positively with N, but it is perhaps not terribly wrong to informally say a higher charge count means a higher luminance in the scene. We will return to this problem when we discuss color sensing, too.

4T Design

The photodiode (PD) technically acts as a capacitor itself (the n-side neutral region holds electrons and the p-side neutral region holds holes), so we could simply use the PD for that purpose. This is indeed how an earlier pixel design works, which we will return to shortly. Modern pixels actually transfer the charges from the PD to a separate measurement node, which we focus on here.

Figure 9.4a shows the circuit diagram of a typical pixel design that detects and measures the charges. The design has a PD and four transistors, so it is usually called the 4T design. The M-TX switch controls the transfer of the charges accumulated in the PD to the Floating

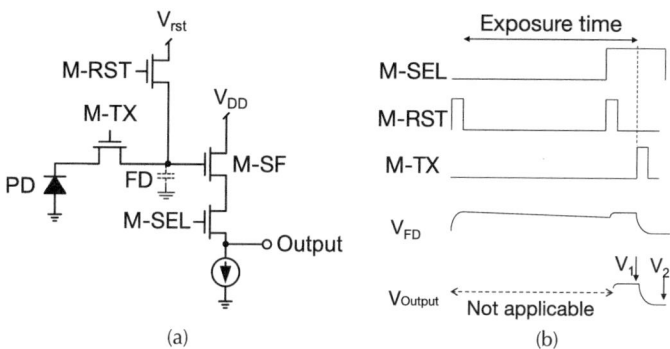

Fig. 9.4 a Circuit diagram of a typical 4T pixel design; adapted from Ma (2024, Fig. 2.5a). **b** Timing diagram of operating a 4T pixel

Diffusion (FD),[1] another capacitive area, and is sometimes called the *measurement node* or the *sense node*, because that is where the charges are actually being measured. The FD is connected to the NMOS Source Follower (SF) transistor M-SF, where the gate terminal is its input and is connected to the FD voltage, the drain is connected to the supply voltage, and the source is the output that faithfully follows/transfers the input with a gain of about 0.9 (g in Eq. 9.5).

The sequence of operation goes roughly like the following, and Fig. 9.4b shows the corresponding timing diagram:

1. Before the exposure, we turn on the M-RST switch *and* the M-TX to drain the charges (electrons) at the PD, which will also, as a byproduct, drain the charges in the FD, resetting their voltage potentials both to V_{RST}. Resetting the FD voltage at this step is of no functional use, as we will shortly see.
2. We then turn off M-RST and M-TX, and the exposure begins, during which the charges are collected inside the PD. We can see from Eq. (9.5) that in order to measure the charges we need to measure the voltage difference *at the FD node* before and after the charges are transferred. So toward the end of the exposure, we turn on the M-RST switch again while, importantly, keeping the M-TX switch off. This would allow us to reset the FD voltage to V_{rst}, which will be measured through M-SF as V_1 in Fig. 9.4b.[2]
3. We then turn on the M-TX switch, which transfers the charges from the PD to the FD. After that, we turn off M-TX and read the voltage from M-SF for the second time, this

---

[1] For the charges collected in PD to be transferable to the FD, the photodiode needs to be "pinned", which means there is another layer of p+ implant above the p-n junction pinned to the ground (0 V). Such a PD is also called the Pinned Photodiode, or PPD (Fossum and Hondongwa 2014).

[2] V_1 and V_{rst} technically are ever so slightly different because the charges might be leaking between resetting and read out.

time for the voltage at FD after the charge transfer. This is the V_2 in Fig. 9.4b. The difference between V_1 and V_2 is the ΔV in Eq. (9.5).

As we can see, we read the voltage of the FD twice to obtain the voltage difference caused by the charges collected during the exposure. This is called **Correlated Double Sampling** (CDS), which turns out to also be very important to mitigate many noise sources, which we will discuss later.

To read out the voltage from the SF, the M-SEL switch needs to be turned on, which is omitted from Fig. 9.4b for simplicity. As we will shortly see in Sect. 9.3, in most cases (although not all), pixels are read out row by row, so the M-SEL switches of all pixels in the same row are connected to the same signal, usually called the row select signal.

The timing diagram in Fig. 9.4b is illustrative of the major operations (omitting M-SF) but not drawn to scale. The exposure time is usually at the tens of milliseconds scale (e.g., 30 FPS means roughly a 33.3 ms exposure time), but the timescale to operate the transistors/switches is at the microsecond level. Also observe, in Fig. 9.4b, that during the exposure the voltage at the FD (V_{FD}) slowly reduces from V_{rst} after the first reset—because of the charge leakage in the FD, just like how DRAM cells leak. This is why we need the second reset to bring the voltage at FD back to V_{rst} before charge transfer. This is also why we say the first reset is of no functional use to the FD (but of course very important to the PD because we want the PD to collect only electrons emitted from the current exposure).

4T APS Versus 3T APS Versus PPS

The (4T) pixel design described above is called an **Active Pixel Sensor** (APS) design, first conceived by Noble (1968) (see Fossum (1993) for a more modern perspective). An APS has a per-pixel SF (a common-drain amplifier) that "actively" reads out the signal for each pixel by turning its charges to voltage. We briefly discuss the other, older pixel designs that are less commonly used now. See El Gamal and Eltoukhy (2005) for a more detailed discussion and visual comparisons.

A simpler and earlier version of the APS design uses only three transistors (3T) without the M-TX gate. Without the transfer gate, the PD is used as the measurement/sensor node itself, so the C_{FD} in Eq. (9.5) is effectively the capacitance of the PD itself. The 3T APS simplifies the pixel design and, thus, increases the fill factor (without the microlenses). It, however, generally suffers from a lower signal-to-noise ratio (SNR) for a variety of reasons. For instance, the PD has a large inherent photodiode capacitance, so the signal (ΔV in Eq. 9.5) read from the PD is low, making it more vulnerable to noise. In contrast, we get to control the FD in the 4T APS, which can be made to have a much lower capacitance, leading to a higher SNR. The CDS for 3T APS is also much less effective in suppressing noise, as we will discuss later.

A precursor to APS was the **Passive Pixel Sensor** (PPS), first suggested in Weckler (1967) and Dyck and Weckler (1968). The PPS has no SF that reads out voltage from the PD charges. Instead, the charges (not voltage) in the PD "passively" flow through a column bus and are turned to voltage there through a charge amplifier (Aoki et al. 1982). The PPS design is simpler (as only one transistor is needed) but leads to a much worse noise profile because of the large (parasitic) capacitance of the column bus. The SF in APS acts as an active amplifier, which isolates the sense node (whether it is the PD or the FD) from the large column bus capacitance, providing a much higher output current and lower output impedance than a PD does and, thus, improving the SNR (Kozlowski et al. 1998; Ohta 2020, Sect. 2.5).

Electronic Shutter

Ideally, when we are not capturing light, the photodiodes should not be exposed to lights. This is achieved by a shutter. **Mechanical shutters** do so by physically blocking lights. The sensor is *not* exposed to light normally, blocked by the shutter. The shutter then mechanically opens to expose the sensor to light. There are many types of mechanical shutters, of which the most popular one is the focal plane shutter shown in Fig. 9.5a. The shutter has two curtains that move in sync with a gap that allows lights in. The size of the shutter opening and the speed of the movement dictate the exposure time: a larger opening and slower speed mean longer exposure time. This is called a focal plane shutter because the shutter is located in front of the focal plane (sensor). There is also the leaf shutter, which is usually located at the aperture plane with the lenses.

The 4T pixel design above essentially implements an **electronic shutter** (ES). With an ES, we expose photodiodes to lights *all the time*. The way we mark the start of the exposure is through the M-RST switch, which resets the PDs, and the way we mark the end of the exposure is through the M-TX switch, which transfers the PD charges for measurement. The time difference between these two steps dictates the exposure time. As you can imagine, the shutter speed (inverse of the exposure time) of an electronic shutter can be much faster than that of a mechanical shutter, since there are no mechanical moving parts.

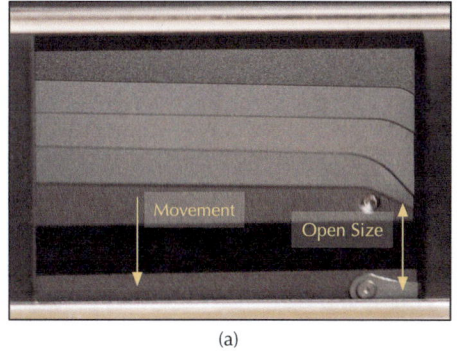 

(a)   (b)

Fig. 9.5 a A mechanical focal-plane shutter, which is inherently a rolling shutter; adapted from Ommnomnomgulp (2008). **b** Rolling shutter artifact; from BrayLockBoy (2018)

9.2.3   Read-Out Circuitry

Following the pixel circuitry is the read-out circuitry, which usually has two main components: the programmable-gain amplifier and the analog-to-digital Converter (ADC). Figure 9.6 illustrates the common, simplified designs of the two components.

The amplifier is there to amplify the voltage read from the pixel, and the **gain** of the amplifier is programmable. A programmable gain is useful in imaging and photography to artificially shorten or extend the exposure time (e.g., through the ISO setting in a digital camera). The particular design shown in Fig. 9.6a combines CDS with a classical amplifier design with two capacitors. Specifically, the two voltages read out from the FD (one right after the reset and the other right after the charge transfer) are sampled by the C_{in} capacitor sequentially, which essentially performs an analog-domain subtraction that is required by CDS. The voltage difference is then amplified with a gain $\frac{C_{in}}{C_{feedback}}$. $C_{feedback}$ is usually programmable, allowing us to control the gain.

The amplified voltage difference then goes through an ADC to obtain the digital value. There is a huge amount of ADC designs (Murmann 2014). The design that is commonly used in image sensors is the single-slope (SS) design, whose simplified diagram is shown in Fig. 9.6b. An SS ADC consists of a comparator, a ramp signal generator, and a counter. The ramp generator provides a monotonically increasing or decreasing ramp signal, which is compared with the to-be-quantized analog signal (output of the amplifier). At every clock cycle, the comparator compares the two inputs while the counter increments. When the two input signals cross, the counter value is recorded and represents the quantized digital value of the analog signal.

The designs in Fig. 9.6 perform CDS in the analog domain (through C_{in}). In many image sensors today, the CDS is performed in the digital domain after the ADC (Nitta et al. 2006). You would think that such a design might require twice the ADC overhead plus the additional digital subtraction overhead. In reality, the design is quite clever. The ADC would first quantize the first sample (before reset), and the resulting counter value represents the digital value of the first sample. For the second sample, instead of counting from scratch,

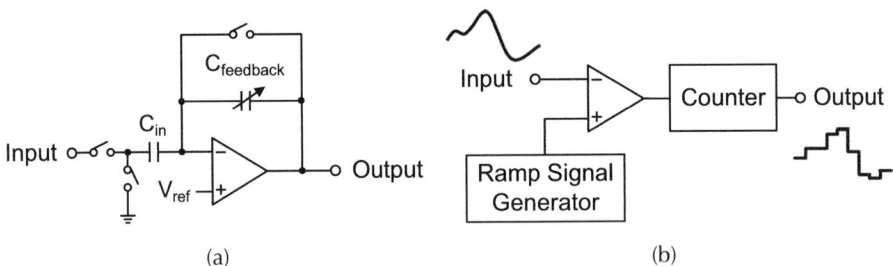

(a)   (b)

Fig. 9.6 a Analog CDS and programmable amplifier; from Ma (2024, Fig. 2.5b). **b** A single-slope ADC typically used in image sensors; adapted from Ma (2024, Fig. 2.5c)

we would simply turn the counter around so that it counts backward. At the end, the counter value is naturally the digital difference of the two samples.

9.3 Global Architecture

We have discussed the individual building blocks that are needed for a pixel to turn lights into digital values, but how are they put together in an actual image sensor supporting tens of millions pixels? This chapter talks about the global architecture of an image sensor. We will start with a common architecture followed by other variants.

9.3.1 Column-Parallel Readout

Figure 9.7a shows a typical arrangement, where pixels are organized as a 2D array, just like a (DRAM/SRAM) memory array, and each column has an amplifier and ADC shared by all the pixels in that column. That is, the Output pin in Fig. 9.4 of all the pixels in the same column are connected to the same amplifier and ADC. The read-out circuit is then connected to digital processing circuitry, which could potentially perform simple image-space operations such as downsampling, scaling, rotation, etc. There is also an I/O unit that transfers the pixels to the host processor, usually through the MIPI-CSI interface, and transfers commands/configuration data from the host processor, usually through the I2C interface, which has a much lower bandwidth than MIPI (Kb/s vs. Gb/s).

The pixels in the pixel array are addressed row by row through a row scanner logic, shown on the left of Fig. 9.7a. Pixels in the same row share three external signals: a reset signal RST, which is connected to all the M-RST transistors in the row, a row-select signal SEL, which is connected to all the M-SEL transistors of the same row, and a transfer signal TX (omitted in the figure) connected to all the M-TX switches in the same row.

The operating sequence of the pixel rows is shown in Fig. 9.7b; the times are not drawn to scale. Each row of pixels goes through the PD reset, exposure, and readout phases under the control of the three external signals (RST, SEL, and TX). Importantly, the three phases are pipelined across rows. That is, while the first row is being exposed, we can start resetting the PDs for the subsequent rows and preparing them for exposure. For instance, in the concrete example of Fig. 9.7a, the first row is starting the read-out sequence, the nth row is starting the exposure, while all other rows in-between are currently under exposure. While the exposure times of different rows can overlap, their readout sequences cannot—pixels in the same column but different rows share the same the read-out circuitry.

We can see that the way the pixel array is addressed and operated is similar to how a memory array (e.g., SRAM/DRAM) is, where the data in an entire row is accessed at once. However, since the pixel rows are operated strictly sequentially (unless random sampling is needed (Feng et al. 2024)), the row scanner logic does not need a decoder, which supports

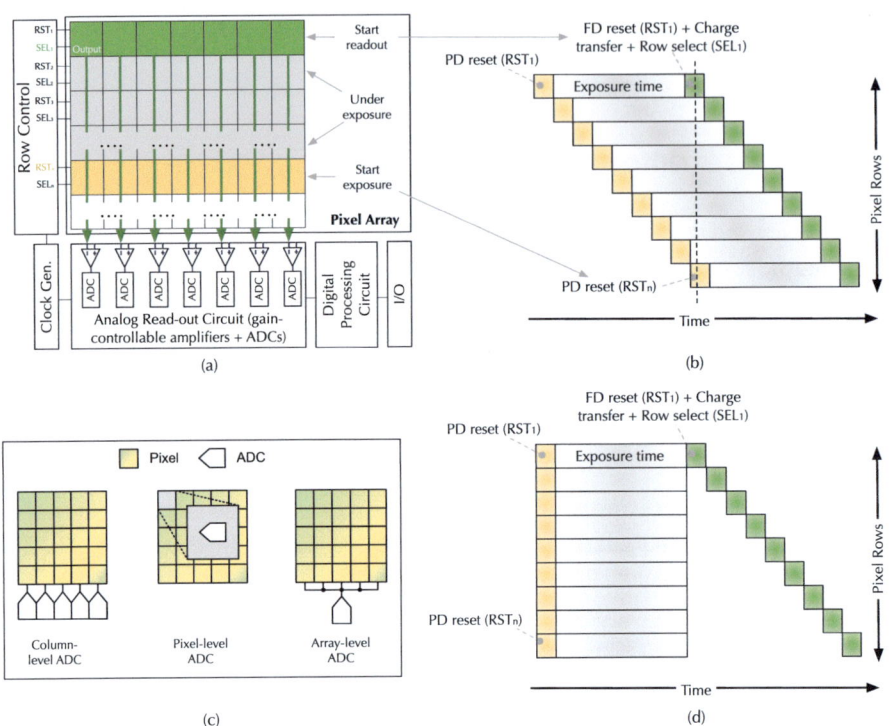

Fig. 9.7 a The block diagram of a typical rolling-shutter image sensor with column-level amplifiers and ADCs, where pixels in the same column share the same amplifier and ADC; pixels are exposed and read out row by row under the control of the RST signal (connecting to the M-RST switches) and the SEL signal (connecting to the M-SEL switches) (for simplicity, we omit the per-row TX signal, which connects to all the M-TX switches in the same row); **b** Timing diagram operating the image sensor in (**a**) with a rolling shutter; technically the FD reset should be overlapped with the exposure time but is lumped into the readout box for simplicity. **c** Comparison of column-level ADC used in (**a**) with pixel-level ADC and array/chip-level ADC. **d** Timing diagram operating the image sensor in (**a**) with a global shutter

random accesses that a typical memory array would need. Instead, one can usually use parallel shift registers to generate the three external signals row by row.

9.3.2   Rolling Versus Global Shutter

The timing diagram suggests that pixels in different rows technically have slightly shifted exposure times, inherently using a **rolling shutter**. The mechanical focal-plane shutter shown in Fig. 9.5a is inherently a rolling shutter. Rolling shutters introduce noticeable artifacts; one such example is shown in Fig. 9.5b, where the photo was taken by a camera traveling in a car driving at about 50 mph. As a result, the fence and gate appear slanted because vertical parts of these objects are taken at different times. Such an artifact is much less visible for more distant objects, such as the cliff (can you reason about why?).

Global shutters address the rolling shutter artifacts by exposing all pixels at the same time. Figure 9.5d shows the timing diagram of a global shutter sensor; compare that with that of the rolling shutter sensor in Fig. 9.5a. All the PDs are reset at the same time and have the same exposure duration.

The pixels are still read out row by row due to the column-level design of the read-out circuitry. This means the pixel values have to be temporarily held in some form of analog buffer after exposure and before they are read out. One could certainly use the FD for this analog buffer—with the caveat that the this prevents the PD from starting a new exposure cycle. This is because starting a new exposure requires resetting the PD, which would also reset the corresponding FD, as shown in Fig. 9.4a. For that reason, it is common to implement an additional analog buffer inside each pixel. The buffer can be implemented either in the charge domain before the FD (Yasutomi et al. 2011; Sakakibara et al. 2012; Tournier et al. 2018; Kumagai et al. 2018b; Yokoyama et al. 2018; Kobayashi et al. 2017) or implemented in the voltage domain after the FD (Kondo et al. 2015; Stark et al. 2018; Miyauchi et al. 2020).

9.3.3 Pixel-Parallel and Chip-Level Readout

We can also arrange the read-out circuitry differently, as illustrated in Fig. 9.7c. For instance, we could have a *per-pixel* (gain-controllable) amplifier and ADC and, consequently, a per-pixel digital memory. This essentially allows each pixel to directly output digital values, giving rise to the so called **Digital Pixel Sensor** (DPS) design, which was first reported in Fowler et al. (1994) and is recently gaining tractions (Liu et al. 2019), where the in-pixel memory can is a 6T SRAM cell and the entire pixel array acts almost like an SRAM array.

DPS increases the pixel design complexity and pixel sizes, which, without microlenses, reduces the fill factor. This can, however, be alleviated with a stacked design, which we will get to in Sect. 9.3.5. The main advantage of the DPS is that it massively increases the readout bandwidth due to pixel-parallel ADCs, which could shorten the frame latency when using a global shutter (see Fig. 9.7d), especially when short exposure time is desirable (e.g., high frame rate or "snap-shot" photography).

Yet another read-out arrangement is to have a single gain-controllable amplifier and ADC for the entire pixel array. In this case, we not only need logic to scan rows one by one but also to scan columns one by one (e.g., through shift registers). This arrangement is not common (thus omitted in Fig. 9.7c) due to its slow read-out speed but is the only option for sensors based on the Charge-coupled Devices (CCD), a design that is different from all the designs we have discussed so far and is our focus next.

9.3.4   CMOS Versus CCD Sensor

All the sensor designs we have covered so far are called Complementary Metal-Oxide-Semiconductor (CMOS) sensors, because they heavily rely on circuitries implemented using the CMOS techonlogies. CCD sensor is the other major category of sensor design, first reported in Boyle and Smith (1970). Both CCD and CMOS sensors use silicon to implement the PDs, although the specific implementations can differ (Nakamura 2006, Sect. 3.1.2). The main difference lies in how the charges generated by the PDs are read out. See Fossum (1993, 1997) and El Gamal and Eltoukhy (2005) for the historical background and comparisons.

A CCD sensor directly reads out charges from pixels by *shifting* the collected charges row by row. When a row reaches the bottom of the pixel array, we then shift the charges column by column to a single, array-level SF amplifier (and potentially a gain-controllable amplifier and ADC afterwards). In CMOS sensors, in contrast, the charges are converted to voltages *within* the pixels, and it is the voltage potentials that are being read out from the pixel array by *addressing*, rather than shifting across, individual rows.

The key to a CCD sensor is the charge-coupled devices themselves. A CCD is a set of connected MOS capacitors that store and transfer, between them, charges (Hu 2009, Sect. 5), invented by Boyle and Smith (1970), who won the Nobel Prize in Physics in 2009. In a CCD image sensor, the CCDs are connected to the PDs. After the exposure, all the PDs simultaneously transfer their charges to the corresponding vertical CCDs. The vertical CCDs in the same column then act as a shift register, transferring the charges downward to the horizontal CCD at the bottom of the chip. When a row of charges reaches the horizontal CCDs, the charges are then transferred horizontally (again, in a shift-register fashion) to the SF amplifier, which turns charges to voltage.

Given this signal read-out architecture, it is perhaps unsurprising to see that CCD sensors inherently support global shutters: the CCDs used for shifting charges naturally store the charges temporarily during the read-out.

CCDs are fabricated using process technologies that are optimized for charge transfer and that are incompatible with the CMOS technologies. In contrast, the read-out architecture of the CMOS sensors can be fabricated using CMOS technologies. This is a huge advantage because non-imaging logics such as control (e.g., clock generation) and analog/digital processing (e.g., ADC, image processing, computer vision tasks) are also based on CMOS technologies. Such logics, in CCD sensors, need to be implemented on a separate chip that interfaces with the CCD chip, rather than integrated with the pixel array on the same chip in a CMOS image sensor.

As modern CMOS technologies mature and gradually take over the semiconductor industry, CMOS image sensors have become more appealing. The main advantage of the CCD sensors is their high SNRs. CCD sensors do not have active devices during read-out and, thus, avoid/minimize many sources of noise that CMOS sensors are vulnerable to, a point we will return to when discussing noise modeling.[3] Because of that, while consumer cameras today mostly use CMOS sensors, CCD sensors are still use widely used in many scenarios where imaging quality is critical, e.g., scientific imaging. For instance, many telescopes for astrophysics (e.g., Sloan Digital Sky Survey) still use CCD sensors.

9.3.5 Computational and Stacked CMOS Image Sensors

Because the imaging circuitries and the logic processing circuitries both use the CMOS process technologies, a clear trend in CMOS Image Sensor (CIS) design is to move into the sensor computations that are traditionally carried out outside the sensor, which gives rise to the notion of **Computational CIS**.

CIS Scaling Trends

Figure 9.8a shows the percentage of computational CIS papers in International Solid-State Circuits Conference (ISSCC) and International Electron Devices Meeting (IEDM), two premier venues for semiconductor circuits and devices, from Year 2000 and Year 2022 with respect to all the CIS papers during the same time range. The trend is clear: increasingly more CIS designs integrate compute capabilities.

A key reason why we could integrate processing/computational capabilities into the CIS chip is because of the advancements in the CMOS technologies that, for instance, have significantly shrunk the feature size, which is the smallest physical dimension that can be reliably fabricated on a semiconductor chip and is proportional to the transistor size. At the same time, however, the PD size itself has not shrunk proportionally, meaning adding CMOS logic to the sensor increases the total chip area minimally in the grand scheme of things.

This is shown in Fig. 9.8b, where triangle markers show the pixel sizes in CIS designs from all ISSCC papers appeared during Yeare 2000 and 2022, which include leading industry CIS designs at different times. We overlay a trend line regressed from these CIS designs to better illustrate the pixel size scaling trend. As a comparison, the blue line at the bottom represents the standard CMOS technology node scaling laid out by the International Roadmap for Devices and Systems (IRDS) (IRDS 2024). We can see that the gap between the pixel size and the standard CMOS feature size steadily increases. In fact, the pixel size scaling stagnates at around $5\,\mu$m, which has long been seen as the practical pixel size limit (Fossum 1997). As semiconductor manufacturers keep pulling rabbits out of a hat, the CMOS feature size is still, miraculously, shrinking (TSMC/Samsung are shipping products with a 2 nm process node in 2025), so the gap would still exist, at least for quite a while.

---

[3] It is worth noting, however, that it is difficult for the CCD sensor to perform CDS because of its read-out architecture (shifting charges to a single SF amplifier).

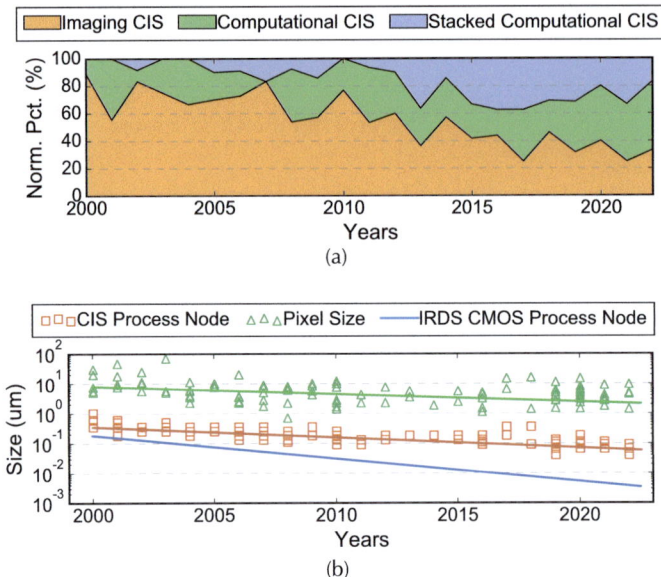

Fig. 9.8 a Percentage of conventional CIS, computational CIS, and stacked computational CIS designs from surveying all ISSCC and IEDM papers published between the year 2000 and 2022. Increasingly more CIS designs are computational. **b** CIS process node always lags behind conventional CMOS process node. This is because CIS node scaling tracks the pixel size scaling, which does not shrink aggressively due to the fundamental need of maintaining photon sensitivity. From Ma et al. (2023, Figs. 1 and 3)

Computational CIS Architectures

The computations inside a CIS could take place in both the analog and the digital domain. Figure 9.9b illustrates one example where analog computing is integrated into a CIS chip before the ADC. Analog operations usually implement primitives for feature extraction (Bong et al. 2017a, b), object detection (Young et al. 2019), and DNN inference (Hsu et al. 2020; Xu et al. 2021). Figure 9.9c illustrates another example that integrates digital processing, such as ISP (Murakami et al. 2022), image filtering (Kim et al. 2005), and DNN (Bong et al. 2017a).

As the processing capabilities become more complex, CIS design has embraced 3D stacking technologies, as is evident by the increasing number of stacked CIS in Fig. 9.8. Figure 9.9d illustrates a typical stacked design, where the processing logic is separated from, and stacked with, the pixel array layer. The different layers communicate through the hybrid bond or the micro Through-Silicon Via (μTSV) (Liu et al. 2022; Tsugawa et al. 2017). The processing layer typically integrates digital processors, such as ISP (Kwon et al. 2020), image processing (Hirata et al. 2021; Kumagai et al. 2018a), and DNN accelerators (Eki et al. 2021; Liu et al. 2022).

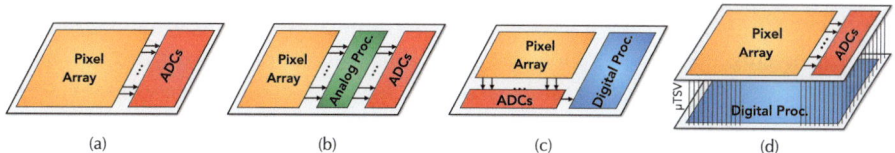

Fig. 9.9 **a** Traditional 2D imaging CIS with the PD array and the ADCs. **b** Computational CIS with analog processing capabilities (before the ADCs). **c** Computational CIS with digital processing. **d** Stacked computational CIS with digital processing in a separate layer. Adapted from Ma et al. (2023, Fig. 2)

Three-layer stacked designs have also been proposed. Sony IMX 400 (Haruta et al. 2017) is a 3-layer design that integrates a pixel layer, a DRAM layer (1 Gbit), and a logic layer with an Image Signal Processor (ISP). The DRAM layer buffers high-rate frames before streaming them out to the host. This enables super slow motion (960 FPS); otherwise, the bandwidth of the MIPI CSI-2 interface limits the capturing rate of the sensor. Meta conceptualizes a three-layer design (Liu et al. 2022) with a pixel array layer, a per-pixel ADC layer, and a digital processing layer that integrates a DNN accelerator—using DPS. Stacking makes it easier to implement DPS: the main disadvantage of DPS is the complexity of the pixel design, but with stacking, the additional pixel processing circuitry (gain amplifier, ADC, etc.) can be "hidden" on a separate layer than the pixel array layer (Liu et al. 2020, 2022).

Challenges of CIS

Moving computation inside a CIS, however, is not without challenges. Most importantly, processing inside the sensor is far less efficient than that outside the sensor. This is because, while the CIS is implemented using the CMOS technologies, it uses significantly *older* process nodes than that of the conventional CMOS.

This is shown in Fig. 9.8b, where the square markers show the process node used in each CIS paper surveyed. As a reference, the IRDS standard CMOS process node scaling line is also shown. At around the year 2000, the CIS process node started lagging behind that of the conventional CMOS node, and the gap is increasing. CIS designs today commonly use 65 nm and older process nodes. This gap is not an artifact of the CIS designs we pick; it is fundamental: there is simply no need to aggressively scale down the process node because the pixel size does not, and can not, shrink much. In fact, from Fig. 9.8b we can see that the slope of CIS process node scaling almost exactly follows that of the pixel size scaling. The reason that pixel size does not shrink much is to ensure light sensitivity: a small pixel reduces the number of photons it can collect, which directly reduces the dynamic range and the SNR.[4]

---

[4] It is interesting to note the fact that there is a fundamental pixel size limit negates one advantage of the CCD sensors, where the pixel design is simpler so one can theoretically make the pixel size smaller, but that is countered by the limit to which the PDs can shrink (Fossum 1997).

Inefficient in-sensor processing can be mitigated through 3D stacking technologies, which allow for heterogeneous integration: the pixel layer and the computing layer(s) can use their respective, optimal process node. Stacking, however, could increase power density, especially when future CIS integrates more processing capabilities. Therefore, harnessing the power of (stacked) computational CIS requires exploring a large design space and is still an active area of research (Ma 2024; Feng et al. 2024; Ma et al. 2023).

9.4   In-Sensor Optics

The on-chip optics serve a few purposes: blocking lights in the IR/UV ranges, boosting photon collection efficiency, anti-aliasing, and filtering for color reproduction.

9.4.1   IR/UV Cut-Off Filters

Many cameras have cut-off filters for infrared (IR) and ultraviolet (UV) lights. Their goals are to remove/block IR or UV lights, as much as possible, from the incident light. These filters are transparent in that they predominantly absorb light while scattering very little light. So their optical behaviors can be adequately captured by their transmittance spectra. Check Melentijevic (2015) for the transmittance spectra of the cut-off filters in a few popular cameras. For instance, the filter in the Nikon D200 essentially blocks lights below 400 nm and above 700 nm.

The reason most photographic cameras want to remove IR and UV lights is because the human visual system is not sensitive to IR and UV lights (recall our earlier discussions about the spectra of the cone fundamentals, which drop to 0 beyond roughly the 380 and 780 nm range). So for a camera to accurately reproduce the color of an object as if the object is directly viewed by the human eyes, the sensor's sensitivity ideally needs to mimic that of the human eyes. Cutting IR and UV lights, to which our photoreceptors are not sensitive, is just the first step. We will discuss in detail in Sect. 9.5 what other mechanisms are in place for accurate color reproduction in image sensors.

Interestingly, thermographic cameras detect optical power in the IR range to estimate object temperature. Any object above absolute zero radiates, and this is call the **blackbody radiation**. Planck's law governs the electromagnetic power emitted at a particular wavelength at a particular temperature. It turns out that at room temperature (about 300 K), most of the radiation power is in the IR range; very little radiation comes from the visible range. That is why thermal cameras use IR radiation for temperature estimation.

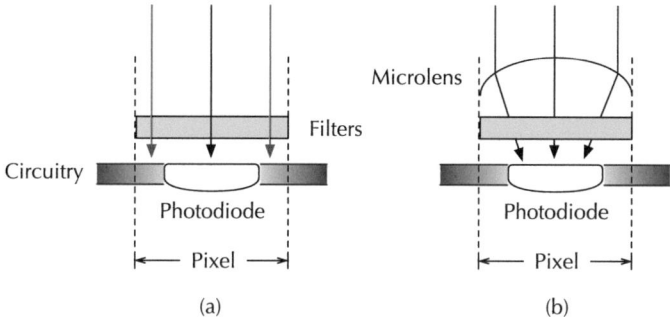

Fig. 9.10 a Without a microlens, the photosensitive area of a pixel is the PD area; many incident lights will not hit the PD, leading to a low fill factor. **b** Microlenses increase the effective fill factor of an image sensor

9.4.2   Microlenses

An important figure of merit of image sensors is the **fill factor** (FF), which is defined as the ratio of the photosensitive area of a pixel to the actual pixel area. Usually the photosensitive area is much smaller than the pixel area. Recall from Fig. 9.1 that, in addition to the actual photodiode, a pixel contains many other electrical components (capacitors, transistors, and other complex logic gates) that take up the area. This is illustrated in Fig. 9.10a, where many incident lights will not reach the PD, leading to a low FF. Given a fixed pixel area, a low FF means the pixel collects fewer photons during exposure, which translates to a higher signal-to-noise ratio, so it is almost always desirable to have a higher FF.

One common way to increase the FF that is prevalent in almost all image sensors is through microlenses. This is illustrated in Fig. 9.10b. Every pixel has a convex lens, which we call a **microlens**, sitting on top of it. The job of the microlens is to, ideally, direct all the photons hitting the pixel to the photodiode, in which case the FF would effectively be 100%, a regime that contemporary image sensors are now very close to achieving.

9.4.3   Anti-aliasing Filters

Many image sensors also have anti-aliasing (AA) filters, especially photographic sensors. Recall that pixels perform spatial sampling of the optical image, which is continuous, thus introducing aliasing. The classic anti-aliasing method is to pre-filter the continuous signal using a low-pass filter, essentially blurring the signal and reducing its peak frequency. Pharr et al. (2023, Chap. 8) and Glassner (1995, Unit II) provide great technical discussions of signal sampling and reconstruction, which we will omit here.

In some sense, the photodiodes themselves and the microlenses act as pre-filters already: they inherently perform spatial 2D box convolutions over the continuous signal impinging

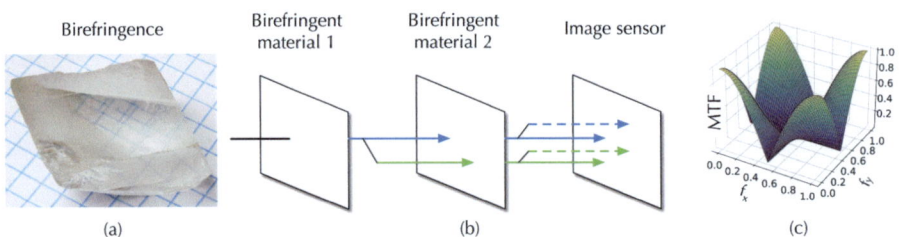

Fig. 9.11 **a** A birefringent material that, through double refraction, splits a ray into two; adapted from APN MJM (2011). **b** Many anti-aliasing filters are made by cascading two birefringent materials that, collectively, split a ray into four; they are called 4-dot AA filters. **c** MTF of a 4-dot AA filter

upon them. Take the photodiode as an example: each photodiode integrates all the incident photons, as we have seen in Sect. 9.2, and integration is equivalent to convolving/filtering the signal with a 2D box filter.

However, the support of the filter carried by the microlens and the photodiode is small: the microlens filter has a size of the pixel area, and the photodiode filter support is even more compact. To more aggressively pre-filter the signal, we need a filter with a wide support. To that end, AA filters use birefringent material, as shown in Fig. 9.11a, which essentially splits a ray into two rays, each with a different polarization and, thus, takes a slightly different path (recall that the refractive index depends on the polarization of light). If we cascade two such materials, a ray gets split into four rays; this is called a 4-dot beam splitting. This is done by, e.g., the Nikon D800e, as shown in Fig. 9.11b.

The birefringent material acts as a low-pass filter. The intuition is that if an incident ray is spread over, say, 4 sensor-plane points, then each sensor-plane point, equivalently, integrates information from 4 incident rays, each coming from a distinct scene point (assuming a pinhole aperture). We know integration is essentially low-pass filtering.

The way to understand the effect of the AA filter is to analyze its Point Spread Function (PSF) and Modulation Transfer Function (MTF), which we have seen in Sect. 8.4.3. Assuming a pinhole aperture, a 4-dot beam-splitting AA filter essentially imposes a PSF where a scene point is spread over 4 sensor-plane points. The PSF is the sum of 4 Dirac Delta functions placed on a regular grid with an offset d between adjacent grid points (which depends on the difference in refractive indices and the relative positions between the two splitting planes):

$$f(x, y) = \frac{1}{4}[\delta(x, y) + \delta(x - d, y) + \delta(x, y - d) + \delta(x - d, y - d)]. \tag{9.7}$$

With a little math, which we omit here, we can show that the MTF of this PSF is:

$$MTF(f_x, f_y) = |\cos(\pi d f_x)||\cos(\pi d f_y)|. \tag{9.8}$$

An example of this MTF is shown in Fig. 9.11c, where the x-axis and y-axis are the two spatial frequencies f_x and f_y, and the a-axis is the MTF. We can see that this particular MTF passes low frequencies and cuts off at a frequency of, in the case where $d = 1, 0.5$. Interestingly, the MTF also passes high frequencies, which is generally not a huge concern because power at high frequencies is usually already attenuated by the PSFs of other optical elements (e.g., the main imaging lens). Of course, in reality the aperture is not a pinhole, so the PSF is not simply a sum of four Delta functions but can nevertheless still be similarly analyzed.

9.4.4 Monochromatic (Noise-Free) Sensor Model

Each in-sensor optical element adds its own spectral transmittance, so the overall transmittance of the in-sensor optics is the product of them. We will simply use $T(\lambda)$ to represent the overall transmittance. Given what we have discussed so far, we can build an analytical model for a monochromatic, noise-free image sensor. The raw pixel value n of a pixel of size $u \times v$ whose top-left corner is (x, y) and is exposed for a duration of t_{exp} is given by:

$$Q = \int_\lambda \int_t^{t+t_{exp}} \int_y^{y+v} \int_x^{x+u} Y(x', y', \lambda, t')T(\lambda)QE(\lambda)dx'dy'dt'd\lambda, \tag{9.9a}$$

$$\Delta V = \frac{Qq}{C_{FD}} \times g, \tag{9.9b}$$

$$n = \left\lfloor \frac{\Delta V}{V_{max}}(2^N - 1) \right\rfloor, \tag{9.9c}$$

where $Y(x', y', \lambda, t')$ is the number of photons incident on position (x', y') at a particular wavelength λ at a particular time t', so it is a quantal counterpart of the spectral irradiance; $T(\lambda)$ is the overall spectral transmittance of the in-sensor optics, $QE(\lambda)$ is the quantum efficiency, and q is the elementary charge; Eq. (9.9a) models the total amount of charges collected at the particular pixel, where we integrate spatially, temporally, and spectrally. Equation (9.9b) is essentially Eq. (9.5), and models the voltage difference sensed before and after the exposure. Equation (9.9c) is a crude ADC model, assuming that the voltage range $[0, v_{max}]$ is quantized into N bits, and the output of the ADC model is the digital number, a.k.a., the raw pixel value.

How do we express $Y(x', y', \lambda, t')$, the quantal counterpart of irradiance? The spectral irradiance at position (x', y') and time t' is:

$$E(x', y', \lambda, t') = \int^{\Omega(p,V)} L(p, \omega, \lambda, t') \cos \theta \, d\omega, \tag{9.10}$$

where $p = (x', y')$, V is the aperture, $\Omega(p, V)$ is the solid angle subtended by p and V; $L(p, \omega, \lambda, t')$ is the radiance with a wavelength λ incident on p from the direction ω at time t', and θ is the polar angle subtended by ω and the pixel normal vector.

Given Planck's equation (Eq. 9.2), we can turn irradiance E (energy per unit area per unit time) into the quantity Y (photon quantity per unit area per unit time):

$$Y(x', y', \lambda, t') = \frac{E(x', y', \lambda, t')\lambda}{hc}. \tag{9.11}$$

Plugging Eqs. (9.10) and (9.11) into (9.9), we have:

$$Q = \int_\lambda \int_t^{t+t_{exp}} \int_y^{y+v} \int_x^{x+u} \int^{\Omega(p,V)} \frac{L(p, \omega, \lambda, t')\cos\theta\, d\omega T(\lambda) QE(\lambda)\lambda}{hc} dx'dy'dt'd\lambda \tag{9.12a}$$

$$= \int_\lambda \left(\int_t^{t+t_{exp}} \int_y^{y+v} \int_x^{x+u} \int^{\Omega(p,V)} L(p, \omega, \lambda, t')\cos\theta\, d\omega dx'dy'dt' \right) T(\lambda) QE(\lambda)\frac{\lambda}{hc} d\lambda \tag{9.12b}$$

$$= \int_\lambda \mathcal{E}(\lambda) T(\lambda) QE(\lambda)\frac{\lambda}{hc} d\lambda. \tag{9.12c}$$

Recall from Sect. 5.3.6, the inner four integrals in Eq. (9.12b) collectively form the so-called camera measurement equation, which calculates $\mathcal{E}(\lambda)$ in Eq. (9.12c), representing the energy at wavelength λ collected by the pixel during the exposure. We have implicitly assumed here that the effects of the in-sensor optics can simply be modeled by the spectral transmittance $T(\lambda)$. This is largely reasonable because (1) in-sensor optics are mostly transparent and (2) they are very close to the pixels, so we can ignore rays that are incident on the edge of the optics and, after refractions, miss the pixels.

Spectral Sensitivity Function

We can make a few assumptions to simplify our discussion. First, we assume the ADC quantization error is negligible. Second, we assume that the irradiance within a pixel is spatially uniform and temporally uniform during a short exposure time. Equation (9.9) is then simplified to:

$$n \approx k \int_\lambda Y(x, y, \lambda, t) T(\lambda) QE(\lambda) d\lambda, \tag{9.13a}$$

$$= k \int_\lambda Y(x, y, \lambda, t) SSF_{quantal}(\lambda) d\lambda, \tag{9.13b}$$

where $Y(x, y, \lambda, t)$ is the (average) number of incident photons at wavelength λ hitting position (x, y) at time t; $k = uvt_{exp}\frac{qg}{C_{FD}}\frac{2^N-1}{V_{max}}$ is a constant.

Let's define a convenient term: **Spectral Sensitivity Function** (SSF), which is the product of $T(\lambda)$ and $QE(\lambda)$. SSF is the only spectral (wavelength-dependent) term in Eq. (9.13b) other than the incident light itself; it represents the phenomenological light sensitivity of the sensor over wavelength. SSF is sometimes also called the camera response function.

The SSF defined in Eq. (9.13b) is an "equal-quantal" function because it tells us the relative responses between different wavelengths under the same amount of incident photons. We can turn it into an "equal-energy" or "equal-power" function that operates on energy or power:

$$n \approx k \int_{\lambda} Y(x, y, \lambda, t) SSF_{quantal}(\lambda) d\lambda, \tag{9.14a}$$

$$= k \int_{\lambda} \frac{\Phi(x, y, \lambda, t)}{t_{exp} \frac{hc}{\lambda}} SSF_{quantal}(\lambda) d\lambda, \tag{9.14b}$$

$$= k' \int_{\lambda} \Phi(x, y, \lambda, t) SSF_{power}(\lambda) d\lambda, \tag{9.14c}$$

where $\Phi(x, y, \lambda, t)$ denotes the spectral power distribution of the light hitting position (x, y) at time t, $k' = uv \frac{qg}{C_{FD}} \frac{2^N - 1}{V_{max}} \frac{1}{hc}$, and $SSF_{power}(\lambda) = SSF_{quantal}(\lambda)\lambda$ is the equal-power SSF. We will omit the subscript because it is usually clear what SSF is being used (e.g., from the quantity that is being multiplied with the SSF). Also note that in some literature, the SSF is used interchangeably with QE, so be very careful.

9.5   Color Sensing

There is one main piece of the on-chip optics we have not discussed: the color filters, which are critical for color sensing and deserve their own section.

9.5.1   Goal of Color Sensing

What does it mean for an image sensor to capture color? We know that colors are subjective sensations caused by cone photoreceptor responses to light; a color can be expressed as a point in a 3D space formed by the L, M, and S cone responses, i.e., the LMS cone space. Ideally, if we can build an image sensor in such a way that it also possesses three kinds of pixels, each of which has a spectral sensitivity matching exactly that of a cone class (i.e., cone fundamental), the sensor would be able to accurately capture and reproduce the color information.

In fact, it is even sufficient for the sensor responses to be just a (linear) transformation away from the cone responses, as long as we can pre-calibrate the transformation matrix offline. This idea is illustrated in Fig. 9.12. We emphasize linear transformation here simply because it is computationally cheaper; nothing prevents you from designing a sensor sensitivity profile that requires a sophisticated transformation from the cone space.

Where do the three classes of spectral sensitivities come? Examine our monochromatic sensing model in Eq. (9.13b); it appears that all the pixels share the same response function and, thus, have the same spectral sensitivity: every pixel has the same quantum efficiency

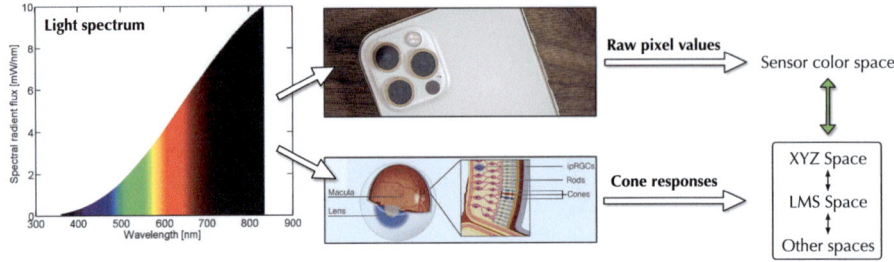

Fig. 9.12 The goal of color sensing is to form a color space from the raw pixel values and for there to exist a (preferably linear) transformation between the sensor color space and a standard color space, typically the CIE XYZ space. Adapted from Blume et al. (2019), Thorseth (2015), ajay_suresh (2021)

and the same optical elements sitting above them (so the same spectral transmittance of the optics).

There are a variety of ways to introduce sensitivity differences across pixels, which we will discuss shortly in Sect. 9.5.2. Assuming, for now, that we have somehow introduced the three classes of SSFs, denoted $SSF_R(\lambda)$, $SSF_G(\lambda)$, and $SSF_B(\lambda)$. Given an incident light with an SPD $\Phi(\lambda)$, the camera responses are:

$$[\int_\lambda \Phi(\lambda)SSF_R(\lambda)d\lambda, \int_\lambda \Phi(\lambda)SSF_G(\lambda)d\lambda, \int_\lambda \Phi(\lambda)SSF_B(\lambda)d\lambda]. \tag{9.15}$$

This is a direct invocation of Eq. (9.14c) with the constant omitted. The color of the light expressed in the LMS cone space is:

$$\left[\int_\lambda \Phi(\lambda)L(\lambda)d\lambda, \int_\lambda \Phi(\lambda)M(\lambda)d\lambda, \int_\lambda \Phi(\lambda)S(\lambda)d\lambda\right]. \tag{9.16}$$

If the cone responses form a 3D cone space, the camera raw responses also form a color space, which is sometimes called the camera's native color space. We provide an interactive tutorial that allows you to interactively explore and compare the native color spaces of various cameras and the LMS cone space. Figure 9.13 (left) shows the SSFs of iPhone 11 (solid lines) and the cone fundamentals. The SSFs are normalized so that SSF_G is peaked at unity, and the cone fundamentals are each normalized to peak at unity, so you could compare the relative sensitivity between the three SSFs in iPhone 11 but could not between the cone classes. Usually the SSF of a camera depends on a variety of factors such as the materials of the optical elements and the photodiodes as well as the pixel design, so it is almost impossible for the three SSFs to match exactly the cone fundamentals. Figure 9.13 (right) shows the spectral locus in iPhone 11's native color space and in the cone space; they evidently do not overlap.

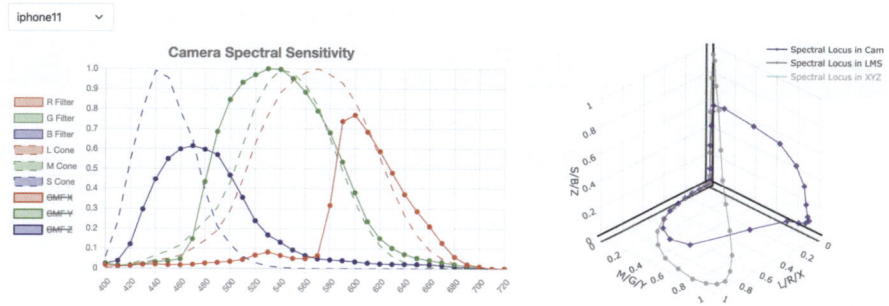

Fig. 9.13 Left: Spectral sensitivity functions of iPhone 11 (the RGB filters; solid lines) in comparison with the LMS cone fundamentals (dashed lines). Right: the spectral locus in the LMS space and in the camera's native color space. Adapted from Zhu (2022b)

A major task in sensor calibration is to identify a transformation matrix M such that the following (approximately) holds:

$$\begin{bmatrix} \int_\lambda \Phi(\lambda)SSF_R(\lambda)d\lambda \\ \int_\lambda \Phi(\lambda)SSF_G(\lambda)d\lambda \\ \int_\lambda \Phi(\lambda)SSF_B(\lambda)d\lambda \end{bmatrix} \times M = \begin{bmatrix} \int_\lambda \Phi(\lambda)L(\lambda)d\lambda \\ \int_\lambda \Phi(\lambda)M(\lambda)d\lambda \\ \int_\lambda \Phi(\lambda)S(\lambda)d\lambda \end{bmatrix} \qquad (9.17)$$

The transformation matrix is then applied in the post-processing pipeline of the raw pixels to turn raw pixel responses into a color value. We will discuss the calibration and the post-processing pipeline in greater details later.

9.5.2   Implementing Three "Classes of Pixels"

Perhaps the most straightforward method to introduce varying SSF is to apply a spectral filter to different pixels. A spectral filter is just a transparent optical element with a wavelength-selective transmittance. We need only three filters to emulate the three cone classes, but ideally each pixel should get all three simultaneously, which is difficult if you think about it, since at any given time you can physically have only one filter sitting on a pixel.

Three-Shot and Three-Chip Methods

There are two ways to go about addressing this issue. We can take three images of the same scene, each with a different filter, and then combine the together. This approach is believed to be pioneered by Sergey Prokudin-Gorsky, who conducted a breathtaking "photographic survey" of the early 20th-century Russia using this method (Prokudin-Gorsky 1948). This is called the "three-shot" approach. Alternatively, one could split the incident lights and send each of them to a different sensor, each with a different filter. This approach would obviously increase the form factor of the camera but avoids having to register and align

Fig. 9.14 Left: the Bayer color filter array; from Cburnett (2006). Middle and Right: a Bayer-domain image where each pixel generates only one response and a full-color image assuming each pixel generates three responses; adapted from Cmglee (2018)

the three separate shots, which is subjective to object motion. These camera are called "three-chip" or "three-CCD/COMS" cameras, which are still very widely used today in broadcasting, film studios, etc.

Color Filter Array (CFA)

Both the three-shot and the three-chip approach allow each incident light to be transformed to three responses needed for color reproduction—at the cost of capturing overhead or bulky system design. A much simpler approach, and the most commonly used approach today, is called Color Filter Array (CFA), which assigns each pixel only *one* filter.

Figure 9.14 shows the most commonly used CFA, where the three classes of filters are tiled in what is called the Bayer filter mosaic, named after Bryce Bayer, who invented this pattern while working for Eastman Kodak in Rochester, NY (Bayer 1976). Each of the three filters has a transmittance spectrum that peaks at, roughly, red-ish, green-ish, and blue-ish wavelengths, similar to the spectra shown in Fig. 9.13 (left).

The three filter classes are organized in 2×2 tiles, where each tile has two green filters. Bayer did so because he wanted to mimic human vision, where the photopic Luminance Efficiency Function (LEF) is most sensitive to green-ish lights (Sharpe et al. 2005, 2011) (see Fig. 3.11). We can see that the CFA approach is actually more similar to human color vision than the three-shot or three-chip approach. In human vision, each cone photoreceptor has a particular sensitivity spectrum, and generates one of the three responses needed to form color vision.

A necessary consequence of using the CFA is that each pixel gets only one color channel information. Figure 9.14 (middle) shows a raw image captured using a CFA, where each pixel evidently has only one color channel. The overall image looks overwhelmingly green because of the sheer amount of green filters. An important step in the post-processing pipeline is to reconstruct the two other missing channels, a process called "demosaicing", i.e., removing the Bayer mosaic artifacts. An example of the reconstructed image is shown in Fig. 9.14 (right).

We will have more to say about the demosaicing process when we get to Sect. 9.6, but for now, let's just observe that demosaicing is nothing more than a signal sampling and reconstruction problem. The CFA allows each pixel to sample only one channel of the three

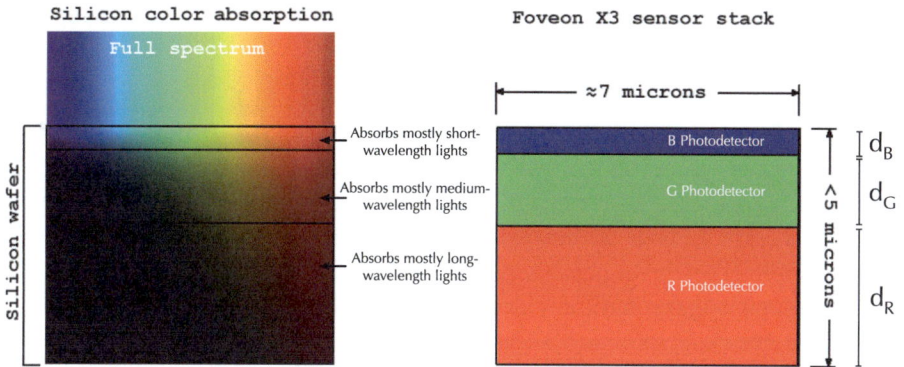

Fig. 9.15 Illustration of the Foveon X3 pixel, which has three PDs made of the same material (silicon) vertically stacked; adapted from Anoneditor (2007). Each PD receives a different light spectrum (due to the depth-varying absorption), effectively creating three different responses of the same light incident on the pixel surface

channels of response. So the green-filter response, for instance, is sampled by half of the pixels,[5] and the other two responses are sampled by one quarter of the pixels each. The job of demosaicing is then to reconstruct the full signal responses from the samples—a well-established problem in signal processing.

Foveon Approach

The final approach does away with optical color filters altogether. Instead, we will use three photodiodes vertically stacked for each pixel. Figure 9.15 illustrates a pixel in the Foveon X3 sensor, which is perhaps the most famous sensor that uses this architecture.

The idea is that the silicon absorption spectrum is wavelength sensitive, as shown in the right panel of Fig. 9.2. Blue-ish lights have a much shorter mean free length than do green-ish lights, which have a shorter mean free length than do red-ish lights. This means most short-wavelength lights will be absorbed after the first photodiode, leaving mostly medium- to long-wavelength lights. Those lights will go through the second photodiode, which absorbs mostly the medium-wavelength lights, leaving mostly long-wavelength lights to the third photodiode. As a result, each PD actually receives a different light spectrum, effectively creating three different responses for the same light incident on the pixel.

Let's assume that the three PDs have a depth of d_B, d_G, and d_R, respectively. The incident light impinging on the pixel (i.e., the first PD surface) has a SPD $\Phi(\lambda)$. The light impinging on the second PD then has a spectrum $\Phi(\lambda)e^{-\sigma(\lambda)d_B}$, where $\sigma(\lambda)$ is the silicon's absorption coefficient spectrum. This is easily derived from the fact that pure absorption (no scattering and emission) leads to an exponential decay of the input signal (Eq. 7.3b). Similarly, the light

---

[5] If we want to be pedantic, each green pixel has a small, but non-infinitesimal, area, so it first performs a low-pass filtering using a box filter whose extent is the pixel area, followed by sampling at the center of the pixel.

impinging on the third PD then has a spectrum $\Phi(\lambda)e^{-\sigma(\lambda)(d_B+d_G)}$. The responses produced by the three PDs are thus (in the order of R, G, and G):

$$\left[\int_\lambda \Phi(\lambda)\eta_R(\lambda)e^{-\sigma(\lambda)(d_B+d_G)}, \int_\lambda \Phi(\lambda)\eta_G(\lambda)e^{-\sigma(\lambda)(d_B)}, \int_\lambda \Phi(\lambda)\eta_B(\lambda) \right], \qquad (9.18)$$

where $\eta_R(\lambda)$, $\eta_G(\lambda)$, and $\eta_B(\lambda)$ are QE spectra of the three PDs (where we consider only photons that reach a PD as the denominator in Eq. (9.3) while ignoring photons that are reflected/absorbed before the photons hit the PD), respectively, and $\Phi(\lambda)$ is the SPD of the light incident on the pixel surface. The three PDs use identical material (so they share the same silicon absorption spectrum) but can still have different $\eta(\lambda)$s because of the thickness differences—due to the differences in the lengths of the depletion and neutral regions in the PD p-n junctions. Can you guess why the thickness tends to increase for deeper PDs in Fig. 9.15 (right)?

Compared to using the CFA, the vertical PD stacking approach is much more complicated to fabricate and more costly, so it is much less commonly used. It avoids color sampling (and the resulting aliasing) and the need for demosaicing, and in theory could also have a higher overall quantum efficiency (and signal-to-noise ratio) since there are no color filters, so it might find uses in scientific imaging (Chen et al. 2023).

9.6   Image Signal Processing

The output of an image sensor is what we usually call the raw pixels. The raw pixels are not the usual RGB images we are used to see. For starters, if we use the common CFA approach for color sensing, each raw pixel has only one color channel response—the two missing channel responses must be recovered. We have also ignored noises, which are introduced every step along the signal transduction chain from incident lights to raw values. Therefore, the raw pixels usually go through a post-processing pipeline to yield a visually pleasing image.

That pipeline in modern cameras is implemented by a special hardware accelerator called the Image Signal Processor (ISP), which is an Intellectual Property (IP) block in a mobile System-on-a-Chip (SoC). Implementing the post-processing algorithms in dedicated hardware makes a lot of sense from an efficiency perspective: when you press a button to capture an image, you certainly do not want to wait for a long time or burn a lot of energy before the image is shown to you. As many mobile vendors do not actually control the optics and the sensor, the ISP increasingly has become the key product differentiator. As a result, many companies have their custom ISP designs; for instance, Qualcomm's Snapdragon SoC has their own Spectra ISP.

Many texts exist on the general ISP algorithm (Ramanath et al. 2005; Karaimer and Brown 2016) and the hardware design (Hegarty et al. 2014), which we refer you to. We also have a pedagogical ISP written in Python (Zhu 2022a) that is a good reference, too. The goal

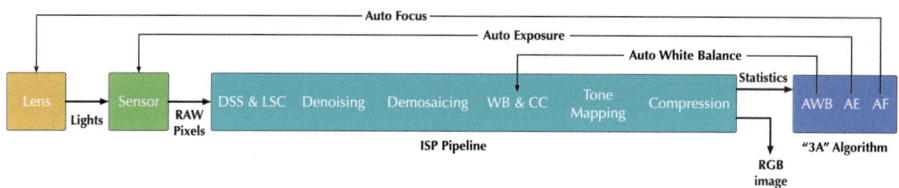

Fig. 9.16 A general ISP pipeline. The exact stages and arrangement of the stages are proprietary. The ISP pipeline outputs both the RGB (or other color spaces) images and image statistics; the latter is used to drive the so-called "3A" algorithms, which are feedback controls over the lens, sensor, and the ISP

of this section is to walk through the general pipeline and point out main ideas. One thing worth emphasizing here is that the ISP design is strongly influenced by the downstream task that consumes the output of the ISP. The two main consumers are human vision and machine vision. The former cares about visually pleasing images while the latter does not—as long as the key semantic information is retained and can be extracted.

9.6.1   General Pipeline

Figure 9.16 shows a general ISP pipeline and how it fits into the entire imaging pipeline. The ISP takes the raw pixels generated by the sensor and generates two types of output: the finished image, usually encoded in sRGB color space and compressed, and statistics of the image that are used to drive the so-called "3A" algorithms, i.e., auto white balance (AWB), auto exposure (AE), and auto focus (AF). We will not have much time to discuss the 3A algorithms, but they can be thought of as feedback controls over the rest of the imaging system: AWB controls the white balancing stage in the ISP, AE controls the exposure time of the image sensor, and AF controls the lens movement in the optics. The 3A algorithms usually run on the host CPU or an MCU because they are relatively simple computationally.

The ISP pipeline shown here is a general architecture that covers roughly what an ISP has to do. Keep in mind that the exact stages and their arrangements are proprietary and vary by vendors. Regardless, all ISPs operate on a set of basic principles.

- Recall that the raw pixel values output by the sensor should ideally be proportional to the scene luminance, but this is hardly the case in reality. The first thing an ISP does is to recover luminance-proportional values from the raw sensor output; this includes three main steps.

    - The first step is called dark signal subtraction (DSS) or back-light subtraction. This is necessary because even when pixels receive no light at all, their raw values are usually not zero. This is because of "dark current", formed by thermally dislodged electrons even in the absence of incident photons. Measuring the raw values of "optical black" pixels (Kameda 2012) per frame and subtracting those values would allow us to eliminate the effect of the dark current.[6] We correct certain known (i.e., pre-calibrated) deviations in the raw pixels.

- The second step is called flat-field correction or lens-shading correction (LSC). It accounts for the fact that the raw pixel values (with dark current subtracted) are spatially non-uniform, a phenomenon called "vignetting", where even under uniform (flat-field) illumination peripheral pixels receive fewer photons. It is caused by a variety of reasons: the mechanical design (including microlenses) of the camera blocks more lights toward the edge of the pixel array, the radiance fall-off (the $\cos\theta$ term) when rays incident in an oblique angles, etc. We can pre-calibrate this non-uniformity, store it in an image, and compensate for the non-uniformity for each frame.

- The final step is denoising. Many excellent discussions of noise sources exist, such as Boukhayma (2018), Nakamura (2006, Sect. 3.3), and Rowlands (2020b, Sects. 3.8 and 3.9), which we refer you to. Regardless of the noise source, the general strategy of denoising is low-pass filtering: blurs are subjectively less objectionable than noises.

It is important that these steps are taken at the very beginning of an ISP; for instance, if the pixel values are noisy, any subsequent manipulations on the pixels also manipulate, sometimes amplify, the noise.

- After that, we can assume that the raw pixels carry physical meanings: they are proportional to luminance, but of course because of the CFA, the color information is spatially sampled. The raw pixels before demosaicing are usually called pixels in the Bayer domain. The next stage is demosaicing, which essentially reconstructs the color information (all three channels) from the single-channel samples. While many reconstruction filters/kernels exist, the easiest and most commonly used filter is the bilinear filter.

- The demosaiced color information is encoded in the sensor's native color space, because the sensor's SSFs almost certainly do not match the cone fundamentals. So the next stage is to transform color from the sensor's native color space to a typical color space such as the CIE XYZ space. We build an interactive tutorial to walk you through this correction process that you are invited to play with (Zhu 2022b). White balancing usually is implemented along with color correction, because both involve linear transformations of colors (Rowlands 2020a; Zhu 2021).

- Usually there is a tone mapping stage in the ISP. The dynamic range of the raw pixels is usually, but not always, different from that of a typical output medium (e.g., a display or

---

[6] Note, however, that DSS does not eliminate the effect of dark current *shot noise*, which results from fluctuations in dark current during the exposure time (so the dark current is in theory different for different pixels even if they have the exact temperature), and the effect of dark current *non-uniformity*, which results from spatial differences in dark current across pixels (because of, for instance, the spatial temperature differences).

a print). Tone mapping operators map signals between the two dynamic ranges so that the output image is visually appealing.

- The final output is usually compressed, either through an image compression algorithm (e.g., JPEG) or, in the case of video capturing, a video compression algorithm (e.g., H264).

9.6.2 Two Trends

Two trends emerge, which we will explore when appropriate. First, it has become increasingly common to co-design ISP algorithms, along with optics and image sensor design, with the downstream tasks. This is particularly important for machine vision, which is not concerned with the traditional goal of an ISP, i.e., generating visually pleasing images. A co-design between the ISP and the machine vision algorithms could potentially improve both task quality and efficiency. Second, a huge amount of recent efforts have been spent on exploring the notion of "neural ISP", which is nothing more than replacing part, or the entirety, of the ISP pipeline with deep neural networks (DNNs). The learning paradigm has two main advantages: it replaces some of the heuristics in traditional ISP designs, and it allows the algorithm to be more easily updated without having to wait until the next generation of the product. The latter point is possible because a neural ISP pipeline can run on a DNN accelerator that almost all modern mobile SoCs have, and updating the algorithm is nothing more than updating the model weights.

The key issue with neural ISP is speed and efficiency: a neural ISP model executed on a generic DNN accelerator is likely much slower and more energy hungry than traditional ISPs. So it is more likely that neural ISPs will find their main uses in offline image processing and photo finishing rather than in the real-time imaging pipeline.

References

ajay_suresh (2021) iPhone 12 cameras; CC BY-SA 2.0 license. https://commons.wikimedia.org/wiki/File:Apple_iPhone_12_Pro_-_Cameras_(50535314721).jpg

Anoneditor (2007) Illustration of the Foveon X3 sensor; CC BY-SA 3.0. https://commons.wikimedia.org/wiki/File:Absorption-X3.png

Aoki M, Ando H, Ohba S, Takemoto I, Nagahara S, Nakano T, Kubo M, Fujita T (1982) 2/3-inch format MOS single-chip color imager. IEEE Trans Electron Dev 29(4):745–750

APN MJM (2011) A calcite crystal displays the double refractive properties while sitting on a sheet of graph paper; CC BY-SA 3.0 license. https://commons.wikimedia.org/wiki/File:Crystal_on_graph_paper.jpg

Bayer BE (1976) Color imaging array. US Patent 3,971,065

Biretta JA, McMaster M (2008) Wide field and planetary camera 2 instrument handbook v. 10.0. Space Telescope Science Institute

Blume, Garbazza, Spitschan (2019) Schematic overview of photorecetors; CC BY-SA 4.0 license.
   https://commons.wikimedia.org/wiki/File:Overview_of_the_retina_photoreceptors_(a).png
Bong K, Choi S, Kim C, Han D, Yoo HJ (2017a) A low-power convolutional neural network face
   recognition processor and a CIS integrated with always-on face detector. IEEE J Solid-State Circ
   53(1):115–123
Bong K, Choi S, Kim C, Kang S, Kim Y, Yoo HJ (2017b) 14.6 a 0.62 mW ultra-low-power
   convolutional-neural-network face-recognition processor and a CIS integrated with always-on
   haar-like face detector. In: 2017 IEEE international solid-state circuits conference (ISSCC), IEEE,
   pp 248–249
Boukhayma A (2018) Ultra low-noise CMOS image sensors. Springer
Boyle WS, Smith GE (1970) Charge coupled semiconductor devices. Bell Syst Tech J 49(4):587–593
BrayLockBoy (2018) An example of the rolling shutter effect in action at Afton Down, Isle of
   Wight, taken by a camera on a car travelling at approximately 50 miles per hour. CC BY-SA 4.0
   license. https://commons.wikimedia.org/wiki/File:Rolling_Shutter_Effect_at_Afton_Down,_21_
   August_2018.jpg
Cburnett (2006) A Bayer pattern on a sensor; CC BY-SA 3.0. https://commons.wikimedia.org/wiki/
   File:Bayer_pattern_on_sensor.svg
Chen C, Wang Z, Wu J, Deng Z, Zhang T, Zhu Z, Jin Y, Lew B, Srivastava I, Liang Z et al (2023)
   Bioinspired, vertically stacked, and perovskite nanocrystal–enhanced CMOS imaging sensors for
   resolving UV spectral signatures. Sci Adv 9(44):eadk3860
Cmglee (2018) Images of a garden with some tulips and narcissus; CC BY-SA 3.0. https://commons.
   wikimedia.org/wiki/File:Colorful_spring_garden_Bayer_%2B_RGB.png
Cmglee (2019) Comparison of front- vs. back-illuminated sensors; CC BY-SA 4.0 license. https://
   commons.wikimedia.org/wiki/File:Comparison_backside_illumination.svg
Dyck RH, Weckler GP (1968) Integrated arrays of silicon photodetectors for image sensing. IEEE
   Trans Electron Dev 15(4):196–201
Einstein A (1905a) On a heuristic point of view about the creation and conversion of light. Annalen
   der Physik 17(6):132–148
Einstein A (1905b) Über einen die erzeugung und verwandlung des lichtes betreffenden heuristischen
   gesichtspunkt
Eki R, Yamada S, Ozawa H, Kai H, Okuike K, Gowtham H, Nakanishi H, Almog E, Livne Y, Yuval G
   et al (2021) 9.6 a 1/2.3 inch 12.3 mpixel with on-chip 4.97 tops/w CNN processor back-illuminated
   stacked CMOS image sensor. In: 2021 IEEE international solid-state circuits conference (ISSCC),
   vol 64. IEEE, pp 154–156
El Gamal A, Eltoukhy H (2005) CMOS image sensors. IEEE Circ Dev Mag 21(3):6–20
Eric Bajart (2010) Quantum efficiency of the CCD sensor "PC1" in the Hubble space telescope's
   wide field and planetary camera WFPC2; CC BY-SA 3.0. https://commons.wikimedia.org/wiki/
   File:Quantum_efficiency_graph_for_WFPC2-en.svg
Feng Y, Ma T, Zhu Y, Zhang X (2024) Blisscam: boosting eye tracking efficiency with learned in-
   sensor sparse sampling. In: 2024 ACM/IEEE 51st annual international symposium on computer
   architecture (ISCA). IEEE, pp 1262–1277
Fossum ER, Hondongwa DB (2014) A review of the pinned photodiode for CCD and CMOS image
   sensors. IEEE J Electron Dev Soc 2(3)
Fossum ER (1993) Active pixel sensors: are CCDS dinosaurs? In: Charge-coupled devices and solid
   state optical sensors III, SPIE, vol 1900, pp 2–14
Fossum ER (1997) CMOS image sensors: electronic camera-on-a-chip. IEEE Trans Electron Dev
   44(10):1689–1698
Fowler B, El Gamal A, Yang DX (1994) A CMOS area image sensor with pixel-level A/D conversion.
   In: Proceedings of IEEE international solid-state circuits conference-ISSCC'94. IEEE, pp 226–227

Glassner AS (1995) Principles of digital image synthesis. Elsevier

Green MA, Keevers MJ (1995) Optical properties of intrinsic silicon at 300 k. Progr Photovoltaics: Res Appl 3(3):189–192

Haruta T, Nakajima T, Hashizume J, Umebayashi T, Takahashi H, Taniguchi K, Kuroda M, Sumihiro H, Enoki K, Yamasaki T et al (2017) 4.6 a 1/2.3 inch 20mpixel 3-layer stacked CMOS image sensor with dram. In: 2017 IEEE international solid-state circuits conference (ISSCC). IEEE, pp 76–77

Hegarty J, Brunhaver JS, DeVito Z, Ragan-Kelley J, Cohen N, Bell S, Vasilyev A, Horowitz M, Hanrahan P (2014) Darkroom: compiling high-level image processing code into hardware pipelines. ACM Trans Graph 33(4):144–1

Hirata T, Murata H, Matsuda H, Tezuka Y, Tsunai S (2021) 7.8 a 1-inch 17mpixel 1000fps block-controlled coded-exposure back-illuminated stacked cmos image sensor for computational imaging and adaptive dynamic range control. In: 2021 IEEE international solid-state circuits conference (ISSCC), vol 64. IEEE, pp 120–122

Hsu TH, Chen YR, Liu RS, Lo CC, Tang KT, Chang MF, Hsieh CC (2020) A 0.5-v real-time computational CMOS image sensor with programmable kernel for feature extraction. IEEE J Solid-State Circ 56(5):1588–1596

Hu C (2009) Modern semiconductor devices for integrated circuits. Prentice Hall

IRDS (2024) International roadmap for devices and systems. https://irds.ieee.org/

Kameda S (2012) Solid state image pickup device having optical black pixels with temperature characteristics above and below temperature characteristics of aperture pixels. US Patent 8,227,734

Karaimer HC, Brown MS (2016) A software platform for manipulating the camera imaging pipeline. In: Computer vision—ECCV 2016: 14th European conference, Amsterdam, The Netherlands, October 11–14, 2016, Proceedings, Part I 14. Springer, pp 429–444

Kevin McCoy (2009) The Jefferson national expansion memorial in St Louis, MO, USA taken at night with an EV +4.09; CC BY-SA 3.0 license. https://commons.wikimedia.org/wiki/File: StLouisArchMultExpEV%2B4.09.JPG

Kim SJ, Lee KH, Han SW, Yoon E (2005) A 200/spl times/160 pixel CMOS fingerprint recognition SOC with adaptable column-parallel processors. In: ISSCC. 2005 IEEE international digest of technical papers. Solid-state circuits conference. IEEE, pp 250–596

Kobayashi M, Onuki Y, Kawabata K, Sekine H, Tsuboi T, Muto T, Akiyama T, Matsuno Y, Takahashi H, Koizumi T, et al. (2017) 4.5a 1.8e-RMS temporal noise over 110 dB dynamic range 3.4μm pixel pitch global-shutter CMOS image sensor with dual-gain amplifiers SS-ADC, light guide structure, and multiple-accumulation shutter. IEEE J Solid-State Circ 53(1):219–228

Kondo T, Takemoto Y, Kobayashi K, Tsukimura M, Takazawa N, Kato H, Suzuki S, Aoki J, Saito H, Gomi Y et al (2015) A 3D stacked CMOS image sensor with 16Mpixel global-shutter mode and 2Mpixel 10000fps mode using 4 million interconnections. In: 2015 symposium on VLSI circuits (VLSI circuits). IEEE, pp C90–C91

Kozlowski LJ, Luo J, Kleinhans W, Liu T (1998) Comparison of passive and active pixel schemes for CMOS visible imagers. In: Infrared readout electronics IV, SPIE, vol 3360, pp 101–110

Kumagai O, Niwa A, Hanzawa K, Kato H, Futami S, Ohyama T, Imoto T, Nakamizo M, Murakami H, Nishino T et al (2018a) A 1/4-inch 3.9 mpixel low-power event-driven back-illuminated stacked CMOS image sensor. In: 2018 IEEE international solid-state circuits conference-(ISSCC). IEEE, pp 86–88

Kumagai Y, Yoshita R, Osawa N, Ikeda H, Yamashita K, Abe T, Kudo S, Yamane J, Idekoba T, Noudo S, et al. (2018b) Back-illuminated 2.74μm-pixel-pitch global shutter CMOS image sensor with charge-domain memory achieving 10k e-saturation signal. In: 2018 IEEE international electron devices meeting (IEDM). IEEE, pp 10–16

Kwon M, Lim S, Lee H, Ha IS, Kim MY, Seo IJ, Lee S, Choi Y, Kim K, Lee H et al (2020) A low-power 65/14nm stacked CMOS image sensor. In: 2020 IEEE international symposium on circuits and systems (ISCAS). IEEE, pp 1–4

Liu C, Bainbridge L, Berkovich A, Chen S, Gao W, Tsai TH, Mori K, Ikeno R, Uno M, Isozaki T, et al. (2020) A 4.6 μm, 512× 512, ultra-low power stacked digital pixel sensor with triple quantization and 127dB dynamic range. In: 2020 IEEE international electron devices meeting (IEDM). IEEE, pp 16–1

Liu C, Berkovich A, Chen S, Reyserhove H, Sarwar SS, Tsai TH (2019) Intelligent vision systems–bringing human-machine interface to AR/VR. In: 2019 IEEE international electron devices meeting (IEDM). IEEE, pp 10–15

Liu C, Chen S, Tsai TH, De Salvo B, Gomez J (2022) Augmented reality-the next frontier of image sensors and compute systems. In: 2022 IEEE international solid-state circuits conference (ISSCC), vol 65. IEEE, pp 426–428

Ma T (2024) Efficient data-driven machine vision: a co-design of circuit, algorithm, and architecture for edge vision sensors. PhD thesis, Washington University in St. Louis

Ma T, Feng Y, Zhang X, Zhu Y (2023) CAMJ: enabling system-level energy modeling and architectural exploration for in-sensor visual computing. In: Proceedings of the 50th annual international symposium on computer architecture, pp 1–14

Melentijevic (2015) DSLR internal cut filter/lowpass filter/hot mirror transmission curves. https://kolarivision.com/articles/internal-cut-filter-transmission/

Miyauchi K, Mori K, Otaka T, Isozaki T, Yasuda N, Tsai A, Sawai Y, Owada H, Takayanagi I, Nakamura J (2020) A stacked back side-illuminated voltage domain global shutter CMOS image sensor with a 4.0 μm multiple gain readout pixel. Sensors 20(2):486

Murakami H, Bohannon E, Childs J, Gui G, Moule E, Hanzawa K, Koda T, Takano C, Shimizu T, Takizawa Y, et al. (2022) A 4.9 mpixel programmable-resolution multi-purpose CMOS image sensor for computer vision. In: 2022 IEEE international solid-state circuits conference (ISSCC), vol 65. IEEE pp 104–106

Murmann B (2014) ADC Performance Survey 1997–2024. https://github.com/bmurmann/ADC-survey

Nakamura J (2006) Image sensors and signal processing for digital still cameras. CRC Press

Nitta Y, Muramatsu Y, Amano K, Toyama T, Mishina K, Suzuki A, Taura T, Kato A, Kikuchi M, Yasui Y, et al. (2006) High-speed digital double sampling with analog CDS on column parallel ADC architecture for low-noise active pixel sensor. In: 2006 IEEE international solid state circuits conference-digest of technical papers. IEEE, pp 2024–2031

Noble PJ (1968) Self-scanned silicon image detector arrays. IEEE Trans Electron Dev 15(4):202–209

Ohta J (2020) Smart CMOS image sensors and applications. CRC Press

Ommnomnomgulp (2008) A focal plane shutter firing at 1/500 of a second with the "gap" clearly visible. This shutter is on a Nikon film SLR. CC BY-SA 3.0 license. https://commons.wikimedia.org/wiki/File:1_500_Sec_Focal_P_Shut.jpg

Pharr M, Jakob W, Humphreys G (2023) Physically based rendering: From theory to implementation, 4th edn. MIT Press

Prokudin-Gorsky S (1948) Library of Congress Prokudin-Gorskii collection. https://www.loc.gov/collections/prokudin-gorskii/about-this-collection/

Ramanath R, Snyder WE, Yoo Y, Drew MS (2005) Color image processing pipeline. IEEE Signal Process Mag 22(1):34–43

Rowlands DA (2020a) Color conversion matrices in digital cameras: a tutorial. Opt Eng 59(11):110801–110801

Rowlands DA (2020b) Physics of digital photography, 2nd edn. IOP Publishing

Sakakibara M, Oike Y, Takatsuka T, Kato A, Honda K, Taura T, Machida T, Okuno J, Ando A, Fukuro T, et al. (2012) An 83dB-dynamic-range single-exposure global-shutter CMOS image sensor with in-pixel dual storage. In: 2012 IEEE international solid-state circuits conference. IEEE, pp 380–382

Sharpe LT, Stockman A, Jagla W, Jägle H (2005) A luminous efficiency function, v*(λ), for daylight adaptation. J Vision 5(11):3–3

Sharpe LT, Stockman A, Jagla W, Jägle H (2011) A luminous efficiency function, vd65*(λ), for daylight adaptation: a correction. Color Res Appl 36(1):42–46

Stark L, Raynor JM, Lalanne F, Henderson RK (2018) A back-illuminated voltage-domain global shutter pixel with dual in-pixel storage. IEEE Trans Electron Dev 65(10):4394–4400

Swain P, Cheskis D (2008) Back-illuminated image sensors come to the forefront. Photonics Spectra 42(8):46

Thorseth (2015) Spectral power distribution of a 25 W incandescent light bulb; CC BY-SA 4.0 license. https://commons.wikimedia.org/wiki/File:Spectral_power_distribution_of_a_25_W_incandescent_light_bulb.png

Tournier A, Roy F, Cazaux Y, Lalanne F, Malinge P, Mcdonald M, Monnot G, Roux N (2018) A HDR 98db 3.2μm charge domain global shutter CMOS image sensor. In: 2018 IEEE international electron devices meeting (IEDM),.IEEE, pp 10–14

Tsugawa H, Takahashi H, Nakamura R, Umebayashi T, Ogita T, Okano H, Iwase K, Kawashima H, Yamasaki T, Yoneyama D, et al. (2017) Pixel/dram/logic 3-layer stacked CMOS image sensor technology. In: 2017 IEEE international electron devices meeting (IEDM). IEEE, pp 3–2

Weckler GP (1967) Operation of PN junction photodetectors in a photon flux integrating mode. IEEE J Solid-State Circ 2(3):65–73

Xu H, Lin N, Luo L, Wei Q, Wang R, Zhuo C, Yin X, Qiao F, Yang H (2021) Senputing: an ultra-low-power always-on vision perception chip featuring the deep fusion of sensing and computing. IEEE Trans Circ Syst I: Regul Pap 69(1):232–243

Yasutomi K, Itoh S, Kawahito S (2011) A two-stage charge transfer active pixel CMOS image sensor with low-noise global shuttering and a dual-shuttering mode. IEEE Trans Electron Dev 58(3):740–747

Yokoyama T, Tsutsui M, Nishi Y, Mizuno I, Dmitry V, Lahav A (2018) High performance 2.5μm global shutter pixel with new designed light-pipe structure. In: 2018 IEEE international electron devices meeting (IEDM). IEEE, pp 10–15

Young C, Omid-Zohoor A, Lajevardi P, Murmann B (2019) A data-compressive 1.5/2.75-bit log-gradient QVGA image sensor with multi-scale readout for always-on object detection. IEEE J Solid-State Circ 54(11):2932–2946

Zhu Y (2021) Principles and practices of chromatic adaptation. https://yuhaozhu.com/blog/chromatic-adaptation.html

Zhu Y (2022a) A pedagogical ISP pipeline in Python. https://github.com/horizon-research/isp

Zhu Y (2022b) Exploring camera color space and color correction. https://horizon-lab.org/colorvis/camcolor.html

Part IV

Research Frontiers: Imaging-Rendering-Human Vision Co-Design

One of the main appeals of doing research in visual computing is the opportunity to work with imaging, rendering, and human vision as parts of a unified, end-to-end system. While these components have traditionally been designed and optimized in isolation, it is only natural to consider them jointly and optimize them holistically. This kind of joint design and optimization is an active and growing area of research.

This part of the book briefly describes a few recent research projects that highlight the potential of such co-optimization. These examples are neither comprehensive nor necessarily the best, but they are ones I am most familiar with, and they illustrate the diverse forms that such joint optimizations can take. We will also briefly touch upon a few other examples to showcase the wealth of the exciting projects in the community.

Gaze-Contingent Rendering in VR

10

10.1 The Basic Idea

AR/VR and, to some extent, robots and self-driving cars are human-facing systems. An important goal of human-facing systems is to stimulate certain percepts from humans. To do so, computing systems act as an encoder, and the HVS acts as a decoder. This is the idea illustrated in Fig. 10.1. For instance, a VR system renders photorealistic images such that humans interpret the rendered objects as if they are from the real, physical world. In this sense, the computer system encodes the percept intended to evoke from humans (e.g., color, objects, depth, motion) as a set of visual stimuli (i.e., lights from the display pixels), which become the inputs to the HVS. The human visual system decodes the target percept from the incident lights. Again, this perspective naturally points to jointly optimizing the computer systems with the HVS.

10.1.1 The Opportunity

Our peripheral visual acuity is extremely bad. If we fixate straight ahead, we will not be able to tell the details of an object in our peripheral vision. A great deal of work leverages the non-uniform spatial visual acuity to improve system performance. As discussed in Sect. 2.3, the fundamental reason for low peripheral acuity is at least three-fold and is well-known.

1. The receptive field (RF) sizes of the RGCs increase with eccentricity, a result of larger dendritic fields (Rodieck et al.1985; Dacey 1993) and sparser RGC density in periphery (Curcio and Allen 1990). A large RF means that an RGC integrates signals from a larger spatial area, i.e., more blurring in the (spatial) frequency domain.

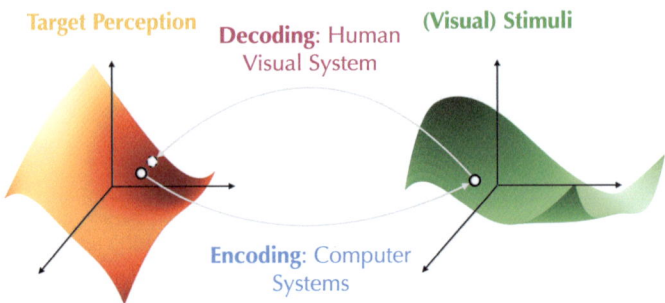

Fig. 10.1 The computer system encodes the percept intended to stimulate from humans (e.g., color, objects, depth, motion) as a set of visual stimuli (i.e., lights from the display pixels), which become the inputs to the HVS. The human visual system decodes the target percept from the incident lights

2. Cone cells (photoreceptors responsible for vision under normal daylight) become larger in size as eccentricity increases (Curcio et al. 1990), also contributing to blurring in spatial frequency.
3. The distribution of cone cells on our retina is extremely non-uniform: over 95% of the cone cells are located in the central region of the retina (i.e., fovea) with an eccentricity of below 5° (Curcio et al. 1990; Song et al.2011). The density of the cone cells decreases drastically in the visual periphery, which is, thus, significantly under-sampled spatially.

The low peripheral vision does not quite affect how computer systems are designed for PCs and smartphones, since the visual content coming from their displays will mostly fall in the fovea. When immersed in a virtual environment (e.g., when a user wears a VR headset), however, much of the visual stimuli generated from the computer systems will fall in the periphery of the retina. This observation gave rise to the now well-established idea of **gaze-contingent rendering**, which is sometimes also called **foveated rendering** (FR), where one could improve the rendering speed by generating low-quality visual stimuli for the periphery with impunity (Guenter et al. 2012; Patney et al. 2016; Sun et al. 2020a). Our community has quickly picked up the idea and proposed hardware extensions to support foveated rendering in AR holograms (Zhao et al. 2021) and cloud-assisted collaborative VR rendering (Xie et al. 2021).

10.1.2 The Conceptual Idea

While conceptually simple, we must answer a basic question: what exactly to render in the periphery without degrading perceptual quality? Perhaps unsurprisingly, today we simply blur or lower the resolution of the peripheral content. These empirical approaches, however, introduce suspicious artifacts (Walton et al. 2021), and it is not clear whether blurring content buys us any computation saving.

A scientifically sound answer requires understanding the complex processing that takes place in the entire human visual pathway, including processing on the retina, in the LGN, and by the visual cortex of the brain. Assume we could model the human visual processing as a function $f(\cdot)$, and model the original input stimulus (without any degradation) as I; what we want to find is an alternative stimulus I' such that $f(I) = f(I')$, all the while minimizing the cost (of the underlying computing systems) to generate I'. This gives the following optimization problem:

$$\min_{I'} \ \mathrm{Cost}(I') \ \ s.t. \ \ f(I) = f(I') \tag{10.1}$$

As one might imagine, the central difficulty is how to model $f(\cdot)$, which is hard since we know $f(\cdot)$ is highly non-linear, dynamically self-adapting, feedback-driven, and most likely non-differentiable; one could even argue that the Holy Grail of neuroscience is to decipher $f(\cdot)$. The way to go about modeling $f(\cdot)$ is, in general, to narrow the scope of $f(\cdot)$ to a particular task, e.g., discriminating between a reference stimulus (ground truth) that is costly to render and an alternative stimulus that is cheaper to render.

Once we narrow the scope of the task we focus on, we then can take one of the two approaches. We could model $f(\cdot)$ from the first principles, building on computational neuro-science models that account for behaviors and interactions of individual neuron populations. This is the approach we will talk about in Sect. 10.3.

Alternative, if we cannot easily derive $f(\cdot)$ from first principles, we look for the next best thing: a phenomenological model that fits experimental data. This is done through psychophysics, where we measure human behaviors under a set of controlled physical stim-uli (Gescheider 2013; Prins et al. 2016) and build/regress models that can robustly correlate behavioral outputs with visuals inputs. This is the approach we will take in Sect. 10.2.

Before moving on, we should note that both techniques fall under the general umbrella of gaze-contingent rendering, which requires tracking user gaze. Gaze tracking could be power-hungry (Feng et al. 2024; Ma et al. 2023b; Singh et al. 2023). While there is every reason to believe that gaze-tracking power will be significantly reduced in the near future, carefully balancing the gaze-tracking power overhead with the potential power saving through gaze-contingent rendering is important (Chen et al. 2024).

10.2   Exploiting Human Color Discrimination

Our recent work makes a good stride in this direction by computationally modeling one spe-cific aspect of human vision—color discrimination—as a function of eccentricity (Duinkhar-jav et al. 2022; Chen et al. 2023). Through over 8000 trials of psychophysical measurements on real participants, we are able to derive the discrimination threshold for a color at a par-

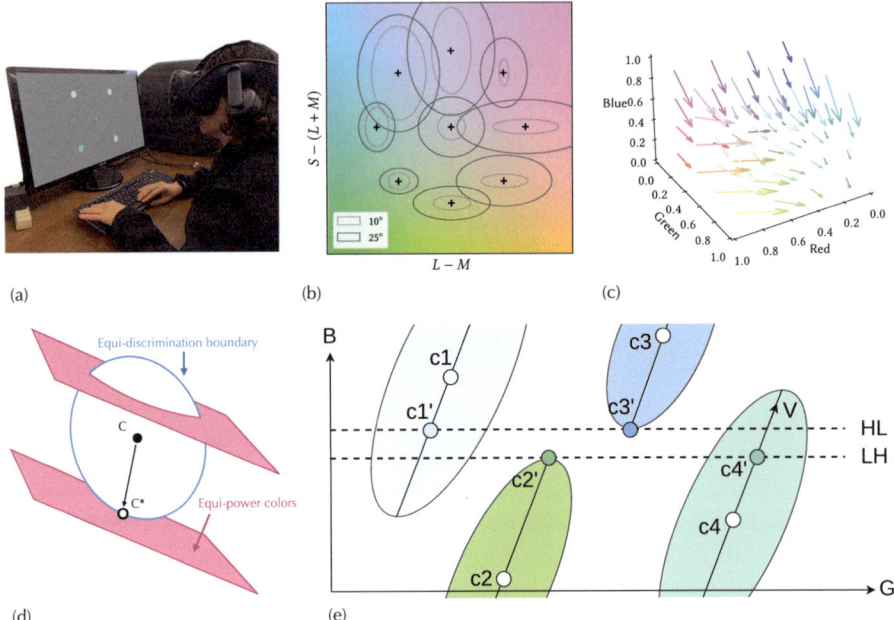

(a)   (b)   (c)

(d)   (e)

Fig. 10.2 a The 4AFC psychophysical paradigm to derive the color discrimination threshold; from Duinkharjav et al. (2022, Fig. 2a). **b** A set of MacAdam ellipses in the (chromatic plane of the) DKL space (Derrington et al. 1984) under two eccentricities; from Duinkharjav et al. (2022, Fig. 4a) and the same as Fig. 4.8 (right). **c** The geometric intuition of our display-power saving color filter; from Duinkharjav et al. (2022, Fig. 4c). **d** The geometric intuition of the analytical solution to the power minimization problem. **e** The geometric intuition of our compression algorithm; from Ujjainkar et al. (2024, Fig. 6a)

ticular eccentricity. Figure 10.2a shows the stimuli in a typical trial, which uses the classic four-alternative forced choice (4AFC) paradigm. In particular, the participant is shown four color patches; three of them have the same color, which is the reference color, and it does not change throughout a trial, and the other patch has a different color (oddball). The participant is asked to identify the oddball The oddball is made closer to the reference color when the participant correctly identifies the oddball and vice versa; eventually, when the participant seems to be taking a random guess, we know we have reached the discrimination threshold.[1]

From the raw psychophysical data, we build a computational model that predicts, for a given reference color at a given eccentricity, the set of colors that are perceptually no different from the reference color. This is illustrated in Fig. 10.2b, where we show the discrimination thresholds under two eccentricities. The reason these discrimination boundaries are elliptical is inspired by the MacAdam ellipses (Sect. 4.7), which originally were used to capture the

---

[1] The actual protocol is slightly more complicated; we use the classic one-up-two-down staircase procedure commonly used in estimating thresholds.

discrimination thresholds at $0°$ eccentricity. Our work can be seen as an extension to arbitrary eccentricities.

Leveraging the perception model, we design a VR rendering system that modulates pixel colors to minimize display power (dictated by colors) without affecting human color perception. Figure 10.2d shows the geometric intuition of finding the optimal solution. Each pixel color has an elliptical discrimination threshold boundary; colors that consume the same display power lie on a plane, and the vertical placement of the plane is proportional to the power consumption, because the power consumption of emissive displays is a linear combination of the pixel colors (Duinkharjav et al. 2022, Sect. 5.2).

All we are looking for is to move the equi-power plane such that it just touches the discrimination thresholds. This optimization is applied to all the pixels. Figure 10.2c shows the geometric intuition of this optimization in the linear sRGB space, where each color is shifted toward an alternative color that is perceptually non-discriminable from the original color while minimizing the display power. It turns out that this optimization is a convex optimization with an analytical solution and, thus, can be implemented in real-time with little overhead. In the end, we get about 20% dynamic display power reduction.

We can take the color discrimination model a step further to optimize for the memory traffic: if all the colors within the discrimination threshold are perceptually no different, there is no need to encode them differently. We propose a compression algorithm that encodes perceptually similar colors together (Ujjainkar et al. 2024). This algorithm, efficiently implemented in hardware, reduces the average memory traffic in a VR SoC by 67%.

10.3   Exploiting Ventral Metamerism

The example before relies on a phenomenological model regressed from psychophysics. We can also make use of models that are derived from first principles. To demonstrate this, we turn to a broader task: instead of discriminating between two colors, a task that is more relevant to FR is discriminating between two images, a high-quality reference image that is costly to render and an alternative image that is ideally cheaper to render. By building a computational model for such a task, we can then determine how much rendering quality to relax without introducing visual artifacts.

10.3.1 Ventral Metamerism-Based Quality Metric

It is well-established that commonly used visual quality metrics such as Peak Signal-to-Noise Ratio (PSNR) or Structural Similarity Index Measure (SSIM) (Hore and Ziou 2010) do not account for the eccentricity-dependent visual acuity drop in HVS (Walton et al. 2021; Rosenholtz 2016; Strasburger et al. 2011) and, thus, are inadequate for FR: an image with a low PSNR at the visual periphery might not introduce visual artifacts. The altered image in Fig. 10.3, when placed in the visual periphery, is visually indistinguishable from the reference image.

We leverage an eccentricity-aware HVS Quality (HVSQ) metric (Walton et al. 2021) inspired by classic neuroscience studies about the ventral pathway in the HVS (Freeman and Simoncelli 2011), which we have briefly touched upon in Sect. 2.5.2. Given a reference image, an altered image, and the eccentricity of each pixel (which depends on the display resolution and the eye-display distance), HVSQ quantifies how similar the two images are as viewed by humans; a lower HVSQ means more similar.

The principle behind the HVSQ metric is as follows. The retina aggregates photoreceptor outputs in spatial regions, called spatial poolings. In the image space, a spatial pooling corresponds to a set of adjacent pixels (e.g., SP in Fig. 10.3). The pooling size increases with eccentricity, usually quadratically. Computational models on HVS (Walton et al. 2021) show that as long as the statistics (mean and standard deviation) of the content in a spatial pooling between two images are close, humans can not discriminate between them. The statistics are calculated in a feature space (as opposed to the pixel space) to emulate the feature extraction in humans' early visual processing.

Computationally, the HVSQ of an altered image with respect to a reference image is calculated as follows:

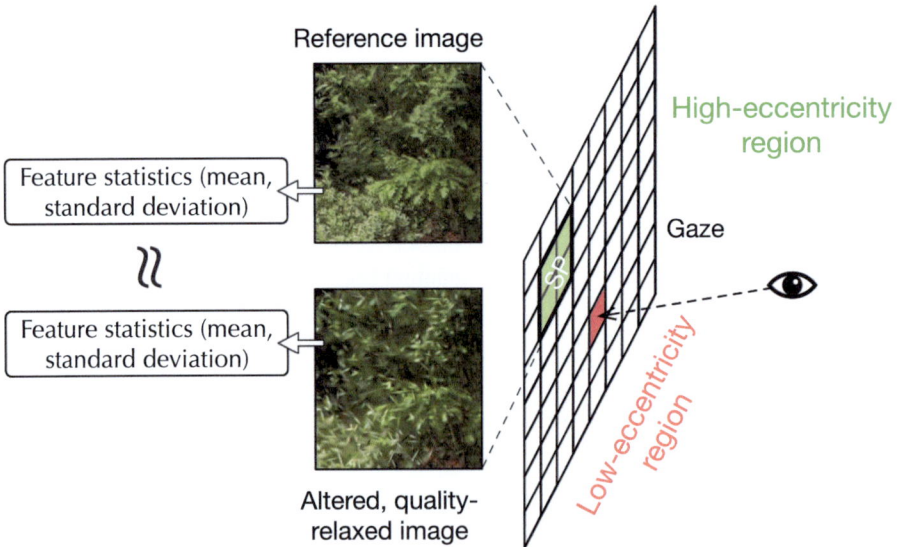

Fig. 10.3 Pixels under the user's gaze have low eccentricities, where the human visual quality is the highest; the peripheral pixels have high eccentricities where human visual acuity is low. In peripheral regions, the visual stimulus (image) can be altered without being discriminable from the reference stimulus if the statistics of the image features are close, as quantified by the HVSQ metric (Eq. 10.2). SP: spatial pooling. Figure from Lin et al. (2025a, Fig. 2)

$$HVSQ = \frac{1}{N} \sum_{i=1}^{N} \left[\left(\mathcal{M}(\mathrm{I}_i^a) - \mathcal{M}(\mathrm{I}_i^r) \right)^2 + \left(\sigma(\mathrm{I}_i^a) - \sigma(\mathrm{I}_i^r) \right)^2 \right] \qquad (10.2)$$

where N is the number of pixels in an image (each pixel has a unique spatial pooling), I_i^r and I_i^a denote the features of the ith spatial pooling in the reference and the altered image, respectively; $\mathcal{M}$ denotes arithmetic mean, and σ denotes standard deviation.

Intuitively, the HVSQ metric calculates the average distance between the two images' statistics across all the spatial poolings. HVSQ makes intuitive sense: as pixel eccentricities increase, the pooling sizes increase, which gives us more "wiggle room" within a spatial pooling to manipulate pixel values to match the feature statistics of the reference image.

10.3.2 FR Algorithm

Now that we have an eccentricity-dependent quality metric, the question is how to leverage it to reduce the rendering cost. We focus on the point-based radiance-field rendering methods discussed in Sect. 7.4.4. A prime example is the 3D Gaussian splatting (3DGS) method (Kerbl et al. 2023), which reconstructs the underlying light field by learning a set of points, each of which is associated with a 3D Gaussian distribution that is splatted to the image plane. Rendering is parameterized using the discrete volume rendering equation by summing the contributions of each splats.

We devise an FR method for 3DGS, shown in Fig. 10.4. As with prior FR work (Deng et al.2022; Guenter et al. 2012; Patney et al. 2016), we divide an image into N regions (4 in the example), each corresponding to a quality level and is rendered by a separate model. The region currently under the user's gaze has the highest quality ($\boxed{R1}$ here). Lower-quality regions are rendered using lighter models, which are obtained by pruning a high-quality model.

Panel $\textbf{\textcircled{E}}$ shows the rendering pipeline augmented to support FR—with two new stages (green). First, after projection, we must *filter* each model's points that are outside the model's quality region. Second, after each region is rendered, we must *blend* the results together to avoid aliasing. Blending is required in all FR algorithms (Guenter et al. 2012; Patney et al. 2016). Due to the quality difference across levels, there is a sharp, undesirable boundary between two adjacent levels in the rendered image (a form of aliasing). To eliminate the boundary, a common technique is for each model to render slightly beyond its assigned boundary; thus, pixels at the boundary will be rendered twice and then are interpolated/blended to provide a smooth transition between the two levels.

We also propose an efficient data representation that allows models at different quality levels to share computation and parameters. The key idea is that points used to train and render a lower quality level are strictly a subset of the points used by a higher quality level. Panel $\textbf{\textcircled{C}}$ in Fig. 10.4 illustrates how the original points in Panel $\textbf{\textcircled{B}}$ are organized after

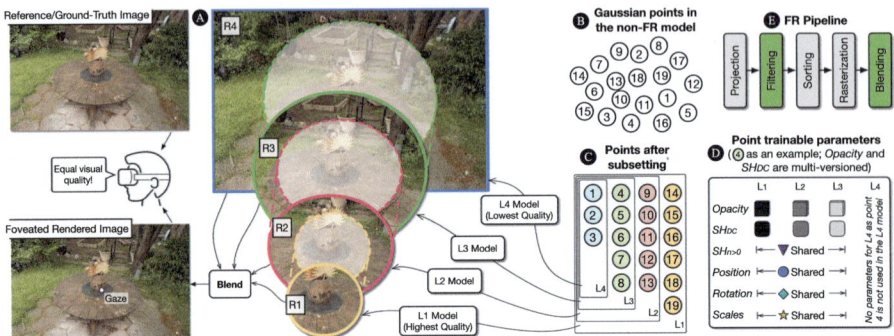

Fig. 10.4 The general idea of FR for 3DGS; from Lin et al. (2025a, Fig. 7). **A**: We train multiple models (four in this example), each with a different quality, and each is responsible for rendering a different quality region in the image (R1 – R4). The four quality regions are blended together to generate the final image. The goal is for the FR-rendered image to have the same visual quality as the reference image (e.g., generated by a dense model) when judged by humans. **B**: Points in the original non-FR model. **C**: Our hierarchical point representation to support compute- and data-efficient FR. We subset the points so that points used to train a higher-level (lower quality) model are strictly a subset of that used by a lower-level model. The *quality bound m* of a point is the highest level that uses the point (e.g., $m = 3$ for Point 4). **D**: To provide more flexibility for training, we selectively allow key trainable parameters to differ across levels; these parameters are the opacity of a point and the Direct Current (DC) component of the SH coefficients (SH_{DC}). Other (trainable) parameters of a point are shared across all the levels *that use the point* (e.g., no parameter in L_4 for Point 4). **E**: The rendering pipeline augmented to support FR (augmentations in green)

subsetting. The Level 1 (L_1) model is trained with the most points and thus would offer the highest quality, and the Level 4 (L_4) model has the fewest points and lowest quality.

Subsetting mitigates both the performance and storage overhead of a naive one-model-per-region approach, because the total number of points across all N models, P_{total}, is the same as that of the highest-quality model, P_1, rather than the sum of all N models. That is, $P_{total} = \max_{i=1}^{N} P_i = P_1 < \sum_{i=1}^{N} P_i$. As a result, there is no storage overhead. The compute overhead is small too, since the Projection and Filtering stages are executed only once, rather than once for each of the N models.

Practically, strict subsetting is likely too restrictive in controlling the rendering quality at different levels. This is because all the trainable parameters of a point would be fixed across all levels, so how a point participates in calculating pixel colors is also fixed at any time. In reality, however, a point's contribution to pixel colors should vary depending on the quality region the point is projected to, which varies with the camera pose and the gaze position. To relax this, we allow multi-versioning as illustrated in panel **D**: a point can maintain m (where m is the quality bound of the point) versions of *some* of its trainable parameters, one version for each level the point is in.

10.3.3 HVSQ-Guided Training and Results

We apply the HVSQ metric in Eq. (10.2) to each quality region—by simply iterating over the spatial poolings (pixels) in the selected region rather than over the entire image. That way, each quality region has a unique HVSQ measure, and our goal is to ensure the HVSQs across all quality levels are similar to the HVSQ of the baseline model. To that end, we first train the highest-quality L_1 model, which itself can be pruned from a dense model. We then prune an L_1 model to obtain an L_2 model, which is pruned down to obtain an L_3 model; this continues until the desired level is achieved. During pruning, we use the HVSQ as the loss function to ensure that the perceptual quality is aligned across eccentricities.

We evaluate our method using both subjective human studies and objective measurements of performance and quality. Across 12 participants, the subjective rendering quality of our method is statistically no worse than that of the state-of-the-art methods. Meanwhile, our method also improves the rendering speed by up to $7.4\times$ on a mobile Volta GPU.

10.4   Other Aspects of Vision

Weier et al. (2017) and Koulieris et al. (2019) are two recent review articles discussing perception issues pertaining to rendering in AR/VR, which we refer you to. We discuss two selected topics here.

10.4.1 Saliency

Complementary to peripheral vision, we can also exploit human visual saliency to reduce the rendering and streaming cost of VR (360°) videos. Informally, saliency refers to stimuli in the scene that attract our attention. Our visual cortex builds a saliency map from the scene to guide our actions, e.g., gaze shifts. In practical terms, this means users will be more attracted to salient objects when watching a video.

Leveraging saliency, EVR is one such cloud-client collaborative rendering system (Sun et al. 2020b; Leng et al. 2019). The cloud service, deployed on Amazon EC2, extracts trajectories of salient objects in a video (i.e., stimuli that most likely attract user attention), pre-render them, and store them as much smaller "videolets". At rendering time, given the real-time visual field of a user, only the best-matching videolets are transmitted. EVR reduces the data transmission cost and avoids expensive on-device rendering, amounting to 58% overall energy reduction. One could also leverage saliency for compression: prioritize bits to perceptually more interesting visual areas. Vignette builds a DNN to predict saliency and presents a system for video compression and storage (Mazumdar et al. 2019).

10.4.2 Temporal Vision

All the discussions so far are concerned with the spatial characteristics of human vision. The temporal dimension provides many interesting opportunities too. The most well-known aspect of temporal vision is saccades?, where our eyes move rapidly when shifting visual attention between targets. Unless purposely trained, e.g., in the military, we simply cannot avoid saccades. On average, saccades occur 3–4 times per second (more frequent than heartbeats) and last 20–200 ms each time, amounting to as many as 15 frames on a 90 FPS device.

Interestingly, human vision during saccades is momentarily blind, a phenomenon widely known as saccadic suppression (Matin 1974; Thiele et al. 2002). Application researchers use saccades to realize many interesting ideas, such as infinite walking in VR (Sun et al. 2018). Saccades also temporally modulate the incident light signals, redistributing power 0 Hz temporal frequency to other temporal frequencies. This power redistribution has been shown to have a significant impact on visual sensitivity right after a saccade lands (Mostofi et al. 2020; Boi et al. 2017). Recent work exploits the post-saccade visual sensitivity change to improve the image resolution during VR rendering (Kwak et al. 2024).

A related phenomenon is blink: our visual perception is also suppressed during eye blinks (Volkmann et al. 1980). Vision research has shown that humans are functionally blind for about ten percent of the time due to blink-induced visual suppression, another opportunity to shave some computation cost. For instance, people have started using blinks for VR redirection/infinite walking (Langbehn et al. 2018).

Finally, keep in mind that the visual stimuli are generated from the displays, which have finite refresh rates. A low refresh rate reduces the computation and display power but introduces many artifacts such as flickering and blur (a low refresh rate is the main reason moving objects look blurry to you on many TVs). A high refresh rate, in contrast, increases the computational load. This contention has led to recent work on variable refresh rate systems (Denes et al. 2020; Jindal et al. 2021).

10.5 Perceptual Imaging

Complementary to improving the computer systems (and perhaps a bit out of place for this section) is to leverage human vision for improving imaging systems. Just like human vision, machine vision applications (e.g., drones and robots) do not require high-quality data at the camera periphery. Foveated image sensing is thus a natural idea: sense the center of the camera field-of-view (FOV) with high quality at the expense of low-quality periphery sensing.

Foveated imaging can be realized in camera optics and/or sensor circuits. For instance, one might use a (3D printed!) micro-lens array to expose different pixels to different FOV sizes (Thiele et al. 2017). Alternatively, one might build the sensor circuit with non-uniform pixel shapes and sizes (Wodnicki et al. 1995; Pardo et al. 1997).

A particularly interesting approach for foveated imaging is to integrate two imagers that share the same aperture in a camera (Hua and Liu 2008). The peripheral imager senses the entire FOV with low resolution, and the other foveated imager provides the "fine high-contrast details and color sensation of a narrow foveated region." Conceptually, this design is reminiscent of three-chip cameras for consumer photography (Kuroda 2017) and multi-chip cameras for astrophysical imaging (Gunn et al. 1998; SDSS 2015), both of which use multiple imagers to accurately capture color/spectrum information of the scene. The dual-sensor foveated imaging system has a similar idea but applies it to foveated imaging.

References

Boi M, Poletti M, Victor JD, Rucci M (2017) Consequences of the oculomotor cycle for the dynamics of perception. Curr Biol 27(9):1268–1277

Chen K, Wan T, Matsuda N, Ninan A, Chapiro A, Sun Q (2024) Pea-pods: perceptual evaluation of algorithms for power optimization in XR displays. ACM Trans Graph (TOG) 43(4):1–17

Chen K, Duinkharjav B, Ujjainkar N, Shahan E, Tyagi A, He J, Zhu Y, Sun Q (2023) Imperceptible color modulation for power saving in VR/AR. In: ACM SIGGRAPH 2023 emerging technologies, pp 1–2

Curcio CA, Allen KA (1990) Topography of ganglion cells in human retina. J Comp Neurol 300(1):5–25

Curcio CA, Sloan KR, Kalina RE, Hendrickson AE (1990) Human photoreceptor topography. J Comp Neurol 292(4):497–523

Dacey DM (1993) The mosaic of midget ganglion cells in the human retina. J Neurosci 13(12):5334–5355

Denes G, Jindal A, Mikhailiuk A, Mantiuk RK (2020) A perceptual model of motion quality for rendering with adaptive refresh-rate and resolution. ACM Trans Graph (TOG) 39(4), Article No.: 133:133:1–133:17

Deng N, He Z, Ye J, Duinkharjav B, Chakravarthula P, Yang X, Sun Q (2022) FoV-NeRF: foveated neural radiance fields for virtual reality. IEEE Trans Visual Comput Graph 28(11):3854–3864

Derrington AM, Krauskopf J, Lennie P (1984) Chromatic mechanisms in lateral geniculate nucleus of macaque. J Physiol 357(1):241–265

Duinkharjav B, Chen K, Tyagi A, He J, Zhu Y, Sun Q (2022) Color-perception-guided display power reduction for virtual reality. ACM Trans Graph (TOG) 41(6):1–16

Feng Y, Ma T, Zhu Y, Zhang X (2024) BlissCam: boosting eye tracking efficiency with learned in-sensor sparse sampling. In: 2024 ACM/IEEE 51st annual international symposium on computer architecture (ISCA). IEEE, pp 1262–1277

Freeman J, Simoncelli EP (2011) Metamers of the ventral stream. Nat Neurosci 14(9):1195–1201

Gescheider GA (2013) Psychophysics: the fundamentals. Psychology Press

Guenter B, Finch M, Drucker S, Tan D, Snyder J (2012) Foveated 3D graphics. ACM Trans Graph (TOG) 31(6):1–10

Gunn JE, Carr M, Rockosi C, Sekiguchi M, Berry K, Elms B, De Haas E, Ivezić Ž, Knapp G, Lupton R et al (1998) The Sloan digital sky survey photometric camera. The Astron J 116(6):3040

Hore A, Ziou D (2010) Image quality metrics: PSNR vs. SSIM. In: 2010 20th international conference on pattern recognition. IEEE, pp 2366–2369

Hua H, Liu S (2008) Dual-sensor foveated imaging system. Appl Opt 47(3):317–327

Jindal A, Wolski K, Myszkowski K, Mantiuk RK (2021) Perceptual model for adaptive local shading and refresh rate. ACM Trans Graph (TOG) 40(6):1–18

Kerbl B, Kopanas G, Leimkühler T, Drettakis G (2023) 3d gaussian splatting for real-time radiance field rendering. ACM Trans Graph 42(4), Article No.: 139:1–14

Koulieris GA, Akşit K, Stengel M, Mantiuk RK, Mania K, Richardt C (2019) Near-eye display and tracking technologies for virtual and augmented reality. Comput Graph Forum. Wiley Online Library 38:493–519

Kuroda T (2017) Essential principles of image sensors. CRC Press

Kwak Y, Penner E, Wang X, Saeedpour-Parizi MR, Mercier O, Wu X, Murdison S, Guan P (2024) Saccade-contingent rendering. In: ACM SIGGRAPH 2024 conference papers, pp 1–9

Langbehn E, Steinicke F, Lappe M, Welch GF, Bruder G (2018) In the blink of an eye: leveraging blink-induced suppression for imperceptible position and orientation redirection in virtual reality. ACM Trans Graph (TOG) 37(4):1–11

Leng Y, Chen CC, Sun Q, Huang J, Zhu Y (2019) Energy-efficient video processing for virtual reality. In: Proceedings of the 46th international symposium on computer architecture, pp 91–103

Lin W, Feng Y, Zhu Y (2025a) MetaSapiens: real-time neural rendering with efficiency-aware pruning and accelerated foveated rendering. In: Proceedings of the 30th ACM international conference on architectural support for programming languages and operating systems, vol 1, pp 669–682

Ma T, Feng Y, Zhang X, Zhu Y (2023b) CamJ: enabling system-level energy modeling and architectural exploration for in-sensor visual computing. In: Proceedings of the 50th annual international symposium on computer architecture, pp 1–14

Matin E (1974) Saccadic suppression: a review and an analysis. Psychol Bull 81(12):899

Mazumdar A, Haynes B, Balazinska M, Ceze L, Cheung A, Oskin M (2019) Perceptual compression for video storage and processing systems. In: Proceedings of the ACM symposium on cloud computing, pp 179–192

Mostofi N, Zhao Z, Intoy J, Boi M, Victor JD, Rucci M (2020) Spatiotemporal content of saccade transients. Curr Biol 30(20):3999–4008

Pardo F, Dierickx B, Scheffer D (1997) CMOS foveated image sensor: signal scaling and small geometry effects. IEEE Trans Electron Dev 44(10):1731–1737

Patney A, Salvi M, Kim J, Kaplanyan A, Wyman C, Benty N, Luebke D, Lefohn A (2016) Towards foveated rendering for gaze-tracked virtual reality. ACM Trans Graph (TOG) 35(6):1–12

Prins N et al (2016) Psychophysics: a practical introduction. Academic Press

Rodieck R, Binmoeller K, Dineen J (1985) Parasol and midget ganglion cells of the human retina. J Comp Neurol 233(1):115–132

Rosenholtz R (2016) Capabilities and limitations of peripheral vision. Ann Rev Vis Sci 2:437–457

SDSS (2015) SDSS camera. https://web.archive.org/web/20220201025926/https://www.sdss.org/instruments/camera/

Singh R, Huzaifa M, Liu J, Patney A, Sharif H, Zhao Y, Adve S (2023) Power, performance, and image quality tradeoffs in foveated rendering. In: 2023 IEEE conference virtual reality and 3D user interfaces (VR). IEEE, pp 205–214

Song H, Chui TYP, Zhong Z, Elsner AE, Burns SA (2011) Variation of cone photoreceptor packing density with retinal eccentricity and age. Invest Ophthal Vis Sci 52(10):7376–7384

Strasburger H, Rentschler I, Jüttner M (2011) Peripheral vision and pattern recognition: a review. J Vis 11(5):13–13

Sun Q, Patney A, Wei LY, Shapira O, Lu J, Asente P, Zhu S, McGuire M, Luebke D, Kaufman A (2018) Towards virtual reality infinite walking: dynamic saccadic redirection. ACM Trans Graph (TOG) 37(4):1–13

Sun Q, Huang FC, Wei LY, Luebke D, Kaufman A, Kim J (2020a) Eccentricity effects on blur and depth perception. Opt Express 28(5):6734–6739

Sun Q, Taherin A, Siatitse Y, Zhu Y (2020b) Energy-efficient 360° video rendering on FPGA via algorithm-architecture co-design. In: Proceedings of the 2020 ACM/SIGDA international symposium on field-programmable gate arrays, pp 97–103

Thiele A, Henning P, Kubischik M, Hoffmann KP (2002) Neural mechanisms of saccadic suppression. Science 295(5564):2460–2462

Thiele S, Arzenbacher K, Gissibl T, Giessen H, Herkommer AM (2017) 3D-printed eagle eye: compound microlens system for foveated imaging. Sci Adv 3(2):e1602655

Ujjainkar N, Shahan E, Chen K, Duinkharjav B, Sun Q, Zhu Y (2024) Exploiting human color discrimination for memory-and energy-efficient image encoding in virtual reality. In: Proceedings of the 29th ACM international conference on architectural support for programming languages and operating systems, vol 1, pp 166–180

Volkmann FC, Riggs LA, Moore RK (1980) Eyeblinks and visual suppression. Science 207(4433):900–902

Walton DR, Dos Anjos RK, Friston S, Swapp D, Akşit K, Steed A, Ritschel T (2021) Beyond blur: real-time ventral metamers for foveated rendering. ACM Trans Graph 40(4):1–14

Weier M, Stengel M, Roth T, Didyk P, Eisemann E, Eisemann M, Grogorick S, Hinkenjann A, Kruijff E, Magnor M et al (2017) Perception-driven accelerated rendering. Comput Graph Forum. Wiley Online Library 36:611–643

Wodnicki R, Roberts GW, Levine MD (1995) A foveated image sensor in standard CMOS technology. In: Proceedings of the IEEE 1995 custom integrated circuits conference. IEEE, pp 357–360

Xie C, Li X, Hu Y, Peng H, Taylor M, Song SL (2021) Q-VR: system-level design for future mobile collaborative virtual reality. In: Proceedings of the 26th ACM international conference on architectural support for programming languages and operating systems, pp 587–599

Zhao S, Zhang H, Mishra CS, Bhuyan S, Ying Z, Kandemir MT, Sivasubramaniam A, Das C (2021) Holoar: on-the-fly optimization of 3D holographic processing for augmented reality. In: MICRO-54: 54th annual IEEE/ACM international symposium on microarchitecture, pp 494–506

In-Sensor Compression

11

11.1 Why and How?

The main power bottleneck of image sensors is the data read-out, mostly the ADC (Sect. 9.2.3), and transmission (LiKamWa et al. 2013; Feng et al. 2024; Ma et al. 2023b), both transmitting the data to the host through MIPI CSI-2 interface and from the host to potentially the cloud (Desai et al. 2022). To address this energy bottleneck, recent research has explored in-sensor compression, where raw pixels are aggressively sampled before being digitized and transmitted out of the sensor (Ma et al. 2023a; Feng et al. 2024; Yoshida et al. 2019; Zhang et al. 2023; Nair et al. 2024).

In-sensor compression must address a fundamental dilemma, where the sensor output is both an *energy* bottleneck and an *information* bottleneck, which are directly in contention with each other. Reducing energy consumption requires aggressive in-sensor compression, but over-compression can lead to significant losses in task accuracy. There are general two strategies:

- Task-specific compression, where we can tailor the compression strategy to a particular downstream task. We will refer you to Feng et al. (2022, 2024) for an example of this approach.
- General-purpose compression, where we compression is realized through task-independent, information-preserving sampling; this is the focus of Sect. 11.2.

11.2   General-Purpose Compression via Efficient-Coding

Ideally, the compressed data should support diverse downstream tasks. For instance, a smart-city camera might need to process the same video stream for both action recognition and traffic monitoring. Similarly, in AR applications, a single camera stream must handle tasks such as hand recognition and scene reconstruction (Kwon et al. 2023).

11.2.1 Sampling Pattern and Mechanism

To design a general compression strategy, we leverage the principle of decorrelation to minimize redundancy among output pixels. This approach is inspired by the classic theory of efficient coding in neuroscience (Barlow 1961; Attneave 1954; Pitkow and Meister 2012; Zbontar et al. 2021), which suggests that the retina efficiently transmits information to the brain by reducing redundancy and increasing decorrelation among the Retina Ganglion Cells (RGCs)—the output neurons of the retina (Dan et al. 1996). This concept is visualized in Fig. 11.1.

Similarly, our compression pattern is trained to maximize information density in the sensor output, as opposed to be tailored to a particular task. The core *mechanism* for compression is *sampling*. In particular, we sample through *coded exposure* (CE) (Reddy et al. 2011), where the sensor selectively exposes pixels both spatially and temporally; pixel values

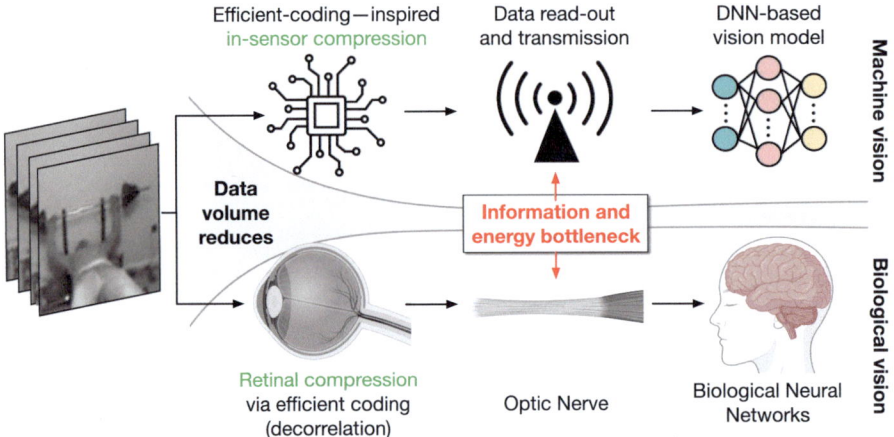

Fig. 11.1 We reduce edge sensing energy through in-sensor compression by decorrelating output pixel values. This is inspired by the mammalian visual system, where the retina compresses information by decorrelating the retinal output neurons; signals carried through the optic nerve, while at a much lower bandwidth than at the initial stage of the retina, encodes essential information that permits the downstream visual cortex to effectively perform visual tasks. Figure from Lin et al. (2025b, Fig. 1)

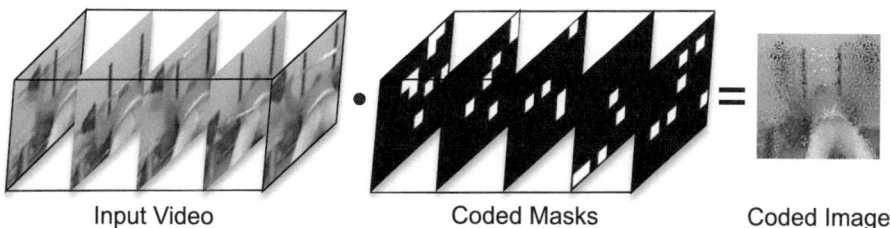

Fig. 11.2 Coded exposure with 5 exposure slots. In each slot, pixels are selectively exposed, controlled by a coded mask. In the end, the values at all the exposure slots are integrated pixel-wise to form one single coded image. Figure from Lin et al. (2025b, Fig. 2)

are integrated across exposure slots into a single coded image before being read out (Yoshida et al. 2019). Figure 11.2 illustrates the fundamental operation of CE. Let Y represent the sequence of images that would have been captured using a conventional image sensor, with dimensions $T \times H \times W$, where T is the number of frames in Y, and H and W are the height and width of each image, respectively.

In the CE process, an exposure mask is applied to each frame (or exposure slot) t to select a subset of pixels to expose during that frame (e.g., 5 exposure slots as shown in Fig. 11.2). The exposed pixel values are then integrated over time for each pixel, resulting in a single coded image of dimensions $1 \times H \times W$ being read out from the sensor. This approach achieves a data reduction factor of T, as T frames are compressed into one. This process can be formulated as follows:

$$X(i, j) = \sum_{t=1}^{T} M(i, j, t) \cdot Y(i, j, t) \tag{11.1}$$

where X is the final coded image, M is the binary masks controlling exposure, i, j, and t index the spatial dimensions and the temporal dimension (frames), respectively.

To maximize the benefits of CE, ideally there should not be any constraint imposed on each pixel's exposure pattern. That, however, means that pixels would carry varying amounts of information and should be treated differently in the downstream model, introducing performance overhead Kumawat et al. (2022), Okawara et al. (2020). Instead, we constrain the sampling pattern to be tile-repetitive—pixels within a tile can have different exposure patterns, but the pattern repeats across tiles—and thus constrains the pixel variation within a tile. To accommodate this tile-repetitive structure, we use Vision Transformers (ViTs) as the backbone. ViTs naturally process inputs tile-by-tile, and the processing of each tile is trained based on the (offline obtained) within-tile pixel variations. With a carefully designed ViT architecture and tailored pre-training, our constrained sampling does not degrade accuracy.

11.2.2 Sensor Hardware Support

We utilize the characteristic of the tile-repetitive decorrelation pattern to reduce both the control footprint and control power. In our design, we replace the global control with local, per-pixel storage to store the CE pattern. We then use a die stacking design (Sect. 9.3.5), where the top layer is the pixel array and the bottom layer hosts the digital logic/storage. Such a stacking design is common in consumer CMOS image sensors (Oike 2021), and our design represents a novel usage of the bottom layer to support CE. By stacking, the per-pixel storage is completely hidden beneath the pixel's exposure circuits, so the area of our proposed pixel is approximately the same as that of the conventional, non-CE pixel.

The proposed pixel design is illustrated in Fig. 11.3, which contains two layers. The top layer is pixel array layer, where each pixel is based on the classic 4T Active Pixel Sensor (APS) design that consists of a photodiode (PD) to acquire incident light and five transistors to reset PD (M1), reset floating diffusion (FD) node (M2), transfer photocharge (M3), and read out photocharge as voltage when the pixel is selected (M4, M5). Different to the conventional 4T pixel design, the additional transistor M1 decouples the reset of PD and FD such that the PD can be exposed across multiple exposure slots but only transfer the photocharge once to the FD, thereby realizing CE function.

At the bottom layer, each pixel is equipped with a D-Flip-Flop (DFF) to buffer the one-bit CE pattern of a given exposure slot. The bit represents whether to accumulate the pixel's exposure during the corresponding exposure slot. The DFFs of all the pixels in a tile are connected in a shift-register style: the *pattern in* wire of the second pixel is connected to the

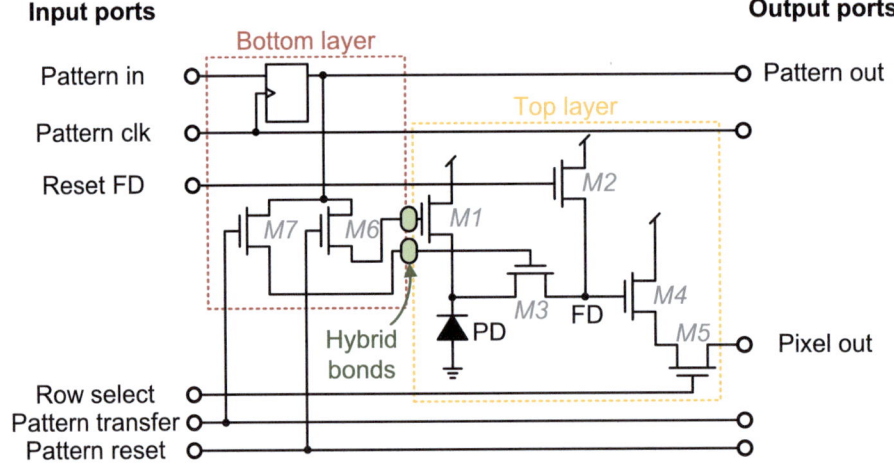

Fig. 11.3 Schematic of the proposed CE pixel. It is based on a stacked design that is commonly used in modern CMOS image sensors. Figure from Lin et al. (2025b, Fig. 5)

pattern out wire of its preceding pixel. Each pixel is also augmented with two additional transistors: M6 (pattern reset) and M7 (pattern transfer).

At the start of every exposure slot, the CE bits of each pixel in a tile are streamed in through the *pattern in* wire and buffered in the corresponding DFFs . Then, M6 is turned on for all the pixels (through the *pattern reset* wire), which allows the CE bit in the DFF to control the reset of the PD. If the CE bit is 1, the PD is reset via M1 (charges accumulated so far is cleared), getting ready for exposure; if the CE bit is 0, the PD is not reset (since M1 will be open). The DFFs can then be powered-gated.

After the exposure, the same CE bits are streamed in and buffered again in the DFFs. We then turn on M7 for all the pixels (through the *pattern transfer* wire). If the CE bit is 1, the charge is transferred from the PD to the FD through M3; otherwise, M3 is open and the FD does not accumulate the charge from the previous exposure. The DFFs are then power-gated again until the next exposure slot. While the DFFs are power-gated, logic 0 is given to both M1 and M3 via a simple reset logic (not shown in Fig. 11.3 for simplicity). The delay between the *pattern reset* and *pattern transfer* signals physically creates the exposure time for the pixel (Yoshida et al. 2019).

11.2.3 Headline Results

We evaluate two distinct downstream tasks: action recognition (AR), a high-level task producing a single classification output, and reconstruction (REC), a low-level task generating a video. REC evaluation addresses scenarios where videos are stored for future, undefined tasks. We refer you to Lin et al. (2025b) for comprehensive results, and highlight two here.

First, simultaneously on both tasks, decorrelation out-performs other task-agnostic CE patterns, including uniforming exposing all pixels with the same duration, randomly exposing each pixel with a given probability, etc. Second, on the AR task, our proposal outperforms task-specific methods specifically tuned for the AR task at the same run-time cost. These methods include earlier CE methods (that are not based on decorrelation) and non-CE, video-based methods.

References

Attneave F (1954) Some informational aspects of visual perception. Psychol Review 61(3):183
Barlow HB (1961) Possible principles underlying the transformation of sensory messages. Sens Commun 1(01):217–233
Dan Y, Atick JJ, Reid RC (1996) Efficient coding of natural scenes in the lateral geniculate nucleus: experimental test of a computational theory. J Neurosci 16(10):3351–3362
Desai H, Nardello M, Brunelli D, Lucia B (2022) Camaroptera: a long-range image sensor with local inference for remote sensing applications. ACM Trans Embed Comput Syst (TECS) 21(3):1–25

Feng Y, Goulding-Hotta N, Khan A, Reyserhove H, Zhu Y (2022) Real-time gaze tracking with event-driven eye segmentation. In: 2022 IEEE conference on virtual reality and 3D user interfaces (VR). IEEE, pp 399–408

Feng Y, Ma T, Zhu Y, Zhang X (2024) BlissCam: boosting eye tracking efficiency with learned in-sensor sparse sampling. In: 2024 ACM/IEEE 51st annual international symposium on computer architecture (ISCA). IEEE, pp 1262–1277

Kumawat S, Okawara T, Yoshida M, Nagahara H, Yagi Y (2022) Action recognition from a single coded image. TPAMI 45(4):4109–4121

Kwon H, Nair K, Seo J, Yik J, Mohapatra D, Zhan D, Song J, Capak P, Zhang P, Vajda P et al (2023) XRBench: an extended reality (XR) machine learning benchmark suite for the metaverse. MLSys 5:1–20

LiKamWa R, Priyantha B, Philipose M, Zhong L, Bahl P (2013) Energy characterization and optimization of image sensing toward continuous mobile vision. In: Proceeding of the 11th annual international conference on mobile systems, applications, and services, pp 69–82

Lin W, Ma T, Boloor A, Feng Y, Xing R, Zhang X, Zhu Y (2025b) SnapPix: efficient-coding–inspired in-sensor compression for edge vision. In: 2025 62nd ACM/IEEE design automation conference (DAC). IEEE

Ma T, Boloor AJ, Yang X, Cao W, Williams P, Sun N, Chakrabarti A, Zhang X (2023a) LeCA: in-sensor learned compressive acquisition for efficient machine vision on the edge. In: ISCA, pp 1–14

Ma T, Feng Y, Zhang X, Zhu Y (2023b) CamJ: enabling system-level energy modeling and architectural exploration for in-sensor visual computing. In: Proceedings of the 50th annual international symposium on computer architecture, pp 1–14

Nair GR, Nalla PS, Krishnan G, Oh J, Hassan A, Yeo I, Kasichainula K, Seok M, Seo J-S, Cao Y, et al (2024) 3D in-sensor computing for real-time DVS data compression: 65 nm hardware-algorithm co-design. SSC-L

Oike Y (2021) Evolution of image sensor architectures with stacked device technologies. IT-ED 69(6):2757–2765

Okawara T, Yoshida M, Nagahara H, Yagi Y (2020) Action recognition from a single coded image. In: ICCP. IEEE, pp 1–11

Pitkow X, Meister M (2012) Decorrelation and efficient coding by retinal ganglion cells. Nat Neurosci 15(4):628–635

Reddy D, Veeraraghavan A, Chellappa R (2011) P2c2: programmable pixel compressive camera for high speed imaging. In: CVPR. IEEE, pp 329–336

Yoshida M, Sonoda T, Nagahara H, Endo K, Sugiyama Y, Taniguchi R (2019) High-speed imaging using CMOS image sensor with quasi pixel-wise exposure. TCI 6:463–476

Zbontar J, Jing L, Misra I, LeCun Y, Deny S (2021) Barlow twins: self-supervised learning via redundancy reduction. In: ICML. PMLR, pp 12310–12320

Zhang T, Kasichainula K, Jee DW, Yeo I, Zhuo Y, Li B, Seo J-S, Cao Y (2023) Improving the efficiency of CMOS image sensors through in-sensor selective attention. In: ISCAS. IEEE, pp 1–4